The Future of Turkish Foreign Policy

D0064499

The BCSIA Studies in International Security book series is edited at the Belfer Center for Science and International Affairs (BCSIA) at Harvard University's John F. Kennedy School of Government and is published by The MIT Press. The series publishes books on contemporary issues in international security policy, as well as their conceptual and historical foundations. Topics of particular interest to the series include the spread of weapons of mass destruction, internal conflict, the international effects of democracy and democratization, and U.S. defense policy.

A complete list of BCSIA Studies and more about the Belfer Center for Science and International Affairs appear at the back of this volume.

The Future of Turkish Foreign Policy

Lenore G. Martin and Dimitris Keridis, editors

BCSIA Studies in International Security

The MIT Press
Cambridge, Massachusetts
London, England

This book was typeset in Palatino by Wellington Graphics and was
printed and bound in the United States of America.

Library of Congress Cataloging-in-Publication Data

The future of Turkish foreign policy / Lenore G. Martin and Dimitris Keridis, editors.
p. cm. — (BCSIA studies in international security)
Includes bibliographical references and index.
ISBN 0-262-13402-0 (alk. paper) — ISBN 0-262-63243-8 (pbk.: alk. paper)
1. Turkey—Foreign relations. I. Martin, Lenore G. II. Keridis, Dimitris.
III. Series.
DR477 .F68 2002
327.561—dc21

2001054628

10 9 8 7 6 5 4 3 2 1

Contents

Foreword

The conference on Turkish foreign policy, held at Harvard University on October 24–25, 1998, was an exceptional case of cooperation among individual scholars and different bodies within the university. Dimitris Keridis, director of the Kokkalis Program on Southeastern and East-Central Europe at the Kennedy School of Government, Lenore Martin, affiliate-in-research at the Center for Middle East Studies (CMES), in addition to her regular position as a professor of political science at Emmanuel College, and I shared ideas and responsibilities in the design of the program and the logistics of the conference—discussing goals, approaches, and organizational matters in all their detail in collegial fashion. The CMES, then under the directorship of Roger Owen, and the Kokkalis Program were joint hosts of the event that brought together two programs in two different schools of the university to engage the eager support of faculty, staff, and students.

The conference was most memorable, not only for the substance of specific papers, but also for the diversity of opinions represented and the spirited exchange around them. The entanglement of international relations issues with matters often related to national or domestic debates was hardly ever disregarded, and this awareness enriched the discussion even beyond the expectations of the conference organizers. Heated debates erupted around Jacobinism, the legacy of Sèvres, Turkey's human rights record, natural resources, and many other issues analyzed in this volume. In all these respects, the meeting was a faithful reflection of the remarkable diversity witnessed in Turkish public opinion as to questions of identity, historical memory, sense of belonging to a civilization or to a

region, and the concomitant choices among alternative foreign policy orientations.

At the same time, the conference dealt with the most salient aspects
of the bewildering variety of concrete issues—such as specific challenges
and opportunities offered by Turkey's neighborhood, and different dimensions of her sweet-and-sour relationship with the European Union—
to which those orientations are meant to provide cogent responses. Discussions around the issues were rooted in the cognizance of the fact that
the world in which Turkey needs to navigate the course of its foreign relations became more complicated in the latter decades of the twentieth century. It is, of course, not only within the country that shifting realities and
emerging complexities have led to reassessments of Turkey's role in the
world. The conference was also concerned with the evolving attitudes
and policies vis-à-vis Turkey of a number of states, policy and opinion
makers, corporations, and non-governmental organizations around the
globe.

This volume is a product and a distillation of those discussions, as it
was shaped under the able hands and watchful eyes of the two editors
into something rather different from simple conference proceedings.
While more selective and focused on original scholarly research, it still retains the spirit of the lively debate that took place among the conference
participants. At the same time, the editors and the authors have gone to
great lengths to bring the book up to date, to the extent possible given the
flux of daily events. Most importantly, the broad outlines of the context
and complexities of Turkish foreign policy at the start of a new era are
carefully analyzed and vividly illuminated here. I am certain that the editors and authors will join me in giving some of the credit to the conference participants whose discussions and comments are among the ingre-
dients of this book.

Cemal Kafadar
—*Director, Center for Middle Eastern Studies, Harvard University*
—*Vehbi Koç Professor of Turkish Studies*

Acknowledgments

We thank the Kokkalis Foundation for its generosity in funding this project. We are also thankful for the support of the Center for Middle Eastern Studies and the Kokkalis Program on Southeastern and East-Central Europe, both at Harvard University. We are especially grateful to Professor Roger Owen and Professor Cemal Kafadar for their interest and participation in planning the conference that preceded this book. The conference benefited greatly from the participation and insightful contributions of İshak Alaton, Kevin Brennan, Yannis Kartalis, Muharrem Kayhan, Hasan Köni, Ambassador Alon Liel, Kalypso Nicolaïdis, Ambassador Thomas Niles, Dani Rodrik, Patrick Seale, Duygu Sezer, and Henry Steiner, as well as the generous support of Niki Tzavella, vice president of the Kokkalis Foundation.

We are most appreciative of all the people who helped with the editing and production of this book. Margaret Owen, our copy editor, kept close watch over us all; with her good humor and great care, she has been essential in bringing this volume to publication. Miriam Avins added a magic touch to several chapters in the editing process. Consulting editor Teresa Lawson stepped in to usher the book through the final stages. Elaine Papoulias, the director of the Kokkalis Program, has given continuous attention and assistance to this project, as has Ayşe Güneş-Ayata, Professor of Political Science and Public Administration at Middle East Technical University, whose enormous support has been invaluable. Mikhala Stein and Nicole Stewart, also of the Kokkalis Program, were very helpful many times in many ways. At the Belfer Center for Science and International Affairs (BCSIA) of Harvard's Kennedy School of Government, Stephen Smith provided diligent proofreading, and our special thanks are due to series editor Sean Lynn-Jones for his encouragement and oversight from beginning to end.

—*Lenore G. Martin*
Cambridge, Mass.

—*Dimitris Keridis*
Athens

Turkey and its Neighbors

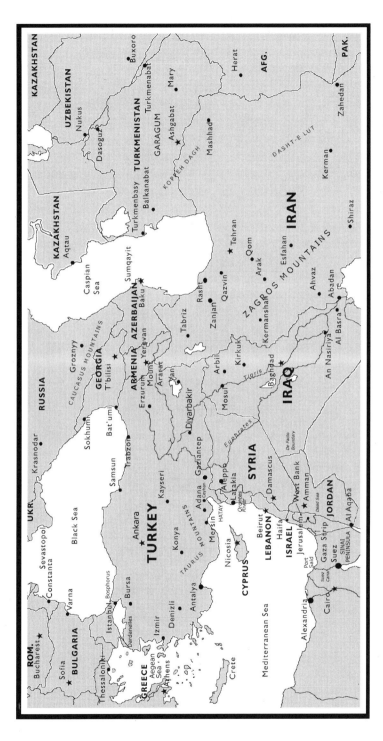

Map drawn by Nicole Stewart, Kokkalis Program, Harvard University, with thanks to the University of Texas at Austin, Perry-Castaneda Library Map Collection.

Introduction

Chapter 1

Introduction

Lenore G. Martin

The tectonic forces that reshaped international relations at the end of the twentieth century—the collapse of the Soviet Union, ethnic conflicts in the Balkans and Eurasia, the growing stridency of Islamic fundamentalism, globalization of national economies, and increasing demands for democratization and civil society—also thrust Turkey into an increasingly pivotal role on the geopolitical stage. The aftershocks at the beginning of the twenty-first century, the events of September 11, 2001, the global spread of anti-Western terrorism, the U.S. invasion of Iraq, and the cracking of consensus in NATO and the UN threw up additional challenges for Turkey that have confirmed and complicated its critical role. How Turkey will react to these external forces and aftershocks and hence shape its destiny in the new international arena raises fundamental questions as to the future of Turkish foreign policy.

Pondering the future in times of transformation and challenge is not intended as a pretentious exercise. It is rather a normal reaction to the unpredictability of what is to come and the desire to pattern it from experience of what has been. This tension is reflected in the aphorisms of two well-known spokesmen from earlier times of global political upheavals, the American and French Revolutions. "I know no way of judging the future but by the past," said Patrick Henry, the American liberal. "You can never plan the future by the past," said his philosophical opponent, Edmund Burke, the British conservative.[1]

---

1.   Jane Carson, *Patrick Henry, Prophet of the Revolution* (Williamsburg: Virginia Independence Bicentennial Commission, 1979), p. 45 (quoting from Henry's Speech to Virginia Convention, Richmond, March 1775); Edmund Burke, *A Letter to a Member of the National Assembly, 1791* (Oxford: Woodstock Books, 1990), p. 73.

In the face of this paradox, the aim of this book is to seek answers to the following fundamental questions: what are the critical foreign policy issues that the Turkish Republic will face in the coming years? What perspectives do its foreign policymakers adopt in order to fashion solutions to those issues? We intend that the answers to these questions will give the reader insights into the formative principles that guide Turkish foreign policymaking and an understanding of the directions that Turkish foreign policy may take in the next decade or so.

The contributors to this work include both analysts and advocates, Turks and non-Turks. Each offers a complex world-view that matches the complexities of foreign policy decision-making in general and Turkey's foreign policy in particular. There are no simplistic or ideological answers to the baffling issues that bedevil the future of Turkish foreign policymaking. Nor do the world-views of the contributors mirror the shifting viewpoints of Turkey's domestic political parties—center left, center right, nationalists, Islamists, "Republicans," and so forth. The experts who advocate solutions to the foreign policy issues posed in this volume are fairly balanced. As a result there are no easy labels that caption their complex philosophies, such as "conservatives" or "liberals." However, for propaedeutic purposes we may refer to the most common opposition of viewpoints as that between advocates of continuity and advocates of change.

To present the guiding principles of Turkish foreign policy and its future challenges, we adopt three perspectives. The first is historical and philosophical. Thus, we open with an outline of the history of modern Turkish foreign policy, then feature the philosophical differences that affect policy choices. The second perspective is geographic and strategic. As befits a state situated at the intersection of Europe, Asia, and the Middle East, we examine challenges from all three directions. First we view the challenges from the West: Turkey's relations with the United States, Europe, and also Greece. Then we look at the challenges from the East: Turkey's relations with Russia and the buffer states, and also challenges from the Middle East. Finally, we consider challenges raised by Turkey's strategic needs and resources: its water supplies and energy demands.

Our third perspective derives from Turkey's domestic politics. We review the challenges to the future of Turkish foreign policy that are raised by the international dimensions of Turkey's development of a civil society: Islamization, the Kurdish question, and human rights. These are the foreign policy determinants that arise from Turkey's vibrant domestic politics and the clash between the advocates of Kemalist continuity within the regime and the advocates of change within its diverse ethnic and religious political community.

Let us take a closer look at what each contribution to the book provides. Feroz Ahmad's contribution, "The Historical Background of Turkey's Foreign Policy," lays the historical groundwork for the conflict of principles in the Republic's foreign policy. He examines the period from the founding of the Republic in 1923 to Turkey's entry into NATO almost thirty years later. With what degree of consistency did the Republic apply its Kemalist principles of foreign policymaking during this period?

How should the Turkish Republic apply these principles after the end of the Cold War, September 11, and the military intrusion of the United States in Iraq? How will Turkey reconcile its Kemalist conservatism in foreign affairs with its new public role as a pivotal actor on the global stage? The contributors reflect a collective endorsement of the need for Turkish activism at the beginning of the twenty-first century. Where they differ is in describing the type of activism that the foreign policy establishment in Ankara should pursue.

This clash of philosophies is evident in the eloquent contributions to the book by Mümtaz Soysal, "The Future of Turkish Foreign Policy," and Cengiz Çandar, "Turkish Foreign Policy and the War on Iraq." Soysal advocates continuity and holding the course. Çandar takes the opposite view and urges reform. They differ on the implications of history, the priorities that the decision makers must consider, and the risks to which they must respond.

What are the foreign policy issues over which the advocates of continuity and of change may clash in seeking to steer the state in the future? Turkey's primary geostrategic goals are to maintain strong relationships in the West, with Europe, and with the United States. Joining the European Union (EU), in fact, represents a cardinal objective of Turkey's Western-oriented foreign policy. Atila Eralp's chapter, "Turkey and the European Union," examines the glacis to the Helsinki Summit of 1999 and considers what steps after Helsinki both the Europeans and Turkey might take to improve Turkey's chances of becoming a full member of the EU.

Ian Lesser's chapter, "Turkey and the United States: Anatomy of a Strategic Relationship," considers the potential dilemma facing Turkey in pursuing accession to the EU at the same time as it maintains a strategic bilateral relationship with the United States. On the one hand, the U.S. relationship is critical for Turkey's achievement of certain security goals in its "dangerous neighborhood." On the other hand, maintaining that relationship where U.S. and European interests diverge may impinge on Turkey's chances of joining the EU.

A similar paradox lies at the heart of Turkey's relations with Greece, which also has a hand on the key to Turkey's entry into the EU. Panayotis Tsakonas and Thanos Dokos, in "Greek-Turkish Relations in the Early

Twenty-first Century: A View from Athens," present the Greek view of the future of this relationship. Is it possible to reduce the tensions and resolve the open issues between these often hostile neighbors?

Looking to the East, Turkey has faced similar risks of hostilities with Russia (and earlier with the Soviet Union) as well as tensions in the Middle East. Oktay Tanrısever's chapter, "Turkey and Russia in Eurasia," lays out succinctly the interplay between cooperation and competition between Ankara and Moscow over economic advantages and influence in the predominantly Muslim Eurasian buffer states between the two powers. Is greater cooperation possible between Turkey and Russia in the future?

My own chapter, "Turkey's Middle East Foreign Policy," explores the dilemmas that confront the Republic resulting from its pursuit of converging and diverging interests with the major Middle Eastern actors in this unstable region, and the additional dilemma created by the introduction of U.S. forces in Iraq. What policies should Ankara implement to further its national interests under such complex conditions?

Some of the dilemmas of Turkey's Middle Eastern policy arise from its strategic advantage in the control of water sources for two neighbors, Syria and Iraq, and its strategic need to import two critical energy sources, oil and gas. İlter Turan's chapter, "Water and Turkish Foreign Policy," explores the foreign policy implications of Turkey's control over the Euphrates and Tigris, as well as Turkey's ability to offer water as an inducement for achieving other foreign policy goals.

Fiona Hill's chapter, "Caspian Conundrum: Pipelines and Energy Networks," explores Turkey's search for energy security through the development of oil and gas supply networks in the Caucasus and Central Asia. This search puts Turkey in direct competition with Russia and Iran over routing pipelines through states troubled by ethnic and religious strife, in regions in which the United States and its allies have strong interests in the outcomes of that competition.

Focusing Turkey's often problematic foreign relations will not suffice to ensure a tension-free future in the new world order. The Turkish Republic's domestic policies in pursuit of a civil society themselves have international dimensions and create challenges for its future foreign policy. For example, Turkey's becoming a full member of the EU also depends upon its achieving significant reforms in its economy, reconciliation of its secular democracy with the demands of its multifaceted Islamic movement, sensitive treatment of its Kurdish minority, and noteworthy improvement of its human rights record.

Sencer Ayata explores the foreign policy ramifications of the increasing strength of the Islamic movement within Turkey in his chapter,

"Changes in Domestic Politics and the Foreign Policy Orientation of the AK Party." What are the implications for Ankara's foreign policy of the new political discourse adopted by the moderate Islamist AK (Justice and Development) Party, after its surprising electoral victory in 2002?

The unwillingness of the Turkish military to prevent or overcome the parliament's decision not to join the United States in its invasion of Iraq in the spring of 2003 contrasts with the military's strong-handed treatment of the Kurdish separatist guerrilla movement, the Kurdish Workers' Party (PKK), and its political supporters. In "The Kurdish Question and Turkish Foreign Policy," Kemal Kirişci examines the multiple foreign policy implications of the Kurdish issue that has troubled the Republic since its inception. Even after the abatement of the activities of the PKK following the capture and trial of the PKK leader, has the Republic been able to come to grips with the demands for recognition of a distinct Kurdish identity and culture within the Turkish state?

If the answer is negative, there will be continuing international criticism of Turkey's human rights record. Elizabeth Andersen's chapter, "The Impact of Foreign Relations on Human Rights in Turkey," describes the inconsistencies of the international criticism of Turkey's human rights record. Is there hope for human rights improvements in the future?

Dimitris Keridis sums up the intersection of Turkish domestic politics and its foreign policymaking in his thought-provoking chapter, "Foreign Strategies and Domestic Choices: Balancing between Power Politics and Interdependence."

In the concluding chapter, the editors challenge the reader to appreciate the complexity of Turkish foreign policy and to consider the ways in which future foreign policy choices may contribute to making Turkey into the dynamic, influential, secure, and prosperous state it has the promise to be.

Chapter 2

The Historical Background of Turkey's Foreign Policy

Feroz Ahmad

Makers of Turkey's foreign policy continue to shoulder the burden of their Ottoman past. To this day they remain apprehensive about the creation of a Kurdish state in the region, fearing that something resembling the abortive Treaty of Sèvres of August 1920 might be imposed upon the Republic should they show any sign of weakness. This fear became even more real after 1991 with the collapse of Yugoslavia followed by the horrendous war in Bosnia. The Treaty of Sèvres, imposed on the sultan's government, partitioned Anatolia and left the Muslim-Turkish population with a rump state in the center. Apart from giving the Greeks extensive rights in western Anatolia and placing both the Bosphorus and Dardanelles straits under League of Nations administration, the treaty created two territories for Armenia and Kurdistan to be placed under Great Power mandate. Though the treaty was never implemented, Turks have continued to live with the phobia that it never quite died and could be revived at any moment; thus their hostile attitude towards the Kurdish and Armenian questions today.

The Treaty of Sèvres was merely the culmination of the so-called Eastern Question, the term used to describe the inter-imperialist rivalry concerning the division of the legacy of the ailing Ottoman Empire, described as the "sick man of Europe." Until the end of the nineteenth century Britain had pursued the policy of supporting Ottoman territorial integrity against Russian encroachments towards Istanbul and the straits, which would have guaranteed Russia free access from the Black Sea to the Mediterranean. But the diplomatic equation changed dramatically in the last quarter of the nineteenth century with German unification and the creation of the German Empire. The balance of power, which had provided stability in Europe after Napoleon's defeat, was damaged irreparably. Faced with the German challenge, Britain began to repair relations with its imperial rivals, France and Russia. The Anglo-French Entente of 1904 settled outstanding colonial differences between London and Paris. The Anglo-Russian Entente of August 1907 achieved the same goal by partitioning Persia into Russian and British spheres of influence, with understandings regarding their mutual interests in Tibet and Afghanistan. The meeting between the English king and the Russian tsar at Reval in June 1908 alarmed the Young Turk revolutionaries, convincing them that Britain and Russia had reached a similar accommodation over the Ottoman Empire. The fear that this meeting aroused is regarded as one of the causes of the constitutional revolution of July 1908.

Sultan Abdülhamid II, who ruled from 1876 to 1909, had attempted to balance British intrusion in Ottoman affairs by involving Germany in the Eastern Question. But the Young Turks who took charge of the constitutional regime were more imaginative and ambitious. Their intention, especially among the Unionist faction, members of the Committee of Union and Progress (CUP), was to reform and modernize the empire so as to abandon the status of client for that of partner to the Great Powers. The Unionists saw their empire as potentially the "Japan of the Middle East" and hoped that Britain would sign an alliance with Istanbul just as it had with Tokyo in 1902. In 1909, when they made this proposal to Sir Edward Grey, the British foreign secretary, he turned them down because he could not afford to alienate Russia and possibly drive it into Germany's arms.[1]

The Turks viewed Russia's southward expansion as the most potent threat to their empire. They had fought many wars against their northern neighbor and the war of 1877–78 had brought the tsarist army to the village of San Stefano and the very gates of the capital. Though Russian pretensions had been partially checked at the Congress of Berlin, the sultan had been forced to cede territories to Russia in the Balkans and the Caucasus. After July 1908, Russia altered its policy and attempted to achieve its goals through conciliation with the constitutional regime. This policy was implemented during the embassy of Nikolai Charykoff but it was abandoned in 1912 when Charykoff was replaced by M. N. de Giers and Russia reverted to its former aggressive policy towards the Ottomans.[2]

---

1.   See Feroz Ahmad, "Great Britain's Relations with the Young Turks, 1908–1914," *Middle Eastern Studies*, Vol. 2, No. 4 (July 1966), pp. 302–329.

2.   On Russian foreign policy towards the Ottoman Empire, see Alan Bodger, "Russia and the End of the Ottoman Empire," in Marian Kent, ed., *The Great Powers and the End of the Ottoman Empire* (London: George Allen and Unwin, 1984). Other articles in this anthology analyze the policies of the other Great Powers. Charykoff had come to love

The constitutional regime suffered a number of setbacks. The declaration of Bulgarian independence, Vienna's annexation of Bosnia-Herzegovina, the declaration of union between Crete and Greece (all in September 1908), the Turkish-Italian war in Libya in 1911–12, and finally the Balkan Wars of 1912–13, all undermined its legitimacy in the eyes of the people. In each case, Istanbul found itself totally isolated and powerless while the Great Powers found diplomatic solutions at the expense of Ottoman territory.

The war with Italy left Istanbul both isolated and bewildered. The Porte had always taken care to remain neutral and impartial in the diplomatic rivalries of Europe and expected to be treated even-handedly when engaged in any conflict. But that had not been the case here and a re-evaluation of policy was called for. When Hüseyin Cahid, an unofficial spokesman for the CUP, examined his country's policy vis-à-vis the two blocs he asked:

Why should Turkey wish to remain neutral? Was it in order to avoid being friendly with any of the Great Powers and sharing interests with them? No! It was to avoid having our friendship for one being regarded as a hostile act by another or all of the others. The aim of Turkey's policy is to achieve something positive rather than something negative; she wants to be friendly with all the Powers but she has not achieved this result.

He concluded that if Germany were unable to intervene on Turkey's behalf with its ally Italy, then Turkey ought to lean towards the Triple Entente.[3]

The poet Mehmet Âkif also issued a warning to Berlin with regard to its Ottoman policy. He wrote:

There is absolutely no doubt that if we are ruined, the key to the East will pass into the hands of her rivals rather than Germany's. . . . Today Germany is tied to Italy by an agreement. If Germany sacrifices us for such a friend, would it not be natural for us to throw ourselves into the arms of Germany's rivals? Our German friends may be certain that if the government of Germany wins over the persevering, loyal, and valiant Ottomans instead of treacherous and cowardly Italy, it will not have lost anything from a moral or material point of view; quite the contrary, it will gain a great deal. It could mean going directly to the East with the Ottomans in order to save and to civ-

---

Istanbul so much that after the revolution he left Russia and sought asylum there, making his home in Bebek. He died there on September 11, 1930. See *The Times* (London), September 13, 1930.

3. "İttifak ve İtilaflar karşisinda Türkiye" (Turkey against the Alliance and the Entente), *Tanin* (Istanbul), September 28, 1911.

ilize it. It could mean making the East a region for the expansion of German commerce and industry. . . . Thus, here is an attractive and important program for the Ottoman and German governments which understand each other.[4]

The catastrophe of the Balkan Wars increased the sense of isolation and created a mood of xenophobia. As war broke out, the Great Powers, anticipating a Turkish victory, declared that they would not permit a change in the status quo as a result of war. But when the Ottoman armies were defeated on all fronts by the Christian coalition, this declaration was disregarded and the Turks were forced to surrender virtually all their European territories. After the setback in Libya, the humiliation in the Balkans was even more traumatic. But the Unionists had no choice but to accept their fate. However, they decided to make a concerted effort to end their diplomatic isolation and seek the protection of one of the blocs. They calculated that the Triple Entente between Britain, France, and Russia was the stronger combination and sought an alliance with each of these powers, but to no avail. The Entente rejected the Unionist offer, convinced that an alliance with the Turks would be a heavy liability in a war against Germany. Berlin had reached the same conclusion and signed the secret alliance with Istanbul on August 2, 1914, only after the war in Europe had broken out. The Unionists preferred an alliance full of risks to neutrality and isolation.

Until the outbreak of war in Europe, most Unionists were pro-Entente. But Britain's naval blockade of the Dardanelles and its decision to confiscate two Turkish battleships built in British yards, and paid for by popular subscription, had a profound effect on the mood of the country.[5] The Porte issued a communiqué accusing Britain of a breach of international law. But the language of the press was much harsher, some newspapers describing Britain's decision as an act of piracy.[6] While Turkey maintained its armed neutrality, its hostility towards the Entente remained guarded. There was still hope of a short war and an early peace and therefore it would be unwise to alienate any of the Great Powers who might well decide Turkey's fate at the peace table. However, with the

---

4. "Osmanli ve İslam Muhibbi Alman'lara Açik Mektup" (Open letter to the Germans, friends of the Ottomans and Islam), in Mehmet Âkif, *Imzasız*, Vol. 7 of *Sirat-i Müstakim* (n.p., n.d.), p. 169, quoted in Cevdet Kudret, "Mehmet Akif," *Yön* (Istanbul), Vol. 6, No. 196 (December 30, 1966), p. 8.

5. Mehmet Cavit, "Mesrutiyet Devrine ait Cavit Beyin Hatiralari" (Cavid Bey's memoirs of the constitutional period), *Tanin*, October 16, 1944.

6. See Yunus Nadi, "Hazar Lanet" (A thousand curses), *Tasvir-i Efkar* (Istanbul), August 7, 1914.

declaration of jihad against the Entente in November 1914, Britain, France, and Russia—the colonizers of Islamic lands—became the enemy. Turkish armies fought on two fronts, in eastern Anatolia against Russia, and at the Dardanelles against Britain and France.

Had the Entente fleet broken through at the Dardanelles, that would have marked the end of the Ottoman Empire. A report presented to the British cabinet on June 30, 1915, entitled "British Desiderata on Turkey-in-Asia" noted that Britain's war aim was to create a "new order in Asiatic Turkey . . . keeping the Ottoman Empire in name but breaking the 'vampire-hold of the metropolis,' providing for local rule in each of the geographic provinces—Anatolia, Armenia, Palestine, and Iraq." Two years later, in response to President Wilson's letter, the Entente stated its own war aims. Concerning the Ottoman Empire they demanded "the liberation of the populations subject to the bloody tyranny of the Turk and the eviction from Europe of the Ottoman Empire."[7] This became one of the Entente's main war aims; Istanbul only learned of it in November 1917, after the Bolsheviks made public the secret treaties.

The Entente failed to force the Dardanelles and this victory gave the Turks a new sense of confidence about their ability to survive as an empire. Instead of being Germany's clients, they saw themselves as allies and partners who had made vital contributions to the war effort. Nevertheless, the situation for the Turks remained desperate until the outbreak of revolution in Russia in March 1917. There was hope of an early peace if Russia left the war. But the provisional government's determination to continue the war and its aggressive war aims led to despair. The Unionists came to the conclusion that even a Russian republic, whether socialist, federalist, or liberal, and ruled according to the ideas of the Cadets, would pursue the traditional policy of the tsars. Thus Russia, while a single political entity, would not be a friendly neighbor. To be a peaceful neighbor, Russia had to become a federal state; only then would the Black Sea be transformed from a battlefield to an arena of harmony and cooperation.[8]

The situation in Russia had the effect of changing the attitude of the Turks towards England. The press began to describe it as the obstacle to peace, continuing the war for its own imperialist war aims, and keeping France and Russia in the war through bribery and duplicity. The Istanbul daily *Tanin* (October 14, 1917) commented:

---

7. Cabinet Papers 27/1, quoted in William Stivers, *Supremacy and Oil: Iraq, Turkey and the Anglo-American World Order, 1918–1930* (Ithaca, N.Y.: Cornell University Press, 1982), pp. 22–23.

8. "Rusya ve Biz" (Russia and us), *Ikdam* (Istanbul), October 9, 1917.

Everyone knows the egotism and vanity of England. Her lack of morality has been proved in this war. The English look upon foreigners as slaves to be exploited for their own purpose. England binds foreign nations to herself through cunning and duplicity so that they cannot break away. This war has finally shown England in her true colors, as the personification of treachery and selfishness.

At the same time, the attitude towards Russia became friendly, especially after the Bolsheviks seized power in November. Lenin's program of peace was welcomed in all quarters and the Turkish response was one of sympathy, even condescension. The speech in the assembly made by Servet Bey, deputy for the province of Trabzon, then under Russian occupation, expressed the sense of sympathy for the new Russia. He said:

I am of the opinion that we must take the first opportunity to listen to the voice of humanitarianism—that is, we must profit by the offer made to neutrals and belligerents by the Russian government. The proclamation which was read yesterday [November 30] in the press is addressed to all governments and all peoples, to the working classes, and to the deputies all over the world. I hope that the Turkish Chamber . . . will not remain indifferent to it. I am also sure that once the moment comes, our government will not fail to make known to us the official communication. . . . For my part, I applaud and congratulate the present rulers of Russia for their humanitarian action.[9]

A few days later, on December 5, 1917, the Russo-Turkish armistice on the Caucasus front was signed at Erzincan.[10] To show their goodwill towards the world of Islam, the Bolsheviks published an appeal to the Muslims of Russia and the East reaffirming their abrogation of the Secret Treaties "regarding the seizure of Constantinople, which was confirmed by Kerensky, the treaty to partition the Ottoman Empire, the Sykes-Picot Agreement which would have deprived the empire of Armenia."[11]

Soviet propaganda found a receptive ear among the Turks. In Soviet revelations, they found irrefutable proof of the Entente's policy of conquest and partition at the expense of the Ottomans. "Each time the Entente found itself faced with the need to promise something to some element or nation which it wished to drag into war on its side, it promised a

---

9. *Tanin*, December 2, 1917.

10. Yusuf Hikmet Bayur, *Türk İnkilabi Tarihi* (History of the Turkish revolution), Vol. 2, Pt. 4 (Ankara, 1952), p. 95.

11. *Izvestia*, November 22/December 5, 1917, pp. 2–3, quoted in Ivar Spector, *The Soviet Union and the Muslim World, 1917–1958* (Seattle: distributed by the University of Washington Press, 1959), pp. 33–34.

piece of our country." The Bolsheviks had exposed the myth that the Entente had been fighting for such humanitarian aims as the freedom of nations. It was time to mend fences with the Russians now that they had put an end to the anti-Turkish intrigues of the tsarist government.[12]

The Bolsheviks had not only put an end to the intrigues of the old regime, but they promised to leave the war and respect the rights of every nation. Such statements were welcomed in Istanbul and Yunus Nadi, a Unionist deputy and journalist, applauded the Bolsheviks for their achievements:

The great revolution which this new government will produce in the Near East and which contains the conditions essential to unlimited confidence in the relations between us may be considered as a fortunate issue for the good of the human race. Tsarist Russia did nothing but cause the greatest misfortunes to humanity with the ambitions, for example, of gaining possession of the Straits. If we do not have to fight for our very survival, it is well known that the Straits are open to the whole world.[13]

Bolshevik declarations of peace coincided with the Entente's Paris declaration that Turkey would be expelled from Europe and restricted to Asia Minor. *Tanin* countered:

Such stupid statements as these—even if intended as a joke—will not be tolerated and their repetition will force us to speak more bluntly once the war is over. The first test of a civilized nation is its attachment to its territory and to the nation. If the Italians, who allowed the enemy to conquer their country, are European why should not the Turks, who defended heroically their capital for months, remain a part of Europe?[14]

The major shift in Turkish foreign policy took place under circumstances of war and revolution. The Western alliance of England and France had already partitioned Ottoman lands and decided that the Turks would be expelled from Europe. Bolshevik Russia, itself a pariah state engaged in civil war and facing Western intervention, provided the

---

12. "Sulh Celsesı" (Peace conference), *Tanin*, December 5, 1917.

13. Yunus Nadi, "İhtilal ve İnkilap Rusyasi ve Biz" (Russia in revolution and reform and us), *Tasvir-i Efkar*, December 4, 1917; Agaoglu Ahmed, a Turk from Azerbaijan who had harbored pan-Turkish aspirations during the war, wrote that there would be no reason for hostility towards Russia now that it had abandoned its expansionist policies. See *Hilal* (Istanbul), December 5, 1917.

14. "Türkiye Avrupadan Kovulacakmış" (Turkey is to be driven out of Europe), *Tanin*, December 10, 1917.

only guarantee for the future. But the territorial basis for the Turkey-to-be was far from clear. At Brest-Litovsk in 1918, the Porte regained territory in eastern Anatolia lost to Russia in 1877–78 but Anatolia was still not well defined in the Turkish mind. When the empire was under siege in 1915, the Unionists "discovered" Anatolia and with it a sense of Anatolian-Turkish patriotism. But as soon as the British had been forced to evacuate the Gallipoli peninsula, the Unionists reverted to their imperial war aims of regaining the Arab provinces, including Egypt, from the British. These aims remained official until the failure of the German offensive of July 1918. Thereafter such ambitions were abandoned and the Nationalists settled for Ottoman territories held by the army at the signing of the armistice at Mudros on October 30, 1918. These boundaries were adopted in the National Pact of 1919. In July 1923, the Treaty of Lausanne gave international recognition to virtually the same borders, thereby creating the new Turkey.

The policy of conciliation with Moscow, begun during the last stages of the First World War, was cemented during Turkey's national struggle and Russia's civil war. The sultan's Istanbul was under Allied occupation and the British were determined to implement their policy of driving the Turks out of Europe. Their Greek allies wanted to go one step further: they not only wanted to drive the Turks out of Europe but they were also determined to incorporate western Anatolia into a greater Greece. To accomplish that goal, a Greek army landed in Izmir on May 15, 1919, launching an invasion that lasted until September 1922. The Greek invasion provoked a resistance movement among the Muslims of Anatolia, which came to be led by Mustafa Kemal Pasha.

The Nationalists and the Bolsheviks were natural allies given the hostility of the West to both movements. But ideologically they were far apart. Mustafa Kemal had no sympathy for communism and took measures necessary to crush it. Nor did he and Stalin have warm regard for each other and he pursued a policy not always in conformity with Stalin's wishes. Thus Stalin did not trust Mustafa Kemal's motives when he agreed to give political asylum to Trotsky. Before Trotsky arrived in Istanbul on February 12, 1929, Maxim Litvinov, Stalin's commissar for foreign affairs, wrote in his journal:

Received a letter from our Embassy in Ankara. Kemal said he saw no objection to granting a visa to Trotsky, but warned that he would have to stay in the Embassy or consulate of the USSR. . . . I had a talk with Koba [Stalin]. He was dissatisfied. "Kemal is a scoundrel," he said. "The offer smacks of provocation." . . . I said there was no hope of getting a visa from other countries. . . .

He retorted that our diplomats were "cobblers" and they should take lessons from the English: the English would have managed to get a visa. . . . In the end he said, "We shall probably have to accept. Let him go to Kemal."[15]

Trotsky's private secretary, Jean van Heijenoort, wrote in his memoirs:

Throughout Trotsky's stay in Turkey there were no difficulties with the Turkish authorities. During the Turkish struggle for national independence in 1920 Kemal Pasha had received arms from Soviet Russia, which had been delivered through the agency of Trotsky as commissar for war. Years later, a visitor reported Trotsky as having said in 1933: "When Turkey was fighting Greece in the war I helped Kemal Pasha with the Red Army. Fellow soldiers don't forget such things. That was why Kemal Pasha didn't lock me up in spite of pressure from Stalin." The words may not be exactly Trotsky's, but he did in fact give military supplies. I also heard it said that in the early years of the Russian Revolution, Lenin and Trotsky had been made honorary members of the Turkish Parliament.[16]

Be that as it may, a working relationship with Moscow had become the main pillar of Turkey's foreign policy and remained so until at least Atatürk's death in November 1938. Falih Rifki Atay, a journalist in Mustafa Kemal's inner circle, wrote, "It was clear that he [Atatürk] did not want Russia and Turkey to ever be enemies again."[17]

The aphorism "Peace at Home, Peace in the World," often used as

---

15.   Maxim Litvinov, *Notes for a Journal* (London: Andre Deutsch, 1955), p. 76.

16.   Jean van Heijenoort, *With Trotsky in Exile: From Prinkipo to Coyoacan* (Cambridge, Mass.: Harvard University Press, 1978), pp. 21–22. While Lenin was alive, relations with the Nationalists were cordial. In November 1921, Lenin sent Mikhail Frunze to Ankara on a mission to provide support to a beleaguered Turkey. In a speech to the assembly, Frunze declared: "The voices which once urged our people to the conquest of Constantinople, the Straits and Anatolia have been stilled for ever." See Raymond Lacoste, *La Russie soviétique et la question d'Orient* (Paris: Les Éditions internationales, 1946), p. 62, quoted by André Fontaine, *History of the Cold War* (New York: Pantheon Books, 1968), p. 285. Mustafa Kemal sent telegrams to Moscow and Kharkov to express his appreciation of the Frunze mission. He wrote: "The mere fact that the Government of the Ukrainian Soviet Republic, for concluding a treaty of friendship in order to further strengthen the political and economic ties between both peoples has chosen Frunze, one of the outstanding political leaders and at the same time one of the valorous generals and heroic leaders of the victorious Red Army, has caused particular gratitude on the part of the National Assembly." *Izvestiya VTsIK*, December 28, 1921, quoted in Makhmut Akhmetovich Gareev, *M.V. Frunze, Military Theorist* (Washington, D.C.: Pergamon-Brassey's, 1988), p. 48.

17.   Falih Rifki Atay, *Inanç* (Belief) (Istanbul: Dünya Yayinları, 1965), p. 21. Mustafa acquired the surname Atatürk by the law of November 1934.

shorthand to describe Kemalist foreign policy, suggests a quietist policy which sought isolation from the rest of the world. Yet that was never the case. Even before the establishment of the Republic, the nationalists had signed agreements with their neighbors to the north as well as with distant Afghanistan. At this point, the goal was to end the isolation imposed upon the new Turkey by the West after the end of the First World War. Even after the signing of the Treaty of Lausanne in July 1923, the Turks had to struggle hard to stop the European powers from treating the new state as they had the former Ottoman Empire. Yusuf Hikmet Bayur in his 1934 study, *Yeni Türkiye Devletinin Harici Siyaseti,* describes how the republican government had to struggle constantly to be treated as an equal in response to some of the indignities the powers tried to heap on Turkey. Thus, even though Ankara was Turkey's new capital, some of the powers refused to move their embassies from Istanbul. The newly appointed American ambassador, Joseph Grew, who arrived in Turkey in August 1927, stayed in Istanbul most of the year, taking the night express to Ankara whenever it was necessary to do so. It is worth quoting from his diary for September 21, 1927, which reveals his casual attitude:

Here I am on the night train from Constantinople to Angora . . . feeling much more on a sight-seeing tour than traveling for the purpose of establishing relations with a new Government. My visit to the Minister for Foreign Affairs tomorrow will be purely incidental; happening to find myself in the capital of Turkey, of course I shall look in on him—that's the way I feel; I ought to be carrying a Turkish Baedeker.[18]

By the late 1920s, Turkey had regained much of its self-confidence, having reconciled itself to the loss of Mosul to British-mandated Iraq. As a result, its entire perception of geopolitics had changed. As far as Tevfik Rüstü Aras and the foreign ministry were concerned, the frontiers of the Near East were no longer the same; they no longer included Iran or the Arab provinces of the now-defunct Ottoman Empire. He defined the Near East as:

the Balkans and Turkey and its frontier is the eastern frontier of Turkey. Persia, Russia, Iraq, and Afghanistan compose the Middle East, and everything east of that is the Far East. Turkey is now a western power; the death of a peasant in the Balkans is of more importance to Turkey than the death of a king in Afghanistan.

---

18. Joseph Grew, *Turbulent Era,* Vol. 2 (Boston: Houghton Mifflin, 1952), p. 717.

He concluded that for Turkey "the Balkan Question exists no longer; it has disappeared and has become the Mediterranean Question."[19]

By the late 1920s and the early 1930s, the Mediterranean Question had come to mean thwarting the dream of Mussolini, Italy's fascist dictator who dreamed of restoring the Roman Empire in Asia and Africa and turning the Mediterranean into an Italian lake. Turkey took such pretensions seriously; not only had it fought the Italians in Libya, but the memory of Italian designs on the Antalya region after the First World War was still very fresh. Moreover, the Italians were still in occupation of the Dodecanese islands off the coast of Anatolia, islands they had occupied in 1912 and were now developing as a major base for expansion in the eastern Mediterranean.

Turkey dealt with the threat from Italy in terms of a policy Tevfik Rüstü Aras often described to Ambassador Grew during his term of five years: "Our foreign policy is simple and direct; we seek friendship with all, alliance or *groupement* with none."[20] This was the spirit in which the Grand National Assembly ratified the Briand-Kellogg Pact in January 1929, renouncing war as an instrument of national policy. Turkey became the first country to do so after the United States, which was a signatory with France. Ankara had already signed an agreement on neutrality with Rome on May 30, 1928, binding both countries to neutrality in case of conflict with a third country and to arbitration should any dispute arise between them. In June 1930, the Turkish-Greek accord cleared the way for friendly relations between the two states, which were still occupied with problems left over from Lausanne. While regional agreements were significant in Turkey's strategic thinking, Ankara recognized that only friendly relations with such major powers as Britain, France, and the Soviet Union could provide true security against another Great Power, even of the second rank, such as Italy. Thus the Turco-Soviet Treaty of Friendship of December 1925 continued to be the basis of the cordial relationship with Moscow. But the warm reception given by the government to the British Mediterranean fleet in October 1929 began the process of reconciliation with London, which was cemented with an alliance in 1939.

Turkey's first venture into European affairs took place in 1930 when it joined a commission of inquiry into European union. Two years later, in

---

19. Ibid., p. 753. Grew's conversation with Tevfik Rüştü took place on January 14, 1928.

20. Ibid., p. 917.

July 1932, Turkey entered the League of Nations and became an ardent supporter of the principle of "collective security" against aggression. If the reaction in the Turkish press is anything to go by, there was great and natural sympathy for Ethiopia when it was attacked by Italy in October 1935. Ethiopia was the last remaining independent state in Africa after the partition of that continent by the European powers, just as the Ottomans had been the last Muslim state to survive the imperialist onslaught before the First World War. The Turks could not help but make the comparison, having been the victims of Italian and Western aggression a generation earlier.

Ankara's policy, based on pragmatism rather than sentimentality, was also principled. Ankara supported "collective security" and it therefore backed the League of Nations sanctions against Italy. Turkey adopted this position even though it sold both cereals and coal to Italy, one of its best customers during the depressed 1930s, and sanctions were therefore a considerable economic sacrifice. Moreover Italy, in occupation of the Dodecanese islands, even posed a military threat to Anatolia.

The Hoare-Laval Pact of December 1935, by which Britain and France abandoned Ethiopia to Mussolini, was bitterly criticized in the press. The Istanbul daily, *Cumhuriyet* (December 15, 1935), noted with heavy sarcasm that Ethiopia would surely have been denounced by the appeasers as the aggressor had it refused to be dismembered and fought back in self-defense. For the Turks, what they were witnessing under the guise of appeasement in the 1930s was virtually the same policy used to dismember the Ottoman Empire and to partition Anatolia. When the League accepted the Anglo-French proposals for Ethiopia, it did just what the Concert of Europe had done to the Ottomans in the past. The Turks could not forget their past so easily and therefore found it natural to sympathize with the victims of aggression.

The Spanish Civil War began virtually at the same moment as the signing of the Montreux Convention on July 20, 1936, permitting Turkey to militarize the straits. Turkey had sought the revision of the Lausanne Treaty in order to defend itself against possible Italian aggression. As the guardian of the straits, Turkey occupied a vital strategic position on the supply line from the Soviet Union to Spain. The war in Spain was seen by many as a European civil war, a struggle between democracy and dictatorship. Mussolini and Hitler came out in open support of General Franco's rebellion against the republican government. England and France proposed that all states refrain from intervening in the conflict and from supplying arms to either party. This became the policy of the League though that did not prevent Rome, Berlin, and Moscow from supplying their clients in the civil war. Ankara followed the League's lead but its sympathies were with the republicans.

Turkey was in no position to play an independent role in Spain, as Hitler and Mussolini were doing on Franco's behalf and Stalin on behalf of the Spanish republic. It continued to support collective security, especially when the Italian threat came closer to home with the sinking of a Spanish ship in Turkish waters in August 1937. The Mediterranean states responded by convening the Nyon conference in September and denouncing "Italian piracy." The Turkish delegation, acting on Atatürk's instructions, went so far as to permit British and French ships to use Turkish naval bases to prevent Italian aggression. Prime Minister İnönü opposed this policy on the grounds that Italy would find it provocative.[21]

Throughout the 1930s, relations with Britain improved dramatically and the desire to be close to the democracies also had an impact on the character of the regime at home. As *The Times* (London) noted on May 25, 1937, "In a sense, Turkey's foreign policy which relied on Moscow, and after 1936 on London and Paris, depended on having a regime at home which did not have a fascist colouring." This may have been a factor in the dismissal of Recep Peker as the ruling party's secretary-general in 1936 for he represented the faction in the Republican People's Party that was responsible for giving the Kemalist regime a "fascist colouring."

Turkey's attitude towards the threat the dictators posed was not restricted merely to diplomatic maneuvers and support for collective security. The government also took measures to deter aggression by strengthening the country's defenses. Not only were the straits refortified but the government also decided to build an air force, the principal instrument of modern warfare. The military maneuvers in Aydin in October 1937, attended by Atatürk, İnönü, and Bayar, were clearly designed to demonstrate the country's determination to resist Italian aggression. The Hitler-Mussolini meetings of these years, where the two dictators were thought to be discussing their spheres of influence, alarmed Ankara and led to greater emphasis on cooperation with neighbors in the Balkans and in the Middle East.

There is much more to explore concerning Turkish policy and attitude towards fascist aggression and the policy of appeasement in the 1930s. Perhaps Turkey's response to the Munich agreement of September 1938 and the Nazi seizure of Czechoslovakia the following spring sums up its position. If we measure this response from the comment of Tur-

21. Dilek Barlas, *Etatism and Diplomacy in Turkey: Economic and Foreign Policy Strategies in an Uncertain World, 1929–1939* (Leiden: E.J. Brill, 1998), pp. 184–185.

key's controlled press, we learn that the Turks were alarmed by the cynicism of Chamberlain and Daladier in signing away Czech territory to the Germans. But they were not surprised by such an act, having witnessed something similar in Ethiopia, and relying on their own past experience. Even though Britain was seen as the main factor in Prague's passivity, there was even greater dismay when the Czechs surrendered their independence without a fight. The Turks remembered their own national struggle and were convinced that if the Czechs had decided to fight they could have maintained their dignity if not their independence. *Cumhuriyet*, the voice of the Kemalist establishment, was quite adamant in stating that if the Czechs had fought the Nazis, their situation would not have been any the worse; indeed, they might have saved the nation.

Throughout the 1930s, Kemalist Turkey took a clear stand against appeasing the dictators. This policy was so rare in Europe of the 1930s that George Orwell was able to write: "In the years 1935–9, when almost any ally against Fascism seemed acceptable, left-wingers found themselves praising Mustafa Kemal."[22] This in itself was a unique achievement in the history of the early Republic and speaks volumes for the foreign policy of the Kemalist regime.

After Atatürk's death in November 1938, Turkey's foreign policy became more cautious and opportunistic. Relations with Moscow, the keystone of Kemalist foreign relations, cooled after the signing of the Nazi-Soviet Pact in August 1939 and Ankara's "orientation in foreign policy now entered a new phase." In October, Foreign Minister Sükrü Saraçoglu visited Moscow to test the waters and was confronted for the first time with Stalin's proposals to revise the Montreux Convention regarding the straits in Russia's favor. Saraçoglu rejected these proposals and "strongly denied any possibility of bilateral revision of a multilateral convention and said Turkey would never allow another Treaty of Hünkar Iskelesi" (of 1833) when Russia was allowed joint defense of the straits.[23] Yet by December 1941, when British Foreign Secretary Anthony Eden arrived in Moscow, soon after the Japanese attack on Pearl Harbor, Stalin made a number of proposals for a postwar settlement. He requested "an immediate agreement to the incorporation of Estonia, Lithuania, Latvia,

---

22. George Orwell, "Who are the War Criminals?" *Tribune*, October 22, 1943, in *The Collected Essays, Journalism and Letters of George Orwell*, ed. Sonia Orwell and Ian Angus, Vol. 3 (London: Secker and Warburg, 1970), p. 367. I owe this reference to my friend, the late Dr. Naim Turfan.

23. Selim Deringil, *Turkish Foreign Policy during the Second World War* (Cambridge: Cambridge University Press, 1989), pp. 85–86. See also Edward Weisband, *Turkish Foreign Policy 1943–1945* (Princeton, N.J.: Princeton University Press, 1973).

and parts of Finland, Poland, and Rumania into the USSR."[24] The straits were not mentioned and there was no request for any concessions from neutral Turkey. In fact, its strategic importance had improved so much that in order to woo Ankara and bring Turkey into the war, Stalin and Molotov proposed that after the war Turkey be given "the Dodecanese Islands and perhaps territories from Bulgaria and Syria."[25]

İnönü's government preferred to remain neutral, possibly gambling on a German victory in the Soviet Union. Perhaps that also explains the discriminatory wealth tax, the notorious *Varlik Vergisi,* imposed on Turkey's minorities. In 1942 the odds favored Germany. It controlled almost all of Europe and its resources, and seemed poised to move into the Middle East. Its ally Japan had destroyed the colonial empires and threatened India and Australia. The Soviet Union had been invaded and lost its industrial base west of the Urals; the United States had yet to mobilize its huge resources.

Until the German surrender at Stalingrad in February 1943, Turkey's neutrality tended to favor Berlin. But soon after the Casablanca meeting between Churchill and Roosevelt (January 12–13, 1943) there was a cautious change. Churchill attempted to bring Turkey into the war with the aim of entering the Balkans behind Ankara, before Stalin was able to do so. But the ever-cautious İnönü preferred to remain neutral.[26]

The question of the straits came up again when Stalin and Churchill met in Moscow in October 1944 to discuss post-war Europe and divide it into spheres of influence. Churchill "expanded the first discussion from Greece and Rumania to include Hungary and Yugoslavia."

Stalin rejoined with a reference to Bulgaria—and, to test the waters at their deepest, Turkey. "What about Russian rights in controlling the Black Sea straits?" [he asked]. The 1936 Montreux Convention covering the entrance to the Black Sea gave Japan as many rights as Russia. If Britain was interested in the Mediterranean, Russia had an equal concern with the Black Sea regime still dominated by Turkey. Suddenly on guard, Churchill asked what changes Stalin had in mind? For the moment, came the answer, agreement that the Montreux Convention must be altered was enough. "What would Britain do if Spain or Egypt were to gain the right to close the Suez Canal, or what would the United States say if some South American Republic had the right to close the Panama Canal? Russia was in a worse situation." Churchill accepted the principle, suggesting that it had to be done in a friendly way so as

---

24. Forrest Pogue, "The Struggle for a New Order," in John Snell, ed., *The Meaning of Yalta* (Baton Rouge: Louisiana State University Press, 1956), p. 18.

25. Ibid.

26. Lloyd Gardner, *Spheres of Influence* (Chicago: I.R. Dee, 1993), pp. 158–159, n. 29.

not to frighten Istanbul. The prime minister then suggested that Stalin take up the Montreux Convention with the United States.[27]

The question of the straits came up at the Yalta Conference in February 1945 when Moscow suggested that the subject be placed on the agenda of the first meeting of foreign ministers after Yalta. The Western powers agreed after observing that Turkey should be informed and assured that its independence would be guaranteed.[28] And that is where the matter rested until the end of the war.

Conventional wisdom concerning Turkish-Soviet relations after the Second World War informs us that Soviet demands and pressure on Turkey forced Ankara to seek Western support and to become an active participant in the Cold War.[29] There may be some truth to this interpretation but it fails to consider domestic factors that led to a radical shift in Ankara's foreign policy. After the war both parties, the ruling Republicans and the opposition Democrats, believed that the fastest way to develop Turkey's economy and modernize its society was by injecting large doses of capital into the economy. Since the country lacked such resources, necessary investment could come only from the United States. Washington would be more forthcoming, analysts in Ankara argued, if Turkey were to be a willing participant in a U.S.-led Cold War. This, then, was the policy the government adopted and it soon began to pay off. The Truman Doctrine and the implementation of the Marshall Plan in Turkey were the first installments, and membership in NATO the last.

Though diplomatic historians tend not to focus on domestic factors in their discussion of foreign policy, their analysis of new documents is often valuable in revising what passes as conventional wisdom. In Turkey, such revisionist writers as Yalçin Küçük questioned the well-established theses on Turkey and the Cold War. But their work, though useful and provocative, was impressionistic, based as it was on secondary sources. Recent studies by a new generation of U.S. diplomatic historians, based primarily on U.S. archival documents, often recently declassified, shed new light on this murky postwar period and help us re-

---

27. Ibid., pp. 198–201.

28. Charles Delzell, "Russian Policy in Central-Eastern Europe," in John Snell, ed., *The Meaning of Yalta* (Baton Rouge: Louisiana State University Press, 1956), p. 118.

29. Bruce Kuniholm, *The Origins of the Cold War in the Near East* (Princeton, N.J.: Princeton University Press, 1980) remains the best conventional account of the origins of the Cold War in the Near East. But, as with earlier diplomatic histories of the Eastern Question, the author uses virtually no Turkish sources and treats Turkey as a passive victim.

consider Turkey's foreign policy. Needless to say, what scholars need are Turkish diplomatic documents to provide a fuller picture. But until we are given access to them, we shall be forced to rely on U.S. State Department and presidential archives.

The conventional story of Turkish-Soviet relations after the war is familiar enough not to bear detailed repetition. Relations between Ankara and Moscow were no longer cordial after the war because the Soviet Union was convinced that Turkey's neutrality had favored Berlin.[30] Thus, when the Soviet-Turkish Treaty of Friendship of 1925 was due to expire in 1945, Moscow placed conditions on its renewal. These included the joint defense of the straits and the return to Georgia of the territories of Kars and Ardahan, which had been recovered by the Ottomans in 1918. The Soviet, and especially the Georgian, press began an anti-Turkish campaign as a part of a war of nerves. However, it is worth emphasizing that there were no official demands from Moscow, there were only proposals.

At the same time, the growth of Soviet influence in the Balkans and northern Iran made Turkey an important asset for American policymakers and the dispatch of the battleship USS *Missouri* was a symbol of Turkey's increasing significance in U.S. strategy. The *Missouri* arrived at Istanbul on April 5, 1946, ostensibly to return the body of Münir Ertegün, the Turkish ambassador who had died in Washington. But the visit was arranged by Secretary of the Navy James Forrestal as a show of force in the Mediterranean designed to intimidate Moscow. Forrestal had wanted to send ships of the Atlantic Eighth Fleet into the Mediterranean to accompany the *Missouri*. Initially, James Byrnes of the State Department had agreed with the proposal, but after the start of the Iranian crisis in March he suggested postponement for fear that the dispatch of such a task force might seem a provocative act. Nevertheless, Forrestal made arrangements for two cruisers from the Eighth Fleet to join the *Missouri*.[31] Despite the alarm over the communist threat, Greece, Turkey, and Iran re-

---

30. It is well known that neutral Turkey supplied such strategic materials to the Nazis during the war. But it also seems to have supplied the Germans with intelligence on Russia. See Reinhard Gehlen, *The Service: The Memoirs of General Reinhard Gehlen*, trans. David Irving (New York: World Publishing, 1972), p. 64: "From decoded Turkish intelligence cables we were extracting information on Russian armoured brigades. On other occasions the Turkish foreign minister supplied us with information of interest to us about Russia."

31. On the significance of the visit of the *Missouri* see David Alvarez, "The Missouri Visit to Turkey: An Alternative Perspective in Cold War Diplomacy," *Balkan Studies*, Vol. 15 (1974), pp. 225–236; and Melvyn Leffler, *A Preponderance of Power: National Security, the Truman Administration, and the Cold War* (Stanford, Calif.: Stanford University Press, 1992), p. 123.

ceived very little financial assistance: Greece received $35 million, Turkey $38 million, and Iran nothing, suggesting that the communist threat was merely for home consumption.[32]

Melvyn Leffler writes that on August 7, 1946, Moscow sent a note to Ankara proposing the revision of the Montreux Convention:

The Soviets advocated a new regime for the Turkish straits limited to the Black Sea powers, and a joint Russo-Turkish defense of the straits. . . . [Ankara] found these terms unacceptable and looked to the United States for support. Because there was no explicit demand for bases on Turkish soil however, Foreign Minister Hasan Saka actually breathed a sigh of relief after reading the Soviet démarche. Not so Ambassador Wilson.[33]

Quoting from contemporary official sources, Leffler notes that Moscow "asked Turkey to alter the rules governing ship movements through the Dardanelles. The Russians maintained that the existing regulations had not protected their interests during World War II. They wanted to get together with other Black Sea powers, formulate a new set of rules, and establish a joint defense of the straits."[34] Interpreting Soviet intentions, the United States embassy in Moscow "did not think that the Kremlin would move aggressively against Turkey. Nor did most other U.S. diplomats, military planners, and intelligence analysts. Moreover reports from Istanbul suggested that the Turks were relieved rather than alarmed by the note." Leffler continues: "American fears did not stem from aggressive Soviet moves against Turkey. The Soviets had done little more than send a diplomatic note. The real problem was that there loomed gaping vacuums of power in this part of the world resulting from the decline of British power."[35]

In fact, Turkey's geopolitical importance was directly related to the evolution of U.S. strategic concepts. On July 27, 1946, Secretary of War Robert Patterson emphasized to President Truman the importance of having "cushions of distance . . . between Soviet areas and areas vital to us." On August 15, the very day Truman approved a tough response to the Soviet note to Turkey, military planners completed a study,

---

32. Chester Pach, *Arming the Free World: The Origins of the United States Military Program, 1945–1950* (Chapel Hill: University of North Carolina Press, 1991), pp. 95 and 255, n. 26.

33. Ibid., pp. 97–98.

34. Leffler, *Preponderance of Power*, p. 123.

35. Ibid., p. 124

code-named GRIDDLE, that called for "every practicable measure . . . to permit the utilization of Turkey as a base for Allied operations in the event of war with the USSR."

The Pentagon noted:

The Turks could slow down a Soviet advance toward Cairo-Suez, thereby affording time for the United States to inaugurate the strategic offensive. Likewise the Soviets could be denied control of the Dardanelles, their submarines might be bottled up in the Black Sea, thereby insuring much safer lines of communications for Allied forces traversing the eastern Mediterranean. If wartime developments permitted, Turkish airfields might even be used to launch raids against vital petroleum areas within the Soviet Union and Romania. At the very least, fighter aircraft, stationed in Turkey, might protect Allied bombers as they ventured into Soviet territory from bases at Cairo-Suez.[36]

Washington took the Soviet démarche to Turkey more seriously than Ankara and used it to fuel the fires of the Cold War at home where the Republicans were reluctant to pay for the arms build-up the Pentagon was striving for. The Soviet démarche was soon blown into a Soviet aggression that had to be resisted at all cost. Chester Pach writes that "Truman vastly exaggerated the danger of war. At the beginning of the straits crisis, Stalin asserted that he had no intention of using force to gain Soviet objectives in Turkey, and analyses by the Central Intelligence Group (CIG) confirmed those assertions."

Truman was informed on August 24, 1946

that the Soviets had not positioned their troops to strike against Turkey, but instead had slightly speeded up their demobilization program. . . . On balance . . . the Soviets were conducting an "intensive war of nerves," probably to "test U.S. determination to . . . sustain its commitment in European affairs." The Soviets still showed no inclination towards military action after the United States and Turkey rejected their proposals for defense of the straits. Another exchange of notes followed, but Soviet pressure for the revision of the Montreux Convention subsided by late October 1946. The only significant deployment of force during the straits crisis came not through the Soviet action but through American dispatch of a naval task force to the Eastern Mediterranean.[37]

---

36. Ibid. For the archival sources used see p. 551, n. 119.

37. Pach, *Free World*, pp. 100–101. Truman's biographer, Robert H. Ferrell, in his *Harry S. Truman: A Life* (Columbia: University of Missouri Press, 1994), writes that President Truman intensified U.S.-Soviet tensions by abruptly canceling Lend-Lease shipments and by overstating his case when announcing U.S. support for Greece and

At the height of the straits crisis, on August 23, 1946,

The Joint Chiefs of Staff recommended the sale of defensive armaments to Turkey. They considered Turkey "the most important military factor" in the Near East because of its strategic location and its apparent determination to fight, if necessary, to preserve its independence. Properly equipped, the Turkish army could mount strong resistance against a Russian attack.[38]

American policymakers were sharply divided over the question of military aid to Turkey. The Pentagon lobby supported the policy of providing military aid to Turkey so as to make it an integral part of U.S. Cold War strategy. In the State Department, such officers as George Kennan, the father of Washington's "containment policy," objected strenuously to such assistance, emphasizing that Turkey faced neither "serious Communist penetration" nor domestic strife. Kennan wanted "the accent . . . on internal morale and firmness of diplomatic stance, not on military preparations." He wanted Truman to make it clear that "there was no cause for alarm over the situation in Turkey."[39]

On February 21, 1947, the British government informed Washington that given their financial woes they could not sustain their assistance to Greece and Turkey. They wanted to pull their troops out of Greece and terminate their aid to both countries. Britain, impoverished by the vast expenditure of the Second World War and faced with a crisis at home, accepted its decline into the ranks of a second rate power. It therefore appealed to the United States government to take over principal responsibility for aiding Greece and Turkey. Leffler observes:

It was taken for granted that Turkey as well as Greece would receive American help. Yet as [Secretary of State Dean] Acheson worked on the draft legislation, he found it difficult to justify assistance to Turkey. Turkey did not need aid for relief or reconstruction, nor was it wracked by financial instability or internal unrest. It was not under any real pressure from the Kremlin. Nevertheless, U.S. officials decided that Turkey must receive assistance. Greece is on the "flank," conceded [Secretary of the Navy James] Forrestal, but if Tur-

---

Turkey. There were domestic economic reasons for fueling the Cold War. Within a month of Japan's surrender, war contracts worth $35 billion were canceled, leading to the unemployment of 2.7 million workers. Demobilization also raised fears of rampant inflation and produced a wave of strikes.

38. Ibid.

39. George F. Kennan, *Memoirs, 1925–1950* (New York: Bantam Books, 1969), pp. 316–317; Pach, *Free World*, p. 111. For a critical evaluation of Kennan's role during these years, see Anders Stephanson, *Kennan and the Art of Foreign Policy* (Cambridge, Mass.: Harvard University Press, 1989).

key falls into the Soviet orbit "you will have an impossible military situation."[40]

On March 12, 1947, President Harry Truman went before a joint session of Congress and delivered the most famous speech of his presidency in which he enunciated what became known as the "Truman Doctrine." "I believe," he declared, "that it must be the policy of the United States to support free people who are resisting attempted subjugation by armed minorities or by external pressures." He requested $400 million in military and economic aid for Greece and Turkey. Washington had assumed Britain's responsibilities in the region.

In the Pentagon, the Joint Chiefs continued to emphasize that Greece, and especially Turkey, were important for controlling the eastern Mediterranean; political analysts added that they were the keys to the future orientation of the entire Near East. This region was considered critical to U.S. interests because of its strategic and economic importance, and because it was the center of vital communications routes and possessed vast oil reserves.[41]

However, Kennan continued to dissent. In his memoirs, he wrote:

I took up the question of Turkey. I pointed out that the situation of Turkey differed quite fundamentally from that of Greece. There was no serious Communist penetration of Turkey—no comparable guerrilla movement. The Turks had nothing to fear but fear: "If . . . the Turks do not lose their nerves, if they keep their internal political life relatively clean and orderly and refuse to become involved in negotiations with the Russians on a bilateral basis over complicated questions such as that of the Straits, they will continue to enjoy a temporary and precarious immunity from Russian pressure." But, I pointed out, should they be increasingly encircled by communist-dominated entities, it would plainly be harder for them to maintain this stance. Aid to Greece was therefore important as a support for stability in Turkey as well.

It should be noted that this view of the problem of Turkey afforded no rationale for the mounting of a special aid program for Turkey itself. The accent was put on internal morale and on firmness of diplomatic stance, not on military preparations. It was for this reason that I was not happy to find in the draft of the President's message to Congress a proposal of aid to Turkey as well as to Greece. I suspected that what was intended was primarily military aid, and that what had really happened was that the Pentagon had exploited a favorable set of circumstances in order to infiltrate a military aid program for Turkey into what was supposed to be primarily a political and economic program for Greece. Since it was important, in my view, that the

---

40. Leffler, *Preponderance of Power*, p. 143–144.

41. Pach, *Free World*, p. 88–90.

Soviet threat be recognized for what it was—primarily a political one and not a threat of military attack—it seemed unfortunate that the picture of what was needed in Greece should be confused by association with something that was not needed—or, if needed, was needed for entirely different purposes—in Turkey.[42]

Despite Kennan's arguments, on May 22, 1947, Truman signed into law the Greek-Turkish Aid Act. Some months later, Congress sanctioned the full appropriation of $400 million. As a result, in 1948, Washington began to implement military aid to Turkey to complement the Middle East strategy envisioned in such military reports as BROILER and HALFMOON. U.S. Army advisers sought to reorganize and modernize the Turkish army, augment its mobility and firepower, improve its communication and transportation infrastructure, and bolster its logistical capabilities. They wanted the Turkish army to retard the Soviet land offensive, thereby affording time for the United States and Great Britain to launch the strategic air campaign from Egyptian bases. The Turkish army was given equipment to blunt a three-pronged Soviet attack across the Bosphorus, the Black Sea, and the Caucasus, to fall back gradually, and to mount a final, large-scale stand in southern Turkey in the Iskenderun pocket. During 1948, the United States also transferred over 180 F-47's, 30 B-26's, and 86 C-47's to the Turkish air force, planes that would assist the Turkish ground forces inside Turkey and help interdict Soviet troops moving toward Persian Gulf oil or sweeping toward Cairo-Suez. The United States also placed a great deal of stress on reconstructing and resurfacing Turkish airfields at such places as Bandirma and Diyarbakir. As a result, Turkey began to develop the ability to attack vital Soviet petroleum resources in Romania and the Caucasus. By the end of 1948 State Department officials endorsed the idea of constructing medium bomber bases in Turkey.[43]

But Turkey's leaders wanted much more than just U.S. military aid; they sought an agreement resembling an alliance. On January 7, 1947, top U.S. military leaders visiting Turkey saw President İnönü and reported that he "wanted a binding commitment either through a political defense pact or through a formal association of military staffs." Later, İnönü wrote directly to Truman stating: "We need assurances now that we would not be abandoned should Turkey be attacked."[44] American diplomats were not eager to make new commitments to Turkey. Yet defense

---

42. Kennan, *Memoirs,* pp. 333–334.

43. Leffler, *Preponderance of Power,* pp. 238–239.

44. Ibid., p. 289.

officials were more inclined than ever to use Turkey in the defense of the Middle East. Its willingness to fight the Soviets continued to impress visitors from the Pentagon.[45]

On April 12, 1949, Dean Acheson reported a conversation with Foreign Minister Necmettin Sadak on a visit to Washington in April.

Acheson was struck by his agitated demeanor. The peacetime military preparations undertaken by Turkey in conjunction with the United States aid meant that, if war should erupt, the Soviet Union would attack Turkey preemptively to forestall its use as a base for United States operations. Why should Turkey take such risks, Sadak inquired, if the United States would not promise to defend it? Why provoke the Kremlin if the Soviets might otherwise avoid war with Turkey, as they had done during the Second World War?

This perspective was so logical that diplomats and military officers feared that Turkey might seek a position of neutrality. The United States might then be unable to capitalize on its investments in Turkey. . . . [Acheson and Truman] preferred strategic advantage without military obligations. But they were also convinced of the need to possess Turkey's allegiance. Turkey thus held considerable bargaining power.[46]

Such was the situation at the time of the outbreak of the Korean War in June 1950. Turkey's willingness to cooperate with Western strategy in the Middle East had become suspect in Washington. After the outbreak of the Korean War, Turkish officials—under a Democrat Party government since mid-May—again tried to ascertain what the United States would do if Turkey were attacked. These overtures agitated Washington. State Department officials could find little evidence that the Kremlin was threatening Turkey. Lewis Jones, one of Paul Nitze's assistants on the Policy Planning Staff, frankly told the first secretary of the Turkish embassy, "Turkey was not being made an object of the Soviet diplomatic offensive or Soviet-inspired pressures."[47]

Although Turkish officials acknowledged that domestic politics had much to do with their insistent demands, there was little doubt among

---

45. Ibid.

46. Ibid., pp. 289–290. In James Chace, *Acheson: The Secretary of State Who Created the American World* (New York: Simon and Schuster, 1998), there is no mention of this conversation with Necmettin Sadak. In retrospect, it was not seen as having any great significance. The British government came to learn of the possibility of Turkish neutrality from a report submitted by the General Staff in May 1951. The diplomats seemed unaware of Turkish sentiments. See Ayşegül Sever, *Soğuk Savaş Kuşatmasinda Türkiye, Batı ve Orta Doğu* (Turkey in the siege of the Cold War, the West, and the Middle East) (Bagcilar, Istanbul: Boyut Kitaplari, 1997), p. 81.

47. Leffler, *Preponderance of Power*, pp. 419–420.

U.S. policymakers that from a geopolitical and strategic perspective the neutralist option constituted a viable possibility for the Turks. Nevertheless, Washington decided that Turkey and Greece would not be taken into NATO because it was not ready for new commitments.

The Turks felt aggrieved. They were contributing troops to the struggle in Korea. They were participating in the containment of communist totalitarianism. Why should they be left in a vulnerable position? Why should they assent to the desires of the U.S. navy to mine the straits in peacetime and why should they make commitments to allow the Americans to use their airfields in wartime if they were not guaranteed protection in return? An associated linkage to NATO was simply a sop. When George McGhee of the State Department, soon to be ambassador to Turkey, visited Turkey in February 1951, President Celal Bayar bluntly expressed his personal displeasure with the existing partnership. If Turkey were not admitted into NATO, Bayar said he would reappraise Turkey's orientation in the Cold War. McGhee wired Secretary of State Acheson: "There is reason to believe that Turkey will veer toward a policy of neutralism, which will always have strong basic appeal. Until commitment is extended to Turkey, there is no assurance that Turkey will declare war unless attacked."[48]

Bayar's threat of neutrality, couched in terms of reappraising "Turkey's orientation in the Cold War," had the desired effect on Washington. Despite European opposition, in September 1951 the NATO council agreed to admit Greece and Turkey into the alliance and both countries became full members on February 18, 1952. For the time being, the lines of Turkish foreign policy were clearly drawn. Ankara remained totally committed to the U.S.-led alliance into the early 1960s. However, in October 1962, President Kennedy's agreement with Premier Khrushchev to remove missiles from Turkey in exchange for the removal of missiles from Cuba alarmed Ankara. The government realized that Turkey's strategic importance was declining and its role and status within NATO would be revised accordingly.

The following year, in November 1963, President Makarios's proposal to amend the 1960 Cypriot constitution led to the threat of Turkish military intervention and the beginning of a crisis between Turkey and Greece. Ankara was disappointed when Washington failed to support the Turkish position. However, President Johnson's letter of June 1964 proved to be traumatic. He warned Prime Minister Ismet İnönü that Turkey could neither use arms provided by the United States without Wash-

---

48. Sever, *Soğuk Savaş Kuşatmasinda Türkiye*, p. 420.

ington's consent against Cyprus, nor could it expect the Atlantic alliance to come to Turkey's aid should Moscow decide to support Makarios. The Johnson letter forced Turkey to reevaluate its policy and to diversify it instead of depending entirely on Washington. The task of diversification was facilitated by the re-emergence of Europe as a political force.

After the foreign ministry's re-evaluation of Turkey's foreign policy in 1967, the government decided to tread a middle path between reliance on the United States and Europe. Turkey has continued to pursue essentially the same cautious policy since the end of the Cold War in the 1990s.

The Philosophical Dimension of
Turkish Foreign Policy

Chapter 3

The Future of Turkish Foreign Policy

Mümtaz Soysal

Few states have a more multifaceted historic destiny and geographic position than the Turkish Republic. Both its past and its location place it at the conjunction of the mainstream in world history and at the meeting point of three continents. It is at the same time in southeastern Europe, in the Black Sea basin, part of the Middle and Near East, and it belongs to the Mediterranean world, which means it is also linked to North Africa. Even in the modern conception of international relations, which minimizes the role of distance and the heritage of the past, geography and history are still the most important factors that determine Turkey's role in world politics.

In contrast, when one considers the global changes in the aftermath of the Cold War, Turkey is perhaps the country that has witnessed the most drastic transformations around its borders: change of regimes, dissolution of defense alliances, and ending of ideological confrontations have affected the whole geopolitical landscape. This fact seems to have reduced Turkey's geostrategic importance from the point of view of East-West military confrontation, but it certainly increases its significance in terms of new challenges emerging from the new set of international relations. These new challenges may seem to open new and tempting options for Turkish foreign policy in the future, but such options need to be examined against the background of the traditional tenets of Turkish diplomacy throughout the republican era.

Realities and Temptations

Turkey's geographic location inevitably gives its inhabitants the illusion of being at the center of the world, although this cartographic impression should, in a way, be common to the schoolchildren of all lands whose country occupies a central position on wall maps. A more sophisticated approach is required, if this impression is not to lead Turkey to international roles exceeding the capabilities of both the state and the nation.

This was the danger inherent in the grandiose scheme that aimed at the creation of a "Turkic bloc" by establishing close ties with Azerbaijan and the newly independent states of Central Asia after the dissolution of the Soviet Union. This flattering idea was the century-old dream of the early Turkish nationalists during the last days of the Ottoman period; it also became very popular among the country's politicians during the first years of the post–Cold War era. Were this scheme to be carried out, not only would it provoke fears of Turkish expansionism in Russian political circles, but it would also outstretch the economic and financial resources of the country. Furthermore, this sudden interest in the fate of distant Asian cousins was not matched by a solid knowledge of their economies, social structures, and cultures on the part of the Turkish establishment. If great damage to the preservation of good relations with Russia and to the pride of peoples in Central Asia was avoided during the pursuit of this clumsy initiative, this was due, as in many other instances, to the restraint and reserve of Turkish diplomacy. Moderation in the conduct of foreign policy prevented the popular enthusiasm for this new relationship from getting out of hand and negatively affecting Turkey's critical good neighbor policies with Russia. But this issue will remain one of the sensitive points of Turkish foreign policy in the future, because the Russian Federation continues to consider the same region within its own sphere of influence and sees the Caucasus as its "backyard." The same considerations seem to have influenced Ankara's measured reaction to the recent events in Chechnya in spite of strong public feelings, especially among the descendants of immigrants from the Caucasus.

Another consequence of the country's geographic position is the frequent use of the "bridge theory" in all projections about the future of its foreign relations. Analysts and policymakers alike never tire of emphasizing the East-West linkage assured by Turkey's position between Asia and Europe. This has often given rise to theories attributing to Turkish diplomacy a role of liaison and mediation between antagonistic spheres of influence in the region, implying thereby the gain of moral and material advantages from the use of the bridge. This view is also very widely shared by many Turkish politicians. But for such a role to be convincing and effective, the essential requirement is a political and ideological neutrality towards the two different worlds, namely the Western or European nations on the one side and the Asian or Middle Eastern countries on the other. It is obvious that Turkey's strong connections with the Western defense mechanisms, its membership in various European organizations, and, in particular, its clear preference for a Western and secular way of life as a standard for its social development weigh heavily against its religious affinities with the Eastern world, thus creating one of the important paradoxes of Turkish society, namely, the ambivalence of its culture. Under these circumstances, which are likely to last for a long time to come, attempting to play this role and trying to benefit from it in an active way risks giving the impression of being used for the promotion of Western interests in the region. Such a role is made all the more difficult by the present state of Turkey's relations with its immediate neighbors in the Middle East (Iran, Iraq, and Syria). This is why it would be wrong to expect a significant initiative by Turkish diplomacy toward the utilization of the bridge theory to assume the role of catalyst in this corner of the world. The rather ineffective role played by Turkish diplomacy in the recent U.S.-Iraqi conflict confirmed once again the fallacy of this presumption.

The most that can be concretely said in the context of Turkey's pivotal location is the likely continuation of its importance for communication and transportation between Europe and Central Asia via the Caucasus. It is obvious that Turkey will continue to attach great importance to the passage of pipelines through its territory for the transport of oil and natural gas from Iraq, Iran, the Caucasus, and Central Asia to European markets. In that respect, the Marmara straits will also continue to be important, though to a lesser degree after the completion of the projected pipelines between the Caspian Sea and the Mediterranean and the construction of a natural gas pipeline between the northern and southern shores of the Black Sea.

Given the geographic location of the country and the fact that Anatolia was the center of an empire stretching over three continents, it is a common assumption that every Turkish mind harbors an unavowed nostalgia for the past grandeur of the nation. Although this assumption runs against the declared non-irredentist philosophy of the Republic, the specter of this fictive imperialist design haunts the writings of most critics of Turkish foreign policy, especially in the neighboring countries.

Even if it does reign in the minds of all Turks, has this feeling of past and future grandeur ever become the driving force of a state policy or the basic pattern of official diplomacy? To say so would be doing a severe injustice to Turkish policymakers: for instance, can the determination of the Republic to defend its treaty rights in the Aegean be taken as a sign of aggressive intentions against its neighbor? Such accusations make sense only if the claim that the Aegean is the national domain of Greece is true.

The best proof of the non-irredentist philosophy of republican foreign policy resides in its constantly underlined attachment to the 1923 Treaty of Lausanne. This is the basic international instrument whereby a people solemnly forsakes its rights in all the territories of its past grandeur and undertakes the never-ending task of creating a nation-state within given borders. This task is so arduous by itself that it excludes any expansionist and expensive foreign adventure. Considering the volume and the intensity of what remains to be done internally, it would certainly be wrong to attribute any intention of reviving the imperial grandeur to the present policymakers of republican Turkey or to their eventual successors.

History and Future

Hostile and mostly distorted views of Turkish foreign policy are usually expressed by analysts and journalists coming from countries whose history bears the scars of some old or recent conflict with the Ottoman Empire or republican Turkey. Although this is also true in the case of most countries, especially those that nourish a certain rancor against their old colonial rulers, in the Turkish case this negative feeling is likely to produce a concrete and direct effect on its relations with its neighbors. This is because Turkey is surrounded by nations that attained independence from the Ottomans relatively recently. Whereas the old possessions of most colonial empires are now independent states far away from the colonizer country, territories that were ceded by the Ottoman Empire at the end of the Balkan Wars in 1912–13, and by the Sèvres Treaty of 1920 or the Lausanne Treaty of 1923 after the end of the First World War, are Turkey's immediate neighbors. All these lands that were once ruled by the Ottomans constitute a periphery of new states in the immediate vicinity of the present Republic—states with whom the conduct of foreign policy requires extreme care and reserve given the sensitivities stemming from the imperial past.

In spite of the fact that Turkish diplomacy will always demonstrate the same cautious respect it has maintained in dealing with these new nation-states, it is not possible ever to be sure that the same attention will be shown by the Turkish media, especially at times of popular reaction of a nationalist nature to some unfortunate incident in this periphery. But it may be safely assumed that the tempering effect of the official line on such occasions will always prevent these reactions from disrupting the constancy of Turkish diplomacy with respect to the historic sensitivities of the neighbors.

In this context, an important particularity of Turkish foreign policy needs to be underlined, especially when speculating about its future lines of development. Although half of the total population of the Republic, estimated to be roughly 12 million at the time of its foundation, were first or second generation refugee families of Muslim ethnic origin from the territories of the empire in the Balkans and the Caucasus, the influence of these ethnic groups on relations with the new states in the region has been minimal, unlike the influence exerted, for instance, by the lobbies of ethnic pressure groups on the foreign policy of the United States. But there are alarming signs for the future, as shown by the involvement of irregular volunteers in the events in Nagorno-Karabakh, Chechnya, Bosnia, and perhaps Kosovo. One can be sure that Turkish diplomacy will do its utmost to prevent these natural ethnic interests from perverting the usual foreign policy lines of the Republic. But the real remedy is elsewhere: the elimination of such conflicts by the eradication of all ethnic discrimination in the countries of the region, especially in the Balkans.

There is, however, one legacy of history that will remain as a determinant factor of future Turkish foreign policy: the collective Turkish feeling that can be called the "Sèvres syndrome." The Treaty of Sèvres, when signed on August 10, 1920, between the victors of the First World War and the representatives of the Ottoman sultan, stipulated, in addition to the dismemberment of the imperial territories outside Anatolia, the establishment of various occupation zones on present day Turkish territory, plus the creation of an independent Armenia in the east and the organization of a referendum for an independent Kurdistan in the southeast. The treaty never came into force, and the Government of the Grand National Assembly of Turkey, as the revolutionary Ankara authority was then called, succeeded, at the end of a war of liberation, in having it replaced by the Treaty of Lausanne on July 24, 1923. But the map of "Anatolia according to Sèvres" remained in the pages of schoolbooks as a symbol of hostile intentions on the last piece of land left to Turks at the end of their historic adventure from the steppes of Central Asia to the center of Europe. The memory of the map is always very vivid in the minds of all those who have gone through the republican educational system and still influences the thinking of both civilian and military cadres, creating a suspicious attitude toward any suggestion of encouraging regionalism or establishing an independent Kurdish state, even outside the present borders of the Republic.

The "Tom and Jerry" Pattern

Relations with Greece are likely to be the most critical aspect of Turkish foreign policy for a long time to come, not only because problems between the two countries are complicated and difficult to solve, but also because these relations reflect a deep-rooted historic confrontation stemming from what may be called "the Byzantine heritage."

Turks are not the autochthonous element in the region. In a way, nobody is. But the Turks are the latest comers. The Ottoman conquest of the Byzantine territories, and of Constantinople in particular, has always been interpreted and presented by Greek historians as the invasion of civilized Christian lands by Asiatic barbarians. Modern Greece, from the early years of its independence in the nineteenth century to the days of the "Asia Minor catastrophe," felt entitled to come back to the same lands as the legitimate heir of the Eastern Roman Empire. Its diplomacy excelled in projecting the "barbaric" image of the Turk against the splendor of Greek antiquity and benefited from this contrast by enlisting the support of Western powers for its territorial expansion throughout the whole history of its independence.

The Treaty of Lausanne put an end to this sterile dispute between the two neighbors and established a balance between them around the Aegean, based primarily on the demilitarization of the islands close to the Turkish shore and an exchange of population between the Greek Orthodox inhabitants of Anatolia and the Turks of Greece, with the mutual exception of the Greek Orthodox population of Istanbul and the Muslim Turks of Western Thrace. The treaty also recognized the transfer of Ottoman sovereignty in Cyprus to Britain, in spite of the presence of Turkish and Greek communities on the island, thereby contributing in a negative way to the maintenance of the equilibrium between their "motherlands" in the eastern Mediterranean.

This equilibrium assured a lasting peace between Turkey and Greece until the events that led in 1960 to the establishment of a bicommunal Republic of Cyprus, which was an endeavor to extend the same conception of equilibrium to the island. But the disruption of this constitutional partnership in 1963 put an end to this and a whole series of disputes arose between the two neighbors, not only on the island, but also in the Aegean, ranging from the demilitarized status of the islands to the extension of the territorial waters and the continental shelf.

The deterioration of Turkish-Greek relations caused the reemergence of Greece's traditional diplomatic strategy vis-à-vis its eastern neighbor: the use of the image of the belligerent, aggressive Turk to enlist the support of the Western world. In order to do this, Greece tried to engineer situations where that image inevitably came to the fore at the end of successive provocations, rather like Tom and Jerry in the famous cartoon series about the "nice little mouse" and the "tomcat": when provocations did not cease after continuous warnings, pleas, diplomatic efforts, and calls for bilateral talks by the Turkish side, the threat to use force became the order of the day. This was the exact moment to expose the cruel, war-mongering "Asiatic barbarian" to the world and use the mastery of Greek diplomacy's skill to mobilize public opinion against the adversary in all fields, not necessarily linked to the issue in question. Turkish diplomacy is very familiar with this strategy, but the unfortunate thing is that because the threat of the use of force is the only effective way to stop the provocations, it is impossible for Turkey not to fall into this vicious circle for the protection of its interests, at the cost of perpetuating the traditional image.

There seemed to be no immediate remedy to this situation, which was, in essence, the result of a very dangerous game that risked serious clashes between two members of the same alliance. Many thought that the solution lay perhaps in the realization by the friends of these two nations of the danger involved, and a serious warning by them to the initiator of the game before the other side felt compelled to use the deterrence of its terrifying image.

Relations between the two countries became even worse when the leader of the separatist Kurdish organization, the infamous Abdullah Öcalan, was captured in Nairobi on February 15, 1999, as he exited the Greek embassy in possession of a Greek Cypriot passport. This event led to the fall of Greek Foreign Minister Pangalos and to a drastic change in Greek foreign policy, particularly in respect to Turkey's application for full membership in the European Union (EU). This change was subsequently instrumental in the decision of the European Council at the Helsinki summit, where the candidacy of Turkey was finally accepted on December 10–11, 1999, without the hindrance of a Greek veto. But Greek diplomacy did succeed in inserting some clauses into that decision regarding the solution of the Aegean and Cyprus disputes as preconditions for the beginning of accession negotiations, thus giving another example of its skill in exploiting every possible international occasion for the solution of its problems with Turkey.

Principles and Prospects

Any speculation on possible future directions that Turkish foreign policy may take has to be conducted according to the basic principles and tenets of Turkish diplomacy, which seem to have resisted the changes, fluctuations, and temptations of more than three-quarters of a century—the life of the Republic.

First, there is a definite emphasis on national defense and security considerations. This primordial concern is due not only to the precarious geostrategic position of the land in a region where the interests of so many big powers compete, sometimes with the risk of involving the country in their violent clashes, but also to the fact that the same land is coveted by so many for exactly the value of its position. This is the reason why the Republic felt the need to initiate political and military alliances for collective defense, as in the case of the Saadabad and Balkan pacts with its neighbors in the Near East and southeastern Europe soon after its foundation, and the Tripartite Alliance with Britain and France on the eve of the Second World War, as well as the need to adhere to an integrated defense scheme, namely NATO, during the Cold War.

Second, there is a clearly noticeable Western orientation to Turkish foreign relations. This orientation is not only a consequence of collective defense engagements and foreign trade links, mostly with Europe and the United States, but also a natural outcome of cultural and social connections with the West, especially Western Europe since the first modernization efforts of the Ottoman state at the end of the eighteenth century. For these reasons, which are closely tied to the realities of international politics and deeply rooted in the history of the last two centuries, this orientation is not likely to change in the long term, in spite of all the difficulties, setbacks, and disillusionments recently experienced with Europe, either in the course of Turkey's application for full membership in the EU and its exclusion from the European Security and Defense Identity initiative, or on the occasion of several issues of human rights that have been the subject of harsh criticism by the West. On the other hand, because the same orientation is in a way an option freely taken by Turkey for reasons of its own social, cultural, and political development, the country's attachment to the West cannot be used by others as leverage to impose policies or political attitudes that would run against Turkey's own interests.

Third, there is a complete absence of any irredentist design in relations with Turkey's neighbors after the Treaty of Lausanne. The annexation of the Alexandretta (Iskenderun) *sanjak* (the province of Hatay) in 1939 and the Cyprus operation of 1974 may seem to be the exceptions to this principle. But a closer analysis of both cases will show that the first was the outcome of peaceful negotiations with France, which was then the mandatory state for Syria, and that the military intervention in Cyprus was made in accordance with an international treaty that guaranteed a bicommunal constitutional order violated by the Greek Cypriot side. On the other hand, strict adherence to the principle of "peace in the world" implied a policy of keeping clear of any adventure in foreign affairs. No promise of an expansionist nature had succeeded in luring the Turkish policymakers into participating in the Second World War, but at the same time, their determination to defend, if necessary by force, the country's independence and territorial integrity was the main factor that helped to dissuade any eventual aggressor during that war. Therefore, a constant military preparedness at any cost became a corollary to the principle of peaceful foreign policy.

Fourth, there is continuous vigilance to ensure that relations with the Russian Federation do not degenerate into a situation of hostility. Turkish diplomacy believes that the enhancement of trade between the two countries is the best way to mitigate any minor friction that may occur in the course of political relations.

Fifth, insistence on the protection of the treaty rights and vital interests in the Eastern Mediterranean is one of the most important preoccupations of the Republic and of its armed forces. The treaty rights include the permanent demilitarized status of the eastern Aegean islands, especially of Lesbos (Midilli), Chios (Sakiz), Samos (Sisam), and Nikaria (Ikarya), whose cession to Greece by the Treaties of London and Athens (1913) at the end of the Balkan Wars was reiterated by the Treaty of Lausanne. To these should be added the Dodecanese islands of Rhodes (Rodos), Kos (Istanköy), Kalimnos (Kilimli), and others, ceded to Italy by the Treaty of Ouchy (1912) at the end of the Tripoli War. This cession was also reiterated at Lausanne, but the sovereignty of the islands was transferred to Greece by the Treaty of Paris (1947) at the end of the Second World War, with the same proviso of retaining a demilitarized status. According to the Treaty of Lausanne, this status should also cover the islands of Lemnos (Limni) and Samothraki (Semendirek) near the entrance of the Dardanelles, but their demilitarization remains a matter of dispute between the two countries; the Greek side claims that the clauses of the 1936 Montreux Convention ending the demilitarized status of the Turkish straits and the neighboring Turkish islands should apply equally to these islands.

Later developments, mostly stemming from the tensions of the Cyprus issue, led Greece to undertake a comprehensive program of establishing military installations throughout the Aegean area, as a "defensive" precaution against alleged Turkish threats. The issue of demilitarization of the islands became one of the major problems that envenom relations between Greece and Turkey. As to the other issues, such as the extension of the territorial waters beyond six nautical miles, delimitation of the continental shelf and of the national air space, definition of the flight information zones, and other matters, Turkey believes that their solution requires extensive bilateral talks between neighbors. Athens generally prefers, in line with its historic orientation, submitting such issues to the mediation or judgment of international organizations, a risk that Ankara is reluctant to take in view of its preconceived belief in those organizations' partiality for Greek causes. Since these topics are closely related to the prospects of Turkey's development as a maritime nation with unhindered access to the Mediterranean, they are seen as threatening the vital interests of future generations and are likely to dominate Turkish foreign policy issues in the early twenty-first century. In December 1999, the European Council at Helsinki stressed "the principle of peaceful settlement of disputes in accordance with the UN charter" and urged candidate states "to make every effort to resolve any outstanding border disputes and other related issues." The following sentences from the same European Council decision seem to make Turkey's acceptance of application to the International Court of Justice (ICJ) a precondition for the start of its accession negotiations with the EU:

Failing this, they should within a reasonable time bring the dispute to the International Court of Justice. The European Council will review the situation relating to any outstanding disputes, in particular concerning the repercussions on the accession process and in order to promote their settlement through the ICJ, at the latest by the end of 2004.[1]

This is another example of Western compliance with the traditional Athens approach of trying to solve its problems with Turkey in the international arena, rather than through bilateral talks, which is definitely the preferred method of Turkish diplomacy.

Finally, there is a realistic and rational attitude toward dealing with all these issues. Rational realism is and will remain the most significant aspect of Turkey's foreign policy. This is the case despite the grave and dramatic nature of the problems faced by the nation in a very difficult corner of the world, and, paradoxically, despite the temptation of lucrative and irredentist involvements.

---

1. European Commission, Bulletin EU 12–1999, at <europa.eu.int/abc/doc/off/bull/en/9912/i1003.htm>.

Chapter 4

Turkish Foreign Policy and the War on Iraq

Cengiz Çandar

During the first quarter of 2003, the unimaginable happened, and the worst case scenario came true: Turkey seemed to depart from its "Western vocation" and lose its track. Its prospects with the European Union (EU) blurred, and its strongest relationship, that with the United States, deteriorated. Turkey had been considered a "strategic partner" of the world's sole superpower. On the path to war in Iraq, the presumed strategic partnership deteriorated when the Turkish parliament, military, and political leadership, unable to agree on how much Turkey should cooperate with the United States, put obstacles in the way of U.S. war planning. Turkey thus deprived its fragile economy of the U.S. offer of $24–30 billion in direct aid and loans, and of the opportunity and liberty to form a "buffer zone" inside northern Iraq's Kurdish zone, which it saw as essential for its security. The Turks had believed that Turkey's strategic value was indispensable for the United States, and that a U.S. military campaign against Iraq without Turkey's participation or active assistance would be too costly for the United States. The outbreak of war on March 20, 2003, without Turkey, proved them wrong. Too little and too late, Turkey opened its airspace—though not its airbases—to U.S. combat aircraft, and its territory was used in the later stages of the war for humanitarian and minor logistical purposes. The impact of this decision will have a major effect upon Turkey's foreign policy, strategic thinking, and the redefinition of geopolitics in the region. No recent event will have as large an effect on Turkey's future as the war in Iraq.

Why did Turkey relinquish its strategic role at the epicenter of a new world, marginalizing itself when its new role in the international system demanded an active contribution?

The Mistakes of March

In one fortnight, Turkey jeopardized its decades-old—if not centuries-old—Western vocation. Because of its pro-Western institutions and establishment, this was not only unpredictable but has always been considered unacceptable, even unthinkable.

The months of the Iraq war, March and April 2003, will probably be registered in history as the most dramatic transitional period of post–Cold War Turkey. Many in the Turkish body politic, including the Turkish intelligentsia, were unaware of the decisive effect of the March–April 2003 period on Turkey's future.

On March 1, 2003, the Turkish parliament blocked a motion that would allow the United States to deploy combat ground forces on Turkish territory on their way into Iraq to remove the regime of Saddam Hussein. Predictably, this was a profound disappointment for Washington and caused a fundamental change in its war plans. In the initial U.S. war plans, a "Northern Front" in Iraq through Turkey was expected to bring a swift military victory by forcing the repressive regime in Baghdad to divide its forces, thus keeping the costs of war, in both human lives and material, to a minimum. Turkey's move also constituted a surprising deviation, if not a break, in the tradition of Turkish-U.S. relations, in a time of pressing need. It led to nervous outbursts from even pro-Turkish circles within or near the U.S. administration.

The move also deprived Turkey of the sizeable economic aid package that Washington had pledged as compensation for the inevitable adverse effects of the war on the Turkish economy. It amounted to $6 billion of grants in cash, or loan guarantees in the range of $24–30 billion with a favorable long-term payment period and low interest rates. Word of the package had sent very encouraging signals to Turkey's once vibrant business community, which was still trying to recover from the devastating consequences of the grave economic crisis of February 2001. It also boosted international investors' confidence in the health of Turkey's economy, which was in dire need of foreign direct investment.

Meanwhile, the already problematic relationship with the EU declined further, thanks to the intransigence of the Turkish Cypriot leader Rauf Denktas, who, with the firm support of the Turkish general staff and the foreign ministry, blocked the approval and the implementation of the plan of UN Secretary-General Kofi Annan to resolve the long-standing Cyprus problem. The Annan Plan would have enabled the Turkish Cypriots to join their Greek counterparts on the island as equal political partners in a reunified State of Cyprus and enter the enlarged EU. It would have paved the road for Turkey to start accession negotiations with the

EU as well. The Annan Plan was generally considered the best chance for resolving the Cyprus problem since Turkey's military intervention in 1974. It was originally scheduled to be accepted at the EU's enlargement summit in Copenhagen on December 12–13, 2002. The date had been postponed until February 28, 2003, but since the intransigence of neither Ankara nor Denktas could be overcome, a final date was set for March 11, 2003. During this time, Kofi Annan shifted his energies from the looming war in Iraq and focused on the Cyprus issue. The Turkish Cypriot sector was rocked with anti-Denktas and pro-settlement street demonstrations that gathered nearly one-third of the inhabitants of Northern Cyprus. For Turkish Cypriots, March 10, 2003, the final date set prior to the accession of new members to the EU on April 16, 2003, became the most important "missed opportunity" for the settlement of the question. In a report presented to the UN Security Council that was unanimously adopted on April 14, Kofi Annan blamed the Turkish side and specifically Rauf Denktas for the failure to reach a settlement prior to Cyprus's accession to the EU on April 16, 2003. While the enlargement ceremony with ten new members, held in Athens on April 16, 2003, in the absence of both Turkey and Turkish Cyprus, was hailed in many European circles as a historic event, the Turkish newspaper headlines and its most respected opinion leaders interpreted the event as the biggest defeat for Turkey's foreign policy in recent history.

In the early hours of March 20, 2003, war in Iraq broke out—the first military conflagration of the twenty-first century and important enough to reshape the entire international system. In the afternoon, the Turkish parliament decided to open Turkish airspace for U.S. overflights and also authorized the government to send Turkish troops into northern Iraq. The overflight rights were far short of U.S. requirements prior to war. Additionally, it would be a nightmare for the United States if Turkey sent its own troops into Iraq, both because the war had already started without Turkey and that would cause a "war within a war," and because the Iraqi Kurds, the new and passionate allies of the U.S. forces on the northern battlefields of Iraq, had declared that they would fight the intruding Turkish troops. Iraqi Kurds even alleged that the Saddam regime was preferable to a Turkish military presence in the north. Thus, the United States tried hard to persuade Turkey not to invade northern Iraq. The Turkish-U.S. relationship, which had been exemplary for decades, immediately became strained. The once highly praised strategic partnership was in the process of evaporating. Turkey seemed more a geopolitical nuisance than a trusted ally of the United States and the United Kingdom in attaining their strategic objectives. As Alan Powell wrote in the *New York Times*, "Without firing a single shot, Turkey's military has had an expensive war. Its commanders have not only lost a special bond with the United States that had endured for half a century, but also forfeited a chance to secure a strategic bridgehead in Kurdish northern Iraq."[1]

Attempts were made to repair the damaged relationship between Turkey and the United States. During the second week of the Iraq war, U.S. Secretary of State Colin Powell visited Ankara, as he had not prior to the war, and declared Turkey "an important member of the coalition [against the Saddam regime]." Turkey had been relegated to the position of "important coalition member" rather than that of "strategic partner" of the United States, the more prestigious status it had enjoyed in the wake of the dissolution of the Soviet Union and the 1990–91 Gulf War.

Turkey's position within Europe looked more enigmatic in the wake of the Iraq war. Its political stand coincided more with that of France and Germany, the two major powers believed to have blocked Turkey's bid for the EU during the December 2002 Copenhagen summit meeting. Ironically, the United States had put pressure on these two countries on behalf of Turkey, though it proved to be counterproductive. Moreover, the United Kingdom, the closest ally of the United States in the war on Iraq, has always been the most passionate advocate of Turkey's place in the EU, supported mainly by Spain and Italy, which were also allied with the United States in the Iraq war. While debating whether to allow U.S. deployment on its soil, Turkey was adamant that British troops would not cross into Iraq from its territory. For Turkey, that evoked memories of the First World War. Thus Turkey had disappointed the United States, alienated its closest European friends, and satisfied those European countries with no interest in seeing it in the EU. This was an unprecedented foreign policy, indeed.

The Rise and Fall of Turkey's Strategic Importance

Some Turks influential in foreign policymaking believed that no large U.S. military initiative in Iraq could take place without the use of Turkish territory. But while the initial U.S. war planning had depended heavily on Turkey, the United States gained control of the entire territory of Iraq in less than one month, making it clear that Turkey was not indispensable.

The acknowledgement of this new fact must lead to new strategic and geopolitical perceptions of Turkey. The exceptional importance of Turkey's geopolitics has increased in post–Cold War thinking. That per-

1. Alan Powell, "Turkey, Spared a War, Still Pays a Heavy Price," *New York Times*, April 19, 2003.

ception served the pragmatic needs of a number of Turkish officials and certain interests of friends of Turkey in the United States. In the wake of the war on Iraq, that perception of Turkey will probably lose its appeal. The disbelief of the Turkish authorities—including some top-ranking commanders in the military—that the United States could ever go to war against the regime in Baghdad without Turkey's active assistance was a result of a peculiar orthodox conviction. Since the end of the Cold War, they believed the United States needed Turkey for its interests and for the control of Eurasia. Any world map indicated clearly the strategic importance of Turkey. But, following September 11, 2001, the United States, prior to and after its campaign in Afghanistan, acquired airbase facilities in Uzbekistan and established a military relationship with Tajikistan and Kyrgyzstan. It could thus move in Turkic Central Asia on its own, without Turkey's support.

The exaggerated perception of Turkey's strategic value that marked the strategic thinking throughout the last decade of the twentieth century was not purely a self-delusion of Turkey's decision-makers and pundits. By the 1990s, Turkey was seen as a unique strategic asset for the sole superpower, the United States, and it was primarily U.S. authorities and experts who emphasized Turkey's strategic value in the wake of the Cold War.[2]

After recovering from the initial shocks of the earlier stage of the post–Cold War era, most of the major global actors reached a quasi-consensus on Turkey's indispensable strategic value. In the eyes of various strategists, Turkey was transformed from a flank country of NATO into a "pivotal state" in the global game. For instance, Richard Holbrooke told Congress in 1995: "Turkey stands at the crossroads of almost every issue of importance to the United States on the Eurasian continent."[3] In 1994, the U.S. Department of Commerce designated Turkey as one of the ten big emerging markets. Zbigniew Brzezinski also attached special importance to Turkey, attributing to it an exclusive role in his forecasts of political and strategic evolution in the twenty-first century.[4] Brzezinski emphasized Turkey as one of two Eurasian powers, the other being Russia. Others regard Turkey as one of the nine pivotal states in the world,

2.   Richard Holbrooke, statement before the U.S. House of Representatives, International Relations Committee, March 9, 1995.

3.   Richard Holbrooke, quoted in Robert Chase, Emily Hill, and Paul Kennedy, eds., *The Pivotal States: A New Framework for United States Policy in the Developing World* (New York: Norton, 1999), p. 9.

4.   Zbigniew K. Brzezinski, *The Grand Chessboard: American Primacy and Its Geostrategic Imperatives* (New York: Basic Books, 1997), p. 41.

defining such a state as "a key country whose future may not only deter-
mine the success or failure of its region but also significantly affect international stability."[5] Simon V. Mayall underlines the peculiar conditions
Turkey was confronted with: "In the new security environment, Turkey's
geographical position and its military strength now made it a European,
Balkan, Middle Eastern, Near Eastern, Caucasian, Mediterranean,
Aegean and Black Sea power."[6] This assessment, mainly shared by the
U.S. foreign policy community, explains more than anything else the ac-
tive U.S. backing for Turkey in the last decade.

In strategic terms, the promotion of Turkey from a peripheral entity
to a pivotal state increased the Western powers' awareness of Turkey's security, territorial integrity, and stability. The United States excelled in taking into consideration pertinent Turkish sensitivities—yet these efforts
fell short of alleviating the insecurity and the fears of the Turkish policymakers. At the geopolitical forefront of the Middle East, Turkey was
drawn into Iraqi politics when "Saddam Hussein's foolish gamble
against Kuwait . . . left Iraq prostrate and threatened by separatism [and]
unleash[ed] a new Kurdish reality in the area," and the war in former
Yugoslavia "raised new questions about the Muslim factor in southeastern Europe and new webs of alliance in that volatile region."[7]

When in 2003 Iraq was again convulsed, this time by an Anglo-
American military campaign that brought down the Saddam regime, Turkey's geographic proximity, and the fact that it has the biggest Kurdish
population in the region, again seriously affected Turkey's strategic interests. This time, however, Turkey was a bystander.

Turkey's Kurdish Problem

Turkey's apparent unwillingness to assist the United States in removing
Saddam's tyrannical regime in Iraq marginalized its role in reshaping the
region, a vital zone in its security perceptions. Furthermore, in the aftermath of the war Turkey faced a nightmare scenario in the regional strategic equation, one that had preoccupied many of its strategic thinkers

---

5. Chase, Hill, and Kennedy, *The Pivotal States*, p. 9.

6. Simon V. Mayall, *Turkey: Thwarted Ambition*, McNair Paper No. 56 (Washington,
D.C.: Institute of National Strategic Studies, National Defense University, January
1997), p. 1.

7. Graham E. Fuller, "Alternative Turkish Roles in the Future Middle East," in Henry
J. Barkey, ed., *Reluctant Neighbor: Turkey's Role in the Middle East* (Washington, D.C.:
United States Institute of Peace Press, 1996), p. 205.

and decision-makers. The Iraqi Kurds in northern Iraq became regional-political actors, and Turkey's interventionist posture in the Iraqi theater of political action, which had earned it the image of a regional power, was restricted. An article in the *Boston Globe* articulated this change in U.S. perceptions of Turkey at the time that Kurdish peshmergas (militias) entered Kirkuk, allegedly violating the "red lines" drawn by Turkey. This exclusive Kurdish control over Kirkuk served as a pretext for Turkey to consider sending its troops to northern Iraq:

From the outset, the behavior of the Kurds has been the model of an ally, and the behavior of the Turks has been the model of the opposite—unacceptable for a fellow NATO member, and borderline suicidal for a new and shaky government facing a mountain of economic woes. . . . Turkey has no right to play sphere-of-influence games in northern Iraq, no right to block autonomy for the Kurds in a new Iraq federation, and no right to object if Kurds seek to return to homes in Kirkuk and Mosul from which they were brutally evicted by Saddam Hussein.[8]

However, the issues on which the article claimed Turkey has no right to act are precisely those issues that have worried Turkey for decades—and they were especially sharpened in the last decade of the twentieth century. The shifting of U.S. regional allegiances transforms those worries into a nightmare. It is almost impossible for Turkish authorities, whether civilian or military, to reconcile themselves to the establishment of direct and warm relations between the United States and the Iraqi Kurdish leadership while Turkey's loyal allied status is devalued. Turkey was deprived by the United States, with whom it had developed close security and military cooperation over half a century, of the ability to undertake military initiatives in a geographic zone it sees as vital for its security. In Turkish security perceptions, there is no real separation between northern Iraq and southeastern Turkey: they are the geographic and ethno-cultural extension of each other. Therefore Turkey feared that the establishment of an autonomous Kurdistan in northern Iraq would rekindle similar yearnings in southeastern Turkey. Though it had been "one of the thorniest and most intractable" of Turkey's foreign policy challenges throughout the 1990s, northern Iraq was not an area to which Turkey's Kemalist elite would have chosen to give priority, preoccupied as they were with Turkey's "European vocation." Nevertheless, "northern Iraq quickly forced

---

8. Thomas Oliphant, "A Lesson for Turkey from Kurdish Allies," *Boston Globe*, April 13, 2003.

itself on policymakers as an area of priority" because it is "adjacent to the epicentre of a violent, secessionist insurgency."[9]

The Sources of Turkey's Perceived Insecurity

Turkey's diplomats and decision-makers should not have been caught off guard in March 2003. Many saw the road to war and its consequences for Turkey with clarity; however, the ruling AK (Justice and Development) Party, which had just won a landslide election victory on November 3, 2002, and its government, an offspring of the former Islamic parties, were not among them. Turkey was unfortunate in having a ruling party ridden with inexperience, amateurishness, and incompetent leadership at a juncture in history that demanded greater resolve, talent, flexibility, and vision than at any other time. With strong *tier-mondist* features and the burden of its Islamic past, Abdullah Gül (and later Tayyip Erdogan) and the governing body of the AK Party seemed simply not up to the gigantic task before them.

Nonetheless, Turkey's major foreign policy blunder at the threshold of a decisive historical period was not only the result of the shortcomings of a new, inexperienced, incompetent government. It was the making of the entire Turkish polity. U.S. diplomats involved at this crucial period defined Turkey's foreign policy blunder to the author as the product of the corporate Turkish entity, ranging from the moderately Islamic ruling party to the arch-secularist main opposition party in the parliament, from the president to the powerful military, from the influential judiciary to the mainstream media. Each had a share in influencing the formulation of the Turkish foreign policy on the eve of war against Iraq. However, an unprecedented U.S. criticism by a high Pentagon official singled out the Turkish military as the main culprit for the failure of the wartime cooperation between the two allies. The backbone of the strong 50-year-old U.S.-Turkish relationship had been the link between the Pentagon and the Turkish General Staff. U.S. Deputy Secretary of Defense Paul Wolfowitz's criticism of the Turkish military for the failure in the expected level of cooperation between Turkey and the United States during the Iraqi campaign resonated strongly in Turkish public opinion for a long period.[10]

---

9. Philip Robins, *Suits and Uniforms: Turkish Foreign Policy since the Cold War* (London: Hurst and Co., 2003), p. 312.

10. DoD News Briefing, Deputy Secretary of Defense Paul Wolfowitz, Monday, May 5, 2003; interview by the author with M. Ali Birand of CNN Turk, Washington, D.C.

The Root of the Problem

The already strained Turkish-U.S. military relationship took a further blow in July 2003, when U.S. troops stormed the headquarters of Turkish Special Forces in the northern Iraqi town of Suleimaniye and arrested a number of Turkish officers allegedly involved in an assassination attempt against the Kurdish mayor of Kirkuk, the city in northern Iraq disputed among Turcomans, Kurds, and Arabs. The event was considered by many Turks to be the gravest crisis between Turkey and the United States since the establishment of their alliance, although the arrested Turkish officers were freed 48 hours after their capture. The damage was already done. The confidence between the two allies had been further eroded.

The root of the problem is structural and needs to be understood in historical perspective. Turkey carries the legacy of one of the longest-lasting empires, the Ottoman Empire. The swift transformation of the empire into a nation-state following the First World War greatly affected the outlook of the Turkish political elite and the subconscious of the Turkish population in general in a way that influences their perception of security as well as the formulation of Turkish foreign policy objectives.

Throughout the nineteenth century, Ottoman Turkey was the focus of the Eastern Question. Turkey's strategic position commanding the Bosphorus and the Dardanelles, and thus controlling the Black Sea–Mediterranean axis, as well as its sovereign power over the Middle East and Balkans, aggravated the Great Power rivalries; the consequence was the gradual disintegration of the empire, which gained momentum after the 1877–78 Turco-Russian War. For over a quarter of a century, until the Balkan Wars of 1912–13, Turkish foreign policy was concentrated on preserving its remaining territories and maintaining the survival of the empire. This experience molded the minds of Turkish policymakers, and Turkish foreign policy acquired a "defensive" spirit. The process of the disintegration of the Ottoman Empire had created a deep xenophobia in the founding fathers of the new Turkish Republic in 1923. They had spent long years as Ottoman civil servants or military commanders, trying to salvage the state from eventual collapse. Not surprisingly, they harbored deep suspicions concerning the intentions of foreign powers—mainly those in the West.

The concept of "security" thus became synonymous with the term "foreign policy" from the founding of the young state. The priorities of Turkish foreign policy were dictated by Turkey's security imperatives, above all that of preserving the "territorial integrity" of the country.

For nearly half a century following the Second World War, Turkish foreign policy was tied to NATO, and security-oriented. Safe under the preemptive nuclear umbrella of NATO, Turkey had no other option. The ambiguities of the post–Cold War order complicated the choices. Foreign policy decision-making became harder and more complex. Fear of the diminishing geopolitical value of Turkey haunted the minds of those in the political community. The new situation demanded new policies from people who were accustomed to act according to tradition and convention. Turgut Özal, prime minister from 1983 to 1989 and president from 1989 until his untimely death in April 1993, was a visionary concerning foreign policy issues. However, as he broke with the traditional reflexes to guide Turkey through the turbulent waters of international politics, his efforts were frequently stalled by various political circles, and above all by the Turkish foreign policy establishment.

Two pillars traditionally constituted the Turkish foreign policy establishment: the military and the ministry of foreign affairs. They usually worked in close coordination. Foreign policy decision-making was their domain, irrespective of changing governments. Turks tended to regard these two institutions not as representatives of "government policy," but as the "state" itself.

The close cooperation and coordination of these institutions predates the foundation of the Turkish Republic. Since the last quarter of the nineteenth century, they jointly tried first to prevent the disintegration of the Ottoman Empire, and then to minimize, if not to contain, territorial losses. They tried hard to secure the survival of the "state." With a very rich institutional memory, they are the most solid and intact segments of the Turkish state. In addition, the military considers itself the institution that formed the Turkish Republic from the vestiges of a devastated empire, and therefore believes that it has an obligation to oversee Turkey's political orientation, whether domestic or international. It acts as the custodian of the secular nation-state founded on the guidelines laid by Kemal Atatürk, who himself was a brilliant general, the hero of the national struggle, and the architect of Turkish nation-building.

Any move that these two institutions interpret as contravening traditional standards, or as being in conflict with perceptions of foreign policy orthodoxy, is regarded as a departure from the untouchable Kemalist principles. In their eyes, if revisionism in Turkish foreign policy is allowed to prevail, the whole "system" would be in jeopardy. Any tendency to change must be prevented at any cost.

This orientation is reflected in the words of former Foreign Minister Mümtaz Soysal, a stalwart of the traditionalist school of Turkish foreign policy. In a Harvard panel, he said:

Ours is a Jacobin republic. Longer lasting than any other of its kind. The history is behind it, the philosophy of its founders. . . . We all have a Sèvres obsession. All of us, from those in the foreign ministry to those at the top echelons of the military, from our elementary school education, we have been introduced to the Sèvres map. We can never forget that map.[11]

Those in key positions in the Turkish establishment in the last decade have often referred to the ill-famed Treaty of Sèvres of 1920. President Süleyman Demirel is in the forefront of stirring the public memory. Sèvres was one in the chain of treaties that ended the First World War, but the only one not implemented and, thanks to the signing of the Treaty of Lausanne in 1923, regarded as null and void. Nonetheless, because it would have carved up the Ottoman territories, leaving an insignificant territory for a Turkish state in central parts of Asia Minor, it is entrenched in Turkish national memory as a curse.

Any reference to Sèvres at the end of the twentieth century, after 80 years of Turkey as a republic is—if not demagogic for domestic political purposes—tantamount to reviving the old nightmare of contraction, repulsion, expulsion, defeat, dismemberment, and disintegration. This residue of the history of the Ottoman Empire has produced an unhealthy mindset, obsessive and paranoid, among the governing elite.

It was this psyche that lay behind the efforts to block and to undo Turgut Özal's initiatives to change the pattern of Turkish foreign policy. Though the post–Cold War era of international relations necessitated a reassessment and a re-evaluation of Turkish foreign policy that would allow it to cope with the underlying dynamics of the new century and the new millennium, Turkey's ruling elite could only demonstrate its incapacity to change in the dazzlingly changing new world. The Turkish authorities' treatment of this complex political issue did not reflect the drastic change required by the new international climate. The Kurdish question was understood merely as a security issue that threatened Turkey's territorial integrity. This banal simplification and recalcitrance on the part of the Turkish establishment only complicated the efforts to resolve it. Turkey's energy is sapped by this myopic prognosis. Inevitably, the pursuit of the Kurdistan Workers' Party (PKK) became the central theme of Turkish foreign policy throughout the latter half of the 1990s. Nearly the whole scope of Turkey's bilateral relations with any country was fixated on the issue of the PKK.

---

11. Mümtaz Soysal, luncheon speech, seminar on "The Future of Turkish Foreign Policy," Harvard University, October 24, 1998.

Finally, signals that Turkey was deviating from its Western vocation preceded the outbreak of the war on Iraq. The nationalist factions in the military entertained the idea of integrating Turkey to an emerging Asian bloc. The Shanghai Five had attracted the attention of those circles. This Asian grouping that included Russia and China lost its political meaning during the U.S. war against Afghanistan when the U.S. military penetrated Central Asia. The Kurdish phobia and the obsession with the emergence of a Kurdish entity in northern Iraq following the U.S. overthrow of the Saddam Hussein regime also influenced Turkish policymakers to probe rapprochement with Syria and Iran. The wisdom and the timing of such a move were highly questionable, since those two countries were subject to stern warnings from the United States during and after the military campaign in Iraq.

If a quest for a policy shift could be attributed to the traditional anti-Western and pro-Islamic axis tendencies of the quasi-Islamists controlling the government, it found an unlikely ally in the nationalistic sections of the arch-secularist establishment, who mistrusted the AK Party and U.S. intentions in Iraq. The impression that Turkey is not wholly dependent on its links with the United States went down well with them. It was as if an implicit Faustian pact existed between the diametrically opposing poles of the Turkish political spectrum. After all, it was a four-star general with the title of the Secretary-General of the National Security Council who had suggested long before the November 2002 elections that Turkey should develop relations with Iran and Russia, as an alternative to pursuing membership of the EU.[12] The war in Iraq and the wartime alliance between the United States and the Iraqi Kurds have stirred antipathy toward the United States within the same circles, and have opened a dangerous internationalist-nationalist rift within the top echelons of the armed forces.

The Glue of Common Interests

In less than four years, Turkey has changed from being a country that was very highly valued by the president of the United States, to one where the common denominator among its most influential authorities has become anti-Americanism in different doses. In November 1999, U.S. President Bill Clinton said:

---

12. Tuncer Kilinç, Secretary-General of the National Security Council, "Türkiye Yeni bir Arayisa Girmeli" (Turkey should be searching for new alternatives), March 7, 2002, <www.ntvmsnbc.com>.

For better or worse, the events of that time when the Ottoman Empire disintegrated and a new Turkey arose have shaped the history of this entire century. . . . Turkey's past is key to understanding the twentieth century. But, more importantly, I believe Turkey's future will be critical to shaping the twenty-first century.[13]

In contrast, in 2003 Turkey is a subject of pragmatic calls to American authorities for mercy—ironically, by the neo-conservative thinker Robert Kagan:

The world's sole superpower doesn't need to hold grudges, and sometimes it can't afford to. No ally imperiled the American war effort more than Turkey, after all, but it would be politically and strategically insane, as the United States works on building a democratic Iraq, to punish the only well-established moderate Muslim democracy in the region.[14]

The post–Cold War dynamics transformed Turkey from a flank country of a collective security mechanism into the epicenter of a new strategic zone. Now it will likely become a backwater of a U.S.-dominated Middle East. This degradation is the result of very bad crisis mismanagement, leadership failures, and to some extent a strange combination of varying and conflicting interests in distancing from the West.

While the relationship between Turkey and the United States was based on mutual concern over the Soviet Union in the post–Second World War period, the war in Iraq might serve as an acid test for the relationship in the post–Cold War period. The Turkish-U.S. partnership was based very much on strategic interests rather than a sharing of worldviews. Their political cultures have emerged from quite different histories, political philosophies, and social and institutional development. Their mutual strategic concerns overrode these differences. In fact Turkey continued to seem to be the most important ally of the United States in the region, cooperating on international issues from the collapse of the Soviet Union until the war in Iraq of 2003. Turkey-Caucasus energy projects, improved relations between Turkey and Israel, Turkey's involvement and support for the United States and the UN in the ethnic crises of former Yugoslavia, even September 11, 2001, and the military campaign in Afghanistan were all good signs of continued friendship. But these incidents were not as demanding as the Iraqi crisis in testing the potency of

---

13. President Bill Clinton, address to the Turkish Grand National Assembly, November 15, 1999.

14. Robert Kagan, "Resisting Superpower Temptations," *Washington Post,* April 9, 2003.

the Turkish-U.S. relationship, which may very well prove to be cathartic for Turkish policy.

The simple truth is that the United States as a global power has an interest in guarding Turkish national interests based on shared U.S.-Turkish visions. Yet the concept of "strategic partnership" between the United States and Turkey is based on no official agreement—it is no more than a remark made by U.S. President Clinton in 1999. Turkey's role was based on protecting interests common to Turkey and the United States. The key point here is the need for "common interests."

Turkey's future foreign policy will be closely linked with the political future and standing of the United States in the region and also with the destinies of the regional actors, both in Iraq and its periphery. There is no doubt that the Iraqi Shi'a and the Kurds will play roles in the history and on the political stage of the Middle East as never before. The redefinition of common interests between Turkey and the United States according to the circumstances following the war on Iraq will determine not only the nature of the bilateral relationship, but also Turkey's status in the international system.

Nevertheless, despite Turkey's strategic and political devaluation by the United States, Turkey can regain its former status in the regional and international system through damage minimization. After all, it is the only functioning Muslim democracy in the Muslim world. Thanks to its imperial heritage and experience in statehood, as well as its reasonably successful experiment in democratic governance, it has a better chance of standing against dangerous turbulence and instability than any other country in the Middle East. Its geopolitics will preserve its importance to a great extent. Turkey is a NATO member, a strategic Janus that the United States cannot afford to see destabilized and weakened.

The real issue for Turkish foreign policy is to address the perennial problem of Turkey's ruling elite's lack of comprehension of the international paradigm shift and thus its inability to adapt to it. The times demand creativity, flexibility, and unconventional approaches, leaving very little room for status-quo thinking, a traditional feature of Turkish foreign policy. Yet given the unpredictability of Turkish politics and a future of international relations pregnant with uncertainties, an entire turnabout in Turkish foreign policy is plausible.

*The Geopolitical Dimension of
Turkish Foreign Policy*

Chapter 5

Turkey and the European Union

Atila Eralp

In this chapter I analyze Turkey's relationship with the European Union (EU) in the changing international climate after the Cold War, showing how major changes in the international system affected the Turkey-EU relationship and its aspirations for membership in the EU.

First, I focus on the major developments in the international system, primarily examining the process of integration of Western and Eastern Europe and the ending of divisions between Europe and Asia. Based on this analysis, I proceed to examine the relationship of Turkey with the EU within the present enlargement process of the EU, illustrating how the issue of Turkey's full membership became contentious. In the following section, I analyze the Turkey-EU relationship in the aftermath of the 1997 Luxembourg Summit. I clarify how the decisions of the summit reinforced the anti-European tendency that became prevalent among the Turkish governing elites in the 1990s—arguing, however, that this situation was to the advantage of neither the EU nor Turkey.

Next I examine the factors that pushed the EU and Turkey to overcome their problematic relationship. Not only larger geopolitical considerations, such as the pivotal role of Turkey in the Eurasian region,[1] but also difficulties in creating boundaries between Europe, the Middle East, and the Eurasian regions, exerted pressure on Turkey and the EU to try and solve their problems and establish a better working relationship. I conclude by examining the prospects for the new relationship between the EU and Turkey.

---

1. Eurasia is defined in this chapter as a region that covers mainly Turkey and the former Soviet republics. See map, p. xiii.

Changes in the International Climate

We are witnessing a period of change in which the internal and external political balances that shaped the Cold War period are rapidly disappearing. Some of the changes started earlier, but the end of the Cold War marked a turning point and created an environment conducive to change.

There are three major developments that affected the post–Cold War period. Foremost, the division of Europe, which shaped European politics for nearly 40 years, ended with the movement toward unity of Western and Eastern Europe. As a consequence, NATO and the EU started a process of enlargement to meet the challenge posed by the political and economic turmoil of Eastern and Central European countries following the collapse of their political regimes. It soon became clear that the worsening of their political and economic situation would lead to political instability and would also adversely affect Western Europe.

The need for a solution to their problems acquired an aspect of immediacy within Western European political circles. Within this context, the rise of a "European vocation" among Central and Eastern European elites was strongly supported by Western European governments and also by important institutions such as NATO and the EU. NATO initiated cooperation and partnership for peace programs before embarking on the enlargement process. The EU first signed European agreements that were mainly associational relationships. This soon led to the full membership applications of the Central and Eastern European countries in the 1994–96 period.

The attention of both NATO and the EU turned toward incorporation of these countries. It was a major task, because their institutional system differed from that of the Western European countries. In this climate, as I argue in this chapter, the Turkish application for full membership lost its significance for the EU. In addition to its economic and political problems, Turkey had also lost its geopolitical significance in comparison to the Central and Eastern European countries.

The end of the Cold War also resulted in the disappearance of the dividing line between Europe and Asia. With the dissolution of the Soviet Union and the end of the Soviet threat, there was a potential for a growing relationship between Europe and Asia, and this development brought forth the geopolitical significance of these relationships within the international system. The discussions of the international orientations of Eurasian countries, mainly Turkey and the former Soviet republics, frozen for a long time, revived. Increased attention was paid to energy resources and pipeline routes (see map, p. 209). Furthermore, there was the realization that Eurasia has a significant role to play in the creation of a new order and stability internationally. Informed analysts pointed out that if Eurasia were not closely linked to the international system, rivalry in the region might lead to the creation of new spheres of influence, as was the case during the Cold War period.[2] Therefore, the economic and political stability of Eurasia was seen as critical for the enhancement of international stability. While Turkey's role in the enlargement process of the EU was rather marginal, it seemed that Turkey had a "pivotal" position in Eurasia.[3] This stemmed not only from Turkey's role as a route for oil, energy, trade, and communication, but also from the fact that Turkey was one of the few countries in the region where Western institutions were the most developed—a valuable attribute where the process of integration with the international system is concerned. I argue in this chapter that this situation created a problem not only for Turkey, but also for the EU: as the attention of the EU turns toward larger geopolitical considerations in addition to the enlargement issue, the case of Turkey will draw more attention. As a result, the EU and Turkey will be moved to overcome their problematic relationship.

Finally, the relationship between the United States and Europe also entered a period of turbulent change.[4] In the Cold War period, close cooperation between the United States and Western Europe resulted in the establishment of the Western alliance under the leadership of the United States. This cooperation secured the political, economic, and military stability of Western Europe. The link weakened during the 1970s with the rise of economic rivalries. The end of the Cold War raised discussions on the need to establish new cooperation between the United States and Eu-

---

2. For a comprehensive analysis of the Eurasian region, see Zbigniew K. Brzezinski, *The Grand Chessboard: American Primacy and Its Geostrategic Imperatives* (New York: Basic Books, 1997), pp. 30–48.

3. In addition to Brzezinski, Chase et al. characterize the position of Turkey as "pivotal"; see Robert Chase, Emily Hill, and Paul Kennedy, eds., *The Pivotal States: A New Framework for U.S. Policy in the Developing World* (New York: W.W. Norton and Company, 1999), p. 8. For an examination of the vital role of Turkey in the international system, see especially the contribution in the same book by Alan Makovsky, "Turkey," pp. 88–120.

4. For the analysis of the transatlantic relationship, see Robert D. Blackwill and Michael Stürmer, eds., *Allies Divided: Transatlantic Policies for the Greater Middle East* (Cambridge, Mass.: MIT Press, 1997); and D. C. Gombert and F. S. Larrabee, eds., *America and Europe: A Partnership for a New Era* (Cambridge: Cambridge University Press, 1997).

rope, on the grounds that the resources of a single country, even the United States, were not enough to meet the challenges of the new international system. This transatlantic cooperation, however, should be based on shared leadership, as opposed to the dominance of the United States during the Cold War. Furthermore, the new relationship should embrace Eurasia as well as Europe.[5]

As the transatlantic relationship evolved, Turkey's relationship with the West went through a major transformation. During the Cold War years, for the Turkish governing elites, the West had largely meant Western Europe and the United States, undifferentiated as the Western alliance. At the end of the Cold War, Turkish elites belatedly realized that the West was no longer an undifferentiated entity: cooperation with the United States no longer ensured an easy relationship with Western Europe. Turkey's relationship with the United States was running smoothly, while relations with Western Europe, and primarily with the EU, were becoming increasingly conflictual.

Turkey's strategic value grew for the United States in the post–Cold War era: Turkey had a key role in the Middle East, the Balkans, and Transcaucasia. As one observer pointed out, the United States wanted "Turkey firmly anchored in the West."[6] As a consequence of this orientation, the United States wanted Turkey to be part of the EU and supported both the Customs Union (CU) arrangement and its full membership application.[7] However, this support was not sufficient to overcome the problems between Turkey and the EU. Europe needed to understand the virtue of anchoring Turkey to the West. Europe may become more cognizant of the role of Turkey, with the changing geopolitical situation regarding Eurasia. Turkey also needed to carry out political and economic reforms to establish a closer relationship with the EU. This was as necessary for the enhancement of stability in Eurasia as was the new relationship between the United States and Europe.

---

5. Brzezinski, *Grand Chessboard*, pp. 30–48.

6. Alan Makovsky, "Turkey's Faded European Dream," in *The Parameters of Partnership: Germany, the U.S. and Turkey*, Conference Report (Washington, D.C.: American Institute for Contemporary German Studies, Johns Hopkins University, 1998), p. 58.

7. The CU is an essential element of a common market that seeks to abolish all the barriers to trade among its members, to introduce a common customs tarriff, and to adopt a common commercial policy as an external dimension of the CU. The CU is different from full EU membership. In most cases, the CU agreement has led to a full membership agreement, although the Turkish case is uncertain.

The Enlargement Process of the EU and Turkey

The EU is involved in the historical process of enlarging to include the countries of Central and Eastern Europe.[8] The present process differs from previous enlargement processes in terms of the number of applicants for EU membership. Furthermore, the nature of the applicants is quite different. Most of them had long-standing command economies and authoritarian political regimes, and only recently started to transform these structures. The international context of the enlargement is also different: divisions in Europe are ending, and this creates a feeling of urgency to unite its separate parts. Most of the applicants realize that the present enlargement of the EU will be the last for some while and that if they are excluded now, it will take a long time for them to be included within the EU.

There are two issues the EU faces in the enlargement process: broadening itself and deepening its base. Examination of the evolution of the EU shows that it has preferred to focus on these two issues at different times. But, because of the dramatic change in the international climate, this time the EU had to face the two simultaneously. It was thought initially that this challenge could not be met by previous models of enlargement, but needed a new, flexible model of integration. It was argued that because of the large number of applicants and the political and economic difficulties in their adjustment to the EU's policies, the integration process at this stage could not be achieved uniformly but had to be differentiated.[9] There were several projections for flexible integration, but most required that it should be a long-term process, and that applicants should be integrated into different mechanisms at different speeds. Under these projections, applicants would not be granted full membership immediately, but would be given a special status that would lead to eventual full membership.

Discussions of the feasibility of the flexible models of integration,

---

8. For a comprehensive analysis of the new enlargement process of the EU, see Christopher Preston, *Enlargement and Integration in the EU* (London: Routledge, 1997); and Graham Avery and Fraser Cameron, *The Enlargement of the EU* (Sheffield, U.K.: Sheffield Academic Press, 1998).

9. For the analysis of flexibility, see Neill Nugent, "The Deepening and Widening of the European Community: Recent Evolution Maastricht and Beyond," *Journal of Common Market Studies*, Vol. 30, No. 3 (September 1992), pp. 311–328; Neill Nugent, "Redefining Europe," *Journal of Common Market Studies*, Vol. 33, No. 1 (August 1995), pp. 1–16; Kirsty Hughes, "The 1996 Intergovernmental Conference and EU Enlargement," *Journal of International Affairs*, Vol. 72, No. 1 (1996), pp. 1–8.

which were quite popular before and during the 1997 intergovernmental conference of the EU, had to be postponed, primarily because they were unable to solve the key problem of institutional reform. Since their viability greatly depended on the realization of institutional reform in the EU, flexible models played no part in the present enlargement process, which started just after the 1997 Luxembourg Summit.

It was understood that not all applicants can be incorporated into all mechanisms at the same time, and it was acknowledged that there was a need for flexibility in terms of areas of integration, as well as transition periods. Nevertheless, the decisions of the Luxembourg Summit on enlargement show that the EU was in the process of granting full membership to the applicant countries based on the existing model of integration and membership. If there was any differentiation, it was made only in terms of grouping countries: six countries were included in the first wave, five in the second, and Turkey was given a special status. It was not clear how and when the EU would achieve its institutional reform. There was also uncertainty as to whether or not institutional reform would lead to the use of more flexible models. It is probable that discussions on institutional reform will continue to proceed simultaneously with negotiations on the enlargement process; thus, a return to the flexible models may be possible during the later phases of the accession process.

In this context of dramatic change, as the EU moved toward the inclusion of the whole of Europe, attention to the issue of Turkey's membership lessened. Turkey's relationship with the EU began to be problematic long before the end of the Cold War, starting with the CU issue in the 1970s, and then the issue of democracy in the 1980s.[10] These problems worsened in the aftermath of the Cold War.

Turkey applied for full membership of the European Community in April 1987. Taking into account its Ankara Association Agreement, which

---

10. For the analysis of Turkey–European Community relations in the 1970s and 1980s, see Atila Eralp, "The Politics of Turkish Development Strategies," in Andrew Finkel and Nukhet Sirman, eds., *Turkish State, Turkish Society* (London: Routledge, 1990), pp. 219–259; Atila Eralp, "Turkey and the EC in the Changing Post-War International System," in Canan Balkir and Allan M. Williams, eds., *Turkey and Europe* (London: Pinter, 1993), pp. 24–45; Atila Eralp, "Turkey and the European Community: Prospects for a New Relationship," in Atila Eralp, Muharrem Tunay, and Birol Yesilada, eds., *The Political and Socioeconomic Transformation of Turkey* (Westport, Conn.: Praeger, 1996), pp. 193–215; İlhan Tekeli and Selim İlkin, *Türkiye ve Avrupa Toplulugu*, 2 vols. (Ankara: Ümit Yayincilik, 1991), pp. 164–247; Mehmet Birand, *Türkiye'nin Ortak Pazar Macerası 1959–1985* (Istanbul: Milliyet Yayinları, 1985), pp. 268–462.

goes back to 1963, Turkey is the longest standing applicant to the EU.[11] In view of the problems centered on competing definitions of democracy and human rights issues in Turkey, the Turkish application for full membership came as a surprise to many observers inside and outside Turkey. While the European Community regarded democracy as a *sine qua non* for inclusion in the community, Turkish leaders saw the transition to democracy as a gradual process. Furthermore, there were problems in financial cooperation. Decision-making bodies such as the European Community–Turkey Association Council and the Joint Turkey–European Community Parliamentary Committee, which supervised and coordinated the Association Agreement[12] between Turkey and the European Community, were not able to meet for a long time after 1981.[13] Another factor in the European Community's reluctance to welcome the Turkish application was that it came at a point when the European Community was facing difficulties of consolidation, concerning the strategy for a single market within Europe by the end of 1992. Furthermore, the European Community usually welcomed applications from groups of countries that have close relations with each other—a pattern visible previously as well as in the present EU enlargement—but Turkey applied as a single country.

Under these circumstances, it took more than two-and-a-half years for the European Commission to prepare its report on Turkey.[14] Compared with the previous Greek, Spanish, and Portuguese applications, this seems rather a long period and shows that the commission was trying to postpone as much as possible the declaration of its opinion of Turkey. When it was delivered on December 17, 1989, the opinion amounted to a recommendation that accession negotiations, with any country, not only with a problematic country such as Turkey, should not start before 1993. In addition to this general assessment, the commission also stated that the specific analysis of the economic and political situation of Turkey showed that it would be hard for Turkey to cope with adjustment prob-

---

11.   The European Community became the EU in 1992.

12.   The Association Agreement, signed in Ankara on September 12, 1993, prescribed the preparatory, transitional, and final stages for Turkey's full membership in the Customs Union.

13.   Turkey's application is discussed in more detail in Eralp, "Turkey and the EC in the Changing Post-War International System"; and Eralp, "Turkey and the European Community: Prospects for a New Relationship."

14.   The European Commission is the EU's executive body with powers of initiative, implementation, management, and control.

lems with which it would be confronted in the medium term if it acceded to the European Community.[15] As a result of this negative opinion on full membership, the Association Agreement and the CU remained the common denominator between Turkey and Europe, and both sides focused their attention on the revitalization of the CU.

When the "frozen" Turkish application for full membership was reactivated in the present enlargement process in the 1994–96 period, there were four possibilities for Turkey's relationship with the EU. The first scenario, which dominated in the beginning, was the exclusion of Turkey from the enlargement process. The EU officials were of the opinion that Turkey should not be included in the present enlargement due to long-standing economic and political problems, as well as its size and the necessity for large financial contributions by the EU. They viewed the CU as the basic mechanism to improve the relationship between Turkey and the EU without linking it to the issue of full membership. This attitude towards Turkey was quite apparent, not only in Greece and Germany, but also within the European Commission, and its reflection is clearly visible in the commission report, "Agenda 2000," which focused on the other applicant countries and omitted consideration of Turkey.

The second scenario was to give Turkey a special status without the commitment of full membership. It was realized during the discussions after the publication of "Agenda 2000" that the exclusion of Turkey, the longest standing applicant to the EU, from the enlargement process would not only aggravate tensions between the EU and Turkey, but would also lead to an increasing anti-European feeling in Turkey. It was argued by some observers of the Turkish case that Turkey could be kept within the emerging European project, short of full membership.[16] As the Luxembourg summit approached, the discussions of the nature of special status became more intense. On the Turkish side, the traditional policies of Westernization made it extremely difficult to give up the idea of full membership; thus there was clear opposition to the idea of special status. The Turkish side also believed that granting the possibility of full membership to some of the applicant countries and putting Turkey in a special

15. See European Commission, *Commission Opinion on Turkey's Request for Accession to the Community* (SEC89, 2290 fin./2, plus annex) (Brussels: December 29, 1989).

16. For analyses that go beyond the CU, but fall short of full membership, see G. Leicester, *Turkey and the EU: The Case for a Special Relationship,* University of Reading Discussion Papers in European and International Social Science Research, No. 55 (October 1995); Peter Ludlow, ed., *Europe and the Mediterranean* (London: Brassey's, 1994); Vojtech Mastny and R. Craig Nation, eds., *Turkey between East and West: New Challenges for a Rising Regional Power* (Boulder, Colo.: Westview, 1995).

category would be extremely discriminatory and unjust. Some EU members, such as France and Italy, which were more interested in seeing the incorporation of the Mediterranean countries into the EU, saw the inherent dangers of this scenario. There was also the mounting U.S. pressure on the EU member countries to include Turkey in the enlargement process. As a result of all this, it became more difficult to put Turkey in a special category without the prospect of full membership.

The third scenario, which predominated in the period leading up to the Luxembourg Summit, was to grant special status to Turkey, but with the prospect of full membership. Turkey would be included in the enlargement process, but not in the pre-accession strategy, which is offered to all other candidate countries to prepare them for accession to the EU. The "when" and "how" of Turkey's membership would be left ambiguous. This strategy was thought to be the best way to solve the Turkish problem. On the one hand, it would give the message to Turkey that it was to be included in the enlargement process. On the other hand, it would not overly commit the EU, primarily in terms of finance, since Turkey would not be included in the pre-accession strategy. The pressure would be on Turkey to reform its political and economic structures.

The fourth scenario, which did not have much chance of success, was to treat Turkey in the same way as all other applicants in terms of full membership. Turkish officials supported this view, but Greece and Germany in particular argued against it. Their arguments gained ground in the discussions because of the prevalent perception of problematic relations between the EU and Turkey, and because of the absence of a political will on the part of other countries to support the Turkish case.

At the Luxembourg Summit, Turkey was given a special status with a long perspective of full membership. It was included in the enlargement process, but not given a pre-accession strategy, as were the other candidate countries. The EU formulated a special "European strategy," which would prepare Turkey for accession by bringing it closer to the EU. This decision was a clear improvement on "Agenda 2000." EU officials were of the opinion that the Turkish case had been approached rather fairly. However, the Turkish government believed that Turkey had been treated unjustly and reacted strongly to the summit decision. Thus, EU expectations and the Turkish attitudes clearly diverged.

Aftermath of the Luxembourg Summit

The Turkish government regarded the Luxembourg decisions as discriminatory and politicized, and made under the influence of Greece. As one close observer of the Turkish case pointed out, "Turkey gauged the EU's views less from what it said than from what it did not."[17] The Turkish government also thought that the Copenhagen criteria, which were said to be objective bases of the Luxembourg Summit, were implemented rather subjectively. Certain countries were put ahead of Turkey, which was more advanced than some countries in terms of economic and political criteria, as well as adaptation to the *acquis communautaire*,[18] because of political considerations and support of such countries among EU members. Primarily, the inclusion of Cyprus created a deep feeling of resentment. Cyprus was not merely a candidate, but was among the first rank of candidates. Ankara thought that this was a clear sign that the EU was taking the Greek side on the Cyprus issue and acting under Greek influence.

The anti-European tendency among the Turkish governing elites, which started after the rejection of Turkey's full membership in 1987, was reinforced after the Luxembourg Summit. For the first time, the parties in the coalition government, and not just some of the opposition parties, distanced themselves from the EU. This attitude was broadly shared by the Turkish political and economic elites in general. This new consensus was clearly seen in the decision of the government to suspend political dialogue with the EU and not to participate in the European conference in 1998, to which Turkey was invited together with the other applicant countries. It was thought that the EU was setting preconditions, both in the invitation to the conference and in the European strategy formulated for Turkey.[19] The government decided to continue the relationship with the EU based on the existing legal arrangements, primarily on the Association Agreement, rather than on the decision of the Luxembourg Summit.

With the deep resentment over Luxembourg, and the resulting coolness towards the EU, key government officials emphasized that the EU was not an "obsession" for Turkey, and that Turkey had other foreign policy alternatives. In this climate, it became more difficult to implement even the Customs Union arrangement between Turkey and the EU. Many of the regulations and laws necessary for its implementation did not go through parliament but waited for attention in different committees. Talks were held to review the CU. Some influential members of the gov-

---

17. Makovsky, "Turkey's Faded European Dream," p. 51.

18. The *acquis communautaire* refers to the full set of rights and obligations deriving from EU treaties.

19. These preconditions included the establishment of satisfactory and stable relations between Greece and Turkey; the settlement of disputes, in particular by legal process; respect for and protection of minorities and human rights; and support for negotiations under the aegis of the UN on a political settlement in Cyprus.

ernment argued against it, pointing out that this relationship was working to the disadvantage of Turkey and increasing Turkey's trade deficit
with the EU. It was also frequently emphasized that Turkey had the disadvantage of implementing the CU without receiving financial assistance
from the EU. It was agreed during the CU negotiations that the EU would
provide financial assistance of 375 million ECU, and the European Investment Bank would extend credits amounting to 750 million ECU.[20] But the
financial aspect of the CU relationship faced major obstacles in the phase
of implementation because of the Greek veto. As a result, while most
countries during this stage received financial assistance from the EU, Turkey experienced difficulties.[21] The most often stated argument was that
the CU for Turkey was linked to the problematic prospect of full membership, and was thus in a vacuum and subject to revision. There were even
suggestions that the CU be turned into a free trade relationship.[22]

The Cardiff and Vienna summits of the European Council in 1998
were not able to overcome the stalemate in the Turkey-EU relationship.[23]
Turkish government officials continued to think there was no major
change in the discriminatory attitude of the EU. Turkey was not given
candidate status, but put in a special category with unspecified financial
resources. Turkish officials acknowledged, however, that there were some
relative improvements over the Luxembourg agreement. These included:
the realization of financial resources for the implementation of the European strategy;[24] the avoidance of the mention of sensitive political issues,
such as Cyprus and human rights; no use of the term "eligible for membership"; and the decision that reporting on Turkey should be based not
only on the conclusions of the Luxembourg Summit, but also on article 28
of the Association Agreement between Turkey and the EU—the article

---

20.   The European Currency Unit (ECU) was replaced by the Euro in 2000.

21.   For a detailed analysis of the CU relationship, see Canan Balkir, "The Customs
Union and Beyond," in Libby Rittenberg, ed., *The Political Economy of Turkey in the
Post-Soviet Era* (Westport, Conn.: Praeger, 1998), pp. 51–79.

22.   In addition to the elimination of trade obstacles among the member countries, the
CU relationship also entails the adoption of a common external trade policy vis-à-vis
third countries. In the Turkish context, suggestions that the CU be turned into a free
trade relationship aim to create a looser type of economic integration that does not entail the adoption of such a policy.

23.   European Council meetings are held regularly among heads of state or government of EU members.

24.   This is the EU strategy for bringing associate countries closer to the EU. It is
based on respect for human rights and democracy, the rule of law, and the market
economy. It is more general than the pre-accession strategy and less supported by
financial resources.

that envisaged Turkey's full membership in the EU, if conditions were met.[25]

The EU officials, on the other hand, believed that Luxembourg and the successive summits marked substantial advances in bringing Turkey closer to the EU and its accession process. To overcome the stalemate in the relationship with Turkey, the European Commission formulated wide-ranging proposals to implement the European strategy for Turkey, outlining areas of cooperation that would make the CU more effective.[26] These included: the intensification of industrial cooperation and stimulation of investment; the extension of the CU to the sectors of agriculture and services; giving greater substance to the CU through technical assistance and administrative cooperation; the establishment of the mechanisms needed to enable Turkey to become involved in certain common community programs and agencies; and the implementation of financial cooperation. The commission primarily emphasized the need to adopt the financial framework, notably the implementation of the assistance for Turkey. By including Turkey with other applicant countries in its *Regular Report* of November 4, 1998, the commission aimed to show that Turkey was being judged on the basis of the same criteria as the other applicants.[27]

This was a clear improvement over Luxembourg—Turkey was no longer in a special category—but it had little effect on Turkey's attitude toward the EU. In responding to the commission report, the government spokesperson, Sükrü Gürel, criticized the inequality shown by the EU towards Turkey. According to him, the inclusion of Turkey in the same report as other applicants did not mean equal treatment of Turkey: the EU had not yet formulated a pre-accession strategy for Turkey. He stressed the lack of financial cooperation and the inability of the EU to carry out its financial obligations. The lack of financial assistance from the EU was one of the issues most emphasized by Turkey. However, the main criticisms of the Turkish government concerned the issue of Turkish "candi-

---

25. At the Cardiff summit, the EU tried to find a way to overcome the stalemate on the issue of financial cooperation and release some of the ECU 375 million for the implementation of the special action for Turkey. In response to this, the European Community adopted a communication on October 21, 1998, that included a regulation regarding the implementation of measures to intensify the CU (ECU 15 million for 1999–2001) as well as a measure to promote economic and social development in Turkey (ECU 135 million for 1999–2001).

26. European Commission, *European Strategy for Turkey,* March 3, 1998.

27. European Commission, *Regular Report from the Commission on Turkey's Progress towards Accession 1998* (at <www.kobinet.org.tr/kosgebabm/english/lib/tr/RR98.pdf>).

dacy." It was strongly pointed out that Turkey would pay little attention to the commission's reports as long as Turkey was not granted candidate status in a summit meeting of the European Council. It seems that the commission's proposals were ineffective in substantially altering the Turkey-EU relationship. While the commission worked towards an incremental change, the Turkish government continued to wait for a major change on the issue of candidacy from the European Council.

From Luxembourg to Helsinki

The analysis of the aftermath of the summit shows the intensification of the problematic Turkey-EU relationship. The deep resentment of the Luxembourg decisions led to the distancing of the Turkish government from the EU. The marginalization of Turkey in the enlargement process, and the increasing anti-European feeling in Turkey pointed to the eventual exclusion of Turkey from the EU, which, it should be noted, was to the advantage of neither the EU nor Turkey. The increasing erosion of traditional distinctions between the European, Middle Eastern, and Eurasian regions on security matters was evident. With the growing inter-relationship, the stability of Europe was linked to the situation in the Middle Eastern and Eurasian regions. It would be difficult for Europe to maintain a stable economic and political system if instability reigned in its adjacent areas. Turkey's role was crucial in the promotion of stability, primarily because it was one of the few countries with long-standing Western links and had remained relatively stable in comparison with the rest the region. The exclusion of Turkey from the European security system could lead not only to instability in Turkey, but might also affect the whole region. In addition to the promotion of stability, Turkey had other crucial roles to play in the linkage of trade, transport, and energy routes of the Middle East, Persian Gulf, and Transcaucasia to Europe. Turkey's role in enhancing regional stability, as well as its efforts to more closely integrate the neighboring regions (the Black Sea region, the Balkans, and the Transcaucasus) with the international system, were limited because of the problematic relations with the EU.

There were concerns among some European policymakers that Turkey was more of a "consumer," than a "producer," of security, as in the Cold War years, and that there were increasing security problems both within Turkey and in its surrounding region. Therefore, the inclusion of Turkey within the EU would expose the EU to unnecessary security risks. These views were based on the assumption of the existence of a clear boundary between Europe and Turkey. But it was extremely difficult to create boundaries between Europe and the Eurasian region within the context of trans-regionalization of security issues. Given Turkey's importance concerning these issues, the exclusion of Turkey would not minimize the security risks to Europe, but would affect the European security system quite adversely. The Öcalan affair clearly showed the impossibility of creating boundaries between Europe and Turkey.[28] Turkey's security problems had already penetrated Europe and become internal to Europe. Equally, European security problems, such as the conflicts in Bosnia and Kosovo have also become Turkey's problems.

These larger geopolitical considerations seemed to have little effect on the EU in the beginning, mainly because it concentrated its attention on the incorporation of Central and Eastern European states. But these matters will gain significance as the EU becomes more sensitive to its adjacent regions. As the EU increasingly realizes the importance of promoting stability in its surrounding regions, the solution to the problematic Turkey-EU relationship will be more evident.

Finding such a solution was also important for Turkey and the integrative process of the region around Turkey. It was important not only economically, but also as a wider project of Westernization. Turkey had followed a policy of Westernization since the establishment of the Republic. In the aftermath of the Cold War, it was evident that Turkey's foreign policy options were increasing in its adjacent region and some analysts argued that Turkey did not have to rely on Europe any more. However, the European link would not adversely affect Turkey's regional orientation. Rather, Turkey would be stronger in its region if it were well connected to Europe, which increasingly means the EU.

This analysis shows that Turkey and the EU have mutual interests in formulating a working relationship that would overcome the problems between them.[29] This should aim beyond the CU toward incorporating political and security considerations. In order to sustain a CU, the Turkish governing elites are geared to a close linkage between it and full membership of the EU. As the recent debate on the CU in Turkey shows, there is even a possibility of backtracking from the CU if the relationship does not improve soon. The process of European integration and the 1963 Ankara

---

28. The Öcalan affair clearly showed the erosion of boundaries between Turkey and Europe on security matters. Öcalan, the head of the Kurdistan Workers' Party (PKK), had to leave Syria under pressure. He ended up in Italy trying to seek political asylum. His stay in Italy created political turmoil all over Europe, not just in the relationship between Turkey and Europe.

29. This section is an updated version of Atila Eralp, "Turkey and the EU in the Aftermath of the Cold War."

Association Agreement with Turkey both envisage a step-by-step pursuit of economic integration gradually leading to political integration.

Turkey would also like to take a more active role in the emerging security architecture of Europe. As NATO emerges as the central institution in security matters in Europe, Turkey's role in the security field cannot be overlooked. Turkey, a full member of NATO and part of the European security system for the last 50 years, could play a greater role in the relationship between NATO and the developing European security system. But Turkey's links with European security institutions also need to be strengthened as the EU establishes its security dimension. Recent developments show that the EU will acquire a more important role in security matters. It is also evident that the EU will work closely with NATO in developing its security. The 1999 Washington summit of NATO and the new "strategic concept" clearly reflect the increasing significance of "out of area" concerns in a broader perspective on European security matters,[30] as shown by the events in Bosnia and Kosovo. Turkey played a crucial role in both conflicts. As the EU becomes more involved in wider security issues of Europe together with NATO, it will be more difficult to overlook Turkey's role in this area. This will increasingly necessitate the creation of a working relationship between Turkey and the EU's emerging European Security and Defence Identity (ESDI). It is essential, however, that Turkey takes part not only in the phase of implementation of security policies, but also in the formulation of these policies. Turkey feels these efforts need to be supported by the EU in terms of its candidacy and of a coherent strategy regarding membership and specific financial resources.

These Turkish concerns were taken into consideration in the 1999 EU Helsinki Summit, and Turkey was offered candidate status within the present enlargement process. Helsinki marked the end of the decade-old impasse in the Turkey-EU relationship, which had been to the advantage of neither side. While the focus of the EU on the incorporation of Central and Eastern European countries in the present enlargement process made the Turkish application somewhat secondary, wider geopolitical considerations gave a pivotal role to Turkey. This anomaly in the Turkish case must be solved through the creation of a more cooperative Turkey-EU relationship.

The Helsinki Summit overcame the long-lasting ambiguity over whether or not Turkey is a European country. Turkey was clearly situated

---

30. For a comprehensive treatment of NATO's new perspective on European security issues, see NATO, "Strategic Concept," NATO Press Release NAC-S (99)65, April 24, 1999.

in the present enlargement process, along with other candidate countries. Turkey also became part of an Accession Partnership, reflecting the willingness on the part of the EU to provide the same financial and technical support to prepare Turkey for membership as the other candidate countries receive. On this issue, there was a major difference from Luxembourg, where Turkey had been treated separately from other candidate countries. The EU proposed to treat Turkey according to the same "Copenhagen criteria" applied to other candidate countries. The Helsinki resolutions differ drastically from those made at Luxembourg: they are more open and inclusive and less discriminatory. As a result, they have been perceived positively by the Turkish elites as resolutions correcting the "mistakes" of Luxembourg.

The change in the relationship between the EU and Turkey, as manifested at Helsinki, mainly emanated from the EU rather than from Turkey. In the aftermath of Luxembourg, there had been increasing criticisms of the Luxembourg framework on enlargement within the EU, including claims that it was narrow and discriminatory and would result in the creation of borders based on geographical and religious-cultural values. The 1998 change in the German government from Christian Democrat to a Social Democrat–Green coalition reflected the new, more open attitude toward the enlargement process, as well as toward Turkey.[31]

The EU governments and the European Commission also manifested a greater awareness of the strategic dimension of enlargement. The EU has focused for a long time on economic and political issues. This attitude started to change after the Kosovo crisis in 1999. EU officials began to realize that instability in the Balkans would have detrimental ramifications for the European integration process. If instability were to reign in adjacent regions, it would be extremely difficult to create a Europe based on the idea of peaceful change. As a result, the EU began to address broader geopolitical questions, starting with the issue of the creation of new patterns of cooperation in the Balkans. With the adoption of a new stability pact in the Balkans, the EU focused more on the problems of the region. This approach in the Balkans necessitated a new relationship between Greece and Turkey. It became evident that the creation of a cooperative relationship in the Balkans would be somewhat difficult if conflicts were to persist between Greece and Turkey. The tragic earthquakes in the two countries in 1999 created a new climate of cooperation and an in-

31. For a more comprehensive analysis, see Kalypso Nicolaidis, "Europe's Tainted Mirror: Reflections on Turkey's Candidacy Status after Helsinki," in Dimitri Keridis and Dimitrios Triantaphyllou, eds., *Greek-Turkish Relations in the Era of Globalization* (Dulles, Va.: Brassey's, 2001), pp. 245–277.

creasing rapprochement between them, as manifested by frequent visits of high officials for the first time in many years.

It is no coincidence that Turkish candidacy was offered at a summit in which important decisions were taken in consolidating the ESDI. The Helsinki Summit decided to create military forces of up to between 50,000 and 60,000 troops to launch and conduct EU-led operations in response to international crises. This attitude showed the determination of the EU to develop an autonomous capacity in the field of security in coordination with NATO. As I have argued in this chapter, it would be increasingly difficult to overlook Turkey's role in the security field as the EU develops its common policy on security and defense. The development of this policy was another reason why there should be a more cooperative relationship between Greece and Turkey.

In brief, the increasing consolidation by the EU of its common policy on security and defense issues indicates the growing significance of geopolitical considerations on the agenda of the EU. It is quite evident that as the attention of the EU turns toward larger geopolitical concerns, the case of Turkey draws more attention after the 1999 Helsinki Summit, and its attitude toward Turkey becomes more inclusive. Turkey's relationship with the EU was at a historical crossroads. Turkey could have been marginalized or even excluded from the emerging European group, or there was the possibility of a working relationship that incorporated Turkey within the EU. The Helsinki Summit decided on the latter, and this decision is to the advantage of both the EU and Turkey.

The Aftermath of the Helsinki Summit

The Helsinki framework required a major mental shift of orientation in the attitudes of both the EU and Turkish officials to create a more cooperative relationship. This mental shift was not easy, primarily because Turkish and EU officials have long been used to an adversarial relationship and treated each other in bilateral "us-them" terms.

It should, however, be mentioned that the Helsinki Summit pressured for major political and economic reforms in Turkey. The EU actively stimulated these reforms through the publication of its Accession Partnership document, which was announced in November 2000. This announcement was important because it led to the inclusion of Turkey in the Accession Partnership relationship with the EU as with other candidate countries. The European Commission listed the short- and medium-term economic and political priorities aimed at the transformation of the Turkish state in line with the Copenhagen criteria. The political measures in the document were designed to create a more liberal and pluralistic order and the economic measures focused on the achievement of macroeconomic stability and an effective regulatory structure.

In response to the AP, the Turkish government prepared the "Turkish National Program for the Adoption of the *Acquis*," which was submitted to the European Commission in March 2001. This was a major attempt to meet the political and economic requirements of the EU. From the EU perspective, the National Program represented significant progress, but officials emphasized that the state of reforms in the report fell rather short of expectations in the political field.

Turkish authorities focused on the political aspects of the National Program in the latter part of 2001 and in 2002. To this purpose, 34 amendments to the constitution were accomplished primarily in the area of human rights and freedom of expression and organization. These were followed by "harmonization laws" designed to translate the constitutional amendments into concrete action by bringing Turkish laws in line with the *acquis*. These measures were dramatic compared with previous efforts and they were engineered by a relatively weak coalition government of three different political orientations, including the nationalist-rightist Nationalist Movement Party (MHP), the nationalist-leftist Democratic Left Party (DSP), and the liberal center-right Motherland Party (ANAP). While dramatic in Turkish terms, critical areas were still left contested between the EU and Turkey, such as the abolishment of the death penalty, the extension of cultural rights of minority groups, the role of the military, and the Cyprus question.

These areas were problematic between Turkey and the EU and they were also at the center of domestic debate in Turkey. EU issues have been at the center of political debate in Turkey ever since the Helsinki Summit, but particularly so in 2002. While all of the major political parties in Turkey displayed a vague commitment on the issue of EU membership, when it came to the sensitive issues mentioned here, there was a lack of consensus. The coalition was clearly fragmented on these issues. The MHP opposed the abolition of the death penalty and the extension of cultural rights, and took a hard line on Cyprus. The DSP was more favorable regarding the death penalty but had serious reservations on other sensitive matters. Only ANAP had a clear pro-EU attitude. Within this climate, it became increasingly difficult for the government to move forward in the reform process on these key political issues.

However, on August 3, 2002, the Turkish Grand National Assembly made some historic decisions regarding the reform process, by large majorities, in order to show Turkey's willingness to join the EU. It abolished the death penalty and granted the right to minorities to learn a mother tongue and to broadcast in it. The early election on October 3, 2002, ended the coalition with the clear victory of the pro-religious Justice and Development Party (AKP). Nevertheless, following the August decisions, there was increasing hope in Turkey that the EU would set a clearer timetable to start negotiations in 2003, or at latest at the beginning of 2004.

The Copenhagen European Council in December 2002 on the current enlargement process did not meet Turkey's expectations. Its decision was that if the European Council of December 2004 finds that Turkey has fulfilled the Copenhagen political criteria, accession negotiations will be opened without delay. This was an improvement for Turkey, but there was still ambiguity over whether negotiations will begin even in 2005. In any event, Turkey's parliament proceeded to address Europe's concerns about Kurdish cultural rights and the role of the military in Turkish politics in the summer of 2003 with the adoption of the sixth and seventh package of legislative reforms.

Turkey's domestic constraints coupled with the EU's ambivalent attitude have put Turkey on a "slow track" compared to other accession candidates in the present enlargement process. Turkey is the only candidate country that has not yet started accession negotiations. It is the only country that has not fulfilled the political expectations of the EU. Not only is it on a slow track, but it also remains the only country without a clear timetable for its accession. In all the other candidate countries, the political and economic processes have accelerated as the EU provided clearer signals to their accession. In the Turkish context, it has not been easy to sustain the political and economic process given the ambivalent, slow track relationship with the EU.

Turkey's relationship with the EU remains unresolved. We have witnessed ups and downs and critical moments in this relationship. The Helsinki Summit provided an important turning point by admitting that Turkey is a European country and extending candidate status to Turkey. However, the Helsinki process remained incomplete because the EU and Turkey were unable to clarify a timetable for Turkey's accession. This chapter argues that this situation has the potential to hamper not only the Turkey-EU relationship but also the EU's role in the regions surrounding Turkey, such as the Balkans and the Eastern Mediterranean. The EU is in the process of extending its security community framework into southeastern Europe. It would be extremely difficult to proceed with this without the inclusion of Turkey in the EU, and without creating a more cooperative relationship between Turkey and Greece and solving the Cyprus problem.

In addition to Turkey's role in the current enlargement process, it is also argued in the chapter that Turkey has a crucial role to play in linking the EU to wider areas of Eurasia. This role became more important after

September 11, 2001. We are witnessing the potential increase of polarization in the international system between the West and Islam, between Eurasia and the West, and between the United States and Europe. Turkey is situated in the middle of most of these tensions. Were Turkey to be clearly situated within the EU framework, this would facilitate the creation of more cooperative relations in the critical regions around her. Turkey's inclusion in the EU would also give Europe more claim to lessen tensions in a multicultural world.

Chapter 6

Turkey and the United States: Anatomy of a Strategic Relationship

Ian O. Lesser

The relationship with the United States has been a key dimension of Turkish foreign policy for six decades.[1] It has also been a defining element in Turkish-Western relations as a whole. In the Cold War years, the relationship had an obvious geostrategic rationale for both countries. Even today, the primacy of security issues continues to shape relations between Ankara and Washington in a changing strategic environment, as underscored by recent bilateral frictions over Iraq. At the same time, Turkey's evolving relationship with Europe, pressures for diversification, changes in Turkish society and politics, regional developments, and uncertainties about the future of transatlantic relations are increasingly important influences. There is also a growing recognition in Ankara— and Washington—that the bilateral relationship requires substantial redefinition and renewal if it is to remain relevant into the twenty-first century.[2]

The opinions expressed here are the author's own, and do not necessarily reflect those of the Pacific Council.

1. The bilateral relationship, is of course, much older, and includes the experience of the extensive nineteenth-century "Turkey trade" with the Ottoman Empire, and U.S. support for Greek independence and later nationalist movements in the Balkans and the Middle East.

2. This discussion, including the question of redefinition in Turkish-U.S. relations, reflects analysis offered in Zalmay Khalilzad, Ian O. Lesser, and F. Stephen Larrabee, *The Future of Turkish-Western Relations: Toward A Strategic Plan* (Santa Monica, Calif.: RAND, 2000).

Contours of U.S. Interest

The U.S. approach to Turkey is often characterized as "strategic," in contrast to Europe's more political—and often more critical—approach to relations with Ankara. Indeed, the relationship continues to be strategic in several senses: strategic in terms of the primacy of security matters; strategic in terms of enduring and broad-based cooperation; and strategic in terms of Turkey's role in the broader geopolitical equation. This last dimension has arguably gained in importance in the wake of the Cold War, as traditional intellectual and political divides between European, Middle Eastern, and Eurasian security have waned. The United States views Turkey, and measures Turkish cooperation, through the lens of a global power, and in this context, Turkey's trans-regional position is significant. This trans-regional quality goes beyond the country's geographic position adjacent to areas of interest—the Balkans, the eastern Mediterranean, the Caucasus, and the Gulf. Analysts and officials, both Turkish and American, often make this point—"location, location, location"—in referring to Turkey's strategic significance.[3] But the more important point concerns Turkey's exposure and role in addressing new trans-regional challenges—functional issues that cut across national and regional borders. These challenges are also some of the most fashionable topics on the post–Cold War security agenda, especially in the United States, and include missile proliferation and defense, refugee movements, transnational crime and terrorism, and energy security in an era of new transport routes.[4]

From the perspective of national interest, the U.S. stake in Turkey has evolved considerably over the past decades.[5] From 1945 through the 1980s, Turkey was a base for power projection, both nuclear and conventional, part of the front line in the political struggle with the Soviet Union, and broadly critical to the containment of Soviet power in Eurasia and the Middle East. Since the end of the Cold War, U.S. interests in Turkey have become more diverse and diffuse, but arguably no less important.

---

3. This "real estate" analogy was made explicitly by Prime Minister Mesut Yılmaz during a December 1997 visit to Washington; Alan Makovsky, "Marching in Step, Mostly!" *Private View* (Istanbul), Spring 1999, p. 30.

4. By virtue of its location, Turkey, along with Israel and Jordan, could play an important role in regional ballistic missile defense architecture, an area in which Washington has a clear interest, and Turkey has been among the most supportive of the U.S. allies.

5. For a comprehensive recent assessment of Turkey's evolution and the meaning for bilateral relations, see Morton Abramowitz, ed., *Turkey's Transformation and American Policy* (New York: Century Foundation Press, 2000).

First, Washington has an interest in the evolution of a stable, prosperous, Western-oriented Turkey that "fits" in Western institutions. This is a
fundamental, enabling objective, to the extent that an unstable, uncertain
Turkey would be a difficult partner for the West—and perhaps no partner
at all. It is, furthermore, an objective that reflects the idea of Turkey as a
"pivotal" state.[6] What happens in Turkey, including the country's political evolution, is assumed to have wider consequences for the regional
and international environment. The continuing debate over the significance of political Islam in Turkey is a part of this equation, as is the notion of Turkey as a developmental model—a notion that has enjoyed considerable popularity among U.S. policymakers. The advent of a new
Turkish government, led by the Justice and Development Party (AKP), a
reform-minded movement with a "recessed" religious background, has
revived the debate about religion and politics. On the whole, Washington
seems far more comfortable with Prime Minister Erdogan and the AKP
than was the case with Turkey's previous experiments with Islamist politics. The current concerns center on Ankara's foreign and security policy
rather than internal politics. On the internal scene, Turkey's prolonged
economic crisis is probably a greater worry from the perspective of U.S.
observers.

Second, Washington will wish to see Ankara play a positive role in
regional development and security, an interest that takes on added importance as societies on Turkey's borders in the Balkans and the Middle
East are in the process of flux and reconstruction. Despite the failure to
reach agreement on a concerted approach to Iraq, Turkey may yet play an
important logistical, commercial, and political role in the reconstruction
of Iraq.

Third, as a global power, the United States wants Turkey to contribute to U.S. freedom of action, diplomatically and militarily. As a practical
matter, this has meant facilitating U.S. power projection in the Balkans
and the Gulf, and contributing to the management of relations with Russia, however these may evolve. However, in the absence of an overarching, common purpose such as the containment of Soviet power, Turkish
support for U.S. power cannot be taken for granted, as bilateral differences over policy toward Iraq and Iran suggest. As the Turkish domestic
debate on foreign and security policy has become more active and far

6.   For an assessment, see Robert S. Chase, Emily Hill, and Paul Kennedy, "Pivotal
States and U.S. Strategy," *Foreign Affairs*, Volume 75, No.1 (January/February 1996),
pp. 33–51; see also Alan O. Makovsky, "Turkey," in Robert S. Chase, Emily Hill, and
Paul Kennedy, eds., *The Pivotal States: A New Framework for U.S. Policy in the Developing
World* (New York: W.W. Norton, 1999), pp. 88–119.

reaching, the measurement of the Turkish interest in promoting U.S. freedom of action has become more transparent, and sometimes more
difficult. Public opinion now has an important role in this process, as revealed in Ankara's strong support, politically, logistically, and militarily,
for NATO's intervention in the Kosovo crisis.

All of these factors were at play in the failure of bilateral diplomacy
over Iraq in the spring of 2003. Turkish public opinion was clearly opposed to U.S. intervention, and a wide range of Turkish elites, including
the security establishment, were ambivalent, at best, regarding U.S. policy. In this sense, Turkey was solidly in the European mainstream. More
broadly, Turks had the sense that Turkish strategic concerns, especially
with regard to Northern Iraq, were not taken seriously. Above all, the notion of deploying some 60,000 U.S. troops on Turkish soil struck a sensitive historical nerve, and was widely perceived as an affront to Turkish
sovereignty. For most Turks, the debate over whether and how to contribute to U.S.-led operations in Iraq was less about practical costs and
benefits, and more about unfulfilled expectations—expectations dating
from the Gulf War of 1990 that Turkey's regional interests would be taken
seriously by the country's leading ally. In the end, Washington had taken
Turkish cooperation for granted, and had been disappointed. The result
has been serious, although not irreparable, damage to the bilateral relationship.

Contours of Turkish Interest

From the perspective of Turkey's foreign and security policy elites, the relationship with Washington is similarly strategic. First, the need for deterrence and reassurance in relations with Russia is deeply imbedded in the
Turkish strategic culture. Concerns about Russian intentions, and risks
flowing from potential chaos inside the former Soviet Union, rank high
on the list of Turkish security concerns. The strategic relationship with
the United States and the NATO security guarantee (the two are closely
linked in Ankara's perception) have traditionally been viewed as indispensable in relation to Russian risks. Ankara may seek closer integration
in nascent European defense initiatives (the European Security and Defence Initiative), but until these arrangements solidify, and unless Turkey
is given a full-fledged place in them, the U.S. link will remain paramount.
In many ways, the Turkish view of Moscow is the most conservative and
security-oriented in NATO. Turkey no longer shares a border with Russia, but political and security vacuums in the Caucasus introduce new
flashpoints for confrontation. In the event of renewed friction between
Russia and the West, and above all the United States, Turkey would be on

the front line in a competition that is more likely to take place on Europe's periphery than in the center of the continent. In this context, Turkish observers are also concerned about the growing emphasis on nuclear weapons in Russian military doctrine. The defense relationship with the United States, including the NATO nuclear guarantee, remains a useful hedge against this.

Second, Turkey confronts instability and risks on its Balkan and Middle Eastern borders that can only be managed effectively in partnership with the United States. This is especially true of ballistic missile risks emanating from Iran, Syria, and, until recently, Iraq. Stability and reconstruction in the Balkans will be strongly affected by European policies, but Washington still has an enormous influence, and has been a persistent advocate for a Turkish role in the region. Similarly, in the Middle East, U.S. involvement provides a measure of reassurance against the worst outcomes in Turkey's relations with its neighbors, even if Ankara is uncomfortable with the containment policy toward Iran, and is troubled by the risks of U.S. strategy in Iraq. In the event of an Israeli-Syrian disengagement, however unlikely in the near term, the United States can be expected to play a leading role in any resulting arrangements with Ankara over water resources, or restrictions on military deployments along the Turkish-Syrian border.

Turkey is in the midst of a major military modernization program, with procurement spending of as much as $100 billion envisioned over the next twenty years. Economic stringency is likely to cut into these plans, but military modernization will remain a priority even at somewhat reduced spending levels over the next few years. The United States has traditionally been the leading supplier of defense goods and services to Turkey, a relationship that has persisted despite the end of formal security assistance (arms sales and credits are now arranged on a commercial basis). Large numbers of Turkish officers have trained in the United States, and military-to-military habits of cooperation are strong. The Turkish military has a strong preference for U.S. technology, but is troubled by the apparent unpredictability of U.S. arms export policies. Disputes over the transfer of major defense systems have been a serious, periodic irritant in the bilateral relationship since the 1960s. The experience of the 1964 "Johnson letter," linking the U.S. security guarantee to Turkey's policy on Cyprus, and the arms embargo in the wake of the 1974 Cyprus conflict, have had an enduring effect on Turkish perceptions. In periods of tension, such as the dispute over the transfer of U.S. frigates at the height of the Kurdistan Workers' Party (PKK) insurgency and human rights problems in the mid-1990s, many Turks came to believe that Turkey faced a *de facto* U.S. arms embargo. The coexistence of supportive and critical policies emanating from the United States often made it difficult to tell if Turkey was being treated as an ally or a rogue state.[7]

Even in the current period of good bilateral relations, détente with Greece, and greater stability in the southeast of Turkey, new arms transfers (for example, the sale of attack helicopters and main battle tanks) remain controversial in Congress, largely as a result of persistent human rights concerns. For these reasons, Ankara has moved to diversify its defense-industrial relationships, with significant new purchases from Israel, Russia, and Europe. Realistically, however, the bulk of Turkey's defense modernization over the next decades is likely to involve cooperation with the United States. As the Turkish military becomes more capable, Turkey will loom even larger as a potential security partner—rather than a base—for the United States in key regions such as the Balkans, the Caucasus, and the Gulf. This may be the case despite the recent frictions over Iraq, if Turkish decision-makers and the Turkish public are persuaded that Turkish and U.S. security interests are convergent.

Third, Washington is capable of facilitating policy objectives that matter to Turks outside the security realm. The United States has been the leading extra-regional proponent of a Turkish route (Baku-Ceyhan) for bringing main Caspian oil supplies to the world market. The completion of the Baku-Ceyhan pipeline remains a cherished objective for Ankara for reasons of regional influence, and economic interest, and to reduce environmental risks in the Bosphorus.[8] Although U.S. policy on Caspian oil continues to favor multiple pipelines (that is, Turkish and Russian, but not Iranian), U.S. diplomacy has unquestionably played a key role in advancing the prospects for a fully operational Baku-Ceyhan line. But there are limits to U.S. policy in this area. Turkish officials argue that the West as a whole has an overriding geostrategic stake in reducing global reliance on oil transport through the Strait of Hormuz, and that the United States should be willing to help subsidize construction of a Turkish route—something Washington has thus far been unwilling to do. To the extent that Iraq wanes as a threat to energy security in the Gulf, the strategic rationale for Baku-Ceyhan may weaken. (It is worth noting here that the restoration of full flow through the existing pipelines from Iraq to the Mediterranean via Turkey would represent roughly double the energy trade envisioned for Baku-Ceyhan—a measure of the Turkish stake in renewed Iraqi oil exports.)

---

7. I am grateful to my RAND colleague Zalmay Khalilzad for this formulation.

8. See Laurent Ruseckas, "Turkey and Eurasia: Opportunities and Risks in the Caspian Pipeline Derby," *Journal of International Affairs,* Vol. 54, No. 1 (Fall 2000), pp. 217–240.

In a similar vein, the United States has been a consistent advocate for Turkish integration in Europe, including membership in the European Union (EU). It has made this case on strategic grounds, arguing that integration in Europe is an essential guarantee of Turkey's Western orientation for the future. This argument parallels the prevailing view among Turkey's foreign policy elites. Lobbying by senior U.S. officials may have played a key role in the European Parliament's eventual approval of a customs union with Turkey in 1996. Ankara has a keen stake in continued U.S. support in its relations with the EU—support that has been unpopular with some of Washington's European allies who question the U.S. standing in matters of EU enlargement.

The offer of candidacy status to Turkey at the EU's December 1999 Helsinki Summit, and the further elaboration of Turkey's candidacy at the 2002 Copenhagen Summit, have changed the context for this policy of advocacy. The Helsinki and Copenhagen outcomes suggest that Europe has adopted a more strategic, if still uncertain, view of relations with Turkey: in short, that Europe's view is becoming more like that of the United States. It also suggests that Turkish-EU relations will be more focused and more closely measured on all sides, and may now be less amenable to U.S. influence. If Europe is serious about Turkey's candidacy, further movement will require tough political decisions, but a fairly technical and legal assessment of Ankara's progress toward accession. There is unlikely to be very much that Washington can do to alter the nature of assessments from the European Commission. If Europe is not serious, and the post-Helsinki candidacy proves "hollow," there is similarly little that Washington can do to advance relations under these conditions.

Europe remains deeply ambivalent about Turkish membership, although the EU has a strong practical interest in ever closer Turkish integration. Turks, too, have serious reservations about the identity and sovereignty implications of membership in Europe. Turkey's sheer scale makes the challenge of integration daunting for all concerned. It is certain to be a long-term project, with the prospects for success dependent on many variables, not least the evolution of the EU itself over the next decades. In terms of U.S.-Turkish relations, the process of convergence between Turkey and Europe is likely to be more important than the issue of EU membership itself. The United States will have a stake in the continued transformation of Turkish society and policy along European lines. To the extent that Turkey enters into the European mainstream, above all the idea of Europe as a liberal order, many aspects of the bilateral relationship, not least frictions over human rights, will be simplified.[9] That

9. For a comprehensive discussion of variables affecting U.S.-Turkish-European rela-

said, a more European-minded Turkey may also be a less predictable security partner when a transatlantic consensus is absent; witness the recent experience with Iraq.

Turkey, the United States, and Regional Security

The primacy of security issues in the relationship will, however, underscore the importance of Turkey's evolving role in European security arrangements. In contrast to other aspects of the Turco-European relationship, this is one area where U.S. interest and engagement is likely to remain high, even if cooperation proves controversial or difficult. It is also a likely area of transatlantic friction in the coming years. Turkey's interest in maximizing the country's role in European defense decision-making is longstanding. In past years, there have been heated debates over the role accorded to Ankara as an associate member of the Western European Union (WEU). Now that the WEU's functions have been transferred to the EU and reinforced as part of the EU's emerging common foreign and security policy and defense initiatives, the question of Turkey's role has become more urgent. European defense efforts are now widely viewed as "serious" and will necessarily involve new approaches to NATO. Ankara shares with the United States a fundamental concern over how these European defense efforts will evolve, their relationship to NATO (which both Ankara and Washington continue to see as the central pillar of transatlantic security arrangements), and the role of non-members in European decision-making.

With many of the potential areas for EU security engagement on or near Turkey's borders, these are hardly theoretical issues for Ankara. Turkey has much to contribute to a more independent European defense identity, including strategic geography and a large and increasingly capable military. But Turkey also brings tangible security needs, on its Middle Eastern borders and elsewhere, that many Europeans will wish to leave to NATO, and by implication the United States.[10] U.S. (and Turkish) arguments about Turkey's strategic role in relation to Middle Eastern and Eurasian risks may actually have the perverse effect of strengthening Euro-

tions, see Hüseyin Bagci, Jackson Janes, and Ludger Kühnhardt, eds., *Parameters of Partnership: The U.S.-Turkey-Europe* (Baden-Baden: Nomos, 1999).

10. This recalls a central dilemma in Turkish-European security relations. Is Turkey a bridge or a barrier in strategic terms? See Ian O. Lesser, "Bridge or Barrier Revisited: Turkish Security Relations with the West," in Alan Makovsky and Sabri Sayari, eds., *Changing Dynamics of Turkish Foreign Policy* (Washington, D.C.: Washington Institute for Near East Policy, 2000).

pean concerns about Turkey as a "consumer" as well as a "producer" of security. The U.S. focus on Turkey's role in the Gulf also poses the highly charged question of whether Turkey is a European or Middle Eastern ally (from Washington's perspective, Turkey is both, but this does not necessarily strengthen the case for Turkey in Europe). For Ankara, EU decisions with regard to Turkey's place in emerging European defense initiatives have become a key test of whether Brussels is serious about Turkey's new candidacy.

Europe continues to hold Turkey at arm's length in the foreign and security policy realm despite strong lobbying from Washington. Americans and Turks tend to regard the question of Turkey's defense role as a strategic, even technical matter ("Ankara has much to contribute, so why is Europe reluctant?"). For Europeans, however, it is arguable that defense too is ultimately about identity ("what is Europe defending?") and here, as in other areas, Europe remains ambivalent about where Turkey fits. This fundamental ambivalence is unlikely to be resolved anytime soon, with the result that Turkish ties to Washington and NATO will remain critical in security terms, and Turks will remain sensitive to the continued viability of NATO and its security guarantee to Turkey vis-à-vis threats on its Middle Eastern borders (here the haggling over specialized reinforcements for Turkey in the Iraq crisis of 2003 was not reassuring).

The U.S. dimension in the evolving Turkish relationship with Israel is also worth noting. Some regional observers are keen to suggest that this manifestly strategic relationship was launched by Washington. To be sure, Washington has been supportive of Turco-Israeli cooperation, and the relationship supports U.S. interests in the Middle East and the eastern Mediterranean. But the impetus for the relationship in its political, economic, and security aspects clearly comes from Turkey and Israel, with strong reasons of their own for developing a more overt partnership. Nonetheless, the United States is almost always an unspoken third partner in Turkish analyses. Strategic cooperation with Israel necessarily has implications for the role of the United States as well as NATO in the region, especially at a time when new Mediterranean security initiatives are underway. It also promised to reinforce Ankara's political standing in Washington—and this may well be the case, but not for the reasons many Turks imagine. The notion that Turco-Israeli cooperation will smooth the path of U.S.-Turkish relations on controversial issues in Congress and elsewhere is uncertain at best. Difficulties in the bilateral relationship with Washington will not evaporate because of visible cooperation with Israel, and the rationale for U.S.-Turkish strategic cooperation stands on its own merits. Over the longer-term however, trilateral cooperation (and perhaps quadrilateral, with Jordan) fits very well with developments in the geopolitical environment that cut across traditional European and Middle Eastern lines. It offers another relevant frame for U.S. analysts and policymakers to assess the importance of relations with Ankara.

Limits to Diversification

The question of how to reshape the bilateral relationship to suit post–Cold War conditions has been a topic of debate for a decade. The first phase of this debate occurred during and after the Gulf War, when Presidents Özal and Bush spoke of a new strategic partnership that would transcend security matters. At the same time, observers in the United States saw a window of opportunity for expanded cooperation across a number of regional issues, mainly in the security area. Despite some stressful periods, the bilateral relationship has retained its importance and utility for both parties in the period since the Gulf War. The heavy emphasis on security issues has provided considerable continuity in relations between countries that, for different reasons, are relatively security conscious. For Turkey, this consciousness springs from a long list of perceived regional and internal risks, and the traditionally central role of the military in Turkish society and policymaking. The United States, as a global power with immense military capability and reach, devotes considerable diplomatic effort to defense cooperation worldwide, with Turkey expected to be in the front rank among regional allies.

Policymakers in Ankara and Washington persist in their determination to diversify the bilateral relationship and to strengthen cooperation outside the security realm. Since the mid-1990s, the U.S. Department of Commerce has identified Turkey as a "Big Emerging Market," and has actively encouraged new investment and exports. These efforts have met with some success, especially in the energy sector. Over the last few years, U.S. companies have embarked on a series of large power generation projects (Enron was particularly active). Given the Turkish concern about meeting future energy requirements, energy-related trade and investment has strategic importance for Ankara. If Turkey's legal and regulatory practices are harmonized to bring the country in line with European norms over the coming years, this will likely facilitate wider U.S. investment in addition to moving the country closer to EU accession negotiations. But the resolution of Turkey's troubled economic situation will be the key factor shaping the outlook for future U.S. trade and investment.

Despite a growing interest in economic ties, efforts to diversify the bilateral relationship by strengthening economic cooperation face certain limits.[11] Europe, rather than the United States, is the natural economic partner for Turkey. In a narrower sense, Russia has emerged as Turkey's leading trade partner on the basis of energy flows, a position occupied by Iraq prior to the Gulf War. Longer-term developments in the Middle East peace process and, perhaps, the full reintegration within the international community of Iraq and Iran, will open further opportunities, as would the normalization of societies in the Balkans. Washington can help to facilitate Turkish involvement in regional trade and investment, but the scope for major bilateral initiatives in these areas is likely to be more limited.

Another, more subtle, factor inhibiting diversification concerns the inherent conservatism of foreign policy elites, especially in Ankara. New issues are difficult to address in a bilateral agenda that is still driven by very traditional geopolitical concerns. Turkish observers have often complained that Turkey lacks a coherent lobby in the United States. In reality, Turkey has benefited for decades from a very strong "strategic lobby" within successive U.S. administrations, especially in defense circles. The focus has naturally been on security matters, and in the wake of the Iraq controversy, some traditional advocates in the U.S. strategic community may be less inclined to lobby on Ankara's behalf. Policymakers in Washington are just becoming accustomed to the expanded range of Turkish interlocutors on foreign policy issues. The overriding importance of defense questions, and the existence of well-established structures for consultation on these issues, put the Turkish General Staff and a handful of non-government specialists at the center of U.S.-Turkish dialogue since 1945. To a remarkable extent, this limited frame for consultation has persisted long after the end of the Cold War, and may have been a source of misperception in Washington regarding the prospects for Turkish cooperation in Iraq.

Changes in Turkey, including the emergence of a highly dynamic private sector with public policy interests, now offer a far wider range of interlocutors for U.S. policymakers and unofficial observers.[12] The U.S. "discovery" of the Turkish private sector has done a great deal to increase

---

11. The volume of U.S. trade with Turkey has more than tripled since 1980, increasing from $1.6 billion in 1985 to $3.4 billion in 1998. See Yılmaz Arguden, "Is Uncle Sam Making the Most of Turkey?" *Private View* (Istanbul), Spring 1999, available online only at <www.tusiad.org.tr/yayin/private/spring99/pdf/>.

12. The Turkish Industrialists' and Businessmen's Association (TÜSIAD), with an office in Washington, is a leading example of a private sector interlocutor capable of dialogue across a spectrum of public policy issues.

awareness of Turkey as an international actor, as well as to expand the range of issues for U.S.-Turkish dialogue to include education, technology policy, healthcare, and other non-traditional areas. Over time, this broader dialogue may help to change a curious aspect of the bilateral relationship: for all of Turkey's strategic significance, even many well-informed Americans know remarkably little about Turkey as a society. Diversification in the relationship, even within limits, could begin to change this situation as new facets of cooperation come to the fore and new faces are brought into U.S.-Turkish dialogue.

To an important degree, the character of the U.S.-Turkish relationship, and the potential for diversification, will be shaped by the evolution of key regions surrounding Turkey. Persistent insecurity in the Balkans and the Middle East, or turmoil or revanchism in Russia, would have the effect of reinforcing the security dimension of the bilateral relationship as Ankara seeks reassurance against regional risks, and as the West seeks Turkish cooperation in managing problems on the European periphery. By contrast, disengagement and normalization on Turkey's borders will encourage the country's Western partners, including the United States, to focus on Ankara's role in economic and political reconstruction. The deepening of Turco-Greek détente is also part of this equation. Turco-Greek brinksmanship has threatened to undermine important U.S. policy objectives, including NATO adaptation and coalition approaches to stability in the Balkans.[13] Continued improvement in relations between Ankara and Athens would remove an enduring complication in U.S. policy toward the eastern Mediterranean as a whole. On balance, détente is likely to enhance relations with Turkey and the region by encouraging a more comprehensive approach that features multilateral as well as bilateral initiatives. In short, the progressive resolution of Turco-Greek differences will help the United States to treat the region as an interdependent whole, rather than as a series of problematic and conflicting relationships.

The Bilateral Relationship in a Global Frame

A traditional Turkish critique asserts that U.S.-Turkish relations are a by-product of Washington's regional policies (for example, toward Russia, the Gulf, NATO, and others) rather than a stand-alone interest. There is, of course, some truth to this statement—and it is equally applicable to

---

13. While U.S. administrations have stressed their concern that Balkan crises could spill over to involve Greece and Turkey, both Athens and Ankara have actually been most cautious and least inclined toward confrontation in their policy toward the Balkans.

Turkey's own outlook in relations with the United States. U.S. and Turkish foreign policy interests are convergent at the broadest level, and aim at the promotion of security and development in key areas, access to energy resources, and the management of regional risks in a multilateral fashion, among other objectives. At the level of specific policy approaches, however, there is scope for considerable divergence. This has certainly been the case with regard to Turkish policy over Cyprus since 1974, and Washington has, at times, been equally critical of Turkish and Greek activities in the Aegean.

As recent developments make clear, Ankara clearly does not favor aspects of U.S. policy toward the Gulf. Turkey has a significant economic stake in relations with Iraq and Iran, and has long been wary of policies that could complicate Ankara's management of the Kurdish issue or prolong a sanctions regime that has damaged the Turkish as well as the Iraqi economy. Turkey permitted U.S. and British aircraft to enforce the no-fly zone and conduct operations over northern Iraq as part of Operation Northern Watch (previously Operations Provide Comfort I and II) until 2003. But the activity was never popular, and raised suspicion even among sophisticated Turkish observers about Western support for Kurdish territorial claims, and even the break-up of the unitary Turkish state—as unthinkable as these suspicions may seem from a NATO perspective. The emergence of nationalism as a more potent force in Turkish politics, together with a much more assertive foreign policy in Ankara over the past few years, suggests that Turkish support for U.S. regional security policy can no longer be taken for granted. The difficult Iraq experience will only underscore the need for more wide-ranging consultation and joint policy planning toward key regions such as the Gulf if confidence in the predictability of the security relationship is to be restored.

On Iran, the Turkish perspective is generally closer to that of Europe than the United States, and favors engagement over containment. To the extent that Turkey moves forward in its EU candidacy, these differences in transatlantic perspective and the consequences of Turkey's own policy choices may acquire greater significance. This will be particularly true if Europe as a whole develops a more active and concerted foreign policy toward Russia, the Middle East, and of course, toward the United States. Closer Turkish integration in Europe may also pose new dilemmas for U.S. policy that has consistently promoted Turkish aspirations in Europe. There will almost certainly continue to be compelling geopolitical reasons for U.S. support of Turkey in Europe as a means of reinforcing Ankara's Western orientation, but the bilateral relationship may become more complex and difficult as a result.

The progressive "Europeanization" of Turkey in policy terms would redress an important asymmetry that has emerged in U.S. relations with southern Europe over the past decades. With the progressive integration of Portugal, Spain, and Greece into the EU and NATO mainstreams, U.S. policy toward these countries has been largely subsumed within the frame of relations with Europe as a whole. As a result, some historically difficult relationships have been normalized. Turkey has remained apart from this trend toward Europeanization, and the bilateral relationship with Washington has retained its relative distinctiveness for both sides. Whether Turkey will go down the path of its southern European counterparts in a post-Helsinki, post-Copenhagen environment remains an open question, and possibly a defining question for the future of Turco-U.S. relations.

The Turkish foreign policy debate is also affected by broad-gauge questions that are shaping attitudes toward international affairs on a global basis, with special implications for perceptions of the United States. Questions of regional integration and globalization, in particular, pose challenges to the Turkish world-view. Both focus attention on long-standing and controversial matters of identity, sovereignty, and the role of the state (always a very strong role in the Atatürkist tradition). The integration dilemma is central to Turkey's relationship with the EU. In a similar fashion, the globalization dilemma highlights the relationship with Washington and attitudes toward U.S. power and influence, whether in the context of military intervention or the pervasiveness of U.S. culture and tastes. In general, aspects of globalization that trouble observers in Europe and the Middle East—the central role of the United States, risks to cultural identity, and implications for power balances—have not been viewed as negatively in Turkey. Until quite recently, many Turks welcomed a U.S. role to balance that of Europe, and broadly regarded U.S. power and influence as supportive of their own interests and role. But as in Europe, the debate over the war in Iraq has also opened a more critical debate in Turkey about the global role of the United States, and the result could well be a less benign view of U.S. power in the years ahead.

In many respects, Turks seem more comfortable with the diffuse challenges posed by the globalization of economic relations than with the more immediate and controversial problems posed by European integration.[14] Given the central place of the United States in perceptions about globalization, the evolution of Turkish attitudes on this question over the

---

14. See, for example, Hakan Aslaneli, "Foreign Minister Cem: The New Revolution is Globalization," *Turkish Daily News*, March 7, 2000.

coming years will be another important factor shaping the future of the bilateral relationship.

There can be little question that the evolution of Turkey as a society will be one of the critical variables affecting relations with the United States for the future. Progress toward liberalization, democratization, more effective governance, and the complex of changes required for Turkey's continued transformation as a modern society will have a profound effect on the country's international relations, not least with the United States. The first and most dramatic effect will be on relations with the EU, and this will in turn affect the balance of Turkey's Euro-Atlantic relationships. But a Turkey that can meet the European *acquis* and the "Copenhagen criteria" will also be in a position to enjoy a more predictable and untroubled relationship with Washington.

A final and very significant variable for the future concerns the evolution of U.S. foreign policy as a whole, and the consequences for relations with Ankara. Barring a collapse of the U.S. foreign policy consensus (and this is most unlikely despite the fractious debate over unilateralism versus multilateralism), the traditional elements compelling U.S. attention to Turkey, including continued engagement in European and Middle Eastern affairs, energy stakes, and the need to hedge against Russian resurgence, should remain. Indeed, as NATO adapts to a new strategic environment in which the most likely demands are in the south, in the Balkans, and around the Mediterranean, Turkey will likely remain a priority for U.S. engagement.[15] Moreover, many of the new and fashionable issues on the international scene, from drug trafficking and transnational crime to nuclear smuggling, affect Turkey and will inevitably become more central to the bilateral agenda.

Overall Observations and Conclusions

After more than a half century in which the contours of Turkish-U.S. relations were well established, the bilateral relationship at the start of the twenty-first century faces a number of important sources of change. The progressive transformation and modernization of Turkish society, politics, and economy is perhaps the most significant element in this equation. Changes on the domestic scene are raising new issues in the relationship, bringing new interlocutors to the fore, and could ultimately eliminate many traditional obstacles in the relationship, including shortcomings in the areas of human rights, democratization, and economic lib-

---

15. See Ian O. Lesser, *NATO Looks South: New Challenges and New Strategies in the Mediterranean* (Santa Monica, Calif.: RAND, 2000).

eralization. The pace of change in these areas will also be critical in shaping the future of Turkey's relationship with the EU, including the prospects for Turkish membership. It will also shape the way Turks perceive broader questions of globalization and integration, in which the roles of the United States and Europe, respectively, loom large.

Regardless of the outcome of Turkey's EU candidacy, the European factor is certain to be a leading influence on bilateral relations in the post-Helsinki environment. European and U.S. interests in Turkish reform and "Europeanization" are essentially convergent. But the longer-term consequences for Washington of a Turkey that is increasingly oriented toward Europe must be considered. The net result is likely to be greater normalization and maturity in relations between Ankara and Washington, on the pattern of developments elsewhere across southern Europe over the past decade. By contrast, a "hollow" Turkish candidacy, and renewed Turkish estrangement from Europe, would tend to reinforce Ankara's reliance on the U.S. connection, but under conditions that would not necessarily make for an easy relationship with Washington. In the current environment, Washington's ability to intervene on Ankara's behalf in EU circles may actually decrease given the technical nature of enlargement deliberations in Brussels, and the troubled nature of transatlantic relations in the wake of the Iraq war. To the extent that Turkey is more closely integrated in Europe, the quality of the bilateral relationship will naturally be even more highly dependent on the evolution of transatlantic relations as a whole, giving Ankara a strong stake in the repair of a badly strained relationship between Europe and Washington.

Regardless of the evolution of Turkish-European relations, many of the basic elements contributing to the strategic character of Turkish-U.S. relations will almost certainly endure. These elements include the need for longer-term reassurance against the potential resurgence of Russian power and the revival of Russian competition with the West, the persistence of energy security interests in the Gulf and the Caspian, and Ankara's natural role in regional security and development in the Balkans, Eurasia, and the Middle East. Together with the promotion of Turkey's European vocation, these elements are also likely to form the basis of collective efforts to refocus and renew the strategic relationship in the post–Cold War, post–Iraq war era. The rationale for the relationship should go beyond geography to reflect the increasingly trans-regional character of many international issues, from energy transport to ballistic missile proliferation, and Ankara's role in relation to these risks and opportunities. Turkey will not be the only key partner for the United States in these areas, but it will be an important one, notwithstanding recent difficulties over Iraq.

Policymakers in Washington and Ankara will continue to seek, probably with some success, a more diverse relationship featuring economic and other forms of cooperation outside the security realm. But the primacy of security issues in Turkish-U.S. relations is likely to endure for structural reasons, including the nature of Turkish and U.S. policy concerns, risks inherent in adjacent regions, the impetus of decades of defense cooperation, and the existence of other, more natural economic partners for Ankara. A stable bilateral relationship will need to reflect the character of the new strategic environment, and more fundamentally, the more rigorous measurement of Turkish national interests that has accompanied the expanded Turkish foreign policy debate and the country's growing regional power. That is the real lesson of the Iraq experience for both countries. Overall, Turkish-U.S. relations in the twenty-first century are likely to be more diverse—within limits—and, above all, more highly dependent on variables outside the bilateral agenda per se.

Chapter 7

Greek-Turkish Relations in the Early Twenty-first Century: A View from Athens

Panayotis J. Tsakonas and
Thanos P. Dokos

Relations between Greece and Turkey, the two NATO allies in the Eastern Mediterranean, remained tense after the end of the Cold War, while the traditional cycle of "conflict-negotiations-conflict" prevailed as the common feature of the new era. In the post–Cold War era, Turkey was still the main concern of Greece's security policy and the driving force behind most of its foreign policy initiatives. In the mid-1990s, Greece began to reformulate its security policy vis-à-vis Turkey in the face of new strategic needs and priorities.

The central argument of this chapter is that Greece's post–Cold War strategic priorities—which focused mainly on its ability to fully integrate into the European Union (EU)—resulted in a realization of the limits of Greece's "internal balancing" efforts vis-à-vis Turkey and a quest for the adoption of sophisticated "external balancing" policies. To this end, the EU appeared as the most appropriate forum. The EU Helsinki Summit, in December 1999, provided Greek decision-makers with the first window of opportunity for engaging Turkey in a medium- and long-term process that would make certain structural changes (that is, democratization) necessary in Turkey, and allow the full endorsement of that country's European *acquis*. It was hoped that this process would eventually lead to the abandonment by the Turkish elite of its aggressive behavior towards Greece, and to the adoption of policies based less on geopolitical instruments of statecraft and more on international law and agreements.

The chapter concludes with a discussion of the future of Greek-

The views expressed in this chapter are those of the authors and may not be attributed to the persons or institutions represented by the authors.

Turkish relations, which may deteriorate due to the process of "problematic democratization" Turkey is expected to experience in order to implement decisions taken at Helsinki and to facilitate the European *acquis*. The need for consolidation and further deepening of the current Greek-Turkish rapprochement appears to be a one-way street. This will establish a less dangerous relationship and create the foundation for the attainment of political stability and, eventually, the resolution of the Greek-Turkish conflict.

The Post–Cold War Setting

The end of the Cold War affected Greek security in a profound way. Although its strategic value was probably enhanced,[1] Greece was faced with considerable fluidity and uncertainty on its northern borders while Turkey continued to be perceived as the state's major security concern. Indeed, besides the unquestionable instability that stems from the fragile Balkan environment, the belief that there is a potential military threat from Turkey has been reflected not only in Greek public opinion but also in debates between experts and in Greek security planning for at least the past two decades.[2] Greek policymakers have perceived Turkey's policy vis-à-vis Greece as influenced by Turkey's ambitions for regional hegemony and by the resentment of the former colonial power/empire over the "difficult" and often "obstinate" behavior of its relatively small neighbor and former part of the Ottoman Empire.

Greek security planners have been concerned about Turkey's revisionist aims toward Greece as expressed in official statements, diplomatic

---

1. The Gulf crisis of 1990–91 confirmed that the Eastern Mediterranean and the Gulf formed a common conflict system, while the collapse of Yugoslavia pointed to Greece's pivotal position in Southeastern Europe and the approach to the Adriatic. Both regions posed new challenges for the role of Greece, NATO, the EU, the WEU, and the United States in regional crises. See Van Coufoudakis, "The Relative Strategic Significance of Greece and Turkey Before and After the Cold War," paper presented at the conference on "The U.S.A., Greece and Turkey in the Emerging International System," Athens, June 19, 1993, p. 9.

2. The results of a poll of June 1994, at a time when the emotionally loaded "Macedonian issue" had become the center of Greece's political and diplomatic concern show that, although Greek public opinion considered the main foreign policy problem faced by Greece to be the issue of Skopje (60.2 percent), the chief threat was still believed to come from Turkey (68.3 percent). For specifics on the 1994 MRB poll, see Yannis Loulis, "Public Opinion and Foreign Policy: 1994 as a Turning Point," in *Yearbook of Defense and Foreign Policy 1995* (Athens: ELIAMEP, 1995), pp. 121–139. Despite differences in style, both major parties (PASOK and New Democracy) have shown remarkable continuity in the last two decades in agreeing that Turkey is Greece's major security concern.

initiatives, and military action, including the deployment of its armed forces.[3] The 1974 Cyprus crisis was regarded as the major turning point in post–Second World War Greek security considerations: the Turkish invasion and subsequent occupation of the northern part of Cyprus in response to the Greek-sponsored coup of 1974 was for Greece not only a traumatic experience but also the basis for "new thinking" in terms of security.[4] Greece's close proximity to Turkey and its much smaller population tend to further increase Greek insecurity. In addition, Turkey has repeatedly rejected Greece's proposal for a bilateral non-use of force pact. This refusal reinforced Greece's belief that, given an opportune moment, Turkey would use military force against a fellow NATO member.[5]

According to Greece, Turkish "revisionist actions" include violations of Greek airspace; refusal to submit the dispute over delimitation of the Aegean continental shelf to the International Court of Justice; threats of war should Greece extend the territorial waters limit from six to twelve miles (as allowed under the 1982 Law of the Sea Convention); and challenges to the Aegean status quo as codified by a number of international treaties: the 1923 Lausanne Peace Treaty, the 1932 Agreement between Turkey and Italy, and the 1947 Paris Treaty. The latter led to a crisis over the sovereignty status of the Aegean islets of Imia in January 1996.[6]

---

3.   As one analyst points out, "Turkish official declarations, usually making headlines in the Greek mass media, have been intensifying Greek fears." Moreover, direct challenges (e.g., "the group of islands that are situated within 50 km of the Turkish coast . . . should belong to Turkey"), as well as indirect questioning of Greek sovereignty over the Aegean islands have been viewed with great alarm. See Yannis Valinakis, *Greece's Security in the Post–Cold War Era* (Ebenhausen: Stiftung Wissenschaft und Politik, S394, April 1994), p. 30. It is also characteristic that Turkey's revisionist claims were repeated in *Turkish Armed Forces, White Paper 2000* (Turkish Ministry of National Defense: Ankara, 2001); see especially chapter 5, "The Aegean Sea and Cyprus," pp. 21–22.

4.   See Valinakis, *Greece's Security*, p. 27. From as early as the late 1950s, NATO's southeast flank has experienced periodic cycles of great tension. The Cyprus problem, which emerged in the 1950s, along with the Greek-Turkish crises of the 1960s, the Greek junta–sponsored coup of 1974, and the Turkish invasion and continued occupation of the island, was complicated by a series of Greek-Turkish frictions in the Aegean region caused by Turkey's insistence on a revision of the Aegean status quo. This led to the reorientation of the Greek defense doctrine, with the official declaration of the "threat from the East" as the main security concern for Greece.

5.   Ibid., p. 30.

6.   As the former Greek Deputy Minister of Foreign Affairs Professor Christos Rozakis puts it: 'The mechanisms Turkey opts for in order to achieve a tipping of balance [in the southeastern Mediterranean region] start with the use of violence (Cyprus), or the threat of the use of violence (as evidenced by the concentration of troops along the Aegean coasts, or with reference to the *casus belli*, or with the display of

In addition, Greek policymakers see Turkey as backing its "non-friendly" intentions with a significant military build-up. From the late 1980s until the economic crisis that began in November 2000, Turkey conducted an impressive program to modernize its armed forces. In an era when other European countries, the United States (until September 11, 2001), and Russia were cutting their defense budgets in an effort to benefit from the "peace dividend," any sizable increase in military expenditure was an additional cause for concern for Turkey's neighbors, especially Greece.

Greece's Balancing Policy vis-à-vis Turkey

Analysts and policymakers in small countries are attempting to identify and to predict trends as well as to recommend policies of adjustment to emerging global patterns which, especially in the post–Cold War era, are in a state of flux. The challenge for Greece, a small, strategically located country, is to safeguard its territorial integrity and to protect its democratic system and values. Greece can be described today as democratic, Western, maintaining its status quo, and free-enterprise oriented. It is also a sensitive strategic outpost of the EU and NATO in the troubled regions of the Balkans and the Eastern Mediterranean.[7]

The dominant theme in the security studies literature approach dealing with state alignment policies, that is, "balance of threat theory," suggests that states, especially the small and weak, have two ideal choices to make when they are confronted with external threats: either to balance against the threat in order to deter it from attacking, and defeat it if it does attack, or to bandwagon with the threat in order to appease it or to profit by getting the spoils of its victory.[8]

---

power, through the constant violations of Greek air space or the Athens FIR), continue through direct or indirect claims over Greek soil (Turkish officials' declarations challenging Greek sovereignty over the islands) and conclude with more sophisticated, diplomatic forms for changing the status quo." See Christos Rozakis, "Greek-Turkish Relations: The Legal Aspect," in Dimitri Constas and Charalambos Tsardanidis, eds., Contemporary Greek Foreign Policy (in Greek) (Athens: Sakkoulas, 1989), p. 65.

7. Although significant on a regional level, Greece's economic capabilities and political-military posture constitute no major (present or future) components of the European or global security system. See Dimitri Constas, "Challenges to Greek Foreign Policy: Domestic and External Parameters," in Dimitri Constas and Nicholaos Stavrou, eds., Greece Prepares for the 21st Century (Baltimore: Johns Hopkins University Press, 1997), p. 72.

8. Thus, balancing is alignment against the threatening state or alliance of states (not the most powerful state or alliance of states, as balance of power theory claims) while

A number of scholars have also attempted to explain small and weak state alignment decisions by examining issues stemming from the domestic level of analysis.[9] The domestic school of alliances emphasizes that small state alignment decisions are but the product of the trade-off between internal mobilization of the state's resources and the formation of alliances, or, to put it simply, between internal and external balancing (or bandwagoning), as the classic "balance of power" theory had, much earlier, suggested.[10] Thus, when confronted with serious external threats, a state may also decide to rely on a combination of internal and external balancing.

Traditionally, to balance threats to its security, Greece has relied on a combination of internal (strong armed forces) and external balancing (participation in all West European security and political organizations—NATO, WEU, EU) and signing and adhering to practically all multilateral arms control agreements and international export control regimes.[11] As small states have fewer options and less freedom of maneuvering than

---

bandwagoning is alignment with the most threatening state or alliance of states. According to Stephen Walt, the concept of threat incorporates both states' power capabilities (i.e., the elements of power, geographic proximity, and offensive capabilities) and, in particular, the perceived intentions of others. Thus, "states ally to balance against threats rather than against power alone." See Stephen M. Walt, *The Origins of Alliances* (Ithaca, N.Y.: Cornell University Press, 1987), p. 5. As is widely known, "balance of threat theory" has managed to refine the "too one-dimensional" classic balance of power theory by adding into the equation the element of threat, the latter defined as a state's aggressive and dangerous intentions and, most importantly, by explicitly separating powerful capabilities and expansionist intentions as independent sources of threat.

9. From the point of view of the "domestic sources challengers," these scholars argued that a state's alignment policy is actually a choice (or a trade-off) between alliances and internal mobilization and thus weak states' alignment policies must be addressed with reference to certain domestic social and political variables. See Michael N. Barnett and Jack S. Levy, "Domestic Sources of Alliances and Alignments," *International Organization*, Vol. 45, No. 3 (Summer 1991), pp. 369–395. See also Michael N. Barnett, *Confronting the Costs of War: Military Power, State, and Society in Egypt and Israel* (Princeton, N.J.: Princeton University Press, 1992); and Jack S. Levy and Michael M. Barnett, "Alliance Formation, Domestic Political Economy, and Third World Security," *Jerusalem Journal of International Relations*, Vol. 14, No. 4 (December 1992), pp. 19–40.

10. For the notions of internal and external balancing, see Kenneth Waltz, *Theory of International Politics* (Reading, Mass.: Addison-Wesley, 1979), p. 168.

11. Greece has signed all major international agreements including the Non-Proliferation Treaty, the Chemical Weapons Convention, the Biological Weapons Convention, the Conventional Forces in Europe Treaty (CFE), and the Ottawa Treaty for the Prohibition of Landmines. Greece has also been a member of the Nuclear Suppliers Group, the Zangger Committee, the Australia Group, the Missile Technology Control Regime (MTCR), and the Wassenaar Arrangement, among others.

the great powers, to promote its security interests more effectively, Greece has sought to aggregate its voice and to integrate its policies with those of its EU partners and NATO allies.[12] Specifically, to deter the perceived threat emanating from its neighboring power, for many years Greece relied mainly on international law and agreements, as well as on the mediating role of the United States, NATO, and the UN.[13]

In Greek security thinking during the Cold War, Greece valued NATO more for its constraint of Turkey than for its contribution to collective security against the Warsaw Pact.[14] In fact, almost since it became a member (along with Turkey) in 1952, Greece has viewed the NATO alliance as a means of counteracting Turkey. It is characteristic of Greek military spending that it has always been more influenced by Turkish military spending than by any considerations of an external threat common to both countries (for example, the former Soviet Union).

For the majority of Greek security analysts and decision-makers, the Turkish invasion of Cyprus aptly demonstrated that Greece had neither institutional nor military safeguards at its disposal against potential Turkish aggression. Thus NATO, as well as other institutions, failed Greece since Cyprus and the Aegean disputes were the results of Turkish expansionism that the West refused to bridle.[15] As reliance on the Western alliance proved rather ineffective after the Turkish invasion of Cyprus, Greece began to place more emphasis on "internal balancing" (through the strengthening of its armed forces)[16] and less on NATO membership and the bilateral relationship with the United States.

---

12. Theodore Couloumbis and Prodromos Yannas, "Greek Security in a Post–Cold War Setting," *The Southeast European Yearbook 1992* (Athens: ELIAMEP, 1993), p. 52.

13. According to one analyst, "the mistaken belief, shared by the Greek and Greek-Cypriot leadership, that diplomacy alone can moderate Turkish behaviour and minimise as much as possible Turkey's political and military gains from the 1974 invasion, coupled with Turkey's intransigence, has eroded the credibility of Greek deterrence." See Constantine Arvanitopoulos, "Greek Defence Policy and the Doctrine of Extended Deterrence," in Andreas Theophanous and Van Coufoudakis, eds., *Security and Cooperation in the Eastern Mediterranean* (Nicosia: Intercollege Press, 1997), p. 157.

14. Kenneth MacKenzie, *Greece and Turkey: Disarray on NATO's Southern Flank* (London: Institute for the Study of Conflict, 1983), p. 117. A recent study on NATO and the Greek-Turkish conflict gives credit to NATO for the fact that the Greek-Turkish dispute has never erupted into a full-scale war. See Ronald R. Krebs, "Perverse Institutionalism: NATO and the Greco-Turkish Conflict," *International Organization,* Vol. 53, No. 2 (Spring 1999), pp. 343–377.

15. Andrew Borowiec, *The Mediterranean Feud* (New York: Praeger, 1983), pp. 29–81.

16. More specifically, the Turkish invasion in Cyprus was interpreted as a situation where Greece found itself both dependent and insecure. See Athanasios Platias,

However, consistent with its policy of relying on a combination of internal and external balancing, Greece soon returned to a policy vis-à-vis Turkey of inclusion in, rather than exclusion from, NATO's structure. Indeed, NATO's potential role as a means of minimizing Greek-Turkish confrontation, due to its interest in consolidating operational normality and cohesion in its Southern Flank, was precisely the reason for Greece's reintegration into the Atlantic Alliance in October 1980, after its withdrawal following the Turkish invasion of Cyprus six years earlier. Still, NATO's objectives with regard to its involvement in the Greek-Turkish conflict were viewed by Greek security analysts as inconsistent with Greece's higher expectations either to turn NATO into a security-providing bulwark or to act as a mediator in resolving the Greek-Turkish dispute.[17]

THE NEED FOR REFORMULATION: REALIZING THE LIMITS OF INTERNAL BALANCING

The 1990s witnessed a number of bilateral crises in relations between Greece and Turkey, including the declaration of the Joint Defense Doctrine between Greece and Cyprus, the October 1994 declaration of a *casus belli* over the possible extension of Greek territorial waters by Turkish Prime Minister Tansu Çiller (which then became official policy through a resolution of the Turkish National Assembly), and, most importantly, a rather serious crisis in January 1996 over the islets of Imia in the eastern Aegean, which brought the two countries to the brink of war. The Imia crisis was followed by the Madrid Declaration in July 1997, when the two countries agreed to refrain from the use of force and to respect each other's vital interests in the Aegean.

Scarcely a month after the signing of the Madrid agreement, which at first seemed to constitute a major positive development in the normalization of Greek-Turkish relations, it became clear that this was not to be

---

"Greece's Strategic Doctrine: In Search of Autonomy and Deterrence," in Dimitri Constas, ed., *The Greek Turkish Conflict in the 1990s* (London: Macmillan, 1991), pp. 91–108.

17. "Instead of enabling them to reconcile their differences by direct negotiation, [the] common alliance [of Greece and Turkey] with the United States and Western Europe often appears to act as an impediment. Bilateral disputes acquired multilateral dimension." Monteagle Stearn, *Entangled Allies: U.S. Policy towards Greece, Turkey and Cyprus* (New York: Council on Foreign Relations, 1992), p. 5. For Greece's misguided expectations that both the Atlantic Alliance and the European security and defense projects could turn into security providers, see Panayotis Tsakonas and Antonis Tournikiotis, "Greece's Elusive Quest for 'Security-Providers': The 'Expectations-Reality Gap'," *Security Dialogue,* Vol. 34, No. 3 (September 2003).

the case as issues over the Aegean and Cyprus heated up. Greece observed a "negative list" of Turkish responses. These included Prime Minister Yılmaz's statement that the principles of international law could not be applied to the Aegean Sea, the "Joining" or "Integration Agreement" concluded between Turkey and the occupied areas of Cyprus, and the challenge to Greek sovereignty over more than one hundred islands and islets in the Aegean Sea, including the island of Gavdos, south of Crete. The picture further deteriorated with the capture of the leader of the Kurdish Workers' Party (PKK), Abdullah Öcalan, at Nairobi airport in February 1999, after a brief stay in the Greek ambassadorial residence in Kenya. For most high officials and analysts in Turkey, the Greek involvement in the Öcalan issue was a clear indication, if not proof, of Greece's plans to bring about Turkey's dismemberment.

On the other hand, Turkey remained highly anxious, due to Cyprus's purchase and planned deployment of the Russian S-300 anti-aircraft missile system. With regard to Turkey's European orientation, decisions made in Luxembourg and Cardiff, in January and June 1998 respectively, also further burdened the already tense and fragile Greek-Turkish security agenda, as the postponement of Turkey's accession negotiations remained linked to Greece's deliberate policy of keeping the doors of the EU closed.

The rise of Costas Simitis and his "modernizers" faction to the leadership of the Pan-Hellenic Socialist Movement (PASOK) in 1996 brought certain changes to Greece's strategic priorities. By placing Greece's quest for convergence with the EU economic prerequisites at the top of the agenda, Greek decision-makers started to question the basic determinant of the Greek-Turkish competition, namely the existing and intensifying arms race. Greek and Turkish defense expenditures—the highest among NATO countries—were kept at extremely high levels, going very much against the average NATO and European trend of falling defense spending (see Figure 7–1).[18] Military expenditures constituted a heavy burden for the Greek economy, especially at the time when Greece was completing the implementation of an economic austerity program in order to enjoy the benefits of full membership in the European Monetary Union. Defense expenditures were, to a certain extent, responsible for the country's

18.   The average defense expenditure, as a percentage of GNP, for the period 1985–98 of the other NATO member-states was 3.1 percent and of the EU 15 member-states 2.6 percent. It is characteristic that in the period of 1989–99 there was a 30 percent increase in Greece's defense spending (from $5.001 million to $6.543 million, 5 percent of its GNP) and a 110 percent increase in Turkey's defense spending (from $4.552 million to $9.588 million, 4.5 percent of its GNP).

Figure 7–1. Trends in Defense Expenditures of Greece, Turkey, NATO, and EU15 Members

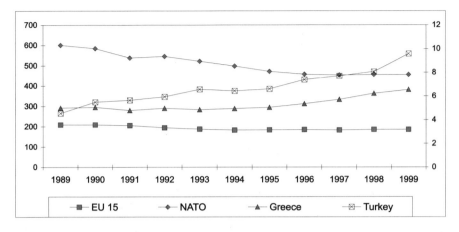

NOTE: Figures on the right are total military expenditures of Greece and Turkey. Figures on the left are total military expenditures of NATO and the EU15. All figures in billions of dollars (stable prices and exchange rates 1995).

SOURCE: Data compiled from various editions of SIPRI (Stockholm International Peace Research Institute) *Yearbooks*.

budget deficit, as well as Greece's lower than desired level of social services. It was also believed that the arms race had resulted in an imbalance of power in favor of Turkey and the risk for Greece of distancing itself from EU economic convergence prerequisites.[19]

Thus, two important goals had to be achieved by Greece in the mid-1990s: the short-term need to restore the balance of power with Turkey and the medium- and/or long-term "escape" from the arms race in a way that would enable it to meet its strategic objective to fully integrate into the EU.[20]

With a view to satisfying its short-term goal, Greece proceeded with the adoption of a series of internal balancing measures in order to deter

---

19. Greece's decision to spend $4.9 billion on buying 60–90 Eurofighters for its air force "is controversial because of fears that high defense outlays would undermine Greece's chances of achieving a budget surplus by 2003 in line with future commitments to the terms of the euro-zone's stability and growth pact." Kerin Hope, "Greece to purchase $5bn European fighters," *Financial Times*, March 9, 2000.

20. In his most recent reference to the need for the achievement of these short and medium-term goals, Greek Prime Minister Costas Simitis stressed that "Greece is neither Ireland nor Portugal. It is the current government, which implements the most extensive armaments program in Greece's modern history in order for its national interests to be secured"; address to the Organizational Congress of PASOK, Athens, December 1, 2000.

the perceived Turkish threat. Based on the fundamental strategic principle that "intentions may change very quickly but [military] capabilities remain," Greece prepared to maintain a relative military balance with Turkey. Therefore, at least until Turkish policy towards Greece changed in a fundamental way, Greece's emphasis had to be on the strengthening of its armed forces through the adoption of a modern strategic and operational doctrine with emphasis on combined/joint operations, improved personnel training, and acquisition of modern weapon systems, including smart weapons and force multipliers. These measures focused on shifting the country's arms procurement policy from quantity to quality to an even greater degree than before.[21] Therefore, the internal balancing of the Turkish threat and the strengthening of Greece's deterrent ability were connected with a series of specific proposals concerning the qualitative upgrading and modernization of the Greek armed forces in the context of the so-called "Revolution in Military Affairs," the cost-effective use of the available economic resources ("more bang for the buck"), the change in the structure of the Greek armed forces, the optimum use of the human resources available, and the like.[22]

Thus, on the level of internal balancing, the qualitative strengthening of the country's deterrent ability—especially for as long as Turkey showed no limiting of its claims—constituted a *sine qua non* for Greece to restore the balance of power, mainly in the Aegean sea, and attain a favorable balance of powers that would convince Turkey that the cost incurred from an eventual attack would be far greater than the expected gains.

Nevertheless, even if the efforts of internally balancing the Turkish threat were crowned with total success and Greece managed to attain its short-term goal of achieving a balance of power with Turkey, the second longer-term goal, that it would escape the arms race and achieve full integration into the EU, remained. Thus, Greece was facing the difficult "guns or butter dilemma." The dilemma came down to Greece's ability to match the need for immediate and considerable defense expenditures with its medium or long-term objective to fulfill the commitments imposed by the terms of the euro-zone's stability and growth pact. There

21. Christos Kollias, *The Political Economy of Defense* (in Greek) (Thessaloniki: Paratiritis, 1998).

22. See Thanos Dokos, "The Balancing of the Turkish Threat: The Military Aspect," in Christodoulos C. Yallourides and Panayotis J. Tsakonas, eds., *Greece and Turkey in the Post–Cold War Era* (in Greek) (Athens: Sideris, 1999), pp. 201–224.

was, in other words, a quest for the achievement of both deterrence and economic development.[23]

THE QUEST FOR SOPHISTICATED "EXTERNAL BALANCING"

To achieve both goals, Greece had to undertake a series of initiatives that would convey to the Turkish cost/benefit strategic calculus that cooperation would be far more beneficial for Turkey than the expansionist policy thus far followed. Thus, Greece started distancing itself from past assessments indicating that diplomacy alone could moderate Turkish behavior (which, coupled with Turkey's intransigence, had eroded the credibility of Greek deterrence) or that Greece's "internal balancing" efforts alone could provide the answer to the "guns or butter dilemma" Greece was facing.

Greece's efforts to effectively balance the Turkish threat without undermining its strategic priorities had to move toward a new position where credible deterrence, mainly achieved by the strengthening of the Greek armed forces, would be coupled with sophisticated diplomatic maneuvering and initiatives. With the election of the Simitis government in 1996, it was made evident that unless successful external balancing—through diplomatic means and maneuvering—could offset the Turkish prospective military superiority, the only option for Greece would be to follow Turkey in a costly and destabilizing arms race. To that end, Greek security policy started relying on a mixture of "internal" and "external balancing" policies that involved the strengthening of Greece's armed forces to offset the current military imbalance with Turkey and, most importantly, the engagement of Turkey in a context where Greece has a comparative advantage, namely the EU.

At least in the minds of Greek decision-makers the EU was the best available forum for setting conditions and placing prerequisites in accordance with certain "European" principles and standards on those countries that wish to become members. They believed that the strengthening of Turkey's European orientation would engage Turkey in a medium

---

23. The *White Paper of the Hellenic Armed Forces 1998–99* (Athens: Hellenic Ministry of National Defense, 2000), p. 150, aptly demonstrated the defense-economy linkage by stressing that "defense and economy constitute the basis, the two main pillars on which the national strategy of the nation stands. . . . Their interweaving plays a determining role in the achievement of the goals of national strategy. The harmonious linking of the two ensures Greece's ability to successfully face the long-term antagonism with Turkey. . . . Without a powerful, dynamically developing and prosperous economy, sooner or later the allocation of resources for the defense shall become very difficult with all that it means to the security of this country."

and long-term process that would eventually lead to the adoption of a less aggressive attitude vis-à-vis an EU member-state, namely Greece. This was in fact the rationale behind Greece's concession to grant the status of candidate country to Turkey.

Greece's decision to lift its veto and grant Turkey candidate status at the 1999 EU Helsinki Summit did not come out of the blue. As early as the Kosovo war in spring 1999 the two governments reached an understanding that an improvement of relations was necessary. Greek Foreign Minister George Papandreou and his Turkish counterpart, Ismail Cem, started preparing the groundwork for an official rapprochement in July 1999, which was greatly facilitated by the catastrophic earthquakes that shook Turkey and Greece, in August and September 1999 respectively. Greece's swift reaction to the Turkish tragedy astoundingly improved relations between the two countries, and led Turkey to reciprocate after the Athens earthquake. Official organizations and private citizens from both countries worked together in dispatching medical supplies, equipment, and rescue teams to alleviate the plight of Greeks and Turks. This "earthquake diplomacy" contributed substantially to an improvement in Greek-Turkish relations by offering policymakers on both sides some latitude in pursuing a détente.[24]

The Helsinki Summit was used by Greece as an opportunity to play the card of external balancing in a more sophisticated manner. Athens accepted the granting of EU candidate status to Turkey, attaching only two conditions (in addition, of course, to the Copenhagen criteria that apply to all candidate countries): first, Turkish claims concerning "gray zones" in the Aegean and the dispute over the delimitation of the continental shelf had to be submitted to the International Court of Justice in the Hague by 2004, if all other efforts failed; and second, the accession of Cyprus to the EU would not be conditional on the resolution of the Cyprus problem.

By insisting on a real—instead of a virtual or *sui generis*—candidacy for Turkey, Greece aimed, in fact, at the engagement of Turkey in an Accession Partnership with the EU. This partnership would put Turkey under the constant screening and monitoring process of certain EU mechanisms and procedures allowing for democratization to take place and encouraging Turkey to more actively use international law and agreements in its foreign policy.

By placing increased importance on its "European card," Greece did

24. In principle, the Conservative Party supports the improvement of relations with Turkey, although it often disagrees with the government's handling of the issue at a tactical level.

not rely solely, as in the past, on the EU's ability to become a "security-providing" hegemon and neither did it see the EU "as a system of political solidarity capable of activating diplomatic and political levers of pressure to deter Ankara from potential adventures in the Aegean."[25] Instead, Greece's medium and long-term policy enmeshed Turkey in the European integration system, where the European norms of behavior and European "rules of the game" had to be followed by Turkey. Thus, by pushing Turkey deeper into the European integration process, Greece aimed at successfully linking Turkey's state interests to certain international, that is, European ways of behavior.[26] "Socialization" from this perspective is the process of reconciling states' individual aspirations with generally accepted standards.[27]

Moreover, at Helsinki, the EU acknowledged the linkage between Turkey's EU orientation, the resolution of the Greek-Turkish conflict over the Aegean issues, and the end of Turkey's occupation of the northern part of Cyprus. Thus, Greece managed to confine both the Cyprus and the Aegean issues within the context of the EU, where Greece enjoys a comparative advantage vis-à-vis an aspiring EU member state, and to closely link them with Turkey's European accession path.

In addition, the engagement of Turkey in the "European project" was expected to transform Turkey's behavior vis-à-vis Greece from a policy based on the "logic of coercive deterrence" to one based on European norms and practices. From this perspective, the notorious *casus belli* issue, namely Turkey's threat to wage war against Greece were the latter to extend its territorial waters in the Aegean, would sooner or later be

---

25. See Yannis Valinakis, *The Security of Europe and Greece* (Athens: Foundation of Political Studies and Training, 1988), p. 55.

26. For a discussion of the pros and cons of Greece's "engagement strategy," see Kostas Ifantis, "Engagement or Containment? For a Greek Strategy towards Turkey in the 2000s," mimeo, University of Athens, Athens, 2000.

27. It is interesting that classical realists such as Henry Kissinger argue that the construction of stable international orders is dependent upon the successful linkage of state interests to international legitimizing principles. See Henry Kissinger, *A World Restored: Metternich, Castlereagh, and the Problems of Peace 1812–22* (Boston: Houghton Mifflin, 1957). In international relations literature, "socialization" has been studied by realist, liberal institutionalist, and constructivist scholars. See, among others, Waltz, *Theory of International Politics,* pp. 74–77, 127–128; John G. Ruggie, "Continuity and Transformation in the World Polity: Toward a Neorealist Synthesis," in Robert O. Keohane, ed., *Neorealism and Its Critics* (New York: Columbia University Press, 1986), pp. 141–148; Henrik Spruyt, "Institutional Selection in International Relations: State Anarchy as Order," *International Organization,* Vol. 48, No. 4 (1994), pp. 527–557; and Alexander Wendt, "Anarchy is What States Make of It: The Social Construction of Power Politics," *International Organization,* Vol. 46, No. 2 (1992), pp. 391–426.

viewed—especially by the "Europeanists" in the Turkish civil-military establishment—as a burden on Turkey's future relations with the EU. Instead, with its integration into the European system, Turkey would reconsider the worth of maintaining a policy of "myopic optimization" before
its medium or long-term goal of becoming a member of the EU.

Greek decision-makers estimated that Turkey's further European integration will entail certain costs for Turkey, especially at the domestic
level. By strengthening the democratization process in Turkey, it was expected that the civil-military establishment would be put under pressure
to make a more rational distribution of the country's economic assets.
Additionally, the military would be put under civilian control, the process of elite circulation would be accelerated, and a new state elite would
eventually be forced to start searching for new definitions of "national interest." With democratization and the broader political participation of
the electorate, which had been more or less indifferent or incapable of reacting to the commands of the military bureaucracy, the pressure exerted
on the Turkish foreign policy elite to redefine the strategic priorities of the
country would intensify.

Greek-Turkish Relations in the Post-Helsinki Era

The Greek-Turkish rapprochement has thus far produced fruitful results.
In January and February 2000, Foreign Ministers Papandreou and Cem
visited each other's capitals and signed a total of nine bilateral agreements on "low politics" or low-confrontation issues. They dealt with
tourism, culture, the environment, trade and commerce, multilateral cooperation (especially with regard to the Black Sea and southeast Europe
regions), organized crime, illegal immigration, drug trafficking, and terrorism. There was also an extension of bilateral cooperation in the fields
of agriculture and energy. A Protocol of Cooperation on Agriculture was
signed in June 2000 and negotiation began on two additional agreements.
In the field of energy, both countries are interested in connecting electricity and gas pipeline networks. Cooperation among businessmen also improved, mainly through the Greek-Turkish Business Forum. According to
Greek data, Greek-Turkish bilateral trade volume increased in 2000, exceeding $930 million.[28]

Both countries also agreed to create the necessary conditions for successfully addressing more sensitive "high politics" issues in the immediate future. To this end, they decided to work together toward the ad-

28. Figure based on data provided by the A4 Directorate (Greek-Turkish Relations) at
the Hellenic Ministry of Foreign Affairs.

vancement of a dialogue on Confidence Building Measures (CBMs) that could form the basis of a more stable relationship. The CBMs enterprise will initially deal with an agreement to adopt specific measures that would eliminate the possibility of a surprise attack and promote stability through the prevention of war inadvertently caused by miscalculations and/or accidents. By agreeing on a dialogue on CBMs, Greece aimed at further strengthening the current status quo, especially in the Aegean, and, most importantly, at integrating the Turkish side into a context based on certain rules and procedures.[29]

The Greek-Turkish CBMs process dates back to January 2000, when the Turkish side submitted a set of exclusively military CBMs that could be agreed upon and implemented by the two countries. The Greek side responded favorably to some of the Turkish proposals while it insisted that the agenda—in line with the broader definition of security in the post–Cold War era—should not be limited to certain military CBMs but should also include certain environmental CBMs. After several official meetings between the ministers of foreign affairs, Greece and Turkey agreed to consider a series of measures included in the following categories of CBMs: measures within the framework of the Papoulias-Yılmaz Memorandum of Understanding (Athens, May 27, 1988); measures of tension reduction; and measures of good neighborliness. The measures included in the first category were to be discussed within the framework of NATO by the permanent representatives in Brussels of each state, while the measures included in the other two categories were to be examined by the political directors of their ministries of foreign affairs.[30] So far

---

29. For a discussion of both the preconditions that should exist in order that any Greek-Turkish CBM enterprise can have a chance of success, and particularly CBMs that could be adopted by the two states, see Panayotis J. Tsakonas, "Security Regimes and Regional Stability: The Case of the Greek-Turkish Arms Race," in Christodoulos P. Yallourides and Panayotis J. Tsakonas, eds., *Greece and Turkey in the Post–Cold War Era* (in Greek) (Athens: Sideris Publications, 1999), pp. 45–71.

30. The first category, entitled "Measures for Confidence Building within the Framework of the Papoulias-Yılmaz Memorandum of Understanding" (Athens, May 27, 1988) included the following five measures: 1. the Turkish Armed Forces are prepared, on the basis of reciprocity, to reduce the number, size, and scope of their exercises in the high seas of the Aegean; 2. all Turkish military aircraft flying in the international airspace of the Aegean will, on a reciprocal basis, operate their identification devices called IFF/SIF; 3. the Interim Combined Air Operation Center (ICAOC) in Eskisehir will be operational and ready for communication and exchange of information with ICAOC in Larissa/Greece on a reciprocal basis on flights conducted by the parties in the international airspace of the Aegean; 4. Turkish and Greek military aircraft may fly unarmed over the Aegean; and 5. notification will be given, in the framework of the Exercise Planning Conference of NATO, yet on a bilateral basis, of the time schedule of

the two countries have agreed on a number of military CBMs, including the prior notification of their scheduled exercises in NATO to be conducted on an annual basis, in order for overlapping to be avoided, and the establishment of a hotline between the ministers of foreign affairs.[31]

Of particular significance in confidence-building was the joint statement made by the Greek and Turkish ministers of foreign affairs in Ankara on April 6, 2001, which stated that the two countries would initiate procedures needed to make them both parties to the 1997 Ottawa Convention regarding the prohibition of the use, stockpiling, production, and transfer of anti-personnel land mines and their destruction.[32]

national exercises for the following year, to avoid possible overlapping. The second category, entitled "Tension Reduction Measures," included the following nine measures: 1. Turkish and Greek military forces could conduct a joint military exercise and/or a Partnership for Peace (PfP) exercise in the Aegean or in the Mediterranean Sea; 2. in addition to naval visits scheduled for NATO exercises, Turkish and Greek Navy vessels could pay mutual port visits; 3. invitations could be extended by both sides to attend national exercises; 4. observation trial flights could be conducted on a reciprocal basis in the context of the Open Skies Agreement; 5. direct communication would be established between the Turkish and Greek Coast Guard Commanders; 6. there would be regular contact between the two chiefs of joint staffs; 7. there would be an implementation-extension of the Papoulias-Yılmaz Agreements (e.g., prolongation of the summer moratorium); 8. the triangular communication line between Athens, Brussels, and Ankara would be transformed into a hotline between Athens and Ankara at the level of foreign ministers and, eventually, prime ministers; and 9. Greek and Turkish armed forces would participate in peace operations in the Balkans, and Greek-Turkish cooperation in the framework of the existing Multinational Peacekeeping Force Southeastern Europe (MPFSEE) would be further intensified. The third category, entitled "Measures of Good Neighborliness," includes the following three measures: 1. exchange of ratification instruments for four protocols and an agreement concerning the border area of Evros, which were signed by Greece and Turkey between 1969 and 1971; 2. implementation of the 1963 Protocol concerning hydraulic work on the basin of the river Evros; and 3. cooperation on the prevention of pollution on the Evros (Maritsa) by establishing a regime of sustainable environmental development of the River Evros. At a later stage, the Bulgarian side could be invited to participate in the project.

31. Although of less importance, Greece and Turkey also agreed in November 2001 on the following CBMs: invitations to officers from both countries to attend one annual large-scale exercise on each side, exchange of views on the activities of international organizations relating to military matters in the margins of meetings of the competent bodies of the said international organizations, and cooperation on the prevention of pollution of the River Evros (information and data provided by the A4 Directorate [Greek-Turkish Relations] at the Hellenic Ministry of Foreign Affairs).

32. According to the Greek-Turkish joint statement, "while Greece initiates the ratification process, Turkey will start accession procedures. It is also agreed that the instruments of ratification and accession will be simultaneously deposited with the Secretary-General of the United Nations in due course." See "Joint Statement by H.E. Mr. Ismail Cem, Minister of Foreign Affairs of the Republic of Turkey, and H.E. Mr. George

It should be stressed at this point that the Greek-Turkish confidence-building enterprise has so far created a framework that could take some of the heat out of Greek-Turkish relations. It was the element of confidence and trust built between the two ministers of foreign affairs, and the consequent strengthening of communication channels between them, that helped the two countries avoid another serious incident in May 2001. The Turkish vessel, *Piri Reis*, which was to conduct a seismic survey from June 4 to June 28 in the less troubled waters of the southeastern Mediterranean (on the Greek and Cypriot continental shelf, according to Greece), cancelled the project after intensive consultations between the two ministers of foreign affairs. Earlier, in 1987, when a seismic vessel undertook a similar voyage towards the disputed continental shelf, a crisis erupted that brought Greece and Turkey to the brink of war.[33]

Parallel to the Greek-Turkish CBMs enterprise, the two meetings by Papandreou and Cem on January 19–22 and February 5–6, 2000, in Ankara and Athens respectively, gave further impetus to bilateral relations by producing ideas that have resulted in successful cooperation between the two countries. One of those initiatives was the creation of a joint task force entrusted with the study and realization of Greek-Turkish cooperation on matters pertaining to Turkey's European *acquis*. After an initial exploratory stage that helped define the main areas of potential collaboration, the task force has focused on developing seminars in order to provide technical know-how to the Turkish side on various issues concerning the European *acquis*.

The seminars cover fields such as banking, the economy, customs, agriculture, the environment, justice and police cooperation, university collaboration, and partnerships in youth projects. As these seminars are intended to bring the two sides together, they are not based on the "teacher and pupil" model. They focus on studying each other's methods and special needs and sharing Greece's experience in dealing with the various aspects of the European *acquis*. The task force has contributed to the tangible and irreversible strengthening of relations between the two countries, and has considerably enhanced mutual understanding and trust between the two administrations.[34]

Papandreou, Minister of Foreign Affairs of the Republic of Greece on Anti-Personnel Landmines" (Ankara, April 6, 2001).

33. See the statement of the Greek minister of foreign affairs along this line of reasoning in "Major Crisis Was Averted through Dialogue and Advanced Channels of Communication," *Athens News Agency*, May 31, 2001.

34. Interviews by the authors with the Greek foreign ministry officials running the Task Force scheme.

COPING WITH THE HURDLES AHEAD

Aside from the progress achieved on issues of "low politics" and on confidence-building efforts initiated by both Greece and Turkey, the Greek-Turkish rapprochement remains fragile, as neither country has been willing to budge on their firm positions regarding "high politics" issues. The Cyprus problem, issues related to the Aegean Sea, and the prospects for conflict resolution of these issues—most of which are considered by Greece as unilateral Turkish revisionist claims—are still not being fully addressed.

Most importantly, the Helsinki Summit, which granted candidate status to Turkey and confirmed Cyprus's path to membership, constituted a major breakthrough for Turkey. Two major processes were put into motion at Helsinki that may decisively affect—and ultimately reverse—the current Greek-Turkish rapprochement.[35] First, Turkey was asked to support a series of internal reforms that are an integral part of a pre-accession strategy.[36] According to the Helsinki terms, Turkey has to fulfill specific short- and medium-term political, economic, legal, and administrative reforms that have been set out in order for accession negotiations to begin. The most notable reforms concern the Kurdish issue, and, by implication, human rights issues; the role of the military in Turkish politics; and certain economic and administrative adjustments.[37]

Second, as already mentioned, according to the Helsinki decisions, both Greek-Turkish relations and the Cyprus issue have become integral

---

35. For an analysis of the domestic shocks—portrayed as "elite turbulence," "societal turbulence," and "economic turbulence"—Turkey is expected to experience due to the Helsinki decisions, see Panayotis J. Tsakonas, "Turkey's Post-Helsinki Turbulence: Implications for Greece and the Cyprus Issue," *Turkish Studies*, Vol. 2, No. 2 (Fall 2001), pp. 1–40.

36. These involve a particular Accession Partnership, drawn up on the basis of the previous European Council resolutions. The Accession Partnership is undoubtedly the key feature of the enhanced pre-accession strategy; Council Decision 2001/235/EC of March 8, 2001, on the principles, priorities, intermediate objectives, and conditions contained in the Accession Partnership with the Republic of Turkey, OJ L 85, March 24, 2001, p. 13.

37. Short-term priorities were selected on the basis that it is realistic to expect that Turkey could complete or take them substantially forward by the end of 2001. Medium-term priorities were expected to take more than one year to complete although work should, wherever possible, have begun on them during 2001. Apparently, the political, economic, and legal issues that were cited by the EU in Helsinki were the ones that legitimized Turkey's traumatic experience of exclusion from the EU Summit in Luxembourg in 1997. Indeed, in its 1997 decision, the EU cited several issues that remained to be resolved, namely the Kurdish conflict and consequent human rights problems, shortcomings in Turkish democracy, and failure to resolve the Cyprus dispute.

to Turkey's European accession goal. At Helsinki the EU acknowledged the link between Turkey's EU orientation, the resolution of Greek-Turkish conflict over the Aegean issues, and the end of Turkey's occupation of the northern part of Cyprus. Turkey's ability to secure EU membership (and even to obtain financial assistance) consequently hinges on its stance on the Cyprus issue as well as on its relations with neighboring Greece.[38]

So far Turkey's response to the EU requirements regarding the internal reforms, as reflected mainly by its National Programme for the Adoption of the Acquis (NPAA), has been rather disappointing, despite the reforms introduced in early August 2002 regarding the abolition of the death penalty in times of peace and the legalization of broadcasting and education in the Kurdish language. The unstable political situation and severe economic crisis has greatly contributed to Turkey's inability to productively realize EU demands. Moreover, the Turkish civil-military elite has proven unwilling to make all the changes necessary for accession. Unfortunately, there has yet to emerge an unequivocal pro-EU party (with the possible exception of the governing Justice and Development Party, AKP, or at least the majority of its members and officials), much

---

38. With regard to Greek-Turkish relations, Helsinki made it clear to Turkey that it had four years—until 2004—to resolve the conflict with neighboring Greece before the rather critical review that would assess Turkey's path towards the EU took place. Paragraph 4 of the Helsinki European Council Conclusions states: "the European Council stresses the principle of peaceful settlement of disputes in accordance with the United Nations Charter and urges candidate States to make every effort to resolve any outstanding border disputes and other related issues. Failing this they should within a reasonable time bring the dispute to the International Court of Justice. The European Council will review the situation relating to any outstanding disputes, in particular concerning the repercussions on the accession process and in order to promote their settlement through the International Court of Justice, at the latest by the end of 2004." See Helsinki European Council Conclusions at <www.europa.eu.int/council/off/conclu/dec99en.htm>. As for the Cyprus issue, the Helsinki European Council, after welcoming the launch of the proximity talks under the auspices of the UN secretary-general, reiterated that although a political settlement of the Cyprus problem would facilitate Cyprus's accession to the EU, this very settlement would not be a precondition for accession. At the same time, the European Council ambiguously stressed that "all relevant factors" would be taken into account for the final decision on accession. Paragraph 9a of the Helsinki European Council Conclusions reads as follows: "The European Council welcomes the launch of the talks aiming at a comprehensive settlement of the Cyprus problem on 3 December in New York and expresses its strong support for the UN Secretary-General's efforts to bring the process to a successful conclusion." Paragraph 9b of the Helsinki European Council Conclusions reads as follows: "The European Council underlines that a political settlement will facilitate the accession of Cyprus to the EU. If no settlement has been reached by the completion of accession negotiations, the Council's decision on accession will be made without the above being a precondition. In this the Council will take account of all relevant factors."

less a pro-EU coalition. Although some members of the elite (including President Ahmet Necdet Sezer and former Economy Minister Kemal Dervis) might be amenable to some of the EU requirements for a democratic breakthrough—and may well favor Turkey's convergence with European standards—they do not support the country's internalization of the European *acquis*.

Moreover, the granting of candidacy status to Turkey reinforced the internal conflict among the various social and ideological groupings (such as the modernizers and Islamists) favorable to Turkey's inclusion as candidate country, each one for its own distinct—and often incompatible—reasons. It is highly likely that Turkey will experience a problematic process of democratic transition, during which basic procedural requirements for democracy will be implemented, and yet societal preconditions for democratic consolidation will be missing.[39] Such a "problematic democratization" may have many negative repercussions: the rise of militant radicalism; the reactivation of Turkey's "Sèvres Syndrome"; and Turkey's adoption of a more regionally-based role, which would depart from EU standards and practices.

Indeed, the Turkish military could be pushed to extremism, since the military views the EU conditions as threatening to the country's ideological foundations and identity. The military has, on many occasions, publicly proclaimed that the state's unity is being jeopardized by the EU's imposed stipulations regarding human and minority rights.[40] Many analysts refer to such concerns as the "Sèvres Syndrome." But this fear of dismemberment by foreign powers with territorial ambitions, as promoted by the Western Powers at Sèvres after the First World War, is not pertinent to this situation. Today's syndrome is instead caused by the consequences of the EU's imposed modernization project on an anachronistic Kemalist elite and a fragmented society. Last but not least, Turkey's "problematic democratization," combined with suspicions that the EU is neo-colonialist and racist (in addition to being intrusive and threatening), may prompt Turkey to adopt a more sovereignty-conscious and regionally-based foreign policy with hegemonic ambitions. This viewpoint is shared by most members of the left and right in Turkey, from the military and the business community to the religious and secular right wing. To

---

39.　Tsakonas, *Turkey's Post-Helsinki Turbulence*, pp. 1–40.

40.　The military has not hesitated to declare that "in case Europe obliges them to take a decision, their preference will, undoubtedly, remain in the unity of the country and the Turkish nation." See the statement made by the Commander of Turkish Military Academies General Nahit Senogul, as quoted in "What the Military Says about EU," *Radikal* (Turkish daily), January 15, 2001.

this end, conservative Kemalists (especially the military) still believe that a special relationship with the United States—much more uncertain after the war in Iraq and related Turkish-U.S. friction—and with Israel would be a positive alternative to EU membership, allowing for a more assertive policy based on a sovereignty-conscious approach in key areas.[41]

The problematic process of the democratic transition Turkey has experienced since Helsinki could lead to foreign policy decisions that will be much more hawkish than those of a successfully consolidated democracy and that may be directed against Turkey's Western neighbor, Greece. It should not be forgotten that contrary to other external fronts (Syria, Iraq, or Iran), where—other than on its postwar Iraqi border—the pressure on Turkey's interests has either relaxed or disappeared,[42] Greek-Turkish relations and the Cyprus issue have both become, after the Helsinki Summit, integral parts of Turkey's European accession path.

Thus, an asphyxiating situation has been created for Turkey with regard to the Cyprus issue while the prospects of Turkey's European path remain rather dim. Turkey was not invited to start accession negotiations in the EU Summit in Seville in June 2002 as it had failed to fulfill the short-term criteria set in the EU-Turkey Accession Partnership as well as the Copenhagen criteria (though some of these reforms were approved in August 2002).[43]

The heads of states and governments of the EU-15 kept sending a clear message to Turkey that the division of Cyprus must end by the next

41. Former Turkish Premier Bülent Ecevit has repeatedly emphasized a "regionally based" foreign policy in which Ankara "seeks to play a more active role in defense of its interests in adjoining areas. Indeed, in practice this has meant a more assertive policy towards Syria, Iran, Northern Iraq, and a strong stance on the Aegean, and Cyprus issues." See Ian O. Lesser, "Changes on the Turkish Domestic Scene and Their Foreign Policy Implications," in Zalmay Khalilzad, Ian O. Lesser, and Stephen Larrabee, eds., *The Future of Turkish-Western Relations: Toward a Strategic Plan* (Santa Monica: RAND, 2000), p. 12.

42. Containment of Iran's potential threat resulting from its programs for the acquisition of weapons of mass destruction and ballistic missiles could be possible through a U.S. missile defense umbrella. The normalization of relations with Syria after Öcalan's forced departure from his residence in Syria seems to be vivid example of the successful exercise of Turkey's coercive diplomacy.

43. The European Council held in Copenhagen in 1993 adopted the following criteria for the evaluation of candidate countries for membership in the EU: 1. political conditions, i.e., the state of democracy and the respect for human rights; 2. economic conditions, i.e., macroeconomic stability, and the ability to deal with competitive pressure; and 3. the ability to adopt the European *acquis*. The council stated that "membership requires that the candidate country has achieved stability of institutions guaranteeing democracy, the rule of law, human rights, and the respect for and protection of minorities." See European Council, *Presidency Conclusions* (Copenhagen, 1993).

EU enlargement date. After that time, even part of a divided Cyprus will become a member of the EU. In this sense, Turkey, which illegally occupies the northern part of the island, can no longer block Cyprus's accession. In addition, the internationally-recognized Greek-Cypriot government, having made rapid advances in its EU accession negotiations, was ahead of all the other candidates in the race to join the EU. The negotiations between the EU and Cyprus were concluded at the end of June 2002 and the *Regular Report* of the European Commission regarding the final assessment of each candidate state was released in October 2002. Unsurprisingly, the final decision regarding EU enlargement was taken in December 2002 at the Copenhagen Summit, while the Accession Treaty was signed in April 2003 in Athens, during the Greek EU Presidency. In Copenhagen it was decided that Cyprus—along with another nine candidates—would become a member of the EU in May 2004. Cyprus will thus participate in the 2004 EU Parliament elections as a full member of the EU. Although the political problem remains unresolved, Turkey may start accession negotiations in December 2004, if certain Copenhagen criteria are first fulfilled.

Thus, Turkey's choices seem limited to the following: it will either make a sincere (but painful) attempt to contribute productively to end the occupation of Northern Cyprus, as well as to resolve its conflict with neighboring Greece, or it will adopt a policy aimed at reversing certain "European-type" rules of political behavior and governance imposed by its Accession Partnership. Unfortunately, Turkey's official (but solely verbal) policy prior to the Copenhagen Summit seemed to be leaning toward the second option. Realizing that Cyprus will be in the first wave of enlargement, Turkey has warned the fourteen EU member-states (excluding Greece) that if the Greek-Cypriot administration is accepted as a full member before the Cyprus problem is resolved, the Turkish Republic of Northern Cyprus (TRNC) may be integrated into Turkey. This warning to the EU was coupled with veiled threats from Turkey that it would withdraw its own EU candidacy.[44] In addition, then Turkish Minister for Foreign Affairs Ismail Cem reminded Europe that Ankara would "do all it could" to block the Republic of Cyprus's accession as an independent state,[45] while stressing that Turkey "would not sacrifice Cyprus in order

---

44. The National Security Council (NSC) noted in a statement released at the end of May 2001 that the full membership of Southern Cyprus in the EU "will make Turkey speed up its efforts to strengthen and deepen the cooperation with the TRNC." See "NSC Releases a Statement," *Anadolu Agency*, May 29, 2001, at <www.anadoluajansi.com.tr>.

45. Simon Tisdall, "Turkey's Friendship Comes at a Cost," *Guardian Unlimited* (elec-

to join the EU."[46] Without doubt, for the first time in many years, Turkey seemed to realize that its Cyprus policy is leading it headlong towards an imbroglio that could jeopardize its own EU bid. Threats to integrate Northern Cyprus with Turkey have not so far materialized, nor are they expected to.

It goes without saying that the solution of the Cyprus problem would lead to a further improvement of Greek-Turkish relations and strengthen Turkey's relations with the EU. Indeed, it is rather unlikely that fundamental progress towards a comprehensive Greek-Turkish settlement will be achieved without a just and mutually acceptable solution of the prickly Cyprus problem. Unfortunately, at least for the decision-makers in Greece, there is an apparent lack of a credible partner on the other side of the Aegean who will be able both to tackle internal problems successfully and to accomplish the difficult task of a rapprochement with Greece up to the very end.

However, at George Papandreou's initiative, Greece and Turkey agreed in April 2002 to initiate a series of "exploratory talks," the aim of which was to sound out each other's intentions and positions on the so-called "high-politics" issues. In other words, the aim was to highlight the issues each side considers as of primary or secondary importance and as negotiable or non-negotiable, as well as the understanding of each other's perceptions, interests, incentives, constraints, preferences, priorities, and bottom lines. For Greece this is a procedure of particular importance since it further enhances Turkey's engagement in the European context while it manages to delegitimize—and even avoid—surprises on the part of Turkey, which, according to some analysts, might decide to proceed along certain exaggerated or excessive lines (for example, full annexation of Northern Cyprus, or military actions against Cyprus or in the Aegean).[47] The exploratory talks were also viewed by Greek decision-makers as the bridge to link progress achieved so far on "low politics" issues with the most demanding next step in Greek-Turkish relations that—according to the Helsinki decisions—should soon follow, namely

---

tronic edition), June 7, 2001 at <www.guardianunlimited.co.uk/elsewhere/journalist/story>.

46. See Alkis Kourkoulas, "Cem Says 'Turkey Will Not Sacrifice Cyprus for EU Membership'," *Athens News Agency,* June 16, 2001 at <www.ana.gr>.

47. See Mehmet Ali Birand, "Is Turkey Preparing to Annex Cyprus?" *Turkish Daily News,* August 26, 2002. On the scenarios generated by Cyprus's accession to the EU, see the thoughtful analysis of Philippos K. Savvides, *Cyprus at the Gate of the European Union: Scenarios, Challenges and Prospects* (Hellenic Foundation for European and Foreign Policy, Policy Paper No. 1: Athens, 2002).

negotiations on the more sensitive "high-politics" issues. Needless to say, the prospects for a successful outcome are highly uncertain, partly as a result of the political power struggle inside Turkey.

In Lieu of Conclusions

More than a dozen years after the end of the Cold War, the truly intriguing question concerning Greek-Turkish relations is whether these two neighboring countries can build a less competitive relationship. Although the Greek political system is still undergoing a significant maturation process, the dominant trend is for a peaceful resolution of the Greek-Turkish conflict based on international law and agreements.

Unsurprisingly, the same degree of unanimity is not found in Turkey, where the use of force, or at least the threat of its use, seems to constitute an integral part of any internal or external policy for tackling difficult situations and solving problems.[48] The exacerbation of conflict among the groups that are to various degrees supportive of Turkey's inclusion in the EU means that Turkey's transition to democracy is unlikely to be smooth and is likely to lead to an aggressive foreign policy directed against Greece.

Thus, some of the "structural" characteristics of Turkey's behavior along with the post-Helsinki internal antinomies do not augur well for Greek-Turkish relations, since, at least for the decision-makers in Greece, they underline the unlikelihood of Turkey's ability to overcome either its internal problems or the difficulties of a rapprochement with Greece.

Moreover, the extent of Euro-skepticism in Turkish politics and society is not clear, at least to outsiders. Furthermore, it is far too early for any predictions about the impact of the rise to power of the moderate Islamic AKP, both for the domestic and the foreign policy scene in Turkey. There are encouraging signals from the new government in Ankara, which is faced, however, with considerable domestic opposition from the "old establishment." Needless to say, Greece will continue to strongly support Turkey's bid for membership to the EU.

Let us conclude with five considerations. First, is it feasible to decouple the Aegean and Cyprus? This might be possible, at least to a certain extent, in terms of implementing agreed CBMs, but the situation in the Aegean has a direct impact on the situation in Cyprus, and vice versa.

---

48. For this argument, see the views of former Deputy Minister of Foreign Affairs Professor Christos Rozakis as they appeared in "Greece, Turkey, and the Path to Peace" (in Greek), speech delivered to the Association for Reflection on the Modernization of Greek Society, March 13, 1997.

It is rather unlikely that fundamental progress towards a comprehensive Greek-Turkish settlement (that is, the establishment of a comprehensive security regime) will be achieved without a just and mutually acceptable solution of the prickly Cyprus problem. To this end, the plan submitted by UN Secretary-General Annan on November 11, 2002, is a rather balanced proposal, demanding compromises by both sides. If accepted and implemented in good faith, it would result in the reunification of the last "divided capital of Europe"—Nicosia. The resolution of the Cyprus problem might radically transform the situation and open the way for the full normalization of Greek-Turkish relations.

If both communities were to join the EU together, the benefits for Turkey would be obvious and significant: it would boost its relationship with the EU, enhance its international prestige as producer rather than a consumer of security, strengthen the détente process with Greece, challenge the perception or allegation that the EU is a Christian club and, in a very symbolic development, render Turkish into an official language of the EU. Thus there is an opportunity for Greece and Turkey to erase a hot spot from the global map of conflicts.

Second, the political and economic costs of the Greek-Turkish conflict for the chief protagonists (Cyprus included), as well as NATO, the EU, and the United States, are considerable. It cannot be overemphasized that a war between Greece and Turkey, whether it involved Cyprus or not, would be a disaster for NATO and the West. Furthermore, a limited 24 or 48-hour conflict should not be seen as the only, or even the most probable scenario. Crises have their own dynamic, are very difficult to control or contain, and escalation would be more likely than not. An armed conflict between Greece and Turkey would result in the collapse of NATO's Southern Flank and would severely disrupt its efforts to play a meaningful role in the post–Cold War world. It is also likely that there would be widespread destruction in both countries as a result of such a conflict.

Third, it is much easier for the stronger side in a conflict to make the first substantive move (to ease concerns about unilateral moves, this could be a largely symbolic and certainly retractable gesture), especially if this is the side that appears unhappy with the status quo. Having said this, the other side should be prepared to quickly recognize such a gesture and respond in kind, without any delay.

Fourth, unfortunately, the short-term prospects for a Davos-III (or Camp David process) between Greece and Turkey are not very good.[49]

---

49. Furthermore, the war against international terrorism is by far the first priority of the Bush administration and in this context U.S. attention will be focused on Iraq and

Problems in EU-Turkish relations could have a negative impact on Greek-Turkish relations. In view of the skepticism in Greece about Turkey's real intentions, what will be the next steps? Expectations should be lowered, but the process continued with careful, well-planned and well-prepared steps involving the civil society, private citizens, and NGOs, but also the businesspersons in both countries to the maximum extent possible.

Finally, Athens does not wish a "lone wolf" Turkey. It is in Greece's interest that Turkey remains firmly anchored in the Western harbor and engaged in a political, economic and social modernization process. Whatever the short-term course of the rapprochement process, relations with Turkey will continue to remain a top priority concern of Greek foreign and security policy well into the twenty-first century.

---

the other members of the "Axis of Evil." U.S. involvement in Greek-Turkish relations is expected to diminish in the immediate future.

Chapter 8

Turkey and Russia in Eurasia

Oktay F. Tanrısever

On November 16, 2001, Turkish and Russian Ministers of Foreign Affairs Ismail Cem and Igor Ivanov signed an "Action Plan for Cooperation between the Republic of Turkey and the Russian Federation in Eurasia: From Bilateral Cooperation to Multidimensional Partnership" in New York.[1] This document called for a Turkish-Russian partnership to cope with the regional problems in Eurasia (this includes the Balkans, Russia, Turkey, the Caucasus, and Central Asia, which are characterized by both European and Asian cultures). The signing of such a document had been unthinkable just five years earlier in 1996, when Turkey and Russia saw each other as rivals in Eurasia. This chapter analyzes the factors that motivated Turkey and Russia to converge their foreign policy orientations in Eurasia, and explores their expectations of their newly-discovered "friendship" to determine the potential to develop healthy bilateral relations.

The chapter examines the Turkish and Russian versions of Eurasianism, and how Eurasianism has affected their orientations toward the Eurasian region. I argue that the rapprochement between Turkey and Russia in Eurasia since 1997 does not mean that they have discarded the long-term objective of integrating themselves fully into the European institutional architecture. Instead, the popularity of Eurasianist perspectives in Turkey and Russia during the post–Cold War era largely stems from their short-term pragmatic interests: until they are fully integrated

1. Hakan Aksay, "Towards a Multidimensional Partnership" (in Russian), *Perspektiva: Evraziiskoe sotrudnichestvo*, No. 31 (2002), p. 5.

into Europe they must find peaceful solutions to their conflict of interests in Eurasia themselves.

Until 1997, Turkey and Russia competed to promote their own versions of Eurasianism. However, subsequent developments showed that they needed each other to cope with the obstacles to full integration into the European system. More specifically, their positions converged concerning regional problems in Eurasia in response to two developments in Europe. The first was the signing in Brussels on December 16, 1997, of accession protocols between NATO and the Czech Republic, Hungary, and Poland, despite Moscow's objections. The second was the 1997 EU Luxembourg Summit decision not to give candidate status to Turkey. Recent developments since September 11, 2001, demonstrate that the Turkish-Russian rapprochement in Eurasia needs to be coordinated with U.S. policies in the region; otherwise, these states could find it very difficult to maintain their newly-discovered "partnership" in the long term because of their conflicting objectives.

The chapter first examines the Turkish and Russian discourses of Eurasianism in the post–Cold War era, and then outlines the positions of Turkey and Russia toward each other in the early 1990s and their competition for influence over Central Asia, the Caucasus, and the Balkans. This is followed by an analysis of the sources of the rapprochement in the positions of Ankara and Moscow toward the Eurasian region since 1997 and an examination of the evolution of relations between Turkey and Russia since 1997. The chapter then looks at the opportunities and risks in Turkish-Russian relations in Central Asia, the Caucasus, and the Balkans since September 11, 2001, and concludes by discussing the limitations of Eurasianism as a basis for "multidimensional partnership" between Turkey and Russia in Eurasia.

Turkish and Russian Discourses of Eurasianism

Ankara and Moscow have sought to project their regional hegemony over Eurasia since the end of the Cold War and, unlike other regional powers, such as China and Iran, both Turkey and Russia have a history of political dominance in some parts of the Eurasian region. Turkish and Russian politicians and intellectuals have developed different versions of Eurasianism, which claims that Eurasia constitutes a geographical region whose population can be united and empowered by a "specific" synthesis of European and Asian cultures. This specific synthesis was developed by either the Turkish or Russian culture, according to who is articulating the ideology. This ideology, which assumes that a number of nations in the Eurasian region need to have a "native Eurasian big brother" to solve their problems, has sometimes been used to justify the ambitious policies of some Turkish and Russian politicians. Unlike Eurasianism in Turkey, Eurasianism in Russia is in reality anti-Western. It formed the ideological framework of the opposition to the pro-Western line of Russian Minister of Foreign Affairs Andrei Kozyrev.[2]

Both Turkey and the Russian Federation are post-imperial states, and their foreign policy orientations cannot be considered in isolation from their attempts to create a post-imperial national identity. The Turkish national identity was constructed in reaction to the Ottoman imperial identity, while the Russian national identity was constructed in opposition to the imperial Tsarist and Soviet identities. Nevertheless, some political groups in both Turkey and Russia challenge the post-imperial Turkish and Russian national identities. For example, Islamic fundamentalists and ultra-nationalists in Turkey and communists and ultra-nationalists in Russia seek to revive a form of imperial relationship between their states and the territories that gained independence from their former imperial center. Such Turkish and Russian groups claim that their states have some historical rights over their former imperial peripheries.

Russian Eurasianists who describe the Eurasian region as Russia's "Near Abroad" claim that no state other than Russia could assert its political dominance in Eurasia. Turkish Eurasianists, by contrast, do not see the former territories of the Ottoman Empire and other Turkic states as their exclusive spheres of influence. Despite this difference, the Turkish discourse of the "historic rights" over some parts of Eurasia clashes with the Russian discourse of Near Abroad.[3]

The diversity of opinions about the nature of Turkey's foreign policy in the post–Cold War era have also characterized Turkish views of Eurasia, since each version of Eurasianism suggests a specific foreign policy orientation.[4] Accordingly, there has been no consensus among Turkish politicians and intellectuals over how Turkey should formulate its foreign policy toward the Eurasian region, where a number of Turkic nations

---

2. Kozyrev's foreign policy line is generally described as "Atlanticism."

3. See Igor Torbakov, "The 'Statists' and the Ideology of Russian Imperial Nationalism," RFE/RL Research Report, December 11, 1992, pp. 10–16; and Hugh Poulton, *Top Hat, Grey Wolf and Crescent: Turkish Nationalism and the Turkish Republic* (London: Hurst, 1997).

4. For a detailed study on the sources of Turkish foreign policy, see Mustafa Aydin, "Determinants of Turkish Foreign Policy: Changing Patterns and Conjunctures during the Cold War," *Middle Eastern Studies*, Vol. 36, No. 1 (2000), pp. 103–140; and Mustafa Aydin, "Determinants of Turkish Foreign Policy: Historical Framework and Traditional Inputs," *Middle Eastern Studies*, Vol. 35, No. 4 (1999), pp. 152–187.

gained their independence following the disintegration of the Soviet Union in 1991. Basically, Turkey's ruling elites have tried to formulate their policies toward Eurasia in coordination with the West, particularly the United States.[5] The elites in modern Turkey are predominantly West-ern-oriented and remain loyal to the non-imperial foreign policy princi-ples of Mustafa Kemal Atatürk, the founder of modern Turkey.[6] These elites are pragmatic and aware that Turkey is too weak economically and politically to become the single dominant power in Eurasia. For this rea-son, they consider Turkey's foreign policy toward Eurasia secondary to its relations with the West. Correspondingly, some members of Turkey's civil and military establishment, such as Necip Torumtay, former chief of staff, believe that the expansion of Turkey's influence in the Eurasian re-gion could attract Western support for Turkey's ambition to join the EU.[7] Bülent Gökay and Richard Langhorne summarized this position as a claim that "there existed a very special relationship between Turkey, the Caucasus and Central Asian republics. This was based on the belief that ethnic, linguistic, religious, and cultural affinities would pave the way for close ties and a major presence."[8]

Right-wing politicians and intellectuals developed a Turkish foreign policy agenda in Eurasia that is more ambitious and radical than that of the civil and military establishment. These groups consider Eurasia to be the region covering Turkey, the Caucasus, Central Asia, the Volga region of the Russian Federation, and Northern Afghanistan, and they claim that this Eurasian region is inhabited predominantly by Turkic peoples.[9] This version of Eurasianism has been popular among many pan-Turkist politicians and intellectuals in Turkey.

Some leftist and Islamic fundamentalist politicians have also pro-moted their own radical and anti-Western versions of Eurasianism as an alternative to the traditionally pro-Western orientation of Turkey's for-eign policymakers. The left-wing groups argue that cooperation between Turkey and Russia as the main Eurasian powers could weaken "Western imperialism." For example, Dogu Perincek, leader of the Workers' Party,

5. See Idris Bal, *Turkey's Relations with the West and the Turkic Republics: The Rise and Fall of the "Turkish Model"* (Aldershot: Ashgate, 2000).

6. William Hale, *Turkish Foreign Policy, 1774–2000* (London: Frank Cass, 2000).

7. Necip Torumtay, *Degisen Stratejilerin Odaginda Türkiye* (Turkey at the center of changing strategies) (Istanbul: A.D. Yayıncılık, 1996).

8. Bülent Gökay and Richard Langhorne, *Turkey and the New States of the Caucasus and Central Asia* (London: HMSO, 1996), p. 32.

9. Ian O. Lesser, *Bridge or Barrier? Turkey and the West After the Cold War* (Santa Monica: RAND, 1992).

argued that Eurasianism could enable Turkey to pursue a more independent foreign policy.[10] In contrast, Islamic fundamentalists, such as Necmettin Erbakan, chairman of the banned fundamentalist Welfare Party, argued that Turkey should promote its own version of Islam among the newly-independent post-Soviet peoples, which have been subjected to the atheistic propaganda of the Soviet Union. Such Islamic fundamentalists support the polarization of post-Soviet peoples along religious lines.

In contrast to public opinion in Turkey, where a variety of radical voices gained popularity during the 1990s, Russian public opinion was predominantly pro-Western during this period since the majority of Russians were critical of the costs of maintaining the Soviet Union, which subsidized a number of Turkic nations at the expense of Russians. Thus, the majority of Russians did not perceive the Caucasus and Central Asia as central to post-Soviet Russia's foreign policy orientation. In their opinion, among the members of the Commonwealth of Independent States (CIS), the Slavic republics of Ukraine and Belarus were more important to Russia's long-term interests than the Turkic republics in the Caucasus and Central Asia. They believed that Russia's long-term interests lay in strengthening its European identity rather than its Asian identity.

Nevertheless, the pro-Western policies of Boris Yeltsin elicited strong criticisms in the Russian parliament. Yeltsin, who dissolved the Russian parliament (Congress of People's Deputies) by force in October 1993, increasingly chose to tailor his policies to meet the criticism of the new Russian parliament elected in 1993. In this period, it became routine, especially in the State Duma (the lower house of the Russian parliament), to criticize the "liberal reformers" for being too naive in shaping Russia's post-Soviet foreign policy. For example, Sergei Stankevich, the political adviser of Yeltsin, criticized Kozyrev's policy of Atlanticism as "a policy of self-abnegation."[11] Moreover, the December 1993 State Duma elections marked the rise of the pragmatic nationalists. The Liberal Democratic Party of Russia (LDPR), which received 22.9 percent of the votes, strengthened the political outlook of Russian nationalists. During the Yeltsin period from 1992 to 1999, LDPR leader Vladimir Zhirinovsky continued to advocate the restoration of the Russian Empire in its previous borders, including even Alaska. According to Zhirinovsky, if Russians failed to revive the Russian Empire, others would revive their own—a

---

10.   Dogu Perinçek, *Avrasya Seçenegi: Türkiye İçin Bagimsiz Dis Politika* (The Eurasian choice: an independent foreign policy for Turkey) (Istanbul: Kaynak Yayınları, 1996).

11.   Sergei Stankevich, "A Great Power in Search of Itself" (in Russian), *Nezavisimaia gazeta*, March 28, 1992.

reference to the United States, China, and Turkey. Zhirinovsky developed a special dislike of Turkey and the Turks, linked to the criticism of Moscow by the Turkic and Muslim minorities in the Middle Volga and the North Caucasus.[12]

In this atmosphere, two major political outlooks toward Russia's foreign policy emerged within Russia's State Duma by the end of 1993: Russian Westernizers, who were united around Boris Yeltsin, and Russian Eurasianists, who represented the coalition of the communists and the ultra-nationalists. Russian Westernizers placed primary emphasis on developing strong ties with the United States, and wanted Russia to be part of Western civilization. They stressed normal diplomatic relations toward Russia's Near Abroad, without Russia's seeking to impose its will from a dominant position.[13] Russian Eurasianists, by contrast, advocated a balanced foreign policy approach for Russia, with equal emphasis on Europe, the Middle East, and the Far East, and they also called for the reestablishment of Moscow's hegemony in the Near Abroad.[14]

This radical right-wing version of Russian Eurasianism gained some popularity among the Russian "national patriots" since it brought under one political roof representatives of all major religions and ethnic groups in Eurasia. Russian Eurasianism, which was first articulated by Count Nikolai Trubetskoi in the 1920s and then developed by anthropologist Lev Gumilev in the 1960s, claims that Russia has a special role to play for Eurasian states and peoples who live together harmoniously. According to this ideology, there is an irreconcilable difference between Eurasia and the West that can be removed only by the victory of one side over the other. Aleksandr Dugin, son of a KGB officer, popularized these views in his journal *Elementy: Evraziiskoe Obozrenie* (Elements: Eurasian review), which began publication in July 1992. In his book *Osnovy geopolitiki* (The basics of geopolitics), Dugin revised this version of Russian Eurasianism by arguing that instead of opposing the West as a whole, Russia should now form an alliance with Europe against the Atlantic powers of Britain and the United States.[15] Dugin continues to advocate the rebirth of the Soviet Union or the Russian Empire in a modern form.

12. Vladimir Zhirinovsky, *Last Push to the South* (in Russian) (Moscow: LDPR, 1993), pp. 63–64.

13. Margot Light, "Foreign Policy Thinking," in Neil Malcolm, et al., *Internal Factors in Russian Foreign Policy* (Oxford: Oxford University Press, 1996), pp. 81–88.

14. Alexander V. Kozhemiakin and Roger E. Kanet, "The Impact of Nationalism on Russian Foreign Policy," in William E. Ferry and Roger E. Kanet, eds., *Post-Communist States in the World Community* (London: Macmillan, 1998), pp. 46–61.

15. Aleksandr G. Dugin, *The Basics of Geopolitics: The Geopolitical Future of Russia* (in

Some versions of Turkish and Russian Eurasianism influenced the orientations of Ankara and Moscow toward Eurasia, depending on changes in the domestic politics of these countries and changes in the international system.

Positions of Turkey and Russia toward Each Other in the Early 1990s

The collapse of the bipolar international system significantly shaped the positions of Turkey and Russia toward each other in the early 1990s. The strategic importance of Turkey's military role in the Western camp declined mainly because of the collapse of the Soviet threat to the West; at the same time the collapse of the Soviet Union created a vacuum of power in Eurasia and offered Turkey an opportunity to exert its economic and political influence over the newly-independent post-Soviet states. Russia was undecided at this time about the nature of its involvement in Eurasian affairs because the imperial form of Russian involvement might further undermine Russia's position in this region, and provoke anti-Russian nationalisms among non-Russian groups in post-Soviet states. In contrast, Russia's integration into the Western institutional structure would create a golden opportunity for Russia to solve its economic and political problems.

In this atmosphere, both Turkey and Russia wished to develop friendly relations with the West in order to become influential in the Eurasian region. For this to happen, Russia would have to carry out several political and economic reforms, and Turkey would have to coordinate its activities with the West. A further obstacle was that the interest of both Turkey and Russia in becoming a "great power" in the Eurasian region was likely to be a problem: it would be very difficult for the West to accommodate Turkey and Russia simultaneously since the accommodation of the interests of one side would likely alienate the other.

Despite these potential problems, Ankara and Moscow sought to improve their relations. The collapse of the Soviet Union, which not only transformed the political regime in Russia but also ended the bipolar international system characterized by the Cold War, removed the ideological rivalry in Moscow's relations with Turkey; this heightened hopes for a better future. In the post–Cold War era, the Westernizing liberals became the dominant political force in Russia. The pro-Western Russian President Boris Yeltsin nominated Andrei Kozyrev, a liberal, as his minister of for-

Russian) (Moscow: Arktogeia, 1999). See also Dmitry Shlapentokh, "Eurasianism: Past and Present," *Communist and Post-Communist Studies,* Vol. 30, No. 2 (1997), pp. 131–132.

eign affairs. Kozyrev saw Russia's membership in the club of developed Western democratic states and the Western international institutions as Russia's main foreign policy objectives. According to Kozyrev, post-Soviet Russia should transform itself into a democratic state, set up an effective economy, and guarantee the rights and freedoms of its citizens.[16]

Turkey shared these values as the basis of its own pro-Western foreign policy orientation, and it was expected that relations between the two states would be affected positively by their similar foreign policy orientations. Thus, Turkish Foreign Minister Hikmet Çetin sought to forge a new start in Turkey's relations with Russia when he visited Moscow on January 20–22, 1992. Russian Foreign Minister Andrei Kozyrev paid a visit to Ankara a month later, in February 1992. An official visit by Turkish Prime Minister Süleyman Demirel to Moscow on May 25–26 of the same year provided the basis for fruitful and comprehensive talks. During the visit, the Turkish-Russian Treaty of Friendship and Cooperation was signed. This declared that the two countries would base their relations on good neighborliness, cooperation, and mutual trust. The treaty, which sets the legal basis and principles of relations between Turkey and Russia, confirmed the commitment of both sides to add new dimensions to their relationship.[17]

The rosy picture of Ankara's relations with Moscow was evident when Russian President Boris Yeltsin visited Istanbul on June 25, 1992, to attend the first summit meeting of the Black Sea Economic Cooperation (BSEC) organization.[18] The diplomatic climate created by BSEC contributed to the development of economic relations between Turkey and Russia. Russian Prime Minister Yegor Gaidar's economic reform program, which was also known as "shock therapy," created many opportunities for foreign investors. To reap the benefits of this reform program through developing and upgrading economic and commercial relations, Ankara and Moscow formed the Turkish-Russian Joint Economic Commission. Its first meeting was held on November 2–6, 1992, in Ankara. Meanwhile, the Russian economy was in a deep crisis, making it difficult for Moscow

16. Richard Sakwa, *Russian Politics and Society* (London: Routledge, 1993; rev. and enl. ed. 1996), p. 278.

17. Duygu Sezer-Bazoğlu, "Turkish-Russian Relations: From Adversity to 'Virtual Rapprochement'," in Alan Makovsky and Sabri Sayarı, eds., *Changing Dynamics of Turkish Foreign Policy* (Washington, D.C.: Washington Institute for Near East Policy, 2000), pp. 92–115, at 95.

18. Serdar Sayan and Osman Zaim, "Black Sea Economic Cooperation Project," in Libby Rittenberg, ed., *The Political Economy of Turkey in the Post-Soviet Era: Going West and Looking East?* (Westport, Conn.: Praeger, 1998), pp. 115–136, at 117.

to repay its Soviet-era $600 million export debts to the Turkish Eximbank. Ankara and Moscow signed two major debt-rescheduling agreements on July 19, 1994, and December 15, 1995, the second one based on the terms and conditions of the Paris Club Agreements.[19]

Unfortunately, positive developments in Turkey's relations with Russia were largely limited to the economic field; since the two countries needed each other economically anyway, this is not indicative of the overall nature of Turkish-Russian relations. The decline of Turkey's trade with the Middle Eastern countries since the end of Iran-Iraq War in 1988 and the Gulf War in 1991 motivated Turkish exporters to look for new markets in Eurasia, particularly the huge Russian market with its great potential. The Russian market was hungry for the cheap semi-manufactured goods of Turkish exporters due to the ongoing economic crisis in Russia. In contrast, in the political sphere both countries sought to become hegemonic powers in the Eurasian region. While the economic dimension of relations between Turkey and Russia, were framed in "win-win" or "non-zero-sum" game terms, their political relations were formulated in "win-lose" or "zero-sum" game terms.

Turkish-Russian Competition for Influence over Central Asia, the Caucasus, and the Balkans

Ankara and Moscow started to compete for influence over Eurasia once hard-liners in Moscow began to view Turkey as one of the main beneficiaries of the Soviet collapse. Moscow sought to pursue a Near Abroad policy, which assumed that the former Soviet republics belonged to the Russian sphere of influence. For example, in 1993 Boris Yeltsin proposed that the UN or the Conference on Security and Cooperation in Europe grant Russia a "security mandate" to preserve order throughout the post-Soviet space.[20] Naturally, Turkey, which lacked the necessary economic and political resources to compete with Russia in the Eurasian region did not welcome this Eurasianist turn in Russian foreign policy. The Western powers were not willing to antagonize Russia and to provoke a Russian nationalist backlash just to please Turkey, whose policies in Eurasia also were not in line with Western expectations.

Hard-line Eurasianists in Moscow viewed Turkish inroads into Cen-

---

19. For further information on the problems in Turkish-Russian economic relations, see Gülten Kazgan, "The Political Economy of Relations between Turkey and Russia," in Rittenberg, *The Political Economy of Turkey in the Post-Soviet Era*, pp. 137–156.

20. Roy Allison, "Military Factors in Foreign Policy," in Malcolm, et al., *Internal Factors in Russian Foreign Policy*, pp. 271–275.

tral Asia as "plots" to encircle Russia by a potentially hostile state. Russian suspicions peaked in summer 1993, when the majority of Central Asian states supported a Turkish idea to create a customs and tariff union. The Russian hard-line Eurasianists viewed this as a vindication of their claim that Turkey and other Western powers sought to isolate Russia from its allies in the Caucasus, Central Asia, and the Middle East. Although Turkey's policy toward the Central Asian states did not seek to remove Russian influence in the region, the Russian side viewed this as a challenge to itself.[21]

Another region that increased Moscow's concerns about the growing Turkish influence in its Near Abroad was the Caucasus. Turkey recognized the independence of Azerbaijan on November 9, 1991, almost two months before the formal disintegration of the Soviet Union at the end of December 1991. Although Turkey recognized the independence of Armenia on December 16, 1991, and invited it to join BSEC as a founding state in 1992, Turkey and Armenia have not established diplomatic relations, mainly because of the Azeri-Armenian dispute over Nagorno-Karabakh. This territorial dispute has given Russia a free hand in manipulating local conflicts in the South Caucasus to its advantage. When Moscow-backed Armenia defeated Azerbaijan militarily in 1992, CIS Military Commander Marshal Evgeny Shaposhnikov warned Turkey of nuclear retaliation if Turkey intervened.[22] This underscored the Russian determination to minimize Turkey's influence in the region. The visit to Moscow by Turkish Prime Minister Süleyman Demirel in May 1992, discussed earlier, took place in this atmosphere. Although the Turkish-Russian Treaty of Friendship and Cooperation declared that the two countries would base their relations on good neighborliness, cooperation, and mutual trust, the developments in the Caucasus showed that the states remained suspicious of each other's motivations.

Moscow controlled Turkey's main gateway to the Turkic states of Central Asia by toppling Azerbaijan's first president, Abulfez Elchibey, in June 1993. Blaming Elchibey for his failure to stop the Armenian aggression in Nagorno-Karabakh, Surat Husseinov, a colonel in the Azeri army, instigated an uprising in the province of Gence. Political instability was avoided by Heidar Aliev's intervention and by Elchibey's exile to a small village in Nakhichevan. For a short period, Aliev's grip on power under-

21. Oktay F. Tanrısever, "Russia and the Independent Turkic States: Discovering the Meaning of Independence," *Eurasian Studies,* No. 20 (Summer 2001), pp. 95–110, at 99.

22. Dmitri Trenin, "Russia's Security Interests and Policies in the Caucasus Region," in Bruno Coppieters, ed., *Contested Borders in the Caucasus* (Brussels: VUB University Press), p. 91.

mined Turkey's influence not only in Azerbaijan, but also in the rest of the Caucasus. Aliev, the former Azerbaijan Communist Party first secretary and first deputy chairman of the USSR council of ministers, thought that the Nagorno-Karabakh problem could only be solved with Russian support, and so pursued a pragmatic policy toward both Moscow and Ankara.[23] In December 1993, Azerbaijan transferred 10 percent of its shares in the exploitation of the Azeri, Chirag, and Guneshli oilfields to the Russian oil company Lukoil. The shares for Turkey, initially set at 1.75 percent, later rose to 6.75 percent. Further concessions to these states were made conditional upon the ability of Moscow and Ankara to convince the Armenians to withdraw from Azeri territory.[24]

The competition between Turkey and Russia in the Caucasus has been generally formulated in zero-sum game terms. As Duygu Bazoğlu-Sezer suggests, the clash of Turkish-Russian interests in the Caucasus stemmed from their differing visions of the regional order in Eurasia. Turkey's Eurasian policy mainly sought to solidify the newly gained independence of the Caucasian states, which might decrease their dependence on Moscow, and to become a major actor in the region to secure economic and security benefits.[25]

In line with this policy, Turkey proposed to transport Caspian crude oil through an overland pipeline to be laid from Baku to Turkey's port of Ceyhan on the Mediterranean (see pipeline map, p. 209). Turkey also sought to block the Baku-Novorossiisk option by questioning the safety of shipping oil through the Turkish straits (oil brought to Novorossiisk through the existing pipelines could only reach the oil markets via the straits). Ankara argued that the Bosphorus is a narrow strait, and there are frequent collisions; an accident with an oil tanker would be highly dangerous. Arguing that the Bosphorus cannot be "used as a pipeline," the environmentalists held protests in the straits against any more tankers being let through.[26] The Turkish parliament adopted a new Straits

---

23. Oktay F. Tanrısever, "Sovyet-Sonrası Dönemde Rusya'nın Kafkasya Politikası" (Russia's policy toward the Caucasus in the post-Soviet era), in Mustafa Türkeş and Ilhan Uzgel, eds., *Türkiye ve Komşulari* (Turkey and its neighbors) (Ankara: İmge Yayinlari, 2001), pp. 391–394.

24. Meliha Altunışık, "Turkey and the Changing Oil Market in Eurasia," in Rittenberg, *The Political Economy of Turkey in the Post-Soviet Era*, pp. 159–162.

25. Professor Duygu Bazoğlu-Sezer is one of the leading experts on Turkish-Russian relations in Turkey. Duygu Bazoğlu-Sezer, "Turkish-Russian Relations: The Challenges of Reconciling Geopolitical Competition with Economic Partnership," *Turkish Studies*, Vol. 1, No. 1 (2000), pp. 59–82, 70.

26. Jon Gorvett, "Pipelines, Tankers and Economics Attempt to Navigate Turkey's

Regulation on July 1, 1994. The new regulation required ships carrying dangerous loads, such as large oil tankers, to follow special rules, which would mean considerable delay and extra costs.[27]

Moscow challenged the legality of these regulations at the International Maritime Organization in March 1994. Moscow argued that Turkey's new Straits Regulation contravened Article 2 of the Montreux Convention, which regulates the regime of the Turkish straits, as well as several other international treaties. Turkey argued that circumstances had changed since the signing of the Montreux Convention in 1936. The number of vessels passing through the straits in both directions had reached almost 50,000 annually by 1994. In fact, the Montreux Convention did not anticipate such heavy traffic.[28] According to Mensur Akgün, Moscow's position was weak since Moscow did not want to risk the collapse of the Montreux Convention, which was essential for Russia's security because it limited the number, type, and weight of non-littoral battleships allowed through the straits. Submarines and aircraft carriers were also banned from sailing to the Black Sea. Akgün argues that any attempt to revise this legally outmoded convention could easily lead to its collapse and thus jeopardize all the rights and privileges of Russia.[29]

Increasingly disillusioned with its weakness and Turkey's growing influence in the Caucasus, Moscow started to give special importance to its military control of Chechnya since it was vital for maintaining control of the Caucasus and Central Asia. Russia's loss of control over Chechnya might greatly encourage other nationalist forces in the Caucasus. Therefore, Russia tried to prevent other regional actors from interfering in the conflict. The Chechen crisis became a critical issue in Russia's relations with Turkey when Russia claimed that the Chechens were obtaining assistance and volunteers from Turkey. However, Turkey, like the rest of the world, officially recognizes Moscow's sovereignty over the republic. Although their public opinion has been sympathetic toward the Chechens, Ankara has refrained from getting involved in this conflict,

---

Narrow Straits," *Washington Report on Middle East Affairs*, Vol. 20, No. 4 (2001), pp. 28–29.

27. Meliha Benli Altunişik, "The Complex Web of Relations in the Caspian Hub," in İsmail Soysal, ed., *Turkish Views of Eurasia* (Istanbul: ISIS Press, 2000), pp. 165–174, at 169.

28. Yücel Güçlü, "Regulation of the Passage through the Turkish Straits," *Perceptions: Journal of International Affairs*, Vol. 6, No. 1 (2001), pp. 125–132.

29. Mensur Akgün, "Turkey and Russia: Burdened by History and Myopia," *Private View*, No. 4 (Winter 1997), pp. 34–39.

apart from offering some humanitarian aid to civilians with the consent of Moscow.[30]

During the first days of 1996, when nine people of Caucasian origin hijacked the Turkish ferryboat *Avrasya* on January 16, 1996, the Chechen question became a very tense issue in Turkey's relations with Russia. The hijackers claimed that they hijacked the ferry to support the "Chechen resistance against Moscow."[31] During an interview by Aleksandr Nadzharov, a correspondent of *Rossiiskaia Gazeta*, with Nikolai Kovalev, director of Russia's federal security service, Kovalev accused Turkey of supporting the Chechens through clandestine activities: "The Russian FSB [Federal Security Service] made an official protest to the leadership of the Turkish special service in connection with the continuation of its intelligence activities in the North Caucasus region."[32]

In return, Turkey suspected that Russia was supporting the Kurdistan Workers' Party (PKK) terrorist organization as a way to increase its influence over Turkey. As Robert Olson argues, Russia's war in Chechnya and the PKK problem in Turkey "are linked more closely than is generally realized and acknowledged."[33] Contrary to the Russian foreign ministry statement that Russians would not "open their arms to the PKK," the Kremlin did not prevent the establishment in Moscow of a "Kurdish House," where the PKK was very influential. A week later, during Turkish Interior Minister Nahit Mentese's January 1995 visit to Moscow, Turkey and Russia signed a Protocol to Prevent Terrorism in which the two countries agreed to exchange intelligence information to prevent terrorism.[34] Nevertheless, Moscow failed to keep its promises to Turkey when it hosted the Second International Congress of Kurdish Organizations with active PKK participation on May 4–8, 1996. During a visit to Moscow in mid-December 1996, Turkish Foreign Minister Tansu Çiller signed a Protocol of Cooperation against Terrorism. According to Olson, "Tur-

30. Paul B. Henze, "Turkey's Caucasian Initiatives," *Orbis: A Journal of World Affairs,* Vol. 45, No. 1 (2001), pp. 81–91.

31. Oktay F. Tanrısever, "The Battle for Chechnia: Russia Confronts Chechen Secessionism," *METU Studies in Development,* Vol. 27, Nos. 3–4 (Autumn 2000), pp. 321–349, at 337.

32. Aleksandr Nadzharov, "Interview with N. Kovalev" (in Russian), *Rossiiskaia Gazeta,* December 20, 1996, pp. 4–5.

33. Robert Olson, "Turkish and Russian Foreign Policies, 1991–1997: The Kurdish and Chechnya Questions," *Journal of Muslim Minority Affairs,* Vol. 18, No. 2 (1998), p. 209.

34. *Hurriyet* (Turkish daily), January 25, 1995.

key was unable to take advantage of the Russian predicament in Chechnya because of its fight against the PKK." Both states are interested in developing a common position in diplomatic forums against secessionist movements, and so Russia has been largely successful in limiting Turkey's involvement in the Caucasus by playing its PKK card against Ankara.[35]

Another area of Turkish-Russian rivalry in Eurasia was the Balkans. The disintegration of Yugoslavia, which was more violent than the relatively peaceful disintegration of the Soviet Union and Czechoslovakia, played a crucial role in the destabilization of the Balkans in the post–Cold War era. Although the official positions of both Turkey and Russia advocated maintaining the territorial integrity of Yugoslavia, they started to pursue different policies when it became evident that Yugoslavia could not exist in its Serbian-dominated form. The Bosnians and Kosovars of former Yugoslavia considered Turkey their natural ally against the authoritarian regime in Belgrade, which was supported mainly by Moscow.

Moscow supported the Serbian position enthusiastically for several reasons. Most Russian communists identified with the Serbs, and believed that the Serbs needed Russian support to avoid the post-socialist disintegration trauma that the Russians suffered after the Soviet collapse. The nationalist Russians needed to promote their Slavic national identity to counterbalance the continuing role of communist ideology in post-Soviet Russia. Russia's military and diplomatic establishments sought to defend the Serbian leadership, Russia's key ally in the Balkans, so that it could play a role in European security and diplomacy. In this atmosphere, the interests that supported the position of Slobodan Milosevic overshadowed the liberal position.

In contrast, Turkey supported the Bosnian and Kosovar sides strongly. Although Turkey was not happy with the Vance-Owen Plan, which dashed hopes for the multiethnic unity of Bosnia Herzegovina by separating the Croat and the Serbian sectors from the Bosnian sector, Turkey supported the full implementation of the Dayton Peace Accords from the outset as a member of the Peace Implementation Council and its Steering Board.[36]

Unlike Russia, Turkey developed very good relations with Bulgaria and Romania, which provided suitable conditions for their Turkish minorities. Turkish entrepreneurs developed very good economic relations with these states, and Turkey supported the entrance of Bulgaria and Ro-

35. Olson, 'Turkish and Russian Foreign Policies," pp. 221–223.

36. Noel Malcolm, *Bosnia: A Short History* (London: Macmillan, 1994).

mania into NATO. Albania, under its President Sali Berisha, also promoted very good relations with Turkey; but Berisha's replacement by former socialist leader Fatos Nano in 1997 led to a cooling of relations between Turkey and Albania.

In its rivalry with Turkey in Eurasia, Moscow had another tool of leverage over Turkey: the sale of missiles to Armenia, Syria, and Cyprus. In January 1997, Russia's arms export company, Rosvooruzhenie, agreed to sell a sophisticated surface-to-air missile system, the SAM-300-PMU-1, to the Greek Cypriot government. With their 150-kilometer range, the missiles could have reached into southern Turkey; if deployed, they would have seriously complicated Turkey's air maneuverability over Cyprus. Turkey took the threat very seriously, warning that it would not allow the missiles to be deployed, and hinting that Cyprus might risk war.[37] During this crisis, Greek Cypriot President Glafkos Clerides sought to apply international pressure on Turkey to help produce a Cyprus solution. But Ankara grew restless as it anticipated the balance of power in Cyprus shifting dramatically against it. In any case, after lengthy negotiations between Greece and Cyprus, the Greek Cypriot government gave up its attempt to install Russia's S-300s on the island, and Greece agreed to put them on Crete instead.[38] All these conflicts convinced Turkey that its rivalry with Moscow could get extremely dangerous and even harm Turkey's relations with its NATO allies.

Sources of Turkish-Russian Rapprochement in Eurasia

Given the predominance of rivalry in Turkish-Russian relations, it was surprising that by the end of 1997 both Ankara and Moscow recognized that their rivalry was unlikely to produce a clear victory in Eurasia, and that it could undermine their national security and their relations with the Western powers. Russia became aware that it was no longer a superpower comparable to the United States, but was instead a regional actor; this made Moscow's relations with the regional actors in Eurasia, such as Turkey, more important. Turkey had already accepted that its capacity to project power throughout Eurasia was very limited, mainly due to its domestic economic and political problems. Thus, economic and political weakness pushed both countries to a more balanced and generally positive relationship. Furthermore, as Dmitri Trenin argues, for Turkey and

37.   Yusuf Kanlı, "Missiles: Provocation or Right of Self Defense?" *Turkish Probe* (Turkish daily), January 17, 1997.

38.   Vladislav Komarov, "Russian Defenses for NATO Member Greece," *Russia Journal* (Moscow daily), December 21, 1999.

Russia, "the nearest pole of attraction has already emerged, and its pull will grow, drawing Ankara and Moscow in the same direction: the European Union."[39] This attraction does not mean that Turkish and Russian relations with the EU in particular, and the West in general, were unproblematic. The leaderships of both countries expressed the need to overcome their differences and to work toward a mutually beneficial "strategic partnership" to improve their positions with the Western powers.

Russia's relations with the West steadily deteriorated between 1993 and 1999, when the pragmatic nationalists in Russia were very vocal in the formulation of Russian foreign policy.[40] NATO's enlargement plans, which began to move forward in 1994, also contributed to the tensions. NATO's Partnership for Peace program was the first step in this direction. Initially, 26 countries, including Russia, became partners in this program by signing the Framework Documents. Despite its involvement, Moscow had strong reservations about the unilateral enlargement of NATO. To accommodate the Russian leadership, the Founding Act on Mutual Relations, Cooperation and Security between NATO and the Russian Federation was signed in Paris on May 27, 1997. Nevertheless, this did not prevent the 16-member NATO from signing accession protocols with the Czech Republic, Hungary, and Poland in Brussels on December 16, 1997, and integrating these three former Warsaw Pact states formally into its institutional structure in March 1999.[41]

NATO's expansion into the former Warsaw Pact territories in Eastern Europe and even into former Soviet territories such as the Baltic states increased suspicions within the Russian leadership that Russia's exclusion from NATO also implied its exclusion from the EU. Indeed, it was feared that Russia would be completely excluded from the West. In fact, the independence of Ukraine and Belarus had already made Russia less European than it was before. Gradually, pragmatic nationalists called for a non-Western Russia, though that did not necessarily mean an anti-Western Russia.[42] In line with the changing political climate, Moscow began to take a cautious stance toward the West. According to Russian Min-

---

39. Dmitri Trenin, "Russia and Turkey: A Cure for Schizophrenia," *Perceptions: Journal of International Affairs*, Vol. 2, No. 2 (1997), pp. 57–65, at 65.

40. See Aleksei K. Pushkov, "Letter from Eurasia: Russia and America: The Honeymoon's Over," *Foreign Policy*, Vol. 93, No. 1 (Winter 1993–94), pp. 88–89.

41. Zsolt Nemeth, "Central Europe: Hungarian Perspectives," *Perceptions: Journal of International Affairs*, Vol. 6, No. 4 (2002), p. 72.

42. Andranik Migranian, *Russia in Search of its Identity* (in Russian) (Moscow: Mezhdunarodnaia otnosheniia, 1997), pp. 399–401.

ister of Foreign Affairs Yevgeny Primakov, Russia's territorial integrity could not be ensured unless Moscow established itself as a great power in international relations. Primakov's geopolitical perception evolved from security concerns related to developments in Russia's Near Abroad. This resulted in criticism of the West and a guarded rapprochement with the East (China, India, Iran, and several Arab states).[43]

To appease Moscow and to get Russian approval for NATO enlargement, the Western powers offered Moscow some modifications in the Conventional Forces in Europe (CFE) Treaty during the CFE Vienna Review Conference in May 1996. This came as a cold shower for Turkey, which had expected that NATO would oppose the increased Russian military presence in the Caucasus. However, NATO's strategy of accommodating rather than antagonizing Russia showed that NATO did not wish to escalate tensions in the Caucasus by siding with Turkey. This convinced the Turkish security establishment that it was in the interest of Turkey to normalize its relations with Moscow in order to strengthen its position in the Western security structures.[44]

The suspicions of the Turkish elite toward the Western powers reached a climax when Turkey's hopes for future membership in the EU were dealt a severe blow at the December 12–13, 1997, EU Luxembourg Summit. Turkey had simply wanted the EU to keep the door open on the basis of the same objective standards and criteria that are applied to the other applicant states.[45] The Luxembourg Summit's decision not to give candidate status to Turkey failed to encourage Turkey to improve its human rights situation and its chronic political instability, and also alienated Turkey from the EU. Not surprisingly, the decision motivated Turkey to become more assertive in its foreign policy; it also made Turkey more receptive to Moscow's overtures, particularly in the area of arms acquisitions.[46]

Changes had also occurred in both Turkish and Russian perceptions of their influence in the region. The rapprochement in Turkey's relations with Russia was fostered by the fact that Turkey's influence in the post-Soviet Caucasus and Central Asia remained very limited due to a

43. Leonid Mlenchik, *Evgeny Primakov: The Story of a Career* (in Russian) (Moscow: Tsentrpoligraf, 1999), pp. 322–329.

44. Gareth M. Winrow, "Turkey's Evolving Role in the Post-Soviet World," in Rittenberg, *The Political Economy of Turkey in the Post-Soviet Era*, pp. 97–113, at 104.

45. Atila Eralp, "Turkey in the Enlargement Process: From Luxembourg to Helsinki," *Perceptions: Journal of International Affairs*, Vol. 5, No. 2 (2000), pp. 17–32, at 18–21.

46. Dominique Moisi, "Dreaming of Europe," *Foreign Policy*, No. 115 (1999), pp. 44–60.

variety of factors, ranging from the limitations in Turkey's economic capacity for influence in the region to the unwillingness of the post-Soviet Turkic states to consider Turkey their new "big brother." Similarly, Moscow also recognized the limits of its influence in the region, which stemmed largely from its ability to manipulate regional ethnic conflicts and economic problems to pressure the central governments to comply with Moscow's demands. This strategy in turn increased anti-Russian sentiments in these states and marginalized Russia's influence. Consequently, both Turkey and Russia recognized that they had to focus on their common interests.

Evolution of Turkish and Russian Positions in Eurasia since 1997

Ankara and Moscow agreed to improve their economic relations as a strategy to minimize their political differences, since their economic relations had been largely satisfactory. Bilateral trade relations reached approximately $10 billion annually in 1997. Official trade made up $3.5 billion of this with Turkish exports to Russia of $1.347 billion and imports of $2.155 billion. Including the non-registered trade carried out by tourists, the volume of trade between the two countries was estimated at around $10 billion in 1997, putting both countries in the second position in their respective overall foreign trade (for Russia, "foreign trade" excludes trade with other CIS states). Moreover, over one million Russians visit Turkey each year, and Turkish contractors continued to consolidate their position in the Russian market.[47]

In the past decade, Turkish business groups made significant investments not only in Russia but also in Central Asia and the Caucasus. For example, Koç Holding, which has opened chains of "Ramstore" supermarkets in these regions, has started to manufacture durable consumer goods in Uzbekistan. Turkish companies are very influential in Turkmenistan's cotton industry. Turkey has investments in the petro-chemical industries in Azerbaijan, where Turkish small businessmen are innumerable. This suggested that Turkey could increase its influence in the region by increasing the volume of trade with Russia and other post-Soviet states and by increasing its investments in these states.

In 1997, Ankara and Moscow took new steps to institutionalize their economic relations. After a three-year break, the third meeting of the Turkish-Russian Joint Economic Council was held in Ankara on Novem-

---

47. All statistics in this paragraph from Sevilay Bayar, *Rusya Federasyonu Ülke Raporu* (Country report on the Russian Federation) (Istanbul: İhracati Gelistirme Merkezi, 2000), p. 39.

ber 4–7, 1997. This meeting served to prepare Russian Prime Minister Viktor Chernomyrdin's December 16–17, 1997, visit to Turkey, the first official visit in the post-Soviet period by a Russian prime minister. Its main objective was to secure a huge natural gas pipeline project. The Blue Stream project, which entailed building underwater pipelines in the Black Sea, started supplying gas to Turkey in 2003 and is expected to supply 16 billion cubic meters of natural gas a year to Turkey by the year 2010. The project involved laying a gas pipeline from Izobilnoe (Stavropol Krai) through Djubga (Krasnodar Krai) and Samsun (Turkey) to Ankara (see pipeline map, p. 209).[48]

During Chernomyrdin's visit to Turkey, the two countries also agreed to abstain from actions likely to harm each other's economic interests or threaten its territorial integrity.[49] This meant that Russia would not interfere with the construction of the Baku-Ceyhan (later the Baku-Tbilisi-Ceyhan, or BTC) pipeline if that route were selected as the main export route from Azerbaijan. In return, Turkey promised to hire Russian companies to help build the pipeline to Ceyhan. Shortly after this agreement, the Russian oil company Lukoil expressed its desire to join the Baku-Ceyhan pipeline project.[50]

Turkey's strategy of rapprochement through economic relations was dealt a serious blow during Russia's August 1998 financial crisis. When the Russian government decided to devalue the Russian ruble dramatically, foreign investors, including many Turkish businessmen, lost a significant amount of money. Russia's strategy of overcoming the financial crisis involved a 90-day moratorium on repayment of debts and some strict measures to control short-term speculative currency exchanges in the financial market.[51] This crisis not only damaged economic relations between Turkey and Russia, but also created a mini crisis in Turkey: Turkish companies lost their comparative advantage over local producers in Russia (due to the devaluation of the ruble) and could not collect money from their partners in Russia.

Although the Russian financial crisis weakened Russia's economic influence in Eurasia, it also weakened Turkey's influence over most of the

---

48. *Hurriyet,* December 17, 1997.

49. Bazoğlu-Sezer, "Turkish-Russian Relations," p. 66.

50. Although Russia formally gave its approval for its oil companies to invest in the BTC pipeline project in April 2002, Moscow soon denied this. Michael Lelyveld, "Russia: Government Approves Investments in Baku-Ceyhan Pipeline Project," *RFE/RL Newsline,* April 17, 2002.

51. Philip Hanson, "The Russian Economic Crisis and the Future of Russian Economic Reform," *Europe-Asia Studies,* Vol. 51, No. 7 (1999), pp. 1154–1157.

states in Central Asia and the Caucasus since Turkish exports suddenly became very expensive in these states. Many Turkish businessmen had to leave Azerbaijan and other states in the Caucasus and Central Asia. Turkey's political influence was also weakened in the region, especially in Uzbekistan, where all Turkish schools were closed by the Uzbek President Islam Karimov for the alleged involvement of some Turkish citizens in a coup plot against Karimov at the end of 1998. Yet Turkey has not been totally marginalized in the Caucasus; it exerts its influence in the region by giving some military help to Azerbaijan and Georgia, and the BTC pipeline project has enabled Turkey to act as an influential regional player in the region.

The most serious blow to Turkey's economic relations with Russia and the Caucasian and Central Asian states has been the Turkish economic downturn since the economic crisis of 2000. This not only weakened Turkey's influence in these regions, but also undermined the whole strategy of improving Turkish-Russian relations by increasing the volume of economic activity between the countries. The most adverse effect of Turkey's economic crisis has been seen in the Blue Stream project. Initially, it was hoped that Turkey would pay for Russian natural gas by selling more goods and services to Russia. But Turkey became unable to buy as much Russian natural gas as it had promised, and Moscow refused to commit itself to buying Turkish goods and services in return for its natural gas sales to Turkey. After lengthy discussions, Turkey succeeded in convincing the Russians to reduce the price of natural gas to levels paid by Russia's European customers.

In the Balkans, unlike in Central Asia and the Caucasus, where Turkey's influence has declined dramatically vis-à-vis Russia, the balance of power shifted in favor of Turkey. When the Kosovars signed the Kosovo peace plan calling for an interim autonomy and 28,000 NATO troops to implement it in the Rambouillet talks in France of February 6–17, 1999, Belgrade's refusal to sign the deal dramatically weakened the Russian position in the Balkans.[52] Russia's position was weakened further in the CIS when some of these states sent their heads of state to Washington to participate in the fiftieth anniversary celebrations for NATO. At the celebration, an agreement to create an informal grouping was signed by Georgia, Ukraine, Uzbekistan, Azerbaijan, and Moldova (GUUAM), the main task of which is to develop and transport to international markets the area's rich oil and gas deposits, bypassing the Russian route.

---

52. "The Rambouillet Text, February 1999," in Kyril Drezov, Bülent Gökay, and Denisa Kostovicova, eds., *Kosovo: Myths, Conflict and War* (Staffordshire, U.K.: Keele European Research Centre, 1999), pp. 96–100.

During the Kosovo war, which started when NATO authorized air strikes on March 24, 1999, the Russian ministries of defense and foreign affairs pursued conflicting policies. The Russian military supported Belgrade enthusiastically. Moscow even sent a military vessel to the Adriatic Sea to provide Belgrade with military intelligence through its satellites. Unlike the military, the Russian ministry of foreign affairs was aware that Belgrade would lose the war eventually. For them, it was better to broker the most favorable peace for Russia and its ally, Serbia, so that Russia's international position would not suffer significantly. Russia therefore played a crucial role in the signing of the Kosovo peace deal. Russia's envoy, Viktor Chernomyrdin, Finnish President Martti Ahtisaari, representing the EU, and U.S. Deputy Secretary of State Strobe Talbott drafted the Kosovo peace plan, which was finally endorsed by Belgrade on June 3, 1999.

Later in June, when talks in Moscow aimed at incorporating Russian troops into a Kosovo peace force stalled, Russian armored vehicles and 200 Russian soldiers entered Kosovo. Under orders from the ministry of defense, these soldiers took control of Pristina Airport in Kosovo. The Russian military backed down when it became clear that the Kosovo Liberation Army (KLA) forces could make things difficult for the Russian troops. In fact, Hashim Thaci, a senior leader of the KLA, warned that rebels considered the Russians an unwelcome addition to the peacekeeping mission, especially after their surprise entry into Pristina Airport.[53]

Unlike Russia, Turkey was always a part of the solution in Kosovo. Along with the United States and other NATO allies, Turkey supported the February 6–17, 1999, Rambouillet talks in France. During the war, Turkey welcomed more than 10,000 refugees from Kosovo. Moreover, Turkish warplanes joined other NATO forces against the forces of Milosevic. Turkey welcomed the end of the Kosovo war, as it stabilized relations between Yugoslavia and Kosovo. The peace deal reinforced the position of Turkey in the Balkans while it weakened the positions of Russia and the Serbian leadership and strengthened the position of Turkey's local allies, the local Turkish minority and the Kosovars. The removal of Slobodan Milosevic from power by a pro-Western government made it possible for Belgrade to carry out economic and political reforms, to fulfill its international obligations, and to normalize its relations with neighbors. Turkey has continued to play an important role in the security and stability of Kosovo by providing troops, civilian police, and other specialists to KFOR (the NATO-led international peacekeeping force in

53. *Moscow Times*, June 12, 1999.

Kosovo) and UNMIK (UN Interim Administration Mission in Kosovo). Turkey considers the protection of acquired rights of the Turkish national minority and their equal representation in the political and administrative structures as its key objectives in Kosovo.

Despite the increased tension between Turkey and Russia in the Balkans, Turkey's political relations with Russia gained new momentum when Prime Minister Bülent Ecevit paid an official visit to Moscow on November 4–6, 1999. During the visit, he met with his Russian counterpart, Vladimir Putin, and the two prime ministers initialed a Joint Declaration on Cooperation in the Struggle against Terrorism; two agreements, "Abolition of Visas for Diplomatic Passports," and "Cooperation in the Veterinary Field"; and a Protocol on Cooperation in the Field of Information. The Protocol on Joint Economic Commission was also signed.[54] During the visit, Ecevit conspicuously remained silent about the Russian forces attacking Grozny in its Second Chechen War, which resumed in September 1999. This gesture was intended to thank then President Boris Yeltsin and Prime Minister Yevgeny Primakov for their prudence in winter 1998–99, which saved Turkey's relations with Russia from diplomatic disaster when Yeltsin vetoed the Duma decision to grant asylum to the PKK leader Abdullah Öcalan.[55] Vladimir Putin's determination to solve the Chechen problem in accordance with the terms set by Moscow was another reason Ecevit remained silent on the issue.[56]

Turkey started to improve its relations with the EU when it was given candidate status during the December 1999 EU Helsinki Summit.[57] This resulted in a more favorable policy environment for Turkey in exerting its influence throughout Eurasia. Many states in Central Asia, the Caucasus,

---

54. *Cumhuriyet* (Turkish daily), November 8, 1999.

55. *Turkish Daily News,* December 27, 1998.

56. Moscow attempted to solve the Chechen problem "on its own terms militarily without accommodating the secessionist Chechen side through a political settlement. Under these circumstances, Ecevit could not have taken any policy line other than supporting the territorial integrity of the Russian Federation. However, it has continuously stated that it supports the 1999 OSCE Istanbul Summit decisions that called for a political, rather than a military, settlement of the Chechen problem with the participation of the both sides." See Oktay F. Tanrısever, "Rusya'daki 2000 Yılı Cumhurbaşkanlığı Seçimlerinin Reform Süreci Açisindan Bir Analizi" (An analysis of Russia's presidential elections in 2000 in the context of the reform process), *Avrasya Dosyasi* (Fall 2000), p. 281.

57. Atila Eralp, "Turkey and the European Union in the Post–Cold War Era," in Makovsky and Sayarı, *Changing Dynamics of Turkish Foreign Policy,* pp. 173–188, at 184–186.

and the Balkans could opt to improve their relations with Turkey once it became a candidate country of the EU. Of course, this is not to say that states in Central Asia, the Caucasus, and the Balkans viewed Turkey as a potential supporter of their bids to join the EU; rather, Turkey's improved relations with the EU increased Turkey's prestige. Although both Ankara and Moscow have many problems that make their membership in the EU a remote possibility, Turkey was given a more realistic prospect of joining the EU than Russia if it meets the Copenhagen criteria, and achieves political and economic stability. Russia's structural political and economic problems, as well as its difficulties in the process of federalization, make its membership very unlikely in the foreseeable future.

Reflecting the improvements in Turkey's international prestige, Russian Prime Minister Mikhail Kasyanov visited Turkey on October 23–25, 2000. During the visit, a Joint Economic Commission Protocol, an Interstate Co-operation Protocol in the Transportation Field, and a Protocol on the Formation of a Joint Committee on Cooperation in Defense Industry were signed by representatives of the two countries.[58] The three-day visit also produced an important agreement on lifting the mutual personnel quotas on their respective embassies. During the visit, Moscow intended to show that it wanted to become Turkey's principal energy provider and a respectable arms supplier in Turkey's ambitious defense acquisition scheme. This policy was in tandem with Russia's new foreign policy concept, which gives a priority to economic factors. Not surprisingly, Moscow avoided talking about the geopolitical rivalry in the Caucasus and Central Asia.[59]

Defense cooperation also moved up the agenda. The two countries shared an understanding that further progress in this sector would increase their mutual trust, as well as their trade. This concern characterized Turkey's attitude during a $4.5 billion tender to build 145 attack helicopters. Although Turkey's history of U.S. arms purchases and experience of working with Bell Helicopter Textron in particular were large advantages for the U.S. candidate, the King Cobra AH-1Z, Turkey took the Russian-Israeli bid, Kamov's helicopter Ka-50-2, very seriously.[60] That the Russian company increased its chances for this tender

---

58. *Cumhuriyet,* October 25, 2000.

59. Kubilay Kultigin, "Turkey and Russia: A Strategic Partnership?" *Biweekly Briefing,* January 31, 2001.

60. "Ankara Opts for Bell to Supply Attack Helicopters," *Financial Times,* July 22, 2000.

shows that Russia could be competitive with the United States, the key ally of Turkey, in providing military technology to Turkey.[61]

Another important attempt to improve relations between Turkey and Russia was the visit by Russian Minister of Foreign Affairs Igor Ivanov to Turkey on June 7–8, 2001. This was the first official visit at this level from Russia to Turkey since 1992. During the visit, the sides shared views on developments regarding the Caucasus, the Middle East, Iraq, and Central Asia and on ways that the two countries could contribute to efforts to resolve current conflicts in the Eurasian region.[62] Significantly, both Ankara and Moscow started to think about extending their bilateral cooperation to include their multilateral relations, though both were aware of the difficulties in coordinating their foreign policies in Eurasia, where they both have potentially conflicting interests.

The level of military cooperation between Ankara and Moscow is likely to determine the potency of Turkey's relations with Russia. This was one of the issues discussed during Kasyanov's visit of October 23–25, 2000, when it was decided that a Military Cooperation Commission be established between Turkey and Russia. The task of the commission was to search for mutually beneficial forms of cooperation between Turkey and Russia in the production of weapons. General Anatoly Kvashnin, chief of staff of the Russian Federation, met his Turkish counterpart General Hüseyin Kivrikoglu in January 2002 to improve the level of military cooperation. They discussed issues relating to bilateral military and military-technical cooperation; Russia-NATO relations; international terrorism; U.S. missile defense plans; and European security. The two generals also signed an agreement for military cooperation and collaboration on military training.[63] The agreement created a strong base for expanded military cooperation.

Although the emerging atmosphere in Turkish-Russian relations could result in greater cooperation in various foreign policy issues, it was far from certain that Turkish-Russian cooperation could reach the level of a "strategic partnership." The strengths and weaknesses of Turkey's rapprochement with Russia were tested by developments following the terrorist attacks in Washington D.C. and New York on September 11, 2001.

---

61.   Jon Wright, "U.S. Government Pressure Seen in Chopper Contest," *Russia Journal,* July 29, 2000.

62.   *Cumhuriyet,* June 8, 2001.

63.   Liz Fuller, "Russian Chief of General Staff Ends Visit to Turkey," *RFE/RL Newsline,* January 17, 2002.

Turkish-Russian Relations in Eurasia since September 11, 2001

United States–led anti-terrorist operations since September 11, 2001, have resulted in significant changes in Central Asia and the Caucasus, increasing the direct involvement of the United States in these regions. Developments undermined Russia's influence in these regions and made the Russian doctrine of Near Abroad obsolete as the former Soviet republics were no longer assumed to be exclusively under the Russian sphere of influence.[64] For example, the countries of Central Asia and the Caucasus gave unreserved support for the war against terrorism without waiting for Russia's official response. To modernize Uzbekistan's Soviet-era Khanabad military airbase, the United States invested around $500 million. In Kyrgyzstan, the Manas airfield facilities were used by the U.S. Air Force for transport aviation. Besides, a small number of U.S. armed forces were stationed in Georgia to train the Georgian military personnel to fight international terrorists.

One of the most important developments since September 11, 2001, has been the inclusion of Russia in the anti-terrorist coalition under U.S. leadership. In fact, Russian President Vladimir Putin has been seeking to improve Russia's relations with the West on Russia's own terms since he took office in May 2000. Nevertheless, Russia's insistence on maintaining its remaining influence in its Near Abroad could be seen in Putin's approach toward the countries in Central Asia and the Caucasus. Putin's first trip after his inauguration was to Turkmenistan and Uzbekistan. Similarly, he appointed a deputy foreign minister for the Caspian as one of his first foreign policy initiatives. He also adopted a more business-like approach to the CIS, promoting the idea that the full integration of the CIS could proceed at multiple speeds and levels. This is compatible with Turkey's intention to act as a role model for the Turkic states of Central Asia and Azerbaijan. Thus, both states could promote their positions without conflict. Moscow could also benefit from the moderating role of Turkey in Central Asia and Caucasus.

The emerging relationship between Turkey and Russia could gain a more solid basis if it were redefined constructively in coordination with the EU and the United States. Such an opportunity emerged when Russian President Vladimir Putin signaled Russia's full support in the fight against terrorism during his meetings with the NATO and EU leader-

---

64. On Turkey's position in the aftermath of September 11, 2001, see Ruben Safrastyan, "Turkey and Eurasia in the Aftermath of the September 11 Tragedy: Some Observations on Geopolitics and Foreign Policy," *Caucasus and Central Asia Newsletter*, No. 1 (Winter 2001–02), pp. 3–8.

ships in Brussels on October 3, 2001; however, Russia has not yet made a historic choice to become a U.S. ally. Although Putin has been sympathetic to U.S. concerns, he seems to be exploiting the U.S. preoccupation in Central Asia and the Middle East to extract concessions on such issues as NATO expansion and the war in Chechnya. Moscow has particularly sought to use the Second Chechen War to increase its pressure on Georgia and Azerbaijan, which it accused of supporting Islamic fundamentalist Chechen terrorists. This worried both Georgia and Azerbaijan; they were more vulnerable to Russian pressure while the United States focused its attention on Afghanistan and they also considered that Moscow had a legitimate right to defend itself against separatists in Chechnya. They worried, too, that Russia could abuse its legitimate right to increase its geopolitical influence in the Caucasus.

In fact, Moscow still strongly rejects the U.S.-centered unipolarity of the post–Cold War world order, insisting on multipolarity as the cornerstone of international peace and stability. According to Russian foreign policymakers, multipolarity can be promoted through cooperation with China, India, and some of the European states, such as Germany and France, powers that share an interest in counterbalancing the influence of the United States in world politics. Putin's strategy of reviving Russia as a strong state and as a great power (*derzhava*) is likely to cause further tensions between Washington and Moscow.[65]

The position of Turkey is closer to that of the United States. In striving for a leading role in Eurasia, Turkey has developed a number of diplomatic initiatives. The visit by former Turkish Minister of Foreign Affairs Ismail Cem to Azerbaijan, Uzbekistan, and Turkmenistan in October 2001 aimed to demonstrate Ankara's engagement in Eurasia, though it did not have tangible results. This visit focused on the general issues of humanitarian aid, inter-religious dialogue, and security cooperation.[66] Ankara's proposal to organize a meeting between representatives of different anti-Taliban forces failed due to the negative response of Pashtun members of the coalition in Afghanistan; nevertheless, Turkey's active role in Afghanistan increased its prestige in Central Asian countries. The coordination of Turkey's policies in the region with those of other Western countries could create a more solid basis for political stability in the region.

---

65. Zbigniew Brzezinski, "A New Age of Solidarity? Don't Count on It," *Washington Post*, November 2, 2001.

66. Steve Bryant, "Turkey Woos Ex-Soviet States over Afghan Crisis," *Reuters*, October 22, 2001.

To benefit from the increasingly positive atmosphere for the United States and Turkey in Central Asia and the Caucasus, Turkey sought to promote its relations with Eurasian countries by accommodating Russian interests. For example, at the UN General Assembly meeting of November 16, 2001, in New York, Turkish and Russian Ministers of Foreign Affairs Ismail Cem and Igor Ivanov signed a document called "Action Plan for Cooperation between the Republic of Turkey and the Russian Federation in Eurasia: From Bilateral Cooperation to Multidimensional Partnership." This stipulated the formation of a Joint Working Group, which held its first meeting, at the level of deputy foreign ministers, in Moscow in January 2002.[67] This Turkish-Russian partnership in Eurasia has made it easier for Turkey to penetrate into the Caucasus and Central Asia without antagonizing Russia.

Turkey has also been keen to maintain its regional political influence in the Caucasus. Turkey proposed that the existing preliminary agreement on economic cooperation between Ankara, Washington, and Tbilisi, concluded in early 2001, be expanded to include political and military affairs as well. A second agreement dealt with military cooperation between Turkey, Georgia, and Azerbaijan to protect the BTC oil pipeline, first discussed in Trabzon in 2001 during the meeting between Ismail Cem and Georgian Foreign Minister Irakli Menagarishvili.[68] While Russia still opposes the BTC pipeline, construction started on November 18, 2002, thanks to the energetic policies of the United States and Turkey.[69] As expected, Russia was quick to denounce this project as economically unfeasible. In fact, in order to get Caspian oil to Ceyhan at a reasonable cost, Turkey must convince Kazakhstan to transport its oil to world markets through the BTC oil pipeline. Russia's influence over Kazakhstan is considerable; Kazakhstan is economically dependent on the Russian market, and almost 40 percent of Kazakhstan's population is composed of ethnic Russians.

The strategic significance of the Balkans to both Ankara and Moscow has declined considerably. Once the political situation in Kosovo and Macedonia became stable, all regional states turned toward the EU. This orientation may further weaken the influence of both Ankara and Mos-

---

67. Hakan Aksay, "Toward a Multidimensional Partnership" (in Russian), *Perspektiva: Evraziiskoe sotrudnichestvo*, No. 31 (2002), p. 5.

68. *Turkish Daily News*, October 18, 2001.

69. Richard Allen Greene, "Work Begins on Oil Pipeline Bypassing Russia and Iran," *New York Times*, September 19, 2002.

cow in this region; in fact, the term "the Balkans" is being replaced by "Southeastern Europe," emphasizing the region's European rather than its Eurasian character.

The Limits of Eurasianism in Turkey's Relations with Russia

Both domestic sources of Turkish and Russian foreign policy behavior and the states' changing positions in the international system influence their foreign policy actions in the Eurasian region. For this reason, relations between Turkey and Russia displayed different characteristics before and after 1997. In 1992–97, relations were characterized by a geopolitical rivalry between the two regional powers; since 1997, both states have moved to normalize their relations as their positions toward the West also started to converge.

Although Ankara and Moscow have enlarged and deepened their relations, there are two structural limitations on their future development. First, the relations of Turkey and Russia with the Western powers have been based on conflicting orientations. While Ankara seeks to join the EU with the help of the United States, Moscow seeks to counterbalance the United States by improving its relations with the EU. Second, the motivations of both Turkey and Russia are pragmatic. Since their strategic goal is to improve their relations with the Western powers, either Turkey and Russia could opt to improve its relations with the Western powers at the expense of the other if it considered this in its self-interest.

This analysis indicates the limitation of Eurasianist foreign policy discourse in both Turkey and Russia. As Dmitri Trenin argues about the Russian version, Eurasianism is a failed project both as an idea and as a physical reality. It was destroyed mainly by the definitive collapse of empires in this region and the rise of new viable states either in Europe or in Asia.[70] Similar arguments could also be made for the Turkish versions of Eurasianism, which have even less of a material and intellectual basis.

It would be fair to say that Turkey has achieved some level of success in projecting its influence into Central Asia and the Caucasus, which Russia considers its backyard. Of course Turkey has not replaced Russia in these regions, but this was not Turkey's real intention; rather it wished to become an influential actor in the region and to consolidate the political independence of post-Soviet states. Since Turkey has been an important actor in the region with influence that varies from country to country, its

---

70. Dmitri Trenin, *The End of Eurasia: Russia on the Border between Geopolitics and Globalization* (Washington, D.C.: Carnegie Endowment for International Peace, 2002).

performance should be considered a partial success. Turkey's influence in Azerbaijan has been greater than its influence in other parts of Central Asia, such as Kazakhstan. Yet the ongoing economic crisis in Turkey has prevented Turkey from fully realizing its potential to increase its influence in Eurasia.

Chapter 9

Turkey's Middle East Foreign Policy

Lenore G. Martin

The realization that the Middle East was creating new risks and opportunities for its national security thrust Turkey into the pursuit of an activist foreign policy in the region in the last decade of the twentieth century. This activism cast off the legacy of the more neutral Kemalist foreign policy in the Middle East.[1] It also plunged the Republic into a vortex of converging and diverging interests that created a series of dilemmas for the pursuit of its national interests in the region.

The complexity of formulating foreign policy in the face of these dilemmas was clearly illustrated in the spring of 2003 when Turkey's parliament, under control of the newly elected Islamist party, the Justice and Development Party (AKP), rejected the U.S. request to use Turkish military bases for its invasion of Iraq. Yet the Republic relies on its U.S. alignment for long-term strategic security in NATO and to deter threats of

The author wishes to thank Kemal Kirisci, Alan Makovsky, and Ayşe Güneş-Ayata for reading earlier drafts of this paper, as well as Sahar Ahmed, Colleen Ammerman, and Chantal Kiami of Emmanuel College for their research assistance.

1. See Soli Özel, "Of Not Being a Lone Wolf: Geography, Domestic Plays, and Turkish Foreign Policy in the Middle East," in Geoffrey Kemp and Janice Gross Stein, eds., *Powder Keg in the Middle East: The Struggle for Gulf Security* (Washington, D.C.: American Association for the Advancement of Science, 1995), p. 162; Sabri Sayari, "Turkey and the Middle East in the 1990s," *Journal of Palestine Studies*, Vol. 27, No. 3 (Spring 1997), pp. 44–45. For Kemal Atatürk's active involvement in European international politics see in this volume, Feroz Ahmad, "The Historical Background of Turkey's Foreign Policy." For the Ottoman legacy and Kemalist influences on Turkish foreign policy generally, see Mustafa Aydin, "Determinants of Turkish Foreign Policy: Historical Framework and Traditional Inputs," *Middle Eastern Studies*, Vol. 35, No. 4 (October 1999), pp. 152–86.

weapons of mass destruction (WMD) in the Middle East. [2] It is likely that the U.S. objectives of ousting the regime of Saddam Hussein and disarming Iraq of its WMD were conducive to that long-term strategic security. By refusing the U.S. request for assistance with the invasion, Turkey risked a diminution of U.S. strategic cooperation with its erstwhile staunch ally. It also risked a diminution in the valuable economic support it had received from Washington, in addition to compensation that Washington offered for Turkey's potential economic losses from another Gulf War. Conversely, had the Turkish military and the government itself compelled parliament to accede to Washington's request, they would have risked serious popular opposition to what many in Turkey and its Middle Eastern neighbors regarded as U.S. imperialism.

The long-term implications of the dilemma were evident in the aftermath of the invasion. There were persistent concerns in Ankara and other regional capitals over the possible establishment of an independent Kurdistan in northern Iraq. Because Turkey had lost its leverage with the United States in bargaining for a post-invasion role in northern Iraq, it was not clear to what extent U.S. goals of democratizing Iraq would favor the degree of autonomy for Iraqi Kurds that could lead to an independent Kurdistan. At the same time, there would be serious danger of hastening the disintegration of Iraq and of additional strains on the U.S. alliance if Turkey were to intervene to prevent the formation of an independent Kurdistan.

This chapter examines the consequences of activism in Turkey's Middle East foreign policy and the dilemmas that it has created. First, the chapter examines the historical precursors and theoretical foundations of that foreign policy. It then explores the dilemmas within Turkey's foreign relations with the Middle Eastern states that most directly affect its interests in the region: Syria, Iraq, Iran, Israel, and the states of the Gulf Cooperation Council (GCC). [3] The chapter concludes with some consideration

---

2. See in this volume, Ian O. Lesser, "Turkey and the United States: Anatomy of a Strategic Relationship." At the outset of the Gulf War of 1990–91 both the United States and NATO promised to defend Turkey against "any attack" from Iraq; William Hale, *Turkish Foreign Policy, 1774–2000* (London: Frank Cass, 2000), p. 221. However, because of divisions within NATO over the U.S. invasion of Iraq in 2003, the North Atlantic Council refused to give Turkey a security guarantee in the event of an Iraqi attack, but NATO's Defense Planning Council did agree to provide defensive weapons: AWACS, Patriot missiles, and chemical and biological protection. Judy Dempsey, "NATO Agrees To Strengthen Country's Border Defense," *Financial Times*, February 20, 2003, p. 3.

3. Turkey does interact with the other Middle Eastern states, including Egypt, Jor-

as to how Turkey's foreign policymakers may seek to resolve these dilemmas in the politically unstable Middle East.

Historical Antecedents of Turkey's Middle East Policy

Kemal Atatürk had no interest in pursuing an active Middle East foreign policy. Inculcating a new "national" identity for an essentially Anatolian Turkey, he rejected the Ottoman Islamic heritage in favor of secularism, and eschewed the Ottoman tradition of despotism in favor of the Western values of democratization and national development. Atatürk's successors continued to pursue his Kemalist principles of virtual neutrality in foreign affairs through the Second World War.

Distancing the Republic from Middle Eastern affairs was also congruent with the Turkish-Arab mistrust that had originated in the first two decades of the twentieth century. From the Turkish perspective, the Arab Revolt, which helped the West destroy the Ottoman Empire during the First World War, had represented an unforgivable stab in the back.[4] From the Arab perspective, the Ottoman imperial domination of most of the Middle East and the repressive regulations of the Young Turks had unforgivably hampered Arab national development.[5]

The specter of a Soviet threat to Turkey in the aftermath of the Second World War was one of the factors that led Turkey's policymakers to join

dan, and Lebanon. For example, Turkey has sought natural gas supplies from Egypt, and it deals with Cairo as a significant spokesman of Arab perspectives on the Middle East, as well as a potential interlocutor in Turkish-Arab disputes. See Erhan Basyurt, "Mubarak's Strategic Visit," *Zaman*, December 6, 1998, FBIS-WEU-98-340 (Egypt assisted in the Syrian-Turkish dispute over the PKK; Egyptian-Turkish trade of $700 million in 1997 was increasing). Turkey has also engaged in some military cooperation with Jordan.

4. The Turkish attitude towards the Arab world during the Atatürk decades is also reflected in this statement: "For the Turkish republic, the Arab world represented the backward ways Turkey itself hoped to shed." Alan Makovsky, "The New Activism in Turkish Foreign Policy," *SAIS Review*, Vol. 19, No. 1 (Winter 1999), pp. 92–113.

5. See Suleiman Mousa, "The Rise of Arab Nationalism and the Emergence of Transjordan," in William W. Haddad and William Ochsenwald, *Nationalism in a Non-National State: The Dissolution of the Ottoman Empire* (Columbus: Ohio State University Press, 1977), pp. 241–243; Hasan Kayali, *Arabs and Young Turks: Ottomanism, Arabism, and Islamism in the Ottoman Empire, 1908–1918* (Berkeley: University of California Press, 1997), pp. 6–9; Philip S. Khoury, "Continuity and Change in Syrian Political Life: The Nineteenth and Twentieth Centuries," *American Historical Review*, Vol. 96, No. 5 (December 1991), pp. 1384–1386. These attitudes were also reflected in numerous interviews conducted by the author with policymakers and bureaucrats in Turkey and the Arab world in the summers of 1997 and 1999.

NATO.[6] The subsequent concern that the Middle East region would be amenable to communist subversion in the 1950s, thereby posing a regional threat to Turkish national security, led Turkey to embrace anti-communist alignments in the Middle East, principally the Baghdad Pact. The rise of Arab nationalism and independent Arab states unraveled Turkey's alignments with Iraq and Iran, and the Republic returned to its Kemalist neutrality in dealing with the new Arab states.

In the 1970s, as Turkey lost Western support for its intervention into northern Cyprus to protect the Turkish Cypriot community, and feared for its economy in the face of oil price escalation by OPEC (the Organization of Petroleum Exporting Countries) aimed at the pro-Israel United States, it sought friendships in the Arab Middle East. The regime in Ankara also tapped into popular sentiment in the overwhelmingly Muslim community for the plight of the Palestinians and downgraded its formal relations with Israel. Nonetheless, Turkey was disappointed by the lack of strong Arab support for its Cyprus policy. Ultimately, in the 1980s Turkey returned to its Kemalist policy of non-entanglement in the Middle East and the Turkish economy profited handsomely by supplying both sides in the Iraq-Iran war of 1980–88.[7]

It was at some risk to these economic benefits that, under Turgut Özal, Turkey opted to join the Western-Arab coalition against Saddam Hussein in the Gulf War of 1990–91. Özal's policy of providing the allies with the use of Turkey's air base at Incirlik to bomb Iraq and blocking the use of the Iraq-Turkish oil pipeline suddenly thrust Turkey into an active role in the international relations of the Middle East. It continued its active role after the Iraq-Kuwait war by participating in the international economic embargo and allowing the United States and the United Kingdom to use Incirlik for Operation Provide Comfort and its successor, Operation Northern Watch.[8] This activism continued through the 1990s, and included Turkey's military and economic cooperation with Israel, its par-

---

6. See Ahmad, "Historical Background," for a more detailed analysis of this period that challenges the conventional wisdom concerning the primacy of the Soviet threats.

7. Turkey's exports to Iraq were 12 percent of its export trade in the middle of the war, 1985. Henri J. Barkey, "Hemmed in by Circumstances: Turkey and Iraq since the Gulf War," *Middle East Policy*, Vol. 7, No. 4 (October 2000), p. 111. Turkey's exports to the Middle East reached 44 percent of its export trade in 1982. Philip J. Robins, "Avoiding the Question," in Henri J. Barkey, ed., *Reluctant Neighbor: Turkey's Role in the Middle East* (Washington, D.C.: U.S. Institute of Peace Press, 1996), p. 198.

8. The change occurred on January 1, 1997, when France left Operation Provide Comfort.

ticipation in the multilateral track of the Arab-Israeli peace process,[9] its use of military threats to compel Syria to renounce support for the Kurdistan Workers' Party (PKK), and its sparring with Iran over the issues of Islamic fundamentalism as well as Iran's support for the PKK.

Theoretical Underpinnings of the New Activism

By the end of the twentieth century, the academic debate and concomitant policymaking quandary over the "new" activism in Turkish Middle East policy had been resolved. Scholars were no longer asking whether Turkey would return to a more neutral Kemalist approach to dealing with its regional neighbors. Instead, analysts were concerned with the costs, benefits, and risks of pursuing a more active role in the Middle East.[10] Turkey was coming to grips with the inherent instability of the international politics of the Middle East and the multidimensionality of the national security issues that Turkey faces in the region.

INSTABILITY IN MIDDLE EAST INTERNATIONAL POLITICS

It is little wonder that the Middle East, with which Turkey shares three of its borders, earns its appellation as a "turbulent" or "unstable" region. The last few decades of the twentieth century witnessed multiple wars, shifting alignments, and fragile settlements of conflicts among the major players on the Middle East stage. After the Arab-Israeli war of 1973, there were ceasefires with Israel without any formal settlements until Camp David produced the Egypt-Israel peace treaty of 1979. Meanwhile, in 1975 at Algiers, Iran and Iraq reached a major settlement of their long-standing border dispute and the Shah renounced his support for Iraqi Kurds challenging the regime. Saddam Hussein repudiated this Algiers agreement and went to war against Iran after he consolidated his

---

9. Turkey participated in the short-lived Arms Control and Regional Security working group and proposed Israeli Conference on Security and Confidence-Building in the Middle East. Makovsky, "New Activism," p. 13.

10. The more extreme version of that question was the academic speculation over the possibility of Turkish predominance in the Middle East—with or without Israel. For consideration of a predominant pan-Turkic foreign policy without Israel, see Graham E. Fuller, "Alternative Turkish Roles in the Future Middle East," in Barkey, *Reluctant Neighbor*, pp. 207–211; for the Arab perception of the possibility of an Israeli-Turkish duumvirate in the Middle East, see Ofra Bengio and Gencer Özcan, "Changing Relations: Turkish-Israeli-Arab Triangle," *Perceptions*, Vol. V, No. 1 (March–May 2000), pp. 136–39; and Alain Gresh, "Turkish-Israeli-Syrian Relations and their Impact on the Middle East," *Middle East Journal*, Vol. 52, No. 2 (Spring 1998), pp. 188–203.

power in Iraq and the Khomeini Revolution weakened the military in Iran. The Iraq-Iran war that began in 1980 ended with a ceasefire in 1988. During the same period, Syria intervened militarily in the civil war in Lebanon that had begun in 1975. And in 1982 the Israelis invaded Lebanon to expel the PLO and eventually created a "security zone" in southern Lebanon. Iraq, following its ceasefire with Iran, continued to build WMD and then invaded Kuwait in 1990. Without fear of Soviet opposition because of the end of the Cold War, the United States led a UN-supported alliance to terminate the conflict by expelling the Iraqis from Kuwait and achieving a ceasefire in 1991. The alliance ultimately imposed international sanctions upon Saddam Hussein's regime seeking to destroy Iraq's capabilities for mass destruction. The United States engaged in active containment of Iraq, with British assistance and the use of the Turkish air base at Incirlik. (The United States also sought, with less international cooperation, to impose economic containment on Iran.) Claiming that sanctions were not working to prevent Iraq from developing WMD and to restrain a potentially aggressive Saddam Hussein from again threatening his neighbors or possibly linking with militant Islamic terrorists, the United States invaded Iraq to forcibly divest it of WMD and to remove Saddam Hussein from power.

During this same period of regional conflict, the continuing Israeli occupation of the West Bank and Gaza engendered the first Palestinian intifada in 1987 and included various terrorist attacks in Israel and against Israelis. The intifada helped convince a larger portion of the Israeli political community of the need to look for peaceful solutions to the Palestinian conflict. With added awareness of the need to stabilize that conflict after the Gulf War, the United States encouraged the Israeli-Palestinian peace process beginning with the Madrid Conference in 1991. Secret negotiations by Israelis and Palestinians in Oslo achieved the Declaration of Principles in 1993.[11] However, despite international mediation efforts and the continuous negotiations that ensued, the Oslo process failed and another intifada began in September 2000. Washington sought to resuscitate the prospect of a Palestinian-Israeli peace by negotiating a "road map for peace" with other members of the international community.[12] Despite

---

11. There were probably other influences in shifting the popular psychology toward peace. These include a willingness to consider a return to Israel's pre–June 1967 borders in the light of the vulnerability of Israel's population centers to Arab missile attacks, as demonstrated by the Iraqi Scud attacks during 1991, as well as the possibility of a "peace dividend," as demonstrated by the willingness of certain GCC states to abandon the Arab-Israeli boycott and engage in open economic relations with Israel.

12. The publication of the road map to peace was delayed until the installation of a

peace treaties with Egypt and Jordan, Israel has none with Syria, nor has its right to exist been formally recognized by other Arab states, and Iran continues to espouse its destruction.

Alignments within the Middle East during the same three decades evidence similar patterns of instability. Egypt's "separate peace" with Israel ruptured its relations with other Arab states for almost a decade. The Gulf Arab states of the GCC, fearing the spread of Islamic revolution, supported Iraq in its war against Iran. Syria aligned with Iran to oppose Iraq during the Iraq-Iran war, then supported the GCC states in opposing Iraq's invasion of Kuwait. The Palestinians and Jordan supported Iraq during the Kuwaiti conflict, and were treated as pariahs for some time thereafter by the Arab opponents of Iraq. The weakened position of the Palestinians encouraged them to engage in the peace process with Israel. As the peace process waxed, it enabled various Arab states to end their economic boycott of Israel, and permitted some of the smaller GCC states to establish economic relations with Israel. The waning of the peace process has disrupted these economic relationships.

Alignments among the Arab states were reformulated to oppose the Israeli-Turkish alignment of the mid-1990s. In the decade following the end of the Iraqi invasion of Kuwait both Syria and Iran took steps to normalize their relations with Iraq in opposition to the U.S.-U.K. policy of Iraqi containment.[13] Other Arab states also resuscitated their relations with Iraq. However, in the aftermath of the U.S. invasion of Iraq, it remains uncertain as to how Iraq's neighbors will deal with the post–Saddam Hussein regime.

Explanations for the region's instability are multifarious.[14] The continuing Palestinian-Israeli conflict creates a potential for confrontation and a focal point for Arab coalitions. Islamist challenges to the political legitimacy of secular and monarchist Arab regimes have created domestic insecurity and the fear of regime overturn, as in Iran and the Sudan, or

---

new Palestinian cabinet under Prime Minister Mahmoud Abbas at the end of April 2003. It was met with considerable skepticism. James Bennet, "U.S. and Partners Present Proposal for Middle East Peace," *New York Times*, May 1, 2003, p. 1; for the full text of the road map, see p. A7.

13. Neil King, Jr., "Oil Smuggling by Iraq Poses Bush Challenge," *Wall Street Journal*, January 24, 2001, p. A6; "First Iraqi Train Reaches Syria after 19-year gap," *Turkish Daily News*, August 14, 2000. See also Ahmad S. Moussalli, "The Geopolitics of Syrian-Iraqi Relations," *Middle East Policy*, Vol. 7, No. 4 (October 2000), pp. 100–109; "Iraq and Iran Reach Accords," *Turkish Daily News*, October 16, 2000.

14. For a theoretical perspective on the instability in the Middle East as a regional system of international politics, see Lenore G. Martin, *The Unstable Gulf: Threats from Within* (Lexington, Mass.: Lexington Books, 1984).

the serious threat of it, as in Algeria. In a number of Middle East states there are significant ethnic minorities who may seek autonomy or separatism and invite subversion or external intervention. These include Kurds in Syria, Iran, and Iraq, as well as in Turkey; Azeris in Iran; Turcomans in Iraq; and Palestinians in Israel. Furthermore, from the perspective of recent international relations theory, most of the states in the Middle East are autocracies, lacking the brakes that democracies impose on a regime's belligerence in disputes with other democratic states.[15]

THE MULTIDIMENSIONALITY OF TURKISH NATIONAL SECURITY AND THE MIDDLE EAST

What are Turkish national interests in this innately unstable region of the Middle East? The most significant interest is Turkey's need for national security. National security in the sense of being able to defend itself against external military threats or withstand internal civil strife is only one dimension of the risks Turkey faces from its Middle Eastern neighbors. This chapter uses a multidimensional concept of national security. The non-military dimensions include challenges to the political legitimacy of the regime, risks of disturbances in the political community from ethnic and religious strife, possibilities of retardation of economic development, and fear of disruption of the availability of essential natural resources such as energy.[16] The unstable Middle East region creates issues for Turkey in all of these dimensions of national security.

From the Turkish perspective, the most salient threats to Turkish national security that emanate from the region have created stresses on the political legitimacy of the regime and risks of ethnic and religious dissension in the political community. The growth of Islamic fundamentalism has challenged the political legitimacy of the secular, democratic, Kemalist regime, and the PKK demand for Kurdish separatism has challenged the ethnic integrity of the Turkish political community.[17] Radical Islamic fundamentalists have engaged in small-scale acts of political terrorism, but have also raised the specter of religious strife against the siz-

15. See Bruce Russett, "Can a Democratic Peace Be Built?" *International Interactions,* Vol. 18, No. 3 (Spring 1993), pp. 277–282; cf. Christopher Layne, "Kant or Cant: The Myth of the Democratic Peace," *International Security,* Vol. 19, No. 2 (Fall 1994), pp. 5–49.

16. See generally Lenore G. Martin, "Towards an Integrated Approach to National Security in the Middle East," in Lenore G. Martin, ed., *New Frontiers in Middle East Security* (New York: St. Martin's Press, 1999), pp. 3–22.

17. See, in this volume, Kirişci, "The Kurdish Question and Turkish Foreign Policy."

able Alevi population in the Turkish political community.[18] PKK terror-ism in Southeast Anatolia—at least until the capture in 1999 of its leader, Abdullah Öcalan—has been tremendously costly for the state in terms of over 30,000 lives lost and great economic and social disruption.[19] And even after Öcalan's renunciation of armed struggle, there are still lingering fears of low-level violence from this extremist Kurdish national-ist group.[20] The Kurdish problem is a persistent one for Turkey though it has been trying to come to grips with the desire within its Kurdish population for cultural identity, and the recognition of cultural rights short of political autonomy.[21] It remains to be seen how the laws allowing Turkish to be taught in schools and private and public broadcasting in Kurdish are implemented and whether these moves by the Turkish par-liament continue to diminish the interest in Kurdish autonomy in the southeast.

With respect to the other regionally generated potential threats to Turkish national security, the risks to economic security and the interrup-tion of the supply of energy resources, there have been lesser strains. The Turkish economy does not depend largely for its development upon

---

18.   The Alevi are a non-mainstream (Sunni) sect of Islam. See Sencer Ayata and Ayşe Güneş-Ayata, "Religious Communities, Secularism, and Security in Turkey," in Mar-tin, *New Frontiers in Middle East Security*, pp. 120–125.

19.   Metin Murin, "New Look—Ocalan Pleads for his Life," *Financial Times*, June 1, 1999, p. 2; Stephen Kinzer, "In Plea for his Life, Kurdish Rebel Offers to Halt War," *New York Times*, June 1, 1999, p. A3. See also Philip Robins, "Turkey and the Kurds: Missing Another Opportunity," in Morton Abramowitz, ed., *Turkey's Transformation and Ameri-can Policy* (New York: Century Foundation, 2000), pp. 69–72. For the less tangible do-mestic political and foreign policy costs, see Kirişci, "Kurdish Question."

20.   The PKK changed its name to the Kurdistan Freedom and Democracy Congress (KADEK) in April 2002. "New PKK Organizations in Turkey, Iraq, Iran and Syria to Unify Kurds," *Turkish Daily News*, October 3, 2002. For convenience, I use the more fa-miliar PKK in this chapter when referring to incidents prior to October 2002 and refer to PKK/KADEK in situations after that date. For lingering fears, see Robins, "Turkey and the Kurds," pp. 79–93; Barkey, "Hemmed in by Circumstances," p. 121.

21.   See Kemal Kirişci and Gareth M. Winrow, *The Kurdish Question and Turkey: An Ex-ample of Trans-state Ethnic Conflict* (London: Frank Cass, 1997). The Turkish government has gradually eased some of its restrictions on Kurdish cultural rights. For example, after August 2002 private schools could offer instruction in Kurdish as long as it took place in a separate branch of the school. Fatma Demirelli, "Lifting Bans is of No Help to Boost Demand for Kurdish Classes," in *Turkish Daily News*, October 9, 2002. In June 2003 the Turkish parliament passed legislation permitting private and public broad-casting in Turkish. "Justice Commission passes sixth package," *Turkish Daily News*, June 19, 2003; and "Sixth package passed, military's status in spotlight," *Turkish Probe*, June 22, 2003.

trade with and investment from its Middle Eastern neighbors.[22] But Turkey does import substantial quantities of its energy resources and, notwithstanding its attempts to diversify these sources, a large percentage of these imports, particularly oil, still comes from the Middle East region.[23] Turkey's economy, therefore, may be vulnerable to disruptions to its oil and gas supplies that could result from Middle East crises.

In sum, because of the inherent instability of the international politics of the Middle East, and because of the multidimensional nature of Turkey's national security interests in the region, the foreign policy challenges it faces are highly complex. This complexity will become more evident from a more detailed examination of the dilemmas created from the simultaneous convergence and divergence of national security interests of Turkey with Iraq, Iran, Syria, Israel, and the GCC states.

Bilateral Foreign Policy Dilemmas

THE IRAQ DILEMMA

The U.S. ouster of Saddam Hussein and his tyrannical Baathist regime in the spring of 2003 has created new dilemmas for Turkey's relations with Iraq. They arise from the uncertainties of Iraq's future and the contending visions of that future by the United States, by factions within Iraq, and by Iraq's neighbors. The U.S. vision is a democratic Iraq with a representative form of elective government that is resistant to Shiite pressure to transform Iraq into an Iranian-style Islamic republic. This vision needs a formula for granting sufficient autonomy and cultural rights to Iraq's Kurds without ceding to them control over oil production or border trade with Turkey, or undermining the authority of a national administration in Baghdad. Within Iraq there are various factions that contend for power and espouse differing visions of the regime, the political community, and

---

22. Turkey's Middle East trade as officially reported (i.e., without accounting for its so-called underground economy) was approximately 8 percent of its worldwide trade in 2001–02. "Foreign Trade by Country Groups" <www.die.gov.tr/english/sonist /disticist/28010306.gif>.

23. Turkish imports of oil in 2001–02 satisfied about 42 percent of its energy requirements, with 90 percent of its oil imports coming from Saudi Arabia, Iran, Iraq, Syria, and Russia, but oil imports were declining vis-à-vis its imports of natural gas. <www.eia.doe.gov>, July 2002, p. 2. Turkish gas imports, reported from the same U.S. Department of Energy source were 70 percent from Russia and 30 percent from Algeria and Nigeria. See, in this volume, Fiona Hill, "Caspian Conundrum: Pipelines and Energy Networks," for Turkey's search for alternative oil and gas supplies in the Caucasus and Central Asia. See also Temel İskit, "Turkey: A New Actor in the Field of Energy Politics?" *Perceptions*, Vol. 3, No. 4 (March–May 1996), pp. 58–82.

the formula for balancing ethnic or religious autonomy with a national administration. These include Iraqi Kurds, Shiites, major Sunni tribes, and politically active Turcomans. There are also factions within factions, and each faction may also reach out for support from Iraq's most powerful neighbors, Turkey, Syria, and Iran (and even Saudi Arabia and the other GCC states).

Furthermore, there are uncertainties as to the longevity of the U.S. commitment to the diplomatic consequences, economic subsidization, and military support for its vision for Iraq. There will be substantial diplomatic pressures on the United States to internationalize the reconstruction of Iraq or simply withdraw from what the Arab world sees as an imperialistic venture. There certainly will be complaints within the United States during economic hard times as to the costs of maintaining a U.S. presence in Iraq. And there could be popular resentment within the United States for casualties to U.S. ground forces caused by Iraqi opponents of the U.S. presence. If these pressures lead to a premature U.S. withdrawal of forces and administrators prior to the achievement of the U.S. vision for Iraq, there is a strong likelihood that civil war may erupt as the various Iraqi factions openly contend for power. In that scenario there will be great temptation for Iraq's neighbors to intervene subversively and even overtly.

Turkey's relations with Iraq were much simpler before the Gulf War of 1990–91. The heyday of Turkish relations with Iraq occurred during the Iraq-Iran war, when Turkey, pursuing a foreign policy of Kemalist neutrality, obtained a significant economic boost from its wartime trade with Iraq. Good relations with Turkey were particularly important for Iraq, because Syria, in solidarity with Iran, had blocked the flow of Iraqi oil to the Mediterranean through the Syrian pipeline, and oil transport through the Persian Gulf was risky. Turkey gained energy resources and transit fees from the flow of Iraqi oil through the Turkish pipeline, as well as through cross-border truck trade.

Özal's proposal to join the allied opposition to Iraq at the outset of the Kuwait war, reversing the policy of Kemalist political disengagement and risking substantial economic losses from the interruption of trade with Iraq, met with considerable opposition within Turkey, including among the Turkish general staff.[24] Turkey in fact complained bitterly about its economic losses from the war and the subsequent economic embargo on Saddam Hussein's regime.[25] With the loosening of the economic

---

24. Clyde Haberman, "Turkey's top official quits over 'Statesmanship'," *New York Times,* December 4, 1990, p. A13.

25. Estimates run to $80–100 billion when taking into account direct losses of trade

embargo to enable Iraq to obtain increased humanitarian supplies, Turkey benefited once again from the reopening of the oil pipeline from Iraq and resumption of trade, including the cross-border truck trade.[26] In the aftermath of the U.S. invasion of Iraq in the spring of 2003, because of Turkey's reluctance to participate fully in the coalition invasion effort, it remains unclear to what extent Turkey will be able to benefit economically by participating in the economic reconstruction of Iraq—at least under U.S. auspices.

Over the longer term, nevertheless, Turkey has a strong interest in improving its economic relations with Iraq. In addition to the benefits from a close source of energy for this energy-hungry state, Iraq is an easy destination for Turkish products.

The prime dilemma created by Turkey's converging and diverging interests in its relations with Iraq centers on the Kurds. Prior to the Gulf War of 1990–91, both Baghdad and Ankara had a mutual interest in repressing Kurdish nationalism with its attendant demands for an autonomous Kurdish state and risks of irredentism in southeastern Turkey and northern Iraq.[27] Iraq even cooperated with Turkey in permitting Turkish forces to conduct limited operations across the border in pursuit of PKK guerrillas.

The Gulf War of 1990–91 and its aftermath gave rise to the central dilemma that was exacerbated by the U.S. ouster of the regime of Saddam Hussein in 2003. During the Gulf War, Operation Provide Comfort and Operation Northern Watch, conducted by the United States and the United Kingdom from Incirlik, were intended to protect the Kurds in the north and contain the Saddam Hussein regime by policing a no-fly zone in the north of Iraq. Operation Provide Comfort originally allowed Iraqi

---

with Iraq, and indirect losses from interruption of the truck trade through Iraq to the Gulf. "Gulf Crisis Continues to Inflict High Cost on Turkey," *Turkish Daily News,* January 17, 2001.

26. Improvements in trade include establishing a Turkey-Iraq Business Council, upgrading the oil pipeline, and negotiating natural gas pipeline agreements. "Turkey and Iraq Sign Agreement to Increase Trade Volume," *Turkish Daily News,* March 2, 2000; and "Full Speed Ahead in Relations with Iraq," *Turkish Daily News,* October 12, 2000. Trade between the two states was expected to reach almost $1 billion in 2002. "Turkey Enhances its Share of Exports to Iraq," *Turkish Daily News,* July 1, 2002.

27. There are an estimated 3.5 million Kurds in northern Iraq, according to Hugh Pope, "Sanctions against Iraq Continue to Erode," *Wall Street Journal,* October 9, 2000, p. A24. Another source estimates the total number of Kurds in Iraq as 4.2 million. David McDowall, *A Modern History of the Kurds* (London: I.B. Tauris, 2000), p. 3. There are some 5 to 6.5 million Kurds in Southeast Anatolia according to Robins, "Turkey and the Kurds," p. 63.

Kurdish refugees to return to Iraq after fleeing into Turkey to escape from Saddam Hussein's repression after the war. However, the rival Iraqi Kurdish factions, most prominently Massoud Barzani's Kurdistan Workers' Party (KDP) and Jalal Talabani's Patriotic Union of Kurdistan (PUK) used the sanctuary of allied air cover to reassert *de facto* autonomy for Iraqi Kurds in the north. This led Ankara to adopt a complicated policy of regulating cross-border trade with Iraq, which benefited the Turkish economy, particularly in the more impoverished southeast. At the same time the cross-border trade improved the lives of Iraqi Kurds and enabled them to sustain their autonomy from Baghdad. Balancing these interests became politically problematic for Ankara. For example, when Turkey imposed trade barriers to discourage economic autonomy of Kurdish northern Iraq, the impoverished economy in Kurdish Southeast Anatolia suffered, leading to political protest against Ankara.[28]

This same sanctuary for Iraqi Kurds in northern Iraq at times also provided the PKK guerrillas with havens and bases of operation to cross into Turkey. Ankara responded by becoming involved in the factional struggles between the Iraqi Kurds to create anti-PKK alignments, and by sending large-scale Turkish military forces into northern Iraq to eliminate the PKK sanctuary. Baghdad, though powerless to prevent Turkish incursions into its sovereign soil, signaled its displeasure by playing a low-level PKK card, permitting the PKK to maintain offices in Baghdad and providing other support to the PKK.[29] Nonetheless, Turkey continued to support Operation Northern Watch despite misgivings within the regime.[30]

Prior to the U.S. invasion of Iraq in the spring of 2003, Turkey attempted to relieve the tension that an invasion could increase by bargain-

---

28.   The protests sought to force Ankara to keep its promises to end trade barriers imposed earlier in 2000; "Border Open But Not for Trade," *Turkish Daily News,* August 14, 2000. Ultimately, Turkey did cut off the diesel fuel trade that was enriching Iraqi Kurds; Dexter Filkins, "Kurds Say a Turkish Crackdown on an Illegal Fuel Trade In Iraq is Aimed at Them," *New York Times,* November 29, 2002, p. A20. Ironically, Turkey's state-owned petroleum company had agreed to build drilling sites in parts of northern Iraq under control of the Kurdish Democratic Party, no doubt with the possibility of enriching that Kurdish faction if successful; Somini Sengupta, "Turkish Business and Kurds Plan Oil Exploration Deal," *New York Times,* December 14, 2001, p. A16.

29.   "Rebel Kurds Open Iraq Office," AP, June 2, 1998; Global Intelligence Update, July 1, 1998; "Saddam Starts to Support PKK against Barzani-Talabani," *Ankara Online,* December 9, 1999, FBIS-WEU-1999-1209.

30.   The misgivings arose within the Turkish military as well as sections of the elite. Barkey, "Hemmed in by Circumstances," pp. 116–117.

ing with the United States for rights to send the Turkish military into northern Iraq to prevent Iraqi Kurds from seizing the oil-rich areas of Kirkuk and Mosul. Iraqi Kurdish control over these areas would certainly strengthen their bid for autonomy. Moreover, Turkish nationalists have claimed that the region was unfairly awarded to Iraq after the First World War.[31] Ankara also sought economic compensation for projected losses from the cut-off of trade with Iraq. In addition, Turkey promoted the interests of Iraqi Turcomans in participating in any post-Saddam regime and indicated its own interests in supporting Turcomans against repression by Kurds and in counterbalancing Kurdish influence in the northern oil region.[32] The bargaining failed with the Turkish parliament's rejection of the request by the United States to use Turkish bases to mount ground and air force attacks against Iraq.

While the United States maintains a military, political, and economic presence in Iraq, it is obviously difficult for Turkey to take direct action to restrain the Iraqi Kurds without diminishing the Republic's vital strategic cooperative relations with the United States. But notwithstanding Ankara's reaffirmation of the need to maintain the integrity of Iraq,[33] Turkey will remain suspicious of any regime in Baghdad that might grant sufficient autonomy to the Kurdish north that could lead to the establishment of an autonomous Kurdistan in Iraq. From Turkey's viewpoint an autonomous Kurdish north within a too loosely federated Iraq could rekindle Kurdish separatism in Turkey and become an irredentist magnet for Turkish Kurds in Southeast Anatolia.

Yet any direct intervention by Turkish forces to prevent Iraqi Kurds from achieving such autonomy risks causing exactly the opposite to occur, namely the disintegration of Iraq. Turkey's intervention, even ostensibly to protect Iraqi Turcomans, would be suspected as a pretext for con-

---

31. Ibid., pp. 123–24; Amberin Zaman, "Turkey prepares to stake claim in Iraq's oil fields," January 7, 2003 <www.telegraph.co.uk>.

32. See General (Ret.) Armagan Kuloğu, *Turkey's Policy Alternatives towards Iraq* (Ankara: ASAM Center for Eurasian Strategic Studies, Summer 2002). It is as difficult to gauge the likely success of such efforts as it is to estimate the size of the Turcoman population in Iraq. Turkey, for example, claims they constitute 13 percent of the Iraqi population; the United States recognizes only 1 percent; and the Iraq Turcoman Council claims almost 3 million, possibly 12 percent of the Iraqi population. Fatma Demirelli, "Turkomans Coming Out of Oblivion," *Turkish Daily News,* October 14, 2002; "Iraq Turcoman Council supports Turcoman Front," *Turkish Daily News,* October 25, 2002; Melik Kaylan, "Iraq's 'Bosnians': The Turkomans as Ethnic Scapegoats," *Wall Street Journal,* December 30, 2002, p. A12.

33. "Iranians and Turkey Discuss Iraq's Economy in Ankara," *Turkish Daily News,* April 26, 2003.

trolling northern Iraqi oilfields. This would alienate Iran, which in the long term shares a converging interest in restraining a militant Iraq and an autonomous Kurdistan. Worse, Turkey's intervention in Iraq could also stimulate the concerted opposition of both Syria and Iran to Turkish predominance in the region. Yet if Turkey refrained from influencing the fate of a disintegrated Iraq, it would risk the predominance of Iran, which has extended its influence throughout Iraq by supporting various Islamic and Kurdish groups. If Iraq were to disintegrate, Iran itself might intervene to support the majority Shiite population of Iraq. If an Iraqi Shiite government, supported by Iran, sought to extend its power over the Sunni Kurds in the north, these Iraqi Kurds might appeal to Turkey to intervene on their behalf. In sum, the dilemmas created by this fluid situation are as conducive to bargaining among the factions and their external allies as they are to the use of military force to achieve their respective visions for the future of Iraq.

Another factor contributing to the dilemma in Turkey's relations with Iraq arises from Turkey's control over the waters of the Euphrates and Tigris rivers, upon which Iraq depends for its water supplies. The control over the Euphrates has tightened as Turkey has developed its Southeast Anatolia Project (GAP), increasing the number of dams and irrigation systems.[34] However, the GAP project does not pose any immediate threat to the bulk of Iraq's water supplies, which come from the Tigris.[35] Nonetheless, this has not deterred Iraq from joining Syria in protesting Turkish domination of these water sources, of which more will be discussed below with respect to Turkey's relations with Syria. A new regime in Baghdad could put economic pressure on Turkey to resolve the Tigris water dispute. If the new regime retains amicable relations with the United States, Turkey may not be able to ignore the demands for resolution.

Turkey's Iraq dilemma, therefore, results from the convergence and divergence of interests. On the one hand is the convergence of Turkey's economic interests with Iraq's, including Ankara's desire to obtain energy resources from Iraq and to balance the costs of imported energy with a thriving export trade. On the other hand, there is a sharp divergence in

---

34. See, in this volume, İlter Turan, "Water and Turkish Foreign Policy"; see also a detailed chronology and discussion of Turkey's negotiations with Iraq and Syria over water in Özden Bilen, *Turkey and Water Issues in the Middle East* (Ankara: Prime Ministry/GAP, 1997, 2nd ed. 2000), pp. 70–80.

35. According to Bilen, Iraq receives 44.4 billion cubic meters (BCM) annually from the Tigris and Euphrates rivers, both of which are sourced in Turkey. Of this, 31.4 BCM of Tigris water flows into Iraq unimpeded and another 3.7 BCM of Tigris waters flows into Iraq after Turkey and Syria have taken a share; Bilen, *Turkey and Water Issues*, p. 60.

strategic interests arising from Turkey's desire to be able to cross over the Iraqi border in force, to root out PKK/KADEK havens and possibly to prevent an autonomous Kurdistan in northern Iraq. Turkey faces the additional dilemma of maintaining its strategic cooperation with the United States at the same time that it fears the possibility that the U.S. vision for a post-Saddam Iraq may bring an autonomous Kurdistan closer to reality. If Turkey aligns too closely with the other Iraqi neighbors, Syria and Iran, in common cause to oppose that reality, it risks losing its valuable alliance with the United States, which is critical for economic, military, and strategic benefits to Turkey.

THE IRAN DILEMMA

Turkey shares some converging economic interests with Iran, as well as diverging political interests, the intersection of which provides the sources of Turkey's Iran dilemma. With respect to their mutual economic interests, Iran is a potential source of cross-border trade and it is particularly a source of energy resources such as oil and gas.[36] In December 2001 Iranian gas started to flow to Turkey through a new pipeline as a result of their 1996 long-term supply agreement (which had incurred U.S. disapproval for violation of the 1996 Iran-Libya Sanctions Act).[37] Turkey and Iran are also potential competitors for alternative oil and gas transit pipelines from the Caucasus and Central Asia.[38] They share, too, a long-term interest in repressing Kurdish nationalism. However, the ideological rivalry between the two Muslim states creates a profound divergence of their political interests. Turkey is a secular democracy, Iran an Islamist theocracy; each represents an alternative model for reformist Middle East states. Their ideological rivalry softened somewhat after the Turkish elec-

---

36. Turkey's trade with Iran in 2001 was approximately $1.2 billion of which approximately $360 million was Turkish exports to Iran. Most of the approximately $840 million imports from Iran were oil and oil products. "Turkey to Send Trade Mission to Iran," *Turkish Daily News,* September 14, 2002. Turkey has contracted with a number of countries in the Middle East (Iran, Egypt, Iraq, Algeria, and Yemen), the Caucasus and Balkans, and Nigeria to diversify its supply of gas, which in 2000 was mainly supplied by Russia. Guzin Yildizcan, "Baku-Ceyhan Project Linked to U.S. Presidential Election," *Turkish Daily News,* August 10, 2000. See also Hill, "Caspian Conundrum," for an account of Turkey's global suppliers of oil and gas. Iran has also agreed to transit gas from Turkmenistan for Turkey; "1,100 Energy Projects to Become Operational in Government Week," *Tehran IRNA,* August 19, 2000, FBIS-NES-2000-0819.

37. Turkey renegotiated the terms of the deal in 2002 because of its prospective oversupply of gas; "Turkey Says Iran Disrupts Gas Supplies," *Turkish Daily News,* December 24, 2002.

38. See Hill, "Caspian Conundrum."

tion in 2002 that brought the Islamist AKP to power. The AKP was the successor to the Welfare Party, which was ousted by the Turkish military in 1997 in part because of its movement toward a closer relationship with Iran.[39]

Turkey has, in the past, accused Iran of attempting to destabilize the Republic by supporting radical Islamist groups such as Hezbollah, Islamist Great Raiders Front, Islamic Action, and the Jerusalem Army, which have been trained in and/or financed by Iran and which engage in terrorist acts in Turkey.[40] Diplomatic relations between the two neighbors were even ruptured for a time in 1997 when the Iranian ambassador to Turkey called for the adoption of the Islamist Sharia system in Turkey at a Jerusalem Day speech in Sincan, a suburb of Ankara.[41] The Turkish military responded by sending in tanks, arresting the Islamist Welfare Party mayor, and expelling the Iranian ambassador. Iran, in turn, had complained of Turkey's harboring Mujahadeen-e-Kalq, violent opponents of the Iranian regime.[42] But diplomatic relations between the two states improved after the AKP gained a majority in parliament, even though the

---

39.   Necmettin Erbekan, the leader of the Welfare Party, had attempted to improve relations with Iran, as well as other Middle Eastern countries, during his short period as prime minister 1996–97, but alienated the Turkish military and others by his friendly relations with Islamic radical groups; see Kemal Kirişci, "The future of Turkish policy toward the Middle East," in Barry Rubin and Kemal Kirişci, eds., *Turkey in World Politics: An Emerging Multiregional Power* (Istanbul: Bogaziçi University Press, 2002), pp. 137–138.

40.   "Iranian Terrorist Connection Once Again on Agenda," *Turkish Daily News*, July 13, 2000; "1,100 Energy Projects to Become Operational in Government Week," *Tehran IRNA*, August 19, 2000, FBIS-NES-2000-0819; "Hizbullah Report to Iranian Mullah," *Istanbul Hurriyet*, August 27, 2000, FBIS-NES-2000-0827; "Iran Sentenced in Absentia," *Istanbul Milliyet* (Ankara edition), August 29, 2000, FBIS-NES-200-0829; Evin Göktab, "Prime Minister N. Erbakan Will Give Information to Iran about the PKK," *Cumhurriyet*, August 10, 1996, pp. 1, 6. It was estimated that there were 20,000 sympathizers and activists of Iranian-supported Hezbollah in Turkey, "The collapse of Hizbullah," *Turkish Daily News*, June 23, 1999, p. A3. Hezbollah members have been accused of multiple murders, personal attacks, abductions, and bombings, with varying estimates of the numbers of their victims, for example, 1,000 crimes since 1991 ("Hizbullah Said to Have Murdered 484 Since 1991," *Ankara Anatolia*, February 12, 2000, FBIS-WEU-2000-0212); 2,000 murders in the southeast since the late 1980s ("Hizbullah is Prime Example of State's 'Playing One against the Other' Policy," *Turkish Daily News*, January 31, 2000); and mass graves and multiple disappearances (Stephen Kinzer, "Mass Graves in Turkey Put Attention on Terror Cell," *New York Times*, January 23, 2000).

41.   Bülent Uzum and Ali Ekeyilmaz, "Call for Sharia in Sincan," *Istanbul Sabah*, February 2, 1997, FBIS-WEU-97–023.

42.   Elif Unal, "Turkey, Iran Agree Anti-Rebel Deal—Turk Official," Reuters, August 12, 1999.

AKP has avoided the rhetorical extremes of the Welfare Party, which led the governmental coalition during the Sincan incident.[43]

Turkey has also accused Iran of surreptitiously aiding the PKK, by providing them with logistical and financial support, guerrilla warfare training, and medical care, as well as arms and sanctuaries.[44] Why has Iran played a PKK card? Certainly Tehran cannot afford to undermine its own interests in repressing Kurdish separatism in northern Iran by openly encouraging it in southeast Turkey. Iran, moreover, needs to be concerned about the expansion of surreptitious ethnic conflict to its own ethnic perimeter where it may be vulnerable to separatist demands from its Azeri population or irredentist demands from Azerbaijan.[45] Furthermore, a more activist Turkey signaled its willingness to use military means to send warnings of Ankara's displeasure with Iran by making aggressive cross-border air raids into Iran against the PKK and also forcing down and searching Iranian planes in Turkish airspace for weapons suspected of being supplied to PKK militants.[46] Still, Ankara has been careful not to create a *casus belli* with its neighbor, and reportedly paid for some of the damage caused by the bombing.[47] Even after the decrease in PKK activity that followed the capture of Abdullah Öcalan in 1999, Iran did not give up support for the PKK. Furthermore, Iran has remained involved in the Kurdish north of Iraq by supporting Islamist groups there.[48]

---

43. See in this volume, Sencer Ayata, "Changes in Domestic Politics and the Foreign Policy Orientation of the AK Party."

44. FBIS-WEU-97-0107; "Scandal in Joint Operation with Iran," *Istanbul Hurriyet*, October 24, 1996, FBIS-TOT-97-0001. In 2002 Turkey also accused Iran of harboring one of Öcalan's successors, Cemil Bayik. "Turkey wants Cemil Bayik from Tehran; Iran Denies His Presence," *Turkish Daily News*, April 4, 2002.

45. Malik Mufti, "Daring and Caution in Turkish Foreign Policy," *Middle East Journal*, Vol. 52, No. 1 (Winter 1998), p. 39; Fuller, "Alternative Turkish Roles," p. 209. For the strategic vulnerability generally of Iran's ethnic perimeter, see Martin, *Unstable Gulf*, pp. 90–93.

46. "Turkey Seen Jockeying for Position in Post-Saddam Iraq," *Mideast Mirror*, July 30, 1999; Charles Recknagel, "Iran: Crisis with Turkey Cools but Relations Remain Volatile," Radio Free Europe/Radio Liberty, August 11, 1999; "Syria's Khaddam to Visit Turkey to Boost Ties," *Turkish Daily News*, November 2, 2000.

47. "Ankara to Pay Damages to Tehran over Delay in Gas Purchase," *Tehran Iran News*, September 5, 2000, FBIS-NES-2000-0905. Turkey also responded with a show of force to Iranian military threats to Azeri oil exploration in parts of the Caspian Sea disputed with Iran. Gyor Ergan, "Turkey Warns Iran on Azerbaijan," *Hurriyet*, FBIS-SOV-2001-0813.

48. C.J. Chivers, "An Iranian-Backed Brigade with Ties to the Kurds Sets Up Camp in

Compare this situation to the game the Shah played in the early 1970s by supporting Iraqi Kurds in opposition to Baghdad in order to pressure Baghdad in the Iraq-Iran border dispute that had flared up. In that instance, the game concluded with a negotiated settlement. The Shah renounced support for the Iraqi Kurds in the 1975 Algiers Agreement in exchange for concessions over the Shatt al-Arab waterway linking the confluence of the Euphrates and Tigris to the Persian Gulf. The situation at the beginning of the twenty-first century remains complex, with many players at the table and with much higher ideological and geopolitical stakes. The major players include Iraq, Turkey, Syria, and the United States. They sometimes support different Kurdish factions, and benefit from inter-factional conflict. Iran wants to make sure that it remains in this game.

From Iran's perspective, the U.S. (and U.K.) presence in Iraq following the overthrow of Saddam Hussein in 2003 brings its most threatening ideological enemy physically closer to the Iranian border and assists in the well publicized U.S. policy of containing Iran. Iran certainly views Turkey as a close ally of the United States that avowedly depends upon its strategic relationship with the United States to deter threats of WMD emanating from Iran. Moreover, the United States remains concerned about Iran's support of Iraqi Shiite demands for a theocratic regime in Baghdad and for the undermining of the U.S. vision for the future of Iraq. While theocracy may not be the only Iranian vision for an Iraqi regime, it is the one most likely to create confrontations with the United States, and also with Turkey. On the other hand, if civil war breaks out in Iraq, Iran shares Turkey's concerns to prevent the Iraqi Kurds from establishing an autonomous Kurdistan. The new Kurdistan might make irredentist appeals to Iranian Kurds as well as Turkish Kurds. Worse, the disintegration in Iraq might also provide opportunities for nationalist Turks to invade the north of Iraq and retake Mosul. It also might embroil Iran in a conflict with Turkey over the reintegration of Iraq under Shiite rule, which Iran would advocate and support.

Equally bad from Iran's perspective is the military cooperation agreement between Turkey and Iran's other ideological enemy, Israel. Turkey and Israel signed a series of military cooperation agreements in 1996, one of which gave the Israeli air force the ability to train in Turkey close to the Iranian border. This has reportedly been modified to restrict Israeli air

Northern Iraq," *New York Times*, March 3, 2003, p. A9; Harvey Morris, "Kurdish Forces Tie Down Iraqi Divisions," *Financial Times*, March 26, 2003, p. 4. The Kurdish Democratic Party of Iran and the Islamic Movement in Kurdistan, located in northern Iraq, are both supported by Iran.

training from Turkey's border areas.[49] Israeli-Turkish military cooperation provides additional support for Turkey's ability to deter long-term
WMD development by Iran.

Surreptitious support for Islamist and other Kurdish groups in northern Iraq, as well as for militant Iraqi Shiites and even factions within the
Iraqi exiles contending for power,[50] enables Iran to demonstrate its opposition to U.S. control over Iraq following the U.S. invasion. Iran thereby
claims a role in the decisions over the fate of Iraq.

Nonetheless, because of their strong mutual interest in avoiding the
establishment of an autonomous Kurdistan in northern Iraq, Turkey and
Iran engage in a delicate balancing of their disparate interests in Kurdish
northern Iraq. Thus Iran has avoided more overt support for the PKK,
and has entered into agreements with Turkey ostensibly to cooperate in
preventing PKK sanctuaries at the border.[51] Furthermore, Iran and Turkey have held high-level diplomatic talks to voice their mutual concerns
over northern Iraq in the wake of the U.S. invasion.[52]

THE SYRIA DILEMMA

Turkey experiences a similar dilemma in its foreign relations with Syria.
Prior to 1998 there appeared to be few converging economic interests between the two neighbors to countervail their long-standing divergent political interests. The divergence stemmed from an entrenched dispute
over the province of Hatay (Alexandretta), and Syria's implacable opposition to Turkey's control over the Euphrates waters.

The Ottoman *sanjak* of Alexandretta had a large Arab population, and
was only approximately 40 percent Turkish. At the end of the First World
War and the break-up of the Ottoman Empire, Alexandretta fell under
French control as part of the mandate over Syria. Atatürk legitimized this

49. Cengiz Çandar, "Israel's Anxiety about Turkey," *Istanbul Sabah,* August 31, 2000,
FBIS-NES-2000-0904.

50. See Judith Miller and Lowell Bergman, "Iraq Opposition is Pursuing Ties with
Iranians," *New York Times,* December 13, 2002, pp. 1, A14. Iran has been suspected
of supporting Islamic militants who have attacked Kurds in the northeast of Iraq;
C.J. Chivers, "Kurds Face a Second Enemy: Islamic Fighters on Iraq Flank," *New York
Times,* January 13, 2003, p. A9.

51. The agreements include controlling the border area, cooperation in locating PKK
guerrillas, simultaneous operations against PKK and Mujahadeen-e-Khalq, installing a
hotline between military commanders, and extraditing PKK guerrillas and Iranian dissidents. FBIS-NES-1995-1009; Reuters, August 12, 1999; Associated Press, August 13,
1999; "What Does Iran Have against Turkey" *Turkish Daily News,* May 17, 2000.

52. Guy Chazan, "Turkey Strengthens Ties with Two U.S. Adversaries: Iran, Syria,"
Wall Street Journal, April 10, 2003, p. 11.

arrangement in a 1921 treaty designed to remove the French from Turkey. On the eve of the Second World War, the tables had turned. The French were eager to secure Turkish assistance against Germany and ceded the *sanjak* to Turkey by treaty in 1939. The Syrians, who had been promised their independence from France at the time, strenuously objected, claiming that this buffer territory should have remained with Syria.[53] This history made it exceedingly difficult to resolve these claims, and inserted a major strain in the relations between Syria and Turkey over the years.

The second cause for difficult relations between these two neighbors was the GAP project that established Turkey's control over the Euphrates. The aim of GAP is to build 22 dams, 19 hydroelectric plants, and 17 irrigation projects, resulting in Turkey's control of the flow of water from the Euphrates and Tigris rivers into Syria and Iraq. Turkey has a great deal at stake in the GAP.[54] It envisions the project as providing both hydroelectric power and irrigation to the underdeveloped southeast, as well as additional electricity to other parts of Turkey.[55] It therefore believes that the GAP will bring economic prosperity to the people of the southeast region, many of whom are Kurds. With economic prosperity, Turkey hopes to overcome the kind of Kurdish separatist appeals that the PKK has voiced.[56]

Interestingly, although the GAP is often referred to as developing resources for the southeast, much of the energy from this area is used to fuel the industrial development of western Turkey. This is simply because much of Turkey's industrial base is located in the west.[57] Although the government encourages industrial development in the southeast, this

---

53. See, generally, George Lenczowski, *The Middle East in World Affairs,* 4th ed. (Ithaca, N.Y.: Cornell University Press [1952], 1980), pp. 319–321.

54. See in this volume Turan, "Water and Turkish Foreign Policy."

55. The GAP dams supplied approximately 41 percent of Turkey's hydroelectricity in 1998 <www.gap.gov.tr/English/Frames/fr8.html>.

56. Mustafa Sönmez, "The Story of Eastern and Southeastern Turkey," *Private View,* Vol. 2, No. 6 (Autumn 1998), p. 34, raises questions as to whether this policy will succeed without significant socioeconomic changes in the region to broaden land ownership. Sönmez notes, however, that landless farmers would have increased opportunities to work in the new agribusinesses in the cities stimulated by the improved productivity resulting from the GAP project. The socioeconomic conditions of the southeast include persistent feudal ownership of land. James Dorsey, "Feudalism Tears at Southeast Turkey and the Government Likes it That Way," *Wall Street Journal,* March 12, 1997, p. A14. See also Ali Çarkoğlu and Mine Eder, "Domestic Concerns and the Water Conflict over the Euphrates-Tigris River Basin," *Middle Eastern Studies,* Vol. 37, No. 1 (January 2001), pp. 41–71.

57. Çarkoğlu and Eder, "Domestic Concerns."

policy has not been successful during the conflict with the PKK in that region, because the instability discouraged Turkish industry from locating there. After Turkey's imprisonment of Abdullah Öcalan in 1999 and the apparent withdrawal of all but a few PKK militants from Turkey, there are greater prospects for inducing Turkish industry into the southeast and for improving the local economy.

The Syrians (and Iraqis) strenuously disputed Turkey's right to control the Euphrates and Tigris waters by means of the GAP project. The dispute has mainly taken the form of appeals to international legal principles and direct negotiations, without resort to overt violence (except for Syrian support for the PKK before 1999, which was a form of indirect violence). The Syrians believe that the Tigris and Euphrates are international watercourses. Accordingly, they claim that, in determining rights to these waters, acquired rights based upon historical usage, as recognized by international law, should govern any agreement on sharing the waters.[58] Turkey, on the other hand, believes that acquired rights of a downstream riparian cannot prevent an upstream state from developing its own water resources. From the Turkish point of view, the Tigris and Euphrates are trans-boundary watercourses. They distinguish international watercourses as only those waters that create borders between countries.[59] Turkey believes that the upstream riparian is entitled to control its waterways until they leave the state. This position conflicts with the position taken by the UN International Law Commission, which defines an international waterway as one with different parts in different states.

Going beyond this issue of definition in trying to fashion an equitable solution to the problem, Turkey maintains that acquired rights constitute only one factor to be considered. Turkey rejects the mathematical formula that has been advocated by Syria and Iraq to settle the issue by calculating the relative demands of each riparian state and the capacity of each waterway. Instead, the Turks invoke the concept of equitable utilization. They would allocate water usage in accordance with several factors including "socio-economic, hydrological, and geopolitical conditions."[60] Thus Turkey has developed a very sophisticated analytical scheme for determining the productive use of the water by measuring soil quality, and so forth. Syria and Iraq, not surprisingly, have rejected this scheme and advocate a different formula for sharing the water.

---

58. Republic of Turkey, Ministry of Foreign Affairs, *Water Issues between Turkey, Syria and Iraq* (January 1995), pp. 3–8.

59. Murhaf Jouejati, "Water Politics as High Politics: The Case of Turkey and Syria," in Barkey, *Reluctant Neighbor,* pp. 136–137.

60. Ministry of Foreign Affairs, *Water Issues,* p. 31.

The Syrians have claimed that they also need the Euphrates as a vital resource for hydro-energy, for manufacturing, for drinking water, and for irrigation.[61] The Syrians claim that their needs have not been met because the GAP project has increased Turkey's consumption from 10 percent to 53 percent of the Euphrates, which, they claim, represents 86 percent of their possible water resources. In addition, they claim that the reduced flow of the Euphrates has limited the energy output of their Tabqa dam.[62]

Syria and Iraq, therefore, have demanded a minimum of 700 cubic meters per second of water from the Euphrates and Tigris. Turkey generally releases a monthly average flow of at least 500 cubic meters per second, as agreed under the Protocol of 1987. However, Turkey has also declared that guaranteeing a supply of 700 cubic meters per second of water to Syria and Iraq would reduce Turkey's own supply of Euphrates and Tigris water to only 30 percent of its needs. In addition, Syria and Iraq have voiced their concerns about the increase in pollution to the Euphrates resulting from the use in Turkey of pesticides and fertilizers in the newly irrigated agricultural areas created by the GAP. Turkey, for its part, claims that Syria mismanages its water resources and that the Syrians are inefficient in their use of the Euphrates waters.[63]

Negotiation of the water dispute has been difficult, in part because of the stiff negotiating positions taken by the disputants. Turkey, for example, demanded that negotiations involve both the Euphrates and the Tigris, a position unfavorable to Iraq. Turkey wants the ability to transfer Tigris water to the Euphrates, to compensate for its lower water levels. Moreover, Turkey demanded that any water treaty encompass all the border crossing rivers with Syria, including the Orontes. Syria is the upstream riparian on the Orontes and, according to the Turks, is using some 90 percent of its water exclusively for Syrian needs.[64] The Syrians rejected this demand because the Orontes flows into Alexandretta/Hatay. Because Syria did not recognize Hatay as Turkish, it did not define the Orontes as an international waterway.

The Syrians sought to strengthen their bargaining power and overcome the impasse over the water issues by supporting the PKK. Syria allowed the PKK to maintain training camps in the Bekaa Valley in Lebanon and allowed the PKK leader, Öcalan, to use Damascus as his base.

61. Jouejati, "Water Politics," p. 133.

62. Ibid.

63. Ibid., p. 133.

64. Ministry of Foreign Affairs, *Water Issues*, pp. 13–14.

Syrian Kurds also fought alongside Turkish Kurds.[65] Ultimately becoming frustrated with Damascus's denials of involvement with the PKK, Turkey massed troops at the border in October 1998 and threatened war with Syria. Chastened, Syria expelled Öcalan and ultimately met all of Turkey's demands, by agreeing at Adana to cease its support for the PKK, and even to permit an intelligence presence in the Turkish Embassy in Damascus to monitor Syrian compliance with the agreement.[66]

Syria had previously sought to increase pressure upon Turkey by signing a Defense Cooperation Agreement with Greece in June 1995. However, that move also backfired because it helped stimulate the Israeli cooperation agreements with Turkey, which will be discussed below. Moreover, Syria has been suspected of developing its own WMD. While from Damascus's perspective Syrian WMD might serve as a deterrent to Israeli nuclear capability, from Ankara's perspective they could also become threats to Turkey.[67]

Since the fall of 1998, the neighbors have sought to improve their relations generally. One principal convergence of interests has been in the economic sphere, principally by increasing their cross-border trade, encouraging transportation and energy links, and even tourism.[68] Significantly, as a result of this general amelioration in relations with Turkey, Syria has also indicated an interest in cooperating with Turkey on the improvement of water use techniques.[69] Even though there has been no formal settlement of the water dispute, together with the increase in their trade relations, these improvements in their overall relations raise the hope that Turkey and Syria may develop a sufficient convergence of economic interests to overcome their diverging interests over Hatay and water.

---

65. Mehmet Ali Birand, "Significant Change in PKK Cadres," *Istanbul Sabah,* January 30, 1997, FBIS-WEU-97-022.

66. "Turkey Cautious on PKK Activities in Syria," *Turkish Daily News,* February 4, 2000.

67. See F. Stephen Larrabee and Ian O. Lesser, *Turkish Foreign Policy in an Age of Uncertainty* (Santa Monica: RAND, 2003), p. 146.

68. Trade between Syria and Turkey in 2001–02 reached approximately $1 billion; "Syrian Chief of Staff in Turkey; relations improving," *Turkish Daily News,* June 20, 2002.

69. In August 2002, GOLD, the Syrian Ministry of Irrigation and Land Development Agency, signed an agreement with GAP to cooperate in training, technology exchange, study missions, and joint projects. Yuksel Soylemez, "Frankly Speaking" (an interview with the president of GAP), *Turkish Daily News,* April 17, 2002.

THE ISRAEL DILEMMA

In the 1990s, Turkey's interests in the Middle East began to strongly converge with those of Israel for political, economic, and military-strategic reasons. Earlier, the Turkey-Israel relationship had waxed and waned with the ebb and flow of Middle East international politics and the Arab-Israeli conflict. Thus Turkey was the first Middle Eastern state to recognize Israel diplomatically, in 1949, soon after Israel's creation. After the failure of the Baghdad Pact in 1958, Turkey entered into a secret strategic pact with Israel, which also included Iran and Ethiopia, intending to pose a counterweight to growing Arab nationalism.[70] After the 1967 Arab-Israeli war, Turkey leaned toward the Arab side, and in 1969 started attending the newly formed Organization of Islamic Conference. During the 1970s Turkey attenuated its relations with Israel in favor of building relations with the Arab Middle East to be able to make purchases of oil on credit, and to gain sympathy for Turkey's Cyprus policies.[71] Turkey's pro-Palestinian sympathies led Ankara in 1980 to downgrade its diplomatic relations with Israel. They were not upgraded to full ambassadorial level until January 1992 after the commencement in 1991 of the Middle East peace process at Madrid.[72]

After the peace process got on track with the Oslo accords of 1993, Turkey's military successfully promoted a series of highly publicized cooperation agreements with Israel in 1996 that simultaneously achieved a number of political, economic, and strategic goals.[73] The first major

70. Amikam Nachmani, *Israel, Turkey, and Greece: Uneasy Relations in the Mediterranean* (London: Frank Cass, 1987), pp. 74–76.

71. Mahmut Bali Aykan, "The Palestinian Question in Turkish Foreign Policy from the 1950s to the 1990s," *International Journal of Middle East Studies,* Vol. 25 (February 1993), pp. 94–102.

72. Turkey also upgraded its relations with the Palestinians to full ambassadorial level. Since 1985, both Turkey and Israel had assigned high-ranking diplomats to maintain these relations informally. Meliha Benli Altunışik, "Turkish Policy toward Israel," in Alan Makovsky and Sabri Sayari, eds., *Turkey's New World: Changing Dynamics in Turkish Foreign Policy* (Washington, D.C.: The Washington Institute for Near East Policy, 2000), p. 60.

73. Prior to 1996, Turkish officials had concluded a number of agreements with Israel, including a Memorandum on Mutual Understanding and Guidelines on Cooperation (November 1993), an agreement on cooperation on international terrorism and crime, a trilateral agreement with the United States on Central Asia, as well as the initialing of an agreement to upgrade Turkey's F-4 fighters (September 1995). Alan Makovsky, "Israeli-Turkish Relations: A Turkish 'Periphery Strategy,'" in Barkey, *Reluctant Neighbor,* pp. 162–64. See also Carol Migdalovitz, "Unprecedented Ties," *Turkistan Newsletter,* Vol. 98, No. 2 (September 23, 1998), pp. 155 et seq.

agreement in February 1996 was for the exchange of military information and joint military training, including personnel exchanges, joint military academy programs, naval access to the ports of both countries, and Israeli air force training flights from Turkish air bases over Turkish territory. In the next month, the two states also signed a free trade agreement. There followed an agreement in April 1996 concerning cooperation in upgrading of weapons and in defense contracts, involving military intelligence equipment, tanks, and Turkey's F4 and F5 fighter planes, as well as an agreement in August 1996 on the co-production of surface to air missiles.[74] Since that time there have been additional agreements on Israeli upgrading of Turkish weaponry and proposed cooperation in the development of a missile shield using the Israeli Arrow, although U.S. approval would be required for Israel to share the Arrow technology with Turkey to enable the project to move forward.[75]

The 1996 agreements had both internal and external political implications for Turkey. Internally, the increasing cooperation with Israel was a signal to the Islamist-led coalition government in Ankara at a time when the Turkish military establishment would not tolerate Welfare Party attempts to create foreign policy alignments with other Islamist governments in the Middle East.[76] Externally, the agreements assisted Ankara by including Turkish interests in Israel's lobbying efforts in Washington to offset the anti-Turkish lobbies of Greeks, Armenians, and Kurds.[77]

---

74. Judy Dempsey, "Forces that Forge Israel-Turkey Ties," *Financial Times,* January 2, 1998, p. 2; Metahin Demir, "Truths Are Hidden between the News Lines," *Turkish Probe,* January 11, 1998, pp. 2–3. Subsequently, the two states agreed to co-produce Popeye II air-to-ground missiles, and have discussed the co-production of other weapons. Altunışık, "Turkish Policy toward Israel," p. 67.

75. "Israel Proposes to Turkey to Take Part in Missile Defense Shield," *Turkish Daily News,* July 10, 2001; "Turkey-Israel Hold Security Meetings," *Israel Line,* February 28, 2002. See also Efraim Inbar, "The Strategic Glue in the Israeli-Turkish Alignment," in Rubin and Kirişci, *Turkey in World Politics,* pp. 156–159. Turkish-Israeli cooperation in weapons production has complicated their individual and joint relations with the United States. For example, Turkey has bowed to pressure from the United States and has cancelled some military procurement contracts with Israel in order to permit U.S. companies to compete for them. "Israeli Companies' Concerns over Defense Tenders Grow," *Turkish Daily News,* August 16, 2000, FBIS-NES-2000-0831. Turkey has limited Israeli training flights from its borders. In contrast, the trilateral naval exercises scheduled for November 2000 were only deferred for two months because of the Palestinian intifada, and were not cancelled. *Israel Line,* January 17, 2001.

76. See M. Hakan Yavuz, "Turkish-Israeli Relations through the Lens of the Turkish Identity Debate," *Journal of Palestinian Studies,* Vol. 27, No. 1 (Autumn 1997), pp. 22–37.

77. For example, the Israel lobby assisted in the defeat of an Armenian genocide resolution in the U.S. House of Representatives in 2000. Sedat Sertoglu, "Behind the Scenes," *Istanbul Sabah* (Ankara Edition), October 23, 2000, FBIS-SOV-2000-1024.

Turkey was also smarting from rejection of its candidacy to the EU and U.S. criticisms of Turkey's human rights policies, and the friendship with Israel offered some political consolation that Turkey would not be completely isolated in the Western-oriented world. From its perspective, Israel hoped to benefit politically by its alignment with a predominantly Muslim state.

Economically, the Turkish-Israeli relationship enabled Turkey to boost its trade with Israel, much to Turkey's benefit.[78] Turkish exports to Israel have increased and substantial numbers of Israelis have visited Turkey as tourists. Israel has benefited in addition by expanding its markets for defense weaponry and gaining access to markets in Turkic Central Asia. Israeli companies, for example, have offered funding for joint projects with Turkish businesses in Kyrgyzstan, Azerbaijan, and Uzbekistan.[79] Israeli companies have been awarded contracts to finance and build irrigation works for the GAP project.[80] In addition, Israel has expressed an interest in purchasing water from Turkey's Manavgat River.[81] Another significant benefit for Turkey from the expanded economic relationship with Israel has been the promise of greater Turkish access to the U.S. markets. Turkish goods that are exported to Israel can be re-exported to the United States after adding 35 percent value to the goods, thereby exceeding the normal U.S. quota for Turkish products.[82]

Strategically, the military linkages of the two states sent a significant signal to their potential Middle Eastern adversaries, Syria, Iraq, and Iran, as well as to Greece. Indeed, from the Turkish perspective, the military cooperation with Israel was first intended as a deterrent to closer Greek

---

78. Turkish trade with Israel just about tripled, from approximately $450 million in 1996 to over $1.2 billion in 2002; <www.foreigntrade.gov.tr/ENGLISH/EU/customs.htm> (1996 figures); <www.die.gov.tr/ENGLISH/SONIST/DISTICIST/28010306.gif> (figures for first eleven months of 2002).

79. "Israel Offers to Find Funds for Joint Projects in Central Asia," *Turkish Daily News,* May 25, 1999.

80. "AA Details Foreign Financing for GAP Project," *Ankara Anatolia,* October 10, 1999, FBIS-WEU-1999-1010 (GAP contract).

81. Negotiations of the projected sale of Manavgat water to Israel have dragged on, with the slowdown ascribed variously to the Israeli desalination lobby complaining about the higher cost of Turkish water and uncertainty as to the receptivity of the Turkish AKP, with its Islamic roots, to signing a deal with the Sharon government. Ozgur Eksi, "Manavgat Still Tests Turkish-Israeli relations," *Turkish Probe,* November 10, 2002. See also Haggai Merom, "Delay in Turkish Water Imports Could Harm Defense Industries," *Globes* (Israel), January 31, 2002

82. John Barham, "Turkey, Israel to Scrap Barriers," *Financial Times,* March 12, 1996, p. 4.

and Syrian relations concluded in 1995.[83] Allowing Israeli planes to fly training missions from Turkish air bases brought Israeli aircraft reconnaissance and striking capability much closer to its adversaries' borders. Cooperation by the two states with what was viewed as superior conventional forces in the region also made Syria vulnerable to threats from opposite fronts and may have contributed to Syria's willingness to enter into the Adana agreement.

In addition, cooperation in defense gave the Turkish military a source other than the United States and Europe for rebuilding its conventional forces. This is significant in the light of the 1997 plan of the Turkish military to update its weaponry at a cost of $150 billion over 25 years.[84] In the United States, anti-Turkish lobbies have interfered with the sales and deliveries of U.S. weaponry to Ankara;[85] and in Europe similar interference has arisen from anti-Turkish lobbies protesting Turkey's human rights violations.[86]

There were disavowals in Ankara and Jerusalem of any hostile intentions toward their neighbors. For example, Israel declared that it was scaling down its military activities at the Syrian border during the Syrian-Turkish crisis in the fall of 1998 to avoid the perception that Israel and Turkey were acting in concert.[87] In general, however, the Turkish-Israeli cooperation agreements stimulated not only denunciations by the Arab states and Iran, but also reformulation of inter-Arab alignments.[88] Fur-

83. Hasan Unal, "Greek Front in Turkey's Relations with Israel," *Istanbul Zaman*, April 18, 1997, FBIS-WEU-97-111; Altunışik, "Turkish Policy toward Israel," p. 64.

84. Metehan Demir, "Turkey Takes Steps for Self-Sufficient Defense Industry in 21st Century," *Turkish Probe*, January 25, 1998, p. 4.

85. See Morton Abramowitz, "The Complexities of American Policymaking on Turkey," in Abramowitz, *Turkey's Transformation*, pp. 153–184. By contrast, U.S. administrations have tried to resist such interference because of the strategic value Turkey has represented to U.S. interests in the Middle East and because Turkey's military cooperation with Israel provides a strategic benefit to the United States. It was believed that such cooperation increases the ability of the United States to respond to Middle East crises that affect U.S. interests, enhanced by coordinated weaponry and planning, as demonstrated by their trilateral military maneuvers in 1998 and 1999. Lesser, "Turkey and the United States"; Alan Makovsky, "U.S. Policy toward Turkey: Progress and Problems," in Abramowitz, *Turkey's Transformation*, pp. 236–237.

86. Altunışik, "Turkish Policy toward Israel," p. 66.

87. Douglas Jehl, "Mubarak Visits Syria in Effort to Defuse Crisis with Turkey," *New York Times*, October 5, 1998.

88. Saudi Arabia denounced the close Israel-Turkey cooperation; FBIS-NES-97-141, May 21, 1997. Syria and Iraq entered into discussions to improve their relations. "Saddam Urges Security Leaders to be Alert, Confirms Positiveness of Relations with Syria and Jordan," *Al-Quds al-'Arabi*, January 6, 1997, FBIS-NES-97-004; "Iraq: Syrian

thermore, Egypt and Syria revived their interest in obtaining Russian arms supplies; Greece and Egypt also joined forces in military training exercises; Syria and Iraq took steps to restore relations by opening up their borders to trade and reopening the Iraqi pipeline Syria had closed during the Iraq-Iran war in 1982; and even Iran and Iraq attempted to resolve the differences they had left open after the end of the 1980–88 war.[89]

The closer its relationship with Israel, the more difficult it becomes for Turkey to resolve its dilemmas with its other Middle Eastern neighbors, such as Iran and Syria, all of whom are relatively hostile to Israel. Furthermore, Turkey's Muslim population has been disturbed by the Israeli occupation of the West Bank and Gaza. Hence, Turkey has also sought ways to distance itself from Israel's heavy-handed response to the new intifada and take a role in ameliorating Israeli-Palestinian relations.[90] In addition, both Turkey and Israel have been concerned to bridge their relations with Greece, in part to decrease the possibility that Greece would align with Arab countries to counterbalance a strong Turkey-Israel alignment, as it did in the mid-1990s. One opportunity for Turkey to improve relations with Greece developed after the disastrous earthquake in 1999 in which Greece provided assistance, and there was a softening of anti-Turkish attitudes in Athens. Israel also repaired its relations with Greece by renewing their 1994 Memorandum of Understanding and Friendship, and by discussing improvements in its defense relations with Greece.

It remains to be seen, however, whether the Islamist AKP government will seek to maintain Turkey's close relations with Israel in the face

---

Businessmen Seek 'Strong Cooperation' with Iraq," *Republic of Iraq Radio Network,* May 20, 1997, FBIS-NES-97-138. Iran and Syria went further, entering into discussion of a defense agreement; Jihad Salim, "Report on Syrian-Iranian Ties, 'Defense Pact'," *Paris al-Watan al-'Arabi,* March 28, 1997, FBIS-NES-97-064. Egypt has denounced the Israel-Turkish relationship and attempted to wean Turkey from it. "Egypt's Musa on Peace Tracks, Arab Ties with Turkey," Cairo MENA, December 12, 1998, FBIS-NES-98-346. On the other hand, Makovsky, "New Activism," p. 12, says that Kuwait and the U.A.E. received ships from Turkey during U.S.-Israeli-Turkish naval exercises in January 1998.

89.   "Russian Arms Deal Might Escalate Syria-Turkey Tension," *Al-Quds al-'Arabi,* December 4, 1998, FBIS-NES-98-338 (Russia-Syria); "Egypt Joins Greece to Counter Israeli-Turkish Bloc—At Russia Prompting?" *Global Intelligence Update;* <www.stratfor. com/service/qiu/112598.asp>, November 25, 1998 (Greece-Egypt); "U.S. Probing Reports of Syria's Importing Iraqi Oil," *Turkish Daily News,* January 25, 2001 (Syria-Iraq); "Iraq and Iran reach accords," *Turkish Daily News,* October 16, 2000 (Iran-Iraq).

90.   For example, former President Demirel has been appointed to the commission investigating the 2000 Israeli-Palestinian violence; "Demirel Likely to Be on the Middle East Committee," *Turkish Daily News,* November 2, 2000.

of the political repercussions of the intifada that began in 2000 and the Israeli responses to it. However, if the AKP were to attenuate Turkey's relationship with Israel, it would add strains to its relationship with the Turkish military.

THE GCC STATES DILEMMA

The GCC states are a good source of energy for Turkey, and to that extent they have converging economic interests. Certainly, during the Gulf crisis of 1990–91, there were also converging political and military interests, which Saudi Arabia and Kuwait recognized by compensating Turkey for some of its wartime losses with one billion dollars each of oil.[91] Furthermore, the GCC pledged $400 million in loans to help Turkey rebuild after the 1999 earthquake.[92] The smaller GCC states of Kuwait, Oman, Qatar, and the U.A.E. have been receptive to promoting better economic relations with Turkey by the formation of joint economic commissions, and U.A.E. fighter pilots have trained in Turkey.[93]

Although there was some commonality of concern over the looming U.S. invasion of Iraq expressed at a meeting in January 2003 coordinated by Turkey that included the Saudis, as well as Egypt, Jordan, Iran, and Syria, Turkey and the GCC states may develop differing visions of the future of Iraq after the invasion.[94] The GCC states themselves may be divided on their support for the continuation of the U.S. presence in Iraq and the degree of risk they face from the potential backlash this could cause in their societies. The Saudis may have differing views as to that risk compared to the other GCC states, all of whom host U.S. military forces in the Gulf.[95] Nonetheless, if U.S. forces withdrew from Iraq and

---

91. Interview with Ambassador Turkekul Kurttekin, director-general of the Turkish foreign ministry, June 1999. Turkey does import some oil from Saudi Arabia, although their trade relations decreased from approximately $2.1 billion in 1992 to approximately $1 billion in 1999. "Turkey, Saudi Target $2 billion in trade," *Turkish Daily News,* May 24, 2000.

92. "Turkey to Get $25 Million in Kuwait Soft Loan," *Turkish Daily News,* September 17, 2002.

93. "Kuwaiti Industry Minister Arrives in Ankara," *Ankara Anatolia,* March 20, 2002, FBIS-NES-2002-0320; "Omani Minister Calls on Kececiler, Departs," *Ankara Anatolia,* July 3, 2001, FBIS-WEU-2001-0703; "Tuzmen Returns from UAE," *Ankara Anatolia,* December 22, 2002, FBIS-NES-2002-1222; "UAE Pilots Given F-16 Flight Training," *Ankara Anatolia,* February 6, 2002, FBIS-WEU-2002-0206.

94. Michael Wines, "6 Neighbors Call on Iraq to Obey U.N. on Weapons," *New York Times,* January 24, 2003, p. A8.

95. In response to those risks, the United States has agreed to withdraw most of its

civil war ensued, there would be a substantial dilemma for the GCC states who would not welcome the prospect of an autonomous Shiite state at their borders with potential irredentist appeals to the Shiites in Bahrain and the Eastern Province of Saudi Arabia. Nor would the GCC states welcome the prospect of a Turkish takeover of Mosul and its ideological implications for the reassertion of Turkish imperialism.

Even without the prospect of civil war in Iraq, there are ideological barriers to close relations of the GCC states with Turkey. The Republic is an avowedly secular Muslim nation and an ideological anti-model for the Gulf autocracies whose legitimacy is tied to both religious and monarchist principles. While it may, therefore, be strategically advantageous for the GCC states to align with their stronger neighbor to the north, it is ideologically difficult for them to do so.[96] Still, the accession to power in 2002 of the AKP may help overcome those difficulties. Also, the ongoing challenges in the Gulf region have increased the awareness of the GCC states of the need for regional cooperation and support. This might lead to more Turkish-Gulf state strategic cooperation in the future.

Future Policy Implications: Resolving the Dilemmas

This analysis of the dilemmas in each of Turkey's bilateral relations with the major Middle East actors makes it clear that Turkey's activism in the region calls for complex decision-making in the formulation of any Middle East foreign policy. What steps should its policymakers therefore consider taking that would facilitate the resolution of current and future dilemmas?

One significant step would be to reduce Turkey's vulnerability to a recrudescence of Kurdish ethnic dissension by implementing the sensible policies to permit Kurdish cultural identity within the Turkish political community that Turkey passed in 2002 and 2003, and to stimulate economic development in Southeast Anatolia.[97] Without that, any one or more of Turkey's neighbors, Syria, Iran, or even a reunited Iraq, could be

---

forces from the kingdom; Eric Schmitt, "U.S. to Withdraw all Combat Units from Saudi Arabia," *New York Times*, April 30, 2003, pp. 1, A14.

96. In interviews in Turkey and Arab states one also encounters expression of the historic mistrust between Arabs and Turks that could impede the development of friendly relations with the GCC states. There was a flare-up of this animosity in Turkey over the Saudi destruction of an Ottoman castle in Mecca in 2001; "Culture Minister Says Turkey No Longer Views Ties with Riyadh Friendly," *Turkish Daily News*, January 10, 2002.

97. See Kirişci, "Kurdish Question"; Robins, "Turkey and the Kurds."

tempted to assist the dissension in order to obtain bargaining advantages in dealing with Turkey. Furthermore, removing the causes for dissension among Turkey's Kurds will assist in resolving Turkey's prime Iraq dilemma in relation to the Iraqi Kurds. A more secure Turkey may be able to live with some measures of greater local autonomy for Iraqi Kurds within the framework of a federated Iraq, if that is the ultimate form of an Iraqi political system.

Another step would be to take advantage of the reduction of tension in Turkey's relations with Syria by seeking long-term resolutions of the issues surrounding Turkey's control over the Euphrates and Tigris. International water issues are amenable to resolution.[98] One immediate benefit for Turkey would be to increase the possibility of international fi- nancial assistance for the completion of the GAP project; a longer-term benefit would be to enable negotiation of water and gas pipelines through Syria to increase Turkish water exports to the water-starved Middle East and to import gas from Egypt. Furthermore, together with the improvement of their general economic relations, Syria's claims to Hatay/Alexandretta might be so significantly reduced that the two neighbors could develop joint economic projects in that border region.[99]

A third step would be to improve Turkey's relations with the GCC states. This would help counterbalance the adverse Arab reactions to the alignment with Israel, encourage GCC investments in the Turkish economy along with other international investments that it seeks, and lay the groundwork for discussions of more strategic cooperation that may be necessary in the uncertain future of this unstable region. While it will by no means be easy to overcome decades of ideological mistrust, improvement of relations would certainly be worthwhile for Turkey, which could benefit from more assured sources of petroleum products, which the GCC states could supply.

There may also be steps that Turkey could take in concert with its Middle East neighbors that would further enhance their bilateral rela-

---

98. There are signs that Syrian-Turkish cooperation, at least at lower bureaucratic levels and with small steps, may be possible on this issue. For one approach to resolving such issues, see the proposals for monetizing the Israel-Syria water dispute in Hillel I. Shuval, "Water and Security in the Middle East: The Israeli-Syrian Water Confrontations as a Case Study," in Martin, ed., *New Frontiers*, pp. 183–213.

99. Sencer Ayata's interviews with Turkish businessmen suggest that there is a strong interest in using Syria's cross-border labor pool to enhance Turkish industrial production, such as textiles. Ayata, "Changes in Domestic Politics." There have also been references in the Turkish press to some Syrian maps that include Hatay in Turkey; "Turkey, Syria Sign Protocol: Official Notes Change in Syrian Policy on Hatay," *Ankara Anatolia*, January 14, 2003, FBIS-NES-2003-0114.

tions. For example, the common interest shared by Iran, Syria, and Turkey in opposing the establishment of an autonomous Kurdistan in northern Iraq lends itself to such concerted action.[100]

Conclusions

The fundamental dilemma for Turkish foreign policy in the Middle East arises on the one hand from the multidimensional risks to Turkey's national security that require it to remain actively involved in the region in order to protect its interests. In this Turkey shares a convergence of strategic interests with its long-standing ally, the United States, and a newer friend, Israel. On the other hand, the inherent instability of Middle East international politics encourages Turkey to balance its interests in countering threats to its national security emanating from the region with maintaining good economic and diplomatic relations with its neighbors, some of whom consider the United States and Israel to be adverse to their own interests. Foreign policymaking in the face of this fundamental dilemma is unlikely to become any less complex in the foreseeable future. Indeed, in pursing its accession to the EU, Turkey has found that its potential European partners are quite ready to demand that Turkey adopt policies that diverge to some degree from the interests of the United States in the Middle East or that attenuate its military cooperation with Israel. Or, Turkey and the United States may develop different visions for the future of Iraq. In addition, there may or may not be final solutions for the Israeli-Palestinian conflict. Both sides of the conflict and their respective allies may pressure Turkey to align more with one camp or the other.

Taking the policy steps of permitting Kurdish cultural identity to be freely expressed in Turkey, resolving remaining differences with Syria, and improving relations with the GCC states will not resolve these future dilemmas. However, they will give Turkey more flexibility in fashioning the complex solutions that its future foreign policymaking in the Middle East will require.

---

100. See Chazan, "Turkey Strengthens Ties with Two U.S. Adversaries," for a report of such concerted actions following the U.S. invasion of Iraq. Similarly, there was concerted action by Turkey, Iran, Saudi Arabia, Kuwait, Egypt, Bahrain, and Jordan to urge the United States and its coalition to quickly stabilize Iraq and withdraw. Sarah Kershaw, "Iraq's Neighbors Issue Declaration Criticizing U.S. Over Syria," *New York Times,* April 19, 2003, p. B6.

Chapter 10

Water and Turkish Foreign Policy

İlter Turan

Long-term observers of Turkish foreign policy and its major concerns did not identify water as a major policy concern until the last two decades. In contrast to Syria and Iraq, its neighbors to the south, Turkey had not used its water resources extensively. This has changed only in recent years, to the extent that, if not water itself, problems that are seen to derive from the utilization of "transboundary" waters have come to occupy a somewhat prominent place on the Turkish foreign policy agenda. The issue of water as a foreign policy concern is the product of changes that gained momentum as the Turkish economy experienced significant growth and became an industrial economy integrated into the world economic system.

The Growth of Demand for Water Utilization

Unlike Syria and Iraq, both of which have histories of irrigated farming, Turkey has not historically used its water potential extensively either for irrigation or for power generation. Such use was not totally lacking, but Turkey's agriculture was typically characterized by dry rather than irrigated farming. Furthermore, the limited amount of irrigated farming that existed was in regions where the water came from sources originating and ending in Turkey. Power generation, in contrast, needed until the 1950s mainly to meet the modest needs of major urban centers, relied on imported fossil fuels and not water.

I would like to thank Gün Kut for helpful remarks on an earlier version of this paper.

The process leading to Turkey's more extensive utilization of its water resources began in the 1950s. After the end of the Second World War, Turkey joined the Western Bloc. With funds from the United States and international agencies, a process of economic development was started, which, at the beginning, took the form of realizing major infrastructural investments. The primary infrastructural activity characterizing the 1950s was the building of a national highway network. Shortly afterward, however, the institutional framework within which water resources would be utilized was also expanded.

It appears that Turkey had envisioned the utilization of its water resources for the generation of power as early as a decade after the founding of the Republic in 1923. In 1935, an independent agency—the Electrical Resources Survey and Development Administration (EIEI)—was created; one of its tasks was to survey water resources in the country with a view to identifying those that were suitable for production of electricity.[1] By 1936, the first measurement station was in operation on the Euphrates to study its flow patterns. Other such stations were added during the 1940s. A nationwide observation station system had been established by 1962.[2]

The establishment of the General Directorate of State Hydraulic Works (DSI) in 1953, whose explicit mission involved the construction of dams for power generation and irrigation,[3] reinforced this modest beginning. The DSI has been the driving force in the development and utilization of Turkey's water resources from its very beginning. To illustrate the growing importance Turkey attached to water utilization and the role the DSI has played in its achievement, it is important to remember that until 1950, in addition to a few small reservoirs built for the collection of water for cities,[4] Turkey possessed a grand total of 3 dams with extremely modest irrigation or power generation capabilities. Six more dams were built during the 1950s. Then came the explosion in numbers with the construc-

1. Law no. 2819, June 14, 1935.

2. Mehmetçik Bayazıt and İlhan Avcı, "Water Resources of Turkey: Potential, Planning, Development and Management," *International Journal of Water Resources Development*, Vol. 13, No. 4 (December 1997), p. 447.

3. Law no. 6200, December 18, 1953.

4. John F. Kolars and William A. Mitchell report that only nine dams were built in Turkey prior to the republican era. These were all located near Istanbul and were mainly reservoirs that supplied the city with fresh water. John F. Kolars and William A. Mitchell, *The Euphrates River and the Southeast Anatolia Development Project* (Carbondale, Ill.: Southern Illinois University Press, 1991), p. 9.

tion of twenty-six dams in 1960–69, thirty-one in 1970–79, and sixty-nine in 1980–89. Another 37 dams were added to the total during 1990–97.[5]

The first major dam to be constructed as Turkey commenced on its path of infrastructural development was the Seyhan Dam, completed in 1956.[6] This dam was built with external support at a time when Turkey had not yet formulated clear-cut policies on water utilization or developed capabilities to undertake the construction of major dam projects. With U.S. support, a dual-purpose dam was completed, providing power for the Adana industrial region and irrigation water for the fertile fields of the Cilician plains. This particular area had a tradition of commercial cotton farming dating back to the middle of the nineteenth century. The cotton produced there had supplied the mills of Manchester and other textile centers in Britain. Irrigation water was welcome. The availability of power also encouraged investments in textile production.

Initial Precedence of Hydroelectric Power Generation

The temporary military takeover in 1960 proved to be a critical moment for policies on water utilization. The military leaders were representatives of the modernizing bureaucratic tradition. These men understood development to mean almost exclusively industrialization; their nationalism gave them an autarkic bent in the policies they followed, while their bureaucratic background made them value economic planning. Quickly, a State Planning Organization was established to guide the economy in the direction of rapid industrialization. Reflecting the mindset of its designers, the principle of economic self-sufficiency would give direction to this effort at planned industrial development. Hence an import substitution strategy was adopted and pursued.

In the preparation of the first five-year development plan, in order to reduce dependence on the outside world, a decision was made to emphasize the utilization of domestic sources for the generation of power.[7] In the second five-year development plan, priority was to be given to the

---

5. I have calculated the numbers from the table listing all the dams and hydroelectric power plants in operation in Turkey at the beginning of 1996 supplied in the desk diary *Ajanda 1997*, published and distributed by the DSI, the General Directorate of State Hydraulics Works.

6. Ibid. The dam was to produce 54 megawatts of power and irrigate 174,000 hectares.

7. Devlet Planlama Teşkilati, *Birinci Beş Yıllık Kalkınma Planı, 1963–1967* (Ankara, 1964), p. 375.

development of hydroelectric sources and sizable investments in that field were promised.[8] Subsequent development plans have all made references to increasing energy production, emphasizing the development of hydroelectric sources as a primary goal. Although it is uncertain how the figure was arrived at, from the first five-year plan onward it has been generally accepted that roughly 40 percent of the country's total energy output should come from hydroelectricity, with the remainder from other sources, mainly fossil fuel. The figure was closely adhered to until the mid-1980s.

The natural outcome of the emphasis on hydroelectric power generation was the initiation of a period of dam construction that has continued to this day. It is interesting that many of the earlier larger dams were built almost exclusively for the generation of power rather than for serving the added purpose of providing irrigation. A classic case is the Keban Dam, completed in 1975, which nearly doubled the electricity produced in Turkey at the time. With a dam that stored such large amounts of water in a region where irrigation would clearly enhance agricultural production, it is surprising that no irrigation was initially envisioned and implemented.[9] This neglect of the irrigation potential of Turkey's rivers derived from a variety of sources, including the high cost of developing irrigation systems, the lack of sufficient funding, the preference of the DSI for building hydroelectric dams, and the pressing need for industrial energy. But prominent among these reasons, and probably above them all, was that Turkey's political leaders and voters alike were fascinated with industrialization while agriculture failed to capture their fancy. Furthermore, Turkey appeared to be reasonably self sufficient in foodstuffs while its lack of sufficient industrial production was all too evident.

The Rising Importance of Irrigation

Turkey first turned to implementing irrigation in those parts of the country that had a long tradition of highly commercialized agriculture. In addition to the Cilician plains, irrigation projects were carried out in the Antalya region as well near Izmir and Aydin. However, hydroelectric power was the overriding priority in the earlier stages of Turkish eco-

---

8. Devlet Planlama Teşkilati, *İkinci Beş Yıllık Kalkınma Planı, 1968–1972* (Ankara, 1970), pp. 558–559.

9. The *Ajanda* published by the DSI does not cite any area that has come under irrigation by the Keban Dam. There is actually some limited irrigation in the region, but since the DSI has not built the irrigation system, it does not appear in its records.

nomic development. This gradually began to change during the 1970s, for the following interrelated reasons.

First, beginning after the Second World War, Turkey had begun to experience a rather rapid population growth, which brought with it a number of outcomes and needs. To begin with the more obvious, a growing population meant a growing demand for foodstuffs. Most land that could be put to agricultural use had already been brought under cultivation during the 1950s. During the 1960s, increases in agricultural yield could only be achieved by increasing productivity. The introduction of irrigated farming appeared to be a natural way of enhancing production. The importance of increasing food production was driven home particularly during the 1970s when Turkey experienced severe shortages of hard currency and found it difficult to meet a growing bill for food including such basics as wheat and vegetable oils.

Second, the import substitution–oriented industrialization led to the conversions in land use where prime agricultural land was often taken over by industrial users. This loss of land (for example, Adana, Bursa, Adapazari, Izmir) meant that other equally productive land had to be brought into use. Provided that this land could be irrigated, it would be possible to compensate for the land that went out of agricultural use.

Third, as Turkey progressed along the road of industrialization, the demands for raw materials used in industry increased. Some of the most impressive growth was registered in textiles, leather goods, and processed foods, all of which had mainly agricultural components. A growing industry influenced agricultural activity in multiple dimensions. One dimension was the sheer increase in need. Another was the need to be more independent of climatic conditions. A third dimension was the requirement that the products be of standard quality. Success in these areas would clearly be facilitated by the expansion of irrigated farming and the ensuing commercialization of agriculture. The introduction of irrigation would promote higher levels of productivity, render production more reliable, and help to standardize the products.

Fourth, the growing market orientation of the Turkish economy and its integration into the world economy after the economic reforms of 1980–83 enhanced the relevance of economic rationales in the planning of investments. For example, the DSI began to give greater weight in its feasibility studies to such concepts as the value added by a particular type of crop or method of agriculture.[10] With the shift in the mode of thinking

---

10. D. Ali Çelik, "Kamu Yatirimlarinin Proje Analizinde Ekonomik Değerlerin Bulunması," in *Su ve Toprak Kaynaklarinin Geliştirilmesi Konferansı Bildirileri,* vol. 1 (An-

from the technical to the economic, irrigation became more important in the minds of the bureaucrats traditionally involved in the making of water policy, mainly in the DSI, but also in other government departments.

Fifth, the rapid growth of population was accompanied by a number of socioeconomic and political pathologies, for which the expansion of irrigated farming was perceived as a cure. From the late 1950s on, many Turkish cities were primary targets for migrants from the countryside in search of gainful employment. The farming areas were unable to support the excess population without changes that would increase the rural need for manpower. Because it reduces the amount of land per unit of labor, and therefore generates employment opportunities for peasants, irrigated farming was favored more and more by successive governments. Briefly, irrigation was seen to generate two outcomes that the Turkish national policymakers find particularly attractive: the expansion of work opportunities in the countryside, and the arrest of substantial population moves toward the cities.[11]

The national government attributed much of the social unrest in Turkey, partly in the east but mainly in the southeast, to the substantial economic disparities between these and other regions of the country. Policymakers have come to believe that major irrigation projects would be key, both to reversing the migration from these regions to the west of the country and to terminating the terrorist movement that kept the Turkish security forces occupied from the mid-1980s until 2000. Policymakers also appear to believe that terror has fed on poverty and unemployment—two related phenomena that major irrigation projects would be highly capable of addressing.

The attraction of irrigated farming as a panacea for dispelling the social and political pathologies originating in rapid population growth has intensified in recent years as those pathologies have come to be felt more closely in Turkish society. Governments have been under ever

---

kara: Bayındırlık ve İskan Bakanlığı, Devlet Su İşleri Genel Müdürlüğü, 1994), pp. 157–168.

11. The socioeconomic expectations tied with integrated regional planning in which dam construction and irrigation are given a primary role are best expressed in documents describing the Güneydoğu Anadolu Projesi (GAP). See Republic of Turkey, Prime Ministry, State Planning Organization, GAP Master Plan, *The Southeastern Anatolia Project, Master Plan Study, Final Master Plan Report, Executive Summary* (Ankara: April, 1989). See also Olcay Ünver, "Southeastern Anatolian Project (GAP)," *International Journal of Water Resources Development*, Vol. 13, No. 4 (December 1997), p. 454 and passim.

growing pressure to address and solve problems. Introducing irrigation has come to be seen, by the politicians and the public alike, as a concrete and convincing way of coping with both a national and a regional problem.

There has been a slow but consistent process in Turkish society, a process that began with the increase in the rate of population growth after the Second World War, which has culminated in the adoption of policies favoring the widespread use of irrigated farming in Turkey in general, and the southeastern region in particular.

Water Becomes a Foreign Policy Concern

Most of Turkey's rivers arise within Turkey and reach the sea without crossing borders. This geographical reality has led both the policymakers and the general public to view all of Turkey's rivers as being national waters irrespective of whether they cross borders. Turkey's plans to develop and exploit its water resources, devised by the DSI, have been made with this assumption. Since the rivers on which the earlier dams were built were those that did not cross boundaries, the assumption that all rivers originating in Turkey are in fact national did not initially give rise to international challenges.

The assumption met its first serious challenge when Turkey announced plans to build the Keban Dam on the Euphrates. This was a considerably larger project than the dams Turkey had previously built. Upon completion, it would nearly double the total power generated in the country. To proceed with its construction, major external funding would be needed. It was thought that financial help for the project could be secured from international agencies that usually supported infrastructural investments in the developing regions of the world, and Turkey duly turned to the World Bank and the U.S. Agency for International Development (USAID) to obtain the long-term credits.

The response of the World Bank to the Turkish request included a dimension to which the Turkish government, or more specifically the DSI, had paid scant attention in its earlier projects. Starting as early as 1950, the bank had developed a set of policy guidelines about the construction of dams that it was being asked to finance. If a dam were to be situated on a river involving more than one state, the bank would work to establish a balance between the water rights of all riparians and the benefits to be derived from the realization of the new project. By the mid-1960s, the bank staff was being instructed to consider the international dimensions of the projects they were asked to evaluate, with a view to ensuring that all riparians would be able to agree among themselves on the utilization of the waters of a river.[12]

Turkey did manage to secure a loan from USAID to finance the construction of the Keban Dam. In getting the loan, Turkey agreed to submit a program to the creditors assuring that a certain amount of water would be released to the downstream countries. The specific assurances the Turkish government extended to USAID have not been publicly confirmed. Private but reliable accounts suggest that Turkey may have agreed to release annually an average of 350 cubic meters per second (approximately 11 billion cubic meters per annum).[13] It is also suggested that when the question of financing the construction of the Karakaya Dam was broached with the World Bank, Turkey made a commitment to release annually an average of 500 cubic meters per second (approximately 16 billion cubic meters per annum),[14] to allay fears that Syria would be left with insufficient water. This was a state of affairs that would clearly escalate tensions between Syria and Turkey.

In 1983, Turkey commenced the construction of the Atatürk Dam on the Euphrates, the fifth largest earth dam in the world. The Atatürk Dam was part of a grand regional development project named the Southeastern Anatolia Project, often referred to by its Turkish acronym as the GAP (Güneydoğu Anadolu Projesi). The overall project aims to substantially increase national agricultural output by opening the plains of the southeast region, most notably the Harran Plain (that is, the northern tip of Mesopotamia), to irrigation. The project comprises a string of dams and irrigation projects on the Tigris and the Euphrates; some are already completed while others are under construction or have the status of future projects.[15]

When the GAP is completed, it is anticipated that the region will offer extensive opportunities for employment not only in agriculture but also

---

12. This paragraph is mainly a summary of Gün Kut, "Burning Waters: The Hydropolitics of the Euphrates and Tigris," *New Perspectives on Turkey*, No. 9 (Fall 1993), p. 4.

13. Özden Bilen, *Ortadoğu Su Sorunlari ve Türkiye* (Ankara: TESAV, 1996), p. 87. In an interview conducted by the author on March 31, 1992, a former minister of energy and natural resources who was working with the EIEI at the time the Keban Dam was to be built remembered: "During the construction of Keban, ICA (AID) confronted us as if it were Syria's attorney. The agency argued that Syria needed 18 billion cubic meters of water annually."

14. Bilen, *Ortadoğu*, p. 89. Bilen notes that the 350 cubic meters was not the product of an agreement but a unilateral declaration.

15. Ünver, "Southeastern Anatolian Project," pp. 462–463; Kolars and Mitchell, *The Euphrates River*, pp. 46–76.

in the industry and commerce such agricultural development is bound to generate. The region will no longer be a net exporter of population to the western regions of the country but one that draws labor and capital from all over Turkey, as well as from outside the country. Increased productivity and the accompanying economic growth, it is hoped, will render the area more prosperous and reduce the income disparities between this region and the western parts of Turkey. This, in turn, is expected to enhance the multiple linkages between the region and the rest of the country, and contribute to the enhancement of regional social and political tranquility.

Although the GAP had been in existence prior to the construction of the Atatürk Dam, it was viewed with only modest alarm by Turkey's neighbors in the Tigris-Euphrates Basin, namely Syria and Iraq. It appears that these countries judged that Turkey could not realize the project and particularly its flagship, the Atatürk Dam, without international financial and technological support. This would give them leverage against Turkey's plans to use the waters of the two rivers, especially those of the Euphrates, that traverse Syria before crossing into Iraq. Syria and Iraq were in fact successful. Turkey's search for international funding for the dam failed. The World Bank asked that the consent of the downstream riparians be secured before considering Turkey's request for financial support.

A unique set of circumstances came together in 1983 that allowed Turkey to decide to build the dam by relying exclusively on its own assets. First, with the economic reforms of 1980, the Turkish economy began to enjoy a period of prosperity and growth, generating new resources that the government could allocate to the construction of the dam. Second, rapid economic growth made it all the more imperative that new sources of power be developed. The Atatürk Dam was a promising way to increase substantially the total power generated in Turkey. There was broad consensus among the relevant constituencies, including the DSI, the government, and the business community, that the project should start and be completed as quickly as possible. It was judged that financing the project entirely from national resources would be a strain and produce hardships and deprivations in other areas, but it was felt that the rewards would be worth the price. Finally, Iran and Iraq had engaged in an exhausting but futile war, reducing not only Iraq's but also Syria's ability to resist the Turkish action: there were concerns that Syria might also be dragged into the conflict. The start of construction was made to coincide with the high point of the Iran-Iraq War, ensuring that neither Iraq nor Syria would be in a strong position to raise objections to Turkey's actions.

The beginning of the construction of the dam was met with alarm in Syria, which was concerned that Turkey would consume such a large portion of the waters of the Euphrates that, in the long run, Syria, as a downstream country, would experience severe shortages.[16] Syria began to extend support to an ethnically based terrorist movement, the Kurdistan Workers' Party (PKK), which operated in the southeastern parts of Turkey. Syria hoped that Turkey's efforts to cope with roving bands of terrorists would sap its energies and resources with the effect of slowing down the construction of the Atatürk Dam and spreading a sense of insecurity in the region. In this way, the Asad regime felt, Turkey might be compelled to negotiate an agreement on sharing the waters of the Euphrates before proceeding with the completion of the Atatürk Dam and then other dams that were included in the GAP project.

In this way, the utilization of water resources, considered by Turkey to be a matter for the domestic domain, worked its way onto the foreign policy agenda. Of course, water as a concern of Turkish foreign policy is not limited to being an issue between just Syria and Turkey, and to a lesser extent between Iraq and Turkey. In the Turkish-Syrian relationship, however, water occupies the center stage. Without it, there is little reason to feel that water would have occupied a prominent position in Turkey's foreign policy agenda.

Water as a Critical Factor in Turkish-Syrian Relations

From the very beginning, Turkey has argued that surface waters that originate in Turkey are national waters and that it is natural for Turkey to use these waters in ways only it deems desirable. Turkey has pursued this point adamantly, abstaining from behaviors that could in any way be interpreted as making concessions or modifying its stand.[17] This determined attitude, for example, has prevented Turkey from reacting favorably to the Convention on the Non-Navigational Uses of International Watercourses or from entertaining any suggestions that the waters of the Tigris and the Euphrates be shared. Rather, Turkey has constantly reiterated the point that while these waters are its own national resources, it will not deprive its neighbors of a resource that they also need.

---

16. Ministry of Foreign Affairs, "Water Issues Between Turkey, Syria and Iraq," *Perceptions*, Vol. 1, No. 2 (June–August 1996), p. 95.

17. See for example Hüseyin Pazarcı, "Su Sorununun Hukuksal Boyutları," in Neşet Akmandor, Hüseyin Pazarcı, and Hasan Köni, *Orta Doğu Ülkelerinde Su Sorunu* (Ankara: TESAV, 1994), pp. 39–54.

Some efforts have been made to hold talks with both Syria and Iraq, separately and jointly, in order to search for a formula that would be acceptable to all parties. At minimum, Turkey hoped that through such talks it would convince its neighbors that in the long run it would not consume most of the waters of the Euphrates, leaving intolerably low quantities for Syria, which, in turn, would reduce the flow into Iraq. But, in most instances, these efforts did not move beyond the stating of irreconcilably divergent positions. The list of fundamental disagreements that would have to be surmounted before talks could proceed included the questions of whether only the Euphrates or also the Tigris should constitute the topic of discussion, and whether waters are to be shared or allocated.[18]

It appears that both Turkey and Syria shy away from making commitments that might restrict their claim to full freedom in the utilization of the waters of the Euphrates. Turkey is concerned that agreeing to share the waters of the river would put it in a position of permanent inferiority vis-à-vis Syria and Iraq. In order to block Turkish projects that aim to make use of Euphrates waters both of these countries are likely to produce with regularity arguments based on user's historical rights.[19] Turkey's committing itself to the provision of a specific amount to the downstream countries would establish a baseline figure that would never go down. Pressures for its upward revision, on the other hand, would never be absent. Syria, for its part, feels that accepting Turkish positions would place it at the mercy of Turkey, which would progressively reduce the water allowed downstream as the GAP moves further towards its completion.

There have actually been a couple of openings in what otherwise has been a highly stalemated situation. First, Turkey agreed in writing, as part of a trade agreement in 1987, to allow annually a minimum average of 500 cubic meters per second of water to Syria until a definitive arrangement for the allocation of water between the three riparians is concluded.[20] Turkey has so far honored this commitment, although the acid test of a genuine drought year has not yet been experienced. Second,

---

18. For a summary of these efforts, see Özden Bilen, *Turkey and the Water Issues in the Middle East* (Ankara: Southeastern Anatolia Project Regional Development Administration, 1997), pp. 108–122. A more detailed account may be found in Ministry of Foreign Affairs, Department of Regional and Transboundary Waters, *Water Issues between Turkey, Syria and Iraq* (Ankara, 1996), pp. 3–15.

19. Ministry of Foreign Affairs, *Water Issues*, pp. 15–16.

20. Bilen, *Turkey and Water Issues*, p. 117. The suggestion that this is an opening is made in many documents, including Kut, "Burning Waters," p. 13.

Turkey has proposed a three-stage plan for the optimum, equitable, and reasonable utilization of the transboundary watercourses of the Tigris-Euphrates Basin. The plan suggests that two preliminary stages should precede a third stage of discussing how the waters could actually be utilized. One stage would be a basin-wide study of the water flows, evaporation losses, water quality, current uses of water, and other similar water-related questions. Another stage would comprise the study of the soils, their quality, the extent to which they lend themselves to being irrigated, and similar items.[21]

By incorporating the three riparians in a basin-wide study, the proposal may have represented a loosening in the Turkish position of claiming full sovereignty over the rivers. But, for a variety of reasons, it was rejected outright by Syria and Iraq. For example, the Tigris, on which Syria is barely a riparian, is of no immediate interest to Syria and therefore it wants to confine the talks to the Euphrates. Similarly, Iraq faces no shortages on the Tigris and is interested in keeping it out of the discussion and focusing on the Euphrates, from which it is supposed to receive 58 percent of the flow that comes into Syria from Turkey. Syria is also afraid that bringing the Tigris into the discussion would provide grounds for Turkey to reduce the amount it releases downstream on the Euphrates. Both Syria and Iraq may be concerned that a study of water-related questions might justify Turkish claims that it is more rational to build dams upstream in Turkey where evaporation losses are much less than in Syria and Iraq. But the study of water usage patterns, soil quality, and other similar questions may well reveal that Syrian and Iraqi claims about the amount of water they need are difficult to substantiate and very likely exaggerated. Whatever the reasons, the Turkish offer of a three-stage plan has so far been left to gather dust.

None of the Turkish efforts have succeeded in allaying Syrian concerns that the full implementation of the GAP will, in the not too distant future, exhaust the usable water potential of the Euphrates and leave Syria in a state of permanent drought.[22] Until very recently, the Syrian response had been to adopt a set of policies that it thought would make

---

21. İlter Turan, "Turkey and the Middle East: Problems and Solutions," *Water International*, Vol. 18, No. 1 (March 1993), p. 28. See also Ministry of Foreign Affairs, *Water Issues*, pp. 21–23.

22. Ministry of Foreign Affairs, "Water Issues," p. 92. Table 4 presents estimates of the amount of irrigable land in Syria and Iraq in which Syrian estimates exceed those made by independent observers by between 200 and 300 percent, indicating that Syrian apprehensions are, to a considerable extent, self-generated.

Turkey's insistence on exercising full sovereignty over the waters of the Euphrates too costly a policy to implement. Toward that end, Syria offered hospitality to the separatist Kurdish organization, the PKK, which had mounted a campaign of rural terror in southeastern Turkey. This strategy has proven to be counterproductive. While it is true that Turkey had to devote significant financial and human resources to fight what it perceived to be a challenge to its territorial integrity, it has modified neither its plans for regional development nor those for the utilization of the waters of the Tigris and the Euphrates. In fact, it may be argued that the uncooperative mood that characterized the Turkish-Syrian relationship has given Turkey an even freer hand in pursuing its plans for the utilization of the rivers' waters.

Syrian aspirations might have been to establish a link between its support for a terrorist movement and its demands for the release of more water by Turkey. Turkey has resisted this link, however, since that would be a way of rewarding terrorism. In the long run, such a strategy is likely to invite more terrorism, not less. Instead, Turkey has chosen to concentrate on improving its military capabilities and isolating Syria from the international system by having it designated as a terrorist state. Syria has remained on the list of states lending support to terrorism as determined by the U.S. Department of State, creating difficulties for Syria in the international arena. Turkey, in contrast, has improved its military capabilities to a level such that rural terrorism, with the exception of isolated occasional incidents, has been brought under control.

In early November 1998, Turkey moved troops to the Syrian border and issued an ultimatum to Syria, asking it to terminate its support of the PKK as evidenced, among other things, by its tolerance of PKK training camps in the Syrian-controlled Beka'a Valley in Lebanon and its allowing the PKK leadership to operate out of Damascus. Sensing that Turkey was determined to back up its demands with military measures, and unable to move significant forces from the Israeli border to the Turkish border, Hafiz al-Asad was left with little option but to accede to Turkey's demands. Turkey rejected initial Syrian suggestions that simultaneous negotiations be conducted on all outstanding issues on the grounds that the termination of support to a terrorist movement is a non-negotiable matter that should not be linked with other issues. Turkey and Syria initiated talks after the PKK headquarters were moved out of Damascus and its leader, Abdullah Öcalan, and his entourage were forced out of Syria. Öcalan was later captured by Turkish agents in Kenya, and brought back to Turkey. He was tried and sentenced to death in 1999. It is too soon to tell whether Syria's change of policy is a tactical shift to defuse the imminent threat of a military intervention by Turkey or whether a longer-term shift has taken place in recognition of the fact that the pro-PKK policy did not produce the intended results (the latter appearing more likely).

Water, and problems connected with water, have been at the heart of Turkey's relations with Syria. As a result of the 1998 confrontation, Syria has abandoned its support for PKK terrorism. The utilization of the waters of the Euphrates will, however, continue to be a major issue of contention between the two countries. Both countries tend to perceive the water relationship in zero-sum terms. They have so far failed to place water in the context of a more comprehensive relationship in which benefits to be derived from extensive cooperation would render water-related issues somewhat less encompassing and more amenable to cooperative solutions. The centrality of water to the relationship is fanned by the emergence of an international context in which frequent references are made to the idea that the next wars in the Middle East will be fought over water. Inevitably, this affects how all actors view the question.

Furthermore, other water problems to which one or another Arab country is a party against a non-Arab country exist in the Middle East. This has reinforced the already existing Arab solidarity against non-Arab parties on questions of water. Syria has engaged in continued efforts to mobilize Arab public opinion in support of its claims to a larger share of the waters of the Euphrates, which it considers to be an Arab river. It is not clear that this effort is producing any particular positive outcome for Syria. While it is true that many Arab countries have expressed public support for the Syrian positions and demands, criticizing Turkey as being the wrongful party, they have left it at that. Turkey's relations with major Arab countries, beginning with Egypt, are multi-faceted and are therefore not shaped exclusively by Syria's complaints about Turkey and how it uses the waters of the Euphrates.

The death of Hafiz al-Asad and the assumption by his son of the presidency has begun to produce positive changes in the Turkish-Syrian relationship, a relationship that had already begun to thaw after Syria was forced to reduce its level of commitment to supporting the PKK. There is a growing desire on both sides to develop commercial relations to much higher levels than exist. There has been talk about Turkey's buying natural gas from Syria. The intensification of trade, tourism, and other contacts may slowly produce not only an atmosphere of confidence but also a web of multi-faceted relations within which a single issue, even if it is that of water, may cease to be the sole determinant of the nature of the relationship. The potential of mutual benefit, and the awareness that each side may impose significant deprivations on the other, might then lead Syria to give greater credit to Turkish claims that it would never let its neighbor go without water. Similarly, Turks might find it easier to believe that Syria has no convincing reason to extend support to separatist terrorism of the PKK.

Only passing references have been made to Iraq, the other riparian on the Euphrates, as well as the major riparian on the Tigris. As is only too evident, Iraq has been plagued with much more important problems in recent years than would allow it to treat the waters of the Euphrates as a major policy concern. The fact that the Tigris carries a larger amount of water and constitutes another lifeline for Iraq also means that it does not experience the same sense of urgency as Syria, which is almost exclusively dependent on the Euphrates. The rivalry between Syria and Iraq, and the competitive and often conflictual character of their relationship, have kept Iraq from acting together with Syria, which, at this particular time, renders Iraq a less significant actor in the politics of the waters of the Euphrates. Finally, there are many other dimensions to the Turkish-Iraqi relationship, with the result that water questions do not receive the attention that they do in the Turkish-Syrian relationship.

Will a favorable outcome of the Middle East peace process affect Turkey's relations with Syria and Iraq? At a time when Palestinian-Israeli relations are at an all time low and following the war in Iraq, this question might appear fanciful. We may, nevertheless, still imagine a future state of affairs when eventually a peace agreement is worked out. While it may be argued that the achievement of a comprehensive Syrian-Israeli accord would create a new political environment conducive to the solution of other contentious problems in the region, it is equally possible to suggest that, because none of the parties appears ready to change its development plans, little improvement should be expected in the situation. It seems ill-advised to assume that there will be any direct effects of the peace process on these relations. Its brokers may well feel, however, that regional peace will not be consolidated until other outstanding issues in the region are solved. Therefore, they may direct their energies to establishing a *modus vivendi* concerning the utilization of the waters of the Tigris-Euphrates system. They may be aided in this process by Syrian President Bashar Asad, who is likely to give priority to settling outstanding issues with neighbors. President Bashar has an interest in achieving external peace in order to have breathing space for consolidating his hold on power and avoiding domestic turmoil.

Water as a Foreign Policy Instrument in the Region

It is evident that water has constituted a negative factor in the shaping of Turkish-Syrian relations, with mild spillover effects into Turkey's relations with other Arab countries. As already noted, in the Turkish-Syrian bilateral relationship, the focus is exclusively on who gets how much of the waters of the Euphrates and on what basis. These are questions that have all the makings of a zero-sum game. Apart from the Syrian context, however, the perception that water is becoming an increasingly scarce resource in the region has led Turkey to search for ways to render water a positive policy instrument, that is, an instrument that may constitute the basis for cooperative relationships or positive-sum games.

The first project in which water was offered as a positive policy instrument was put forth by the late Turgut Özal, prime minister and later president of Turkey. As prime minister, Özal came out with a proposal to construct a pipeline that would carry fresh water from the Seyhan and Ceyhan rivers to the water-hungry states of the Middle East, including Jordan, Palestine, the Gulf States, Saudi Arabia, and possibly Israel.[23] Although imaginative, both the cost of the project, dubbed the "Peace Pipeline," and the price of water thus supplied were found to be high. Arab states did not like the idea of becoming dependent on water from a non-Arab country. They also found the possibility that Israel might get some of the water wholly unacceptable. In addition, the pipeline would have to traverse Syria, a country that argued that it did not get enough water from the Euphrates because Turkey would not let sufficient water down. Syria would not allow the pipeline to go through without extracting an acceptable concession from Turkey in return. It soon became apparent that too many impediments had to be overcome before the project could even be entertained as a genuine possibility.

The Peace Pipeline was but one example of the idea that excess Turkish water could be made available to other countries of the region, mainly on a commercial basis. An example of an undertaking where some success has been registered is the Manavgat River Project. On the Mediterranean coast of Turkey, mountains run parallel to the coastline and the distances between the sea and the mountains are small. Rivers originating in the mountains carry substantial quantities of water, exceeding any local need, to the sea. One such river, the Manavgat, was selected as a pilot for development.[24] The Manavgat Dam and a water treatment plant are al-

---

23. The Peace Pipeline is discussed in Harp Akademileri Komutanlığı, *Siniraşan Sular ve Ortadoğu'da Su Sorunu* (Istanbul: Harp Akademileri, 1994), pp. 147–149. See also Turan, "Turkey and the Middle East," p. 26.

24. See Hüseyin Yavuz, "The Manavgat Project of Turkey: Water, an Economic Good," *International Journal of Water Resources Development*, Vol. 13, No. 4 (December 1997), pp. 561–566.

ready in operation. Turkey has offered to sell the water from the Manavgat Dam to anyone interested in buying it. Interested parties have included Israel, Jordan, and the Palestinians. After initial explorations, it has become apparent that Jordan is interested only if the price is symbolic, a position that Turkey does not treat with favor since it views the sale of water mainly as a commercial proposition. There have been no concrete discussions with the Palestinians. The negotiations with Israel have followed an uneven path. Apparently there has been some Israeli concern about the reliability of supply in view of the volatile nature of Turkish politics. Turks, for their part, have sometimes wondered whether there exists a genuine Israeli interest since Israel seems to be in no rush to reach an agreement with Turkey. Major differences concerning price have also emerged. At the time of this writing, however, the two countries seem to be drawing closer to an agreement. Earlier reports that a private Turkish investor would also set up a corporation that would bottle the Manavgat water and offer it as drinking water in the Gaza Strip appear to have been mainly statements of intent.[25]

Turkey has also engaged in shipping water to the Turkish Republic of Northern Cyprus (TRNC) using balloons. The particular technology of transport has proven problematical since balloons tend often to puncture. In any case, the water for this destination no longer comes from Manavgat, but from the Göksu River near Silike, Turkey. There is a project that envisions the construction of an underwater pipeline traversing the Mediterranean to transport major quantities of water to the TRNC, which experiences water shortages for agriculture and is dependent on the Greek administration in the South to meet some of its city water needs. Since the entire island suffers water shortages, making water from Turkey available to the whole of the island may serve as a modest enticement in motivating the Greek side to reach accommodation with the TRNC.

There are several rivers that flow into the Mediterranean whose waters cannot be consumed on the narrow coastal strips. As long as the shortage of water characterizes the southern coast of the Mediterranean, Turkey may serve as a source of water for those who experience severe shortages. And, as long as the shortage of water continues to constitute a critical stumbling block to the advancement of the Israeli-Palestinian peace process, water from Turkey may carry some potential in helping overcome it.

---

25. *Milliyet*, January 21, 1999, 11.

Conclusion

The issue of water has developed gradually but steadily to become both a foreign policy concern and a foreign policy instrument for Turkey. Turkey has viewed waters originating within the country, including those that leave its borders before reaching the sea, as falling fully within its national jurisdiction. It has rejected any claims to the contrary, and has therefore shied away from arrangements that would undermine its claims. This general direction of policy appears unlikely to change totally. There are some signs, however, that while preserving its essence, Turkey may be softening its position somewhat to reduce the hostile relations between it and Syria. So far, in any case, claims of full sovereignty over transboundary waters, particularly the Euphrates, have not been used to deprive neighbors of water. Since the planned irrigation networks have not yet been fully constructed, quantities released downstream have generally exceeded the amounts to which Turkey has committed itself. While the quantity released may vary over time, it appears difficult to perceive a future state of affairs where less than the promised amounts of water would be released across the border.

Commercial sales of water by Turkey may take place more widely in the future. Since the determination of price, as opposed to cost, is a policy prerogative, Turkey retains the option of using water as an instrument to elicit favorable foreign policy behaviors from those who are interested in buying the water. The quantities involved, however, are unlikely to render commercially available Turkish water a potent policy instrument. Rather, it may be used for making goodwill gestures, for reconfirming a desirable state of affairs, and for initiating better relations with other societies.

The development plans of all countries in the Middle East, the current demographic trends, and the patterns of economic development all point to the likelihood that the importance of water will increase as a vital commodity in the future. This means that tensions emanating from shortages will continue. These tensions will likely produce conflictual relations between those who are perceived to have more water and are inclined to exercise control over it, and those who feel that they are short of water. This creates both problems and opportunities for Turkish foreign policy. While Turkey is not itself a water-rich country, its water sources are more varied and it has higher capabilities than some of its neighbors of using its resources efficiently. This gives it a comparative advantage in the forming and conduct of its external relations, freeing them from being shaped exclusively by questions of water.

Pipelines of the Caspian

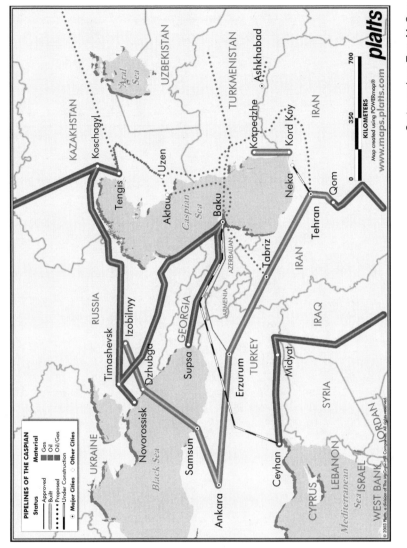

Cartographer: Tara McCoy.

Used by permission.

Chapter 11

Caspian Conundrum: Pipelines and Energy Networks

Fiona Hill

Energy issues are of critical importance to Turkey and are closely tied to its foreign policy. By virtue of its location in Asia Minor, Turkey is the land bridge between the Middle East, the Caucasus, Central Asia, and Europe, and physically controls the passage between the Black and Mediterranean Seas through the Bosphorus and Dardanelles straits. It is thus able to serve as a transit state for pipelines from both the established oil fields of the Persian Gulf and the new fields of the Caspian Basin. (See map, p. 209.) Since the early 1990s, the twin goals of Turkey's foreign policy in the region have been to secure new energy supplies, and to establish itself as the transit country for energy flows from the Caspian to consumer markets in Europe. It has sought to achieve these goals through the dual exploitation of its position at the crossroads of Asia and Europe, and of the strategic partnership with the United States it has developed during and since the end of the Cold War through membership in NATO and other Western political and economic institutions.[1]

The achievement of these goals has been challenged by several factors, including pendulum swings in the international oil industry's interest in the Caspian region; the complications of the very location that offers Turkey such geopolitical advantage; disputes over the legal status of the Caspian Sea; persistent regional conflicts; the growing assertiveness of Iran in the region; the political obstacles posed by U.S. policy against

---

1. See Alan Makovsky, "The New Activism in Turkish Foreign Policy," *SAIS Review*, Vol. 19, No. 1 (Winter 1999), pp. 92–113; and Marios Evriviades, "Turkey's Role in United States Strategy During and After the Cold War," *Mediterranean Quarterly*, Vol. 9, No. 2 (Spring 1998), pp. 30–51.

cooperative relations with Turkey's energy-rich neighbors, Iran and Iraq; and competition with the Russian Federation. Fluctuating oil prices, the volumes of oil ultimately produced by Caspian states, choices made by the Turkish government regarding preferential transport tariffs, and the consistency of U.S. policy in the region will all determine the final outcome.

Turkey's Energy Needs

In the 1990s, as a result of urbanization and strong economic growth of around 5 percent per year, Turkey's energy demand was high and increasing—with a projected growth of 200–300 percent over the next ten to fifteen years.[2] The country currently relies on imports for 60 percent of its total energy needs, a proportion that is projected to rise to 75 percent by the year 2010.[3] Oil provides almost half of these energy requirements, and approximately 90 percent of oil supplies is imported, primarily from the Middle East and Russia. In 1996, natural gas accounted for only around one sixth of Turkey's energy consumption, but demand for gas is projected to increase four-fold over the next twenty years.[4] Again, more than 90 percent of gas supplies must be imported, with the bulk of this from Russia, which first began to supply Turkey in 1987 and has since made successive agreements to increase its exports by the year 2010.

Before 1990, Turkey's immediate Middle Eastern neighbor, Iraq, was the central supplier of oil to Turkey, and also played a major role in its international trade. Iraq exported almost one third of its oil production through Turkey, with twin pipelines supplying 250,000 barrels per day to Turkish refineries and extending to Turkey's primary oil terminal and major port of Ceyhan in the eastern Mediterranean. After Iraq's invasion of Kuwait in August 1990, the flow of oil to Ceyhan was ruptured by UN sanctions against Iraq and the Gulf War. This resulted in Turkey's loss of an estimated $30–60 billion dollars in revenue from transit and storage fees, and trade and business opportunities, over the following decade.[5]

---

2.   Cited in Kelly Couturier, "Turkey Aims to Satisfy Its Fuel Needs: International Politics Rewrites Pipeline Deals," *Washington Post,* October 20, 1997, p. A17.

3.   Cited in Christopher Parkes, "United States to Mediate in Conflicts over Caspian Oil," *Financial Times,* September 16, 1998, p. 4.

4.   Figures cited from U.S. Department of Energy, Energy Information Administration Country Report on Turkey, July 1998, at <www.doe.gov/emeu/international/turkey/html>.

5.   Ibid.

Given its growing energy needs, and the discovery of giant gas fields in the Middle East, Russia, and Central Asia, Turkey has chosen to increase the share of natural gas in domestic energy consumption and to diversify its supply. It has therefore signed energy import deals with Algeria, Egypt, Iran, Iraq, Kazakhstan, Nigeria, Qatar, Russia, Turkmenistan, Uzbekistan, and Yemen. Transit fees from oil and gas exports through Turkish territory from these countries are expected to play an important role in offsetting part of the high energy import bill.

While Iraqi exports were limited under the UN's "food for oil" agreement, Turkey has looked increasingly to the oil and gas reserves of the Caspian Sea as a source of energy supplies, revenues from transportation tariffs, and regional influence through the control of transportation routes, and an alliance with the United States in the development of these reserves. Beginning in September 1994, Turkey's state petroleum company (TPAO) has been an active member of foreign oil consortia exploring and developing oil fields in Azerbaijan and Kazakhstan—the two countries in the Caucasus and Central Asia possessing the bulk of Caspian oil reserves.

Pendulum Swings in the Caspian

In a world that is increasingly depleting its known stocks of reserves, the Caspian Sea currently represents the largest untapped oil and gas resource, and an important prospect for the diversification of energy supply away from the Middle East. In the late 1990s, the Persian Gulf supplied one in every three barrels of the world's daily consumption of oil, and experts projected that it would achieve and surpass 35 percent of world oil production within ten years.[6] The cost of oil extraction in the Persian Gulf is significantly cheaper than anywhere else in the world; when oil prices are low, market share and foreign investment in the Gulf increases. This increases the vulnerability of world energy consumers to another disruption in supply along the lines of the 1973–74 oil shock. In this period, in response to U.S. support of Israel in the Yom Kippur War, Arab countries imposed an oil embargo on the United States and its allies—sending the price of oil rocketing and leading to a rise in inflation, increased trade deficits, and a serious recession in the United States and Western Europe.

In the late 1980s and early 1990s, expert estimates, based on Soviet figures, suggested that the Caspian held somewhere in the range of 16–19

6. United States Department of Energy forecasts, *BP Statistical Review of World Energy* (London: British Petroleum Company, 1997) at <www.bp.com>.

billion barrels of oil and 12–16 trillion cubic meters of natural gas. Oil-fields off Azerbaijan were estimated to have 3–4 billion barrels of recoverable oil reserves, while the Tengiz field in Kazakhstan was identified as the largest discovery of crude oil since that in Prudhoe Bay in Alaska, with proven crude reserves of 6 billion barrels, and a possible additional recoverable reserve of 3 billion barrels (9 billion barrels in total).[7] As far as natural gas was concerned, by the 1990s the Central Asian state of Turkmenistan was the world's fourth largest natural gas producer, producing 120 billion cubic meters per year. Given projected global energy demand, this was sufficient to meet fully one half of Europe's near-term energy needs from natural gas, which were expected to reach approximately 240 billion cubic meters by 2005.[8] As well as helping to diversify world energy supplies and reduce dependence on the Persian Gulf, the exploitation of these Caspian resources offers a major source of hard currency for the fragile economies of the new states of the Caspian region, particularly Azerbaijan, Kazakhstan, and Turkmenistan.

Since the early 1990s, however, when the first major contracts were signed between international oil companies and the governments of Azerbaijan and Kazakhstan for the exploration and production of oil, the stress has been on oil rather than gas, and the Caspian Sea has been subject to pendulum swings in expectations about the potential of its oil supplies. These have ranged from the wildly optimistic forecast of 200 billion barrels of total oil reserves, to the pessimistic prognosis of 30 billion barrels. Just as the estimations of reserves have fluctuated, so have world oil prices. Interest in the Caspian waxed in 1995–97 with a rise in prices to over $20 per barrel, and waned in 1998–99, as average world oil prices fell to around $10 per barrel before rebounding to almost $40 per barrel and a ten-year high in 2000 in response to production cuts in the Gulf States.

Although very early estimates that the Caspian might possess the resources of "another Persian Gulf" proved to be incorrect,[9] careful studies of the region's oil potential in the late 1990s concluded that the Caspian

---

7.   See Mark Lewis, "The Implications of the Development of Caspian Sea Oil on the International Crude Oil Market," presentation at conference on "Oil and Caviar in the Caspian," School of Oriental and African Studies, London University, February 24, 1995.

8.   See presentation by Boris Shikhmuradov, deputy prime minister and foreign minister of Turkmenistan, "Geopolitics of the Caspian Sea Region," Nixon Center for Peace and Freedom Program Brief, November 1995.

9.   Saudi Arabia alone possesses 260 billion barrels of proven reserves, and the Gulf States together possess over 670 billion barrels. In total, the Middle East holds about 60 percent of known global oil reserves. Christopher Cooper and Hugh Pope, "Dry Wells Belie Hope for Big Caspian Reserves," *Wall Street Journal,* October 12, 1998, p. A13.

could possess up to 90 billion barrels of oil. This is the reserve equivalent of Iran or Kuwait and would certainly establish the Caspian as a more important energy resource than the North Sea.[10] The stakes for oil development in the Caspian are, therefore, high—even by the more pessimistic prognoses. The United States imports around 50 percent of its oil supplies, while Europe collectively imports approximately 56 percent, and Japan almost 100 percent.[11] Oil is a vital interest for the world's developed countries, and one that took the United States and the international coalition to war in the Persian Gulf in 1991 to ensure its uninterrupted flow from the region.

These calculations of vital interest have greatly enhanced Turkey's post–Cold War role in the broader region encompassed by the Caspian, Black, and Mediterranean Seas. As the Caspian is landlocked, the shortest route to the world's major seaways is overland through the Caucasus by pipeline or rail, by tanker across the Black Sea, and from there to the Mediterranean. On the Black Sea, the Russian ports of Novorossiisk and Tuapse and the Georgian ports of Batumi and Poti are the main existing and potential termini for oil pipelines or rail tankers from the Caspian, with Novorossiisk being the largest and most important of these ports.[12] Turkey, however, dominates access to the Mediterranean through the straits and thus all the sea routes from the Black Sea, and also offers an overland route from the Black Sea to the eastern Mediterranean, with alternative overland routes to the Aegean and the Adriatic across the Balkans. Since 1995, Turkey has thus become a central player in projects to develop a new East-West energy transportation corridor in the Caspian region that will reduce or eliminate dependence on the existing, Soviet-era, South-North transportation corridor through Russia. Turkish oil and gas markets are also seen as potentially lucrative by U.S. and other international energy companies, and as a prize in themselves.

Turkey's Policy in the Caspian

The advantage of Turkey's geography is also its dilemma. The Bosphorus may be the gateway to Europe, but it is also a choke point, and an obstacle to increased flows of oil from the Caspian as fields are developed and

---

10. See K.T. (Terry) Koonce, president, Exxon Ventures (CIS) Inc., "Caspian Infrastructure," presentation at a meeting of the Central Asia–Caucasus Institute, Johns Hopkins School of Advanced International Studies, Washington, D.C., December 1998.

11. BP Statistical Review of World Energy (1997) at <www.bp.com>.

12. Novorossiisk has a major disadvantage in the form of poor weather conditions, which result in the closure of the port for a period equivalent to two months a year.

brought to full production.[13] A narrow isthmus between the Black and
Marmara Seas, and ultimately the Mediterranean, the strait is just over 30
kilometers long and only 0.8 kilometers wide at the narrowest point. The
Bosphorus is also one of the world's busiest waterways and most difficult
to navigate, with 45,000 ships traveling annually through the heart of Istanbul—one of Turkey's most historic and densely populated cities, with
a population of 12 million people. This traffic, which has increased by
over 150 percent in the last 30 years to a volume that is three times that of
the Suez Canal, is augmented by local ferries, fishing, and other craft
crossing the Bosphorus on a daily basis.[14] In the 1990s, the hazards and
heavy usage of the strait resulted in more than 200 shipping accidents, including collisions, fires, and oil spillages and leakages.

In accordance with the 1936 Montreux Convention, all commercial
vessels are guaranteed free passage through the straits. Seventy-five percent of the traffic moves south from the Black Sea to the Mediterranean,
with an estimated 1.4 million barrels of oil a day shipped through the
straits. Over half of Russia's total oil exports—between 30 and 35 million
tons annually—travels through them. By the year 2010, projected output
from Azerbaijan could more than double these shipments from Russia's
Black Sea ports. Even greater amounts are expected to be transported
from Kazakhstan's oil fields to Novorossiisk for shipment to Europe. The
Turkish government has repeatedly expressed serious concern about the
risks to shipping, safety, the marine ecosystem, and the well-being of the
local community posed by any potential increase in tanker traffic through
the straits.[15]

The Turkish government's concern is shared by international environmental groups, and most importantly by the inhabitants of Istanbul
and the majority of the Turkish population.[16] The issue of shipping safety
in the Bosphorus is not simply a maritime or political issue in Turkey. It
is a social issue of great potency that unites the Turkish political, busi-

---

13. See United States Energy Information Administration report on "World Oil Transit Choke Points," May 1998, at <www.eia.doe.gov/emeu/cabs/choke.html>.

14. See "Transporting Caspian Sea Region Oil the Mediterranean Route: The Challenge of the Bosphorus," materials provided by the Turkish Embassy in the United
States at <www.turkey.org/politics/pipeline.html>.

15. See "The Bosphorus: A Waterway at Risk," at <www.access.ch/tuerkei/
GRUPF/caspian>.

16. See Jon Gorvett, "How Safe is the Bosphorus?" *Middle East* (London), April 1999,
pp. 31–32; Thomas Land, "Pollution and Politics in the Black Sea," *Contemporary Review,* May 1999, pp. 230–235; and Owen Bowcott, "Istanbul at Risk from Oil Tanker
Boom," *Guardian* (London), March 27, 2000, p. 14.

ness, and cultural elite, whose fine homes line the Bosphorus, with the rest of the urban population. As one Turkish analyst noted, "the Bosphorus is the most cherished piece of land in this country. . . . Dining on the Bosphorus, living on the Bosphorus are universally ranked at the top of the list for everyone."[17] In the summer of 2000, these attitudes were underscored by public protests against the passage of a Romanian freighter carrying 200,000 tons of iron ore through the straits, after the freighter was deemed to be too long to safely navigate the waterway. The freighter was ultimately granted passage only after the intervention of the Romanian foreign ministry and an agreement that the vessel would accept security measures stipulated by Turkey.[18]

This deep-rooted concern, and the desire to collect lucrative transit tariffs which cannot be levied on Bosphorus shipping, have led to a Turkish policy of deflecting oil to overland routes across Turkey itself to the Mediterranean port of Ceyhan, which has the capacity to handle the largest tankers and store large volumes of oil. In promoting this policy, Turkey has stressed the dual geostrategic and security benefits to the West of having the final terminal for Caspian Sea oil located in a NATO country, free from shipping accidents in the Bosphorus. Turkish proposals for Caspian Sea oil transportation have thus involved tankers departing from Georgian ports, with off-loading at Turkish Black Sea ports for pipeline transportation across Turkey, or pipelines extending directly from Azerbaijan through Georgia and Turkey to terminate in Ceyhan.

The major problem here in the 1990s was that the shipping routes from Black Sea terminals in Novorossiisk to the Mediterranean were in full operation, while trans-Turkey pipelines had yet to be constructed. Turkey's proposals were also in competition with other potential overland routes from the Black Sea that would bypass the Bosphorus through littoral states such as Bulgaria, Romania, and even Ukraine. All of these states were, or still are, in the process of constructing oil terminals and large capacity ports, and have planned pipeline routes to link in with existing pipeline systems, such as the Druzhba or Adria lines, which transport Russian oil to both European and Mediterranean markets.[19] If world

17.   Hakan Altinay, executive director of the Open Society Institute, Turkey, during personal interview with the author, August 23, 2000.

18.   See "Turkey Clears Ship to Sail through Straits of Bosphorus," *Agence France Presse,* July 28, 2000. For a visual description of the activities of one of the environmentalist groups involved in these protests see <www.dogasavascilari.org/bogaz.htm>.

19.   See Mikhail Klasson, "Yukos and Transneft Join Forces," *Moscow News,* January 21–27, 1999, p. 7; "Accidents May Push Turkey to Renew Calls for Limits on Tanker

oil prices are low, financing these pipelines becomes a key issue for energy companies and investors.

Turkey thus actively pursued an alliance with the United States in the Caspian to capitalize on the presence of the U.S. oil majors in the region, the public and private financial power that the United States commands, and the U.S. government's post–Cold War calculation that Turkey is a "front-line state . . . at the crossroads of almost every issue of importance to the United States on the Eurasian continent."[20] In December 1997, Turkey and the United States formalized a "strategic energy alliance" to promote energy diversity and security, develop Caspian resources, transport oil and gas through Turkey to international markets, and facilitate international investment in energy projects in Turkey.[21]

Turkey at the Center of U.S. Policy in the Caspian

Transportation is the major obstacle to the development of Caspian oil and the smooth export of oil from the region. In the absence of pipelines, a number of costly alternative overland routes to the Black Sea were used in the 1990s, including combinations of rail and barge. The U.S. oil company, Mobil, for example, transported oil from ports in Turkmenistan, across the Caspian Sea by tanker to the port of Makhachkala in the Russian republic of Dagestan, and from there by rail to the Russian ports of Novorossiisk and Tuapse. In early 1999, the cost of the railway transportation alone was $34 per ton, or about $4.60 per barrel, which is a serious issue if oil prices drop to around $10 per barrel, as they did in 1998.[22] Prior to opening the rail route, Mobil had been forced to suspend oil production in Turkmenistan because of a lack of transportation options. A

Traffic," Newsbase, *FSU Oil and Gas Monitor,* February 16, 1999, p. 4; "AMBO Seeks to Cut Through Caspian Oil Export Muddle With Balkan Pipeline Plan," Newsbase, *FSU Oil and Gas Monitor,* March 9, 1999, pp. 4–5; "Trans-Balkan Pipeline Complicates U.S.-Turkey Relations," STRATFOR.COM, January 14, 2000, <www.stratfor.com/SERVICES/GIU/011400.ASP>; and "Trans-Balkan Pipeline Construction Starts One Year After NATO Bombing Ended," *Associated Press,* May 30, 2000.

20. Richard Holbrooke, Assistant Secretary of State for European Affairs, Statement before the House International Relations Committee, March 9, 1995, cited in Makovsky, "The New Activism in Turkish Foreign Policy," pp. 108–109.

21. "United States, Turkey, Pledge Dialogue on Energy Cooperation," Department of Energy News, Press Release, December 19, 1997, at <www.etde.org/html/news/releases97/decpr/pr97140.htm>.

22. Cited from Russian pipeline company Transneft's figures in *Neft i Kapital,* January 1999, p. 51.

second U.S. oil company, Chevron, also shipped oil from Kazakhstan via Azerbaijan and Georgia using barges, short pipelines, and rail, and made plans to transport crude oil by rail across Russia.

The construction of pipelines from the Caspian is, therefore, a commercial imperative, and the U.S. government made the creation of an East-West transportation corridor in the region, and the construction of multiple oil and gas pipelines, the centerpiece of its policy in the 1990s. The policy was underpinned by the promotion in the U.S. Congress, in early 1999, of the Silk Road Strategy Act, which amended the U.S. Foreign Assistance Act to provide a mandate for the support of the economic and political independence of the countries of the Caucasus and Central Asia.

The bill specifically emphasized a U.S. preference for the development of infrastructure along an East-West axis in order to build strong international relations and commerce between the countries of the Caucasus and Central Asia, as well as to support U.S. business interests and investments in the region. The bill provided for insurance, reinsurance, financing, and other assistance activities from U.S. public sector agencies such as the Export-Import Bank (Ex-Im), the Overseas Private Investment Corporation (OPIC), and the Trade and Development Agency (TDA). The bill offered encouragement to international financial institutions such as the International Bank for Reconstruction and Development (World Bank), the International Finance Corporation (IFC), and the European Bank for Reconstruction and Development (EBRD) to lend to the countries of the region. It also actively promoted "the participation of United States companies and investors in the planning, financing, and construction of infrastructure for communications, transportation, including air transportation, and energy and trade, including highways, railroads, port facilities, shipping, banking, insurance, telecommunications networks, and gas and oil pipelines."[23]

U.S. support for the corridor followed a similar strategy on the part of the European Union (EU), manifested in the European Commission's Transport Corridor Europe Caucasus Asia (TRACECA) project to fund the development of a transportation corridor from the Black Sea to Central Asia, which would link the region into existing trans-European networks.[24] This project, which was launched by the EU at a conference

---

23. See United States Senate Bill S.579, sponsor Senator Sam Brownback (Kansas), introduced March 10, 1999.

24. For more information on TRACECA, see the project's website at <www.traceca.org>.

with the Caucasus and Central Asian states in Brussels in May 1993, circumvented Turkey to some degree. However, it also complemented other cooperative regional initiatives with Turkey at the core, such as the Black Sea Economic Cooperation zone (BSEC), which was established in Istanbul in 1992. Overall, the development of the East-West corridor is viewed as a tool for reorienting the broader Caspian region away from its former dependence on Russia, and for cementing Turkey's position as a bridge between the new states of the Caucasus and Central Asia, and Europe.

Pipeline Networks in the East-West Transportation Corridor

In the late 1990s, under the auspices of its Caspian policy, the United States emphasized five major pipelines across the East-West transportation corridor: Tengiz-Novorossiisk (the Caspian Pipeline Consortium, or CPC), a new pipeline from Kazakhstan to the Russian Black Sea port of Novorossiisk for the transportation of oil from Kazakhstan's Tengiz field; Baku-Supsa, a pipeline running from Baku in Azerbaijan to the Georgian Black Sea port of Supsa for the transportation of "early oil," or the initial oil production, from the Azerbaijan sector of the Caspian Sea; Baku-Novorossiisk, the existing, Soviet-era, pipeline from Baku in Azerbaijan to the Russian Black Sea port of Novorossiisk for the transportation of "early oil" from Azerbaijan; Baku-Ceyhan (Main Export Pipeline, or MEP), a new pipeline stretching from Baku in Azerbaijan across Georgia to Turkey's eastern Mediterranean port of Ceyhan for the transportation of "main oil," or the long-term oil production, from Azerbaijan; and Trans-Caspian, a proposed pipeline extending from Turkmenistan to Azerbaijan under the Caspian Sea for the transportation of gas to markets in Turkey.

The first pipeline, from Tengiz to Novorossiisk, originated in April 1993 when the U.S. oil company, Chevron, concluded a $20 billion joint venture agreement with the government of Kazakhstan to develop the huge Tengiz oilfield that lies adjacent to the Caspian Sea. Chevron then established the CPC to arrange for the transport of this oil to the Black Sea. Under pressure from Moscow, the CPC agreed to export Tengiz oil through a pipeline of approximately 1,500 kilometers that traverses several southern regions of the Russian Federation en route to Novorossiisk. After several years of negotiation, the CPC was finally officially endorsed by the Russian and Kazakh governments in November 1998 and construction began in February 1999. The pipeline came into full operation in October 2001. By 2010, the fully expanded CPC line should export 1.34 million barrels per day from Kazakhstan to world markets.[25]

Subsequent to Chevron's agreement with the government of Kazakhstan, in September 1994, a consortium of major international oil companies called the Azerbaijan International Operating Company (AIOC) signed a $7.5 billion contract with Azerbaijan's state oil company (SOCAR) to exploit three Azeri oilfields in the Caspian Sea. Production from this project was projected to reach between 800,000 and 1 million barrels per day by the end of the next decade. In the interim, production would be divided into two stages referred to as "early" and "main" oil. The purpose of producing "early oil" was to help finance ongoing production and development activities and allow the AIOC to test the transport, tax, and investment climate in the region before investing more substantial funds in the long-term production of "main oil."

In October 1995, amidst pressure from Moscow to choose Russian pipeline routes, Azerbaijan and the AIOC announced that they had chosen not one but two routes for the transport of the early Azeri oil to the Black Sea. The first, a new pipeline from Baku to Georgia's port of Supsa; and the second, the existing Soviet pipeline from Baku through Chechnya to Russia's port of Novorossiisk on the Black Sea. By 1999, these two pipelines scheduled for "early oil" production from Azerbaijan were in operation. However, with the AIOC expected to produce 800,000 barrels per day by 2010, these pipelines would not be sufficient to serve as the main Caspian oil export pipeline (MEP).

Following the October 1995 decision, the Azerbaijan government initially considered three routes for the MEP. The first was the proposed new pipeline from Baku to Ceyhan. This pipeline had three additional possible variations: from Baku to the Georgian Black Sea Coast at Supsa, then by ship to Turkey's northern coast at Samsun, then by pipeline to Ceyhan on Turkey's southern coast; from Baku to Tbilisi, Georgia and then by spur pipeline across eastern Anatolia to Ceyhan; or from Baku via a spur pipeline through Armenia to Ceyhan. The third variation could only receive serious consideration with the resolution of the Azeri-Armenian conflict over Nagorno-Karabakh. The other two routes were expanded versions of the Baku to Novorossiisk and Baku to Supsa "early oil" pipelines.

---

25. See Michael Gordon, "Oil Pipeline Agreed on for Caspian Area," *New York Times*, November 25, 1998, p. C1; and "As CPC Work Begins—Why Build More?" *Caspian Investor*, January 1999, p. 1.

In the period from 1995 to 1999, the Turkish government consistently pushed for the MEP to be constructed through eastern Anatolia to link in with its existing pipelines from Iraq to Ceyhan. It was bolstered by popular support for a policy and a pipeline that would save the Bosphorus from increased tanker traffic. Turkey's pressure was broad-ranging and included government sponsored English-language websites that stated the case for the construction of the Baku-Ceyhan pipeline,[26] ordering oil refineries to boycott oil from international companies seen to be blocking the construction of the pipeline, and threatening to impose unilateral restrictions on tanker access to the Bosphorus.[27]

Azerbaijani President Heidar Aliev also indicated his support for the Baku-Ceyhan option, which the U.S. government described as the most geopolitically desirable and commercially viable route that would create "robust economic linkage between Central Asia, the Caucasus, and Turkey, . . . ensure that Turkey remains an integral player in the region's economic development, . . . [and] ensure the sovereignty and independence of the new independent states in the region."[28] This statement illustrated the centrality of Turkey in U.S. regional policy. Russia, not surprisingly, opposed the selection of Baku-Ceyhan for the MEP, and pushed for the routing of "main" Caspian oil through Novorossiisk.

As the second central pillar of its Caspian policy in the 1990s, the U.S. government also supported the construction of Trans-Caspian pipelines for the transport of Turkmen and Kazakh gas and oil to Turkey. The Turkish gas market is especially important internationally because the supplier that succeeds in acquiring it will be the best positioned to access the expanding European gas market. Together with Baku-Ceyhan, support for the Trans-Caspian pipelines underscored the U.S. government's emphasis on the East-West commercial and geopolitical orientation of Caspian energy, breaking the monopoly of Russian transportation routes for exports.

---

26. See <www.turkishembassy.org/governmentpolitics/issuesoil.htm>.

27. In November 1998, the Turkish government instructed state refineries not to buy oil from BP and Amoco because of frustration over lack of progress on the pipeline. A month earlier, in October 1998, the government declared its intention to restrict passage through the Bosphorus. Cited in Paul Sampson, "Lubricating the Caspian: Disputes over an Azerbaijani Oil Pipeline are Causing a Geopolitical Stampede," *Transitions*, February 1999, pp. 25–29.

28. Ambassador Richard Morningstar, special advisor to the president and secretary of state for Caspian Basin Energy Diplomacy, in testimony before the Senate Foreign Relations Committee Subcommittee on International Economic Policy, Exports and Trade Promotion, March 3, 1999.

Plans for the construction of the Trans-Caspian gas pipeline moved ahead in November 1998, when the U.S. energy company, Enron, produced a feasibility study funded by the TDA for a 2,000 kilometer pipeline that would carry 30 billion cubic meters of gas, at a construction cost of around $2.5–3 billion.[29] In February 1999, the government of Turkmenistan subsequently signed an agreement with a U.S. consortium, PSG International, for the construction of the pipeline. The U.S. government also lent concrete support in the form of an Ex-Im contribution toward the estimated construction costs of the pipeline. This activity culminated in the conclusion of a basic framework agreement among the respective governments in November 1999 during a summit meeting of the Organization for Security and Cooperation in Europe (OSCE) in Istanbul.

The future of the Trans-Caspian gas pipeline was, however, thrown into serious question almost immediately by a number of major issues. These include a competing proposal by the Russian gas monopoly, Gazprom, and the Italian energy company, ENI, to transport Russian gas 1,400 kilometers across the Black Sea to Turkey (the Trans–Black Sea pipeline, or "Blue Stream" project), disagreements over the capacity of the Turkish gas market, and the political vagaries of the Turkmen government.

The Blue Stream project—which was launched as the result of a 25-year agreement signed by the Russian and Turkish governments in December 1997—concluded a series of crucial intergovernmental agreements in 1999, secured sufficient funding to move ahead with construction in 2000, and was completed in October 2002. The goal of the Turkish government was to establish a direct supply line with Russia to replace an existing gas pipeline that traversed Ukraine, Romania, and Bulgaria and was frequently tapped by the three countries, leading to power shortages in Turkey.[30] Major technical difficulties in construction, given the depth of the Black Sea along the proposed route, forced final costs up to $3.3 billion. The Blue Stream pipeline is now the world's deepest underwater pipeline, hitting an unprecedented depth of 2,150 meters.[31]

---

29. Cited in "Baku-Ceyhan Pipeline Plans May Be Losing Support . . . But Ashgabat Gives Trans-Caspian Gas Pipeline Project a Boost," Newsbase, *FSU Oil and Gas Monitor*, February 16, 1999, p. 5.

30. Reuters, "Turk PM Says Gas Shortage Underpins Pipeline Bid," *Russia Today, Business News*, December 1, 1999, at <einnews.com/russia/business>.

31. See Hugh Pope, "Russian-Italian Pipeline to Turkey Wins Support; ABN-Amro Backs Plan in Blow to United States," *Wall Street Journal*, February 25, 1999, p. A10; and Michael Lelyveld, "Russia: Blue Stream Pipeline a Technological Feat, but an Economic Misadventure," RFE/RL, October 23, 2002.

Initially, Turkey had actively supported both the Blue Stream project and the Trans-Caspian gas pipeline on the basis that its demand for natural gas would quadruple over the next two decades, and that "it [would] need all the gas it can get."[32] Many Turkish and international analysts suggested, however, that there was insufficient gas demand in Turkey to merit two pipelines for gas from both Russia and the Caspian, especially with a faltering economy. The ratification of the Blue Stream agreements in the Turkish parliament was intensely debated in the National Security Council, cabinet, legislature, and in the media.[33] And, in 2001, Turkish Energy Minister Cumhur Ersümer resigned after a series of corruption charges against his ministry related to the Blue Stream negotiations.[34] In addition, in June 1999, a major natural gas discovery was announced in Azerbaijan's offshore Shah Deniz field. This introduced an entirely new element into regional energy calculations, with Azerbaijan now seeking to supply Turkey with gas, competing with supplies from Turkmenistan and Russia, and also demanding the use of any pipeline traversing Azeri territory for the transportation of its own gas.[35]

Turkmenistan also demonstrated itself to be an increasingly unreliable negotiating partner for international energy companies and gas supplier for Turkey. In Turkmenistan, an insular political regime emerged in the 1990s with an extreme Soviet-style personality cult around President Saparmurad Niyazov—the self-styled "Father of the Turkmen" (Turkmenbashi) and "President for Life"—who asserted extraordinary decision-making power over every facet of public life. The president vacillated among pursuit of relations with the United States, Russia, and Iran. In June 2000, Niyazov's refusal to move forward in honoring his commitments to the Trans-Caspian pipeline, his conclusion of gas export agreements with Russia, and efforts to increase gas sales to Iran, led to the ef-

---

32. See Leyla Boulton and Robert Corzine, "Playing Pipeline Politics in Turkey," *Financial Times,* March 16, 1999, p. 3.

33. See Bhushan Bahree, "Gazprom and ENI Set to Build Gas Pipeline," *Wall Street Journal,* February 4, 1999, p. A17; Edward Smith, president and chief executive officer of PSG International, Prepared Statement before the Senate Foreign Relations Committee Subcommittee on International Economic Policy, Export and Trade Promotion, March 3, 1999, published by the Federal News Service, March 4, 1999; and Lally Weymouth, "Turkey's Pipeline Provocation," *Washington Post,* November 24, 1999, p. A23.

34. See Energy Information Administration, "Russia: Oil and Natural Gas Export Pipelines," November 2002, at <www.eia.doe.gov/emeu/cabs/russpip.html>.

35. See Michael Lelyveld, "Caspian Gridlock: Failures of Policy and the Press," paper presented at Caspian Studies Program conference, Harvard University, October 27, 1999.

fective withdrawal of PSG from its operations in Turkmenistan. Although concerns over Azerbaijani and Iranian subsequent efforts to pipe gas to Turkey at Turkmenistan's expense prompted Niyazov to express renewed interest in the Trans-Caspian pipeline in August 2000, his personal commitment to the ultimate realization of the project remained uncertain. Turkmenistan also failed to maintain its agreed level of gas supplies to Iran, which raised questions about its ability to supply any additional pipelines.[36] Plans for the Trans-Caspian pipeline stalled entirely in 2001, with the energy industry's focus shifting to the prospect of gas exports from Azerbaijan to Turkey and a gas pipeline that would run along the line of the MEP.

Although the discussion of a Trans-Caspian pipeline mainly focused on gas transportation, there were also plans in the 1990s for a dual oil and gas pipeline that would serve both Kazakhstan and Turkmenistan, taking advantage of economies of scale and dual-use technology. In December 1998, for example, the Kazakh government, Chevron, Mobil, and Shell all agreed on a feasibility study for dual pipelines.[37] A Trans-Caspian oil pipeline, however, was seen as contingent on increased oil output and the maintenance of that increase from Kazakhstan, and would require at least 35 million tons of oil to be available each year. In the late 1990s, Kazakh oil production was only around 26 million tons annually,[38] and was not projected to increase appreciably before 2005 in spite of announcements by the Kazakh government about a huge find in its offshore East Kashagan oil field in July 2000.[39]

Challenges to Caspian Pipeline Networks

The success or failure of U.S. government policy in the Caspian, and the extent of Turkey's influence in the region, will be determined by the ultimate fate of the MEP, the Baku-Ceyhan pipeline, which in 1999 was slated to be routed through Georgia, becoming the Baku-Tbilisi-Ceyhan

---

36. See Michael Lelyveld, "Turkmenistan: Trans-Caspian Consortium Closing," RFE/RL, June 20 2000, at <www.rferl.org/nca/features/2000/06/F.RU.000620135831.html>; and "Turkmenistan: Is Unpredictable President Ready to Reconsider Pipeline Project?" RFE/RL, August 10, 2000, at <www.rferl.org/nca/features/2000/08/F.RU.000810143351.html>.

37. See Michael Gordon, "As CPC Work Begins—Why Build More?"

38. Ibid.

39. See "Kazakh officials remain optimistic about Kashagan prospect," Oil-Online, July 10, 2000, at <www.oilonline.com/news/news_international_hotline_ka0171000.html>.

pipeline project, or BTC. Since the early 1990s, five major issues have posed challenges to the development of Caspian pipeline networks: disputes over the legal status of the Caspian Sea; persistent regional conflicts; the growing assertiveness of Iran in the region; obstacles posed by U.S. policy; and competition with Russia.

DISPUTES OVER THE LEGAL STATUS OF THE CASPIAN SEA

Disputes have surrounded the legal status of the Caspian Sea since the dissolution of the Soviet Union in 1991. The central point of contention has revolved around whether the Caspian is a sea, and thus subject to the terms of the 1982 International Law of the Sea, or a lake. If the Law of the Sea convention is applied to the Caspian, then full maritime boundaries of the five littoral states—Russia, Kazakhstan, Turkmenistan, Iran, and Azerbaijan—would be established based upon the division of the sea and undersea resources into national sectors. If the law is not applied, the Caspian and its resources would be jointly owned.

In negotiations that began in 1994, Russia and Iran—with some support from Turkmenistan—argued that the Caspian should be subject to joint ownership. By contrast, Azerbaijan and Kazakhstan argued that the Caspian should be delineated into national sectors drawn equidistant from the respective coastlines. In summer 1994, Russian President Yeltsin and Foreign Minister Andrei Kozyrev signed a directive "On Protecting the Interests of the Russian Federation in the Caspian Sea."[40] This marked a Russian foreign ministry policy of pushing for a post-Soviet renegotiation of the status of the land-locked Caspian that would result in the international recognition of the sea as a lake, prevent its division into national sectors, and ensure a Russian veto over all oil deals.[41]

---

40. See Robert V. Barylski, "Russia, the West and the Caspian Energy Hub," *Middle East Journal*, Vol. 49, No. 2 (Spring 1995), pp. 217–233.

41. Caspian Sea oilfields are claimed by Azerbaijan, Kazakhstan, and other littoral states on the basis that, under the provisions of the 1982 Law of the Sea, the Caspian is divided into national sectors. The Russian foreign ministry's summer 1994 counterclaim rejected this division, asserting that the Caspian is not a sea, but an inland lake, and therefore not subject to the Law of the Sea. The foreign ministry, furthermore, insisted on retaining the Soviet-era legal regimes that governed the Caspian. These consisted of treaties signed by the Bolshevik government and Persia in 1921, and by the Soviet Union and Iran in 1940, in which the Caspian was recognized as a "condominium." Although these two treaties dealt specifically with freedom of navigation and fishing rights, and not specifically with resource exploitation, Russia claimed the privilege of rejecting any off-shore development deals in which its interests were not taken into account. On October 5, 1994, for example, the Russian foreign ministry sent a letter to the UN secretary-general stressing that a new legal status for the Caspian had not been determined since the dissolution of the Soviet Union, and therefore no single

Despite the serious legal disputes concerning ownership, the disagreement did not stop offshore exploration and development of the Caspian's resources. Although boundary lines for the sea were not officially demarcated, the littoral states—particularly Azerbaijan, Kazakhstan, and Turkmenistan—negotiated contracts in the 1990s with international oil companies to explore and develop offshore oilfields that fell within *de facto* national sectors. Moscow and Tehran opposed these steps, but permitted Russian and Iranian companies to be parties to Caspian oil contracts. Indeed, both Russia and Iran used the Caspian dispute manipulatively, and each modified its position on the legal issue when its companies seemed likely to be included in major projects.

Russia's position, for example, softened considerably after 1994, in part because of discoveries in its own northern sector of the Caspian that indicated substantial oil reserves. Beginning in late 1996, the foreign ministry began to back away from its hard-line stance on the Caspian Sea regime and in July 1998 announced an agreement with Kazakhstan recognizing national sectors, drawn equidistant from the respective coastlines, for sub-sea development. This resulted in increased tension with Iran, which was left to defend the hard-line legal stance alone. Russia still argued, however, that the sea itself should be subject to common ownership. For its part, the government of Azerbaijan indicated in April and May 1998 that it would agree only to a complete division of the Caspian Sea and its sub-sea resources, but then also began to back away from this position toward a division of the seabed in 2001.

By 2002, the Caspian had undergone a *de facto,* but not entirely stable, division on the basis of sovereignty rather than joint ownership. Russia and Azerbaijan concluded their own bilateral agreement on demarcation in September 2002, during a visit by Azeri President Aliev to Moscow.[42] Residual instability now stemmed from a number of specific, and at times vocal, boundary disputes over the jurisdiction of key oil fields—particularly between Azerbaijan and Turkmenistan in the southern Caspian—which were left without any formal resolution. These remaining disputes and the uncertain legal status of the Caspian Sea could pose a threat to long-term projects in both oil and gas. This point was brought

country bordering the Caspian could make unilateral claims to its resources. In the letter, Russia rejected the claims of Azerbaijan and Kazakhstan as illegitimate and issued a threat to the two countries that it would take all necessary measures against other states to enforce its view. See, for example, Steve LeVine, "Iran Backs Russia on Caspian Sea Claim," *Financial Times,* May 17, 1995, p. 3.

42.   Farz Ismailzade, "Aliyev Balances U.S. and Russian Interests in Turbulent Caucasus," Eurasianet.org, September 25, 2002, at <eurasianet.org/departments/business/articles/eav092502a_pr.shtml>.

into stark relief in 2001, when Iranian gunboats confronted a British Petroleum (BP) exploration ship in an area of the Caspian claimed by
Azerbaijan but disputed by Iran. The incident resulted in sharp exchanges between the two neighbors as well as Turkish and Russian intervention in support of Azerbaijan.[43]

As far as gas projects were concerned, Iran opposed the construction
of any Trans-Caspian lines, arguing that they were a violation of the existing agreements on the delimitation of the Caspian Sea. If a Trans-Caspian
gas pipeline to Turkey were ever to proceed, Azerbaijan and Turkmenistan would also have to conclude agreements on the demarcation of
their respective sectors of the Caspian Sea. In addition, in the 1990s Russia repeatedly voiced its strong opposition to dual Trans-Caspian pipelines, which would divert both Turkmenistan's gas and Kazakhstan's oil
from the Russian pipeline systems. Russia used arguments similar to
those of Iran in opposing their construction, and in 2002, Moscow concluded an energy agreement with Kazakhstan that could be extended to
other Central Asian states, and that would guarantee the export of
Kazakh and Central Asian gas through Russian pipelines.[44]

Russia's opposition to Trans-Caspian pipelines could have serious
consequences for the disposition and flow of Caspian oil over the long
term—especially in any future low oil price environment. Although the
exact cost of the BTC line will not be known until construction is complete, estimates have varied from $2.4 to $3.8 billion. Reports in January
1999 indicated that the AIOC had projected that, if oil prices were as low
as they had been in 1998, it could lose as much as $3 billion in potential
profit over the 30-year life of its Caspian oil projects in using BTC for the
transport of "main oil" from Azerbaijan.[45] To be profitable, the AIOC sug-

---

43. Michael Lelyveld, "Iran: Hurdles Remain in Improving Ties with Azerbaijan,"
RFE/RL Newsline, August 21, 2001; and Arkady Dubnov, "Tehran Guns for Caspian
Oil," Institute for War and Peace Reporting, CRS Number 95, August 24, 2001, at
<www.iwpr.net/index.pl?archive/cau/cau_200108_95_3_eng.txt>.

44. Anna Raff, "President Gets a Grip on Central Asia Gas," *Moscow Times*, Tuesday,
January 22, 2002, p. 1; Vladimir Socor, "Move Over OPEC: Putin's Got a Bigger Idea,"
Wall Street Journal, February 1, 2002; Michael Denison, "Putin Aims to Lock Up Cas-
pian Gas With or Without Niyazov," *Central Asia Caucasus Analyst*, Biweekly Briefing,
Wednesday, February 27, 2002, at <cesww.fas.harvard.edu/calarc/calarc_publ34.
html>; "Russian, Kazakh Leaders Discuss Gas Project, Need for Fresh Look at CIS,"
BBC Monitoring, Former Soviet Union—Political, Monday, March 4, 2002 (Source: Russian Public TV [ORT], Moscow, in Russian, 0700 gmt March 2, 2002).

45. Reported in "Pipelines: Azerbaijan," *Caspian Investor*, January 1999, p. 28. With
estimated construction costs of $3.8 billion and low crude oil prices, Baku-Ceyhan
would generate $14.5 billion in profit, in contrast to Baku-Supsa, which would offer
$17.5 billion in profit.

gested that BTC would need a flow-through of 1 million barrels per day, although a break-even point could come at a much lower volume depending on oil prices.[46] In March 1999, AIOC Chairman David Woodward announced that the consortium did not anticipate sufficient volumes of oil production to warrant construction of the MEP before 2005.[47] Considerations such as these led the Turkish government to offer some of its own funds for construction costs of the pipeline in excess of the lower estimated figure of $2.4 billion.

High construction costs for the BTC pipeline, unstable oil prices, and the projected requirement of 1 million barrels per day flow-through for profitability have suggested that the flow of additional volumes of oil to Baku from Kazakhstan, through the Trans-Caspian oil pipeline, may be essential for the long-term commercial feasibility of the BTC pipeline once it is constructed. In 1999, Kazakhstan joined the general host government agreements for BTC, signed in Istanbul. But it was not until early 2003 that Kazakhstan began to initiate discussions with Azerbaijan for a draft framework agreement to transport oil from Kazakhstan to Baku for transportation through BTC. In the course of the discussions, Kazakh energy officials also noted that they did not anticipate requiring access to BTC for their additional oil production until 2008–09.[48] They would continue to use existing routes—including the CPC from Tengiz to Novorossiisk—for oil production in the meantime. This is a sufficiently long period of time for circumstances to change again, especially in light of the close cooperation between Kazakhstan and Russia on oil and gas development cemented in 2002. If Kazakhstan ultimately decides to expand the relationship with Russia at the expense of its participation in BTC, this could thwart the geopolitical and commercial goals Turkey and the United States laid out for themselves in the Caspian in the 1990s.

PERSISTENT REGIONAL CONFLICTS

Regional instability adds a further impediment to the flow of Caspian region energy resources. Since the beginning of the disintegration of the Soviet Union in the late 1980s, the Caspian region, and the Caucasus in particular, has been the scene of the most violent of the post-Soviet

46. Steve Levine, "The U.S. and the Struggle for Control of Caspian Oil," *New York Times,* November 20, 1999, p. A5.

47. See "Turkey, AIOC Begin New Round of Discussions on Baku-Ceyhan," *Newsbase, FSU Oil and Gas Monitor,* March 30, 1999, p. 5; and "AIOC Head Says MEP Will Only Be Profitable," ibid., April 27, 1999, p. 17.

48. "Kazakhstan to Transport Oil Via Baku-Tbilisi-Ceyhan Pipeline," Interfax News Agency Bulletin, Tuesday, March 11, 2003.

ethno-political conflicts and civil wars. These include the undeclared war between Armenia and Azerbaijan over the political jurisdiction of Nagorno-Karabakh, the war between Georgia and Abkhazia, and the outbreaks of war between Russia and Chechnya in the North Caucasus. The regional conflicts and instability in Turkey's Kurdish regions in the southeast have complicated the choice of route for the MEP from Azerbaijan and threaten the security of all pipeline routes from the Caspian.

Outside intervention by the international community has contributed little to defusing these conflicts. In some instances, it has actually aggravated them by creating false expectations on the part of one party or another of the resolution of a conflict in their favor. The violence in the Caucasus has abated only as a result of the military collapse of one of the protagonists, mutual exhaustion, or the dictates of political expediency.

In Nagorno-Karabakh, the warring parties ran out of steam and a ceasefire has held since May 1994. Both Armenia and Azerbaijan have gradually been moved toward a compromise solution brokered by OSCE, but the final resolution has remained elusive, the hostage of political circumstance—including, in October 1999, the assassination of both the prime minister and the speaker of the parliament of Armenia, who were critical figures in the negotiations.

In Georgia, Russian support for Abkhazian forces, civil war, and military collapse forced Tbilisi to end its assault on Abkhazia. Neither pressure from Moscow nor a UN mission has since been able to bring the two sides together. In Abkhazia, as in the case of Nagorno-Karabakh, the problem of political status and the relationship between the majority group and the minority are the major obstacles to the resolution of the conflict.

In Chechnya, the collapse of the Russian military, the fierce resistance of the Chechens, and a popular backlash in Moscow against the war resulted in a tentative peace treaty in August 1996. This proved to be little more than a prolonged ceasefire in October 1999. The Russian government launched a second military offensive against Chechnya following Chechen militant incursions into the neighboring Russian republic of Dagestan, and terrorist bomb attacks in Moscow and other Russian cities in August and September 1999 that were blamed on the Chechens.

Each pipeline from the Caspian to the Black and Mediterranean Seas must pass through one of these conflict or multiple-conflict zones. The Baku-Novorossiisk route, for example, passes through Chechnya. In 1999, flows of oil through the Baku-Novorossiisk pipeline were halted repeatedly in Chechnya by accidents and by disputes between the Chechen and Russian authorities over transit payments, before being completely cut off by the renewed outbreak of war. The Russian government thus constructed a 280-kilometer bypass pipeline to take oil from Azerbaijan through the neighboring Russian republic of Dagestan and then on to Novorossiisk. Although this was brought into operation in spring 2000, persistent instability in Russia's North Caucasus region raises serious questions about the long-term reliability of the Baku-Novorossiisk route.

The Baku-Supsa route is beset by conflicts in both Azerbaijan and Georgia. In Azerbaijan, although there has been progress with Armenia and Azerbaijan in the OSCE negotiations over Nagorno-Karabakh, the Karabakh Armenians remain skeptical. They do not foresee any prospects of benefiting from future oil-based regional prosperity and are reluctant to cede any of the territory seized around Karabakh or to allow the return of Azeri refugees to these regions. In Georgia—especially Abkhazia—again there is stalemate in relations. Georgia and Abkhazia are embroiled in a dispute over the return of Georgian refugees to the Gali region and the role of 1,500 Russian peacekeepers in Abkhazia. There are also tensions between the central and local governments in Georgia's Muslim enclave of Adjaria, and its Armenian autonomous district in the south near the border with Turkey. The Baku-Supsa pipeline runs about 40 kilometers south of Abkhazia, and Georgia's key Black Sea port of Batumi, which would serve as a second terminal for Caspian oil, is in Adjaria.

The BTC route encounters not only the same problems in Azerbaijan and Georgia as the Baku-Supsa pipeline, but faces an additional potential threat from the Kurdish separatist movement, led by the Kurdistan Workers' Party (PKK), in southeastern Turkey. Since 1984, the PKK has waged an armed insurrection and engaged in terrorist activity against the state, targeting pipelines and other energy projects in its attacks. In 1996, the PKK's leader, Abdullah Öcalan, announced that the group would not permit any pipelines from the Caspian to run across Kurdish territory, and in April 1997, Kurdish militants blew up a small oil pipeline from one of Turkey's domestic oilfields operated by the U.S. oil company, Mobil, disrupting production at this field. Although two subsequent events—Öcalan's capture and trial in June 1999 and the EU's decision to include Turkey in the list of candidates for future accession in December 1999—have considerably changed the domestic dynamic and encouraged a rapprochement with the Kurds, a BTC line that runs through Kurdish territory is not an attractive option if the conflict in southeastern Turkey is reignited. The greatest fear is that the war in Iraq will result in the creation of an independent Kurdish state in northern Iraq, which will become a magnet for Turkish Kurds. Turkey's most serious domestic security problem, therefore, affects its energy security, commercial interests, and larger geopolitical goals.

If conflicts in the region remain unresolved, or there are renewed outbreaks of war, as in Chechnya, extra measures to ensure pipeline security
will increase construction and operating costs. Costly bypasses, such as
the Russian government's pipeline through Dagestan, may also eventually become necessary to maintain an uninterrupted flow of oil.

THE GROWING ASSERTIVENESS OF IRAN

An additional challenge to Turkey's commercial interests and geopolitical
goals over the long term is posed by Iran, which experts have agreed is
the cheapest, most efficient, and most secure route for the transport of
Caspian oil to world markets. Pipelines through Iran have been projected
to offer the most competitive options with the lowest capital costs—as
low as $50 million for one proposed combination of pipeline and oil
swaps at the Persian Gulf.[49] If Caspian oil is routed through Iran in the
future, this will undercut Turkey's role as the transit route for energy exports from the region. Iran, with its own considerable energy reserves
and substantial production, is also a major competitor with the Caspian
for international investment. A significant improvement in Iran's relations with the United States might at some point lead not only to the routing of Caspian pipelines through Iran, but to the re-routing of U.S. direct
investment dollars from the Caspian to Iran.

In the late 1990s, Iran became increasingly assertive in Caspian oil
ventures. Commercial and political pressures also began to undermine
the existing U.S. sanctions policy toward Iran. The Iran-Libya Sanctions
Act (ILSA), signed into law by President Clinton on August 5, 1996, requires the president to impose at least two out of seven possible sanctions
on citizens or companies who have made investments over $20 million in
Iran's oil and gas industry that "directly and significantly contribute to
the enhancement of Iran's ability to develop" its petroleum resources.
However, in 1998, the U.S. government decided not to impose sanctions
on Russia's gas monopoly, Gazprom, and its French and Malaysian partners, Total and Petronas, when they announced a project to develop
Iran's South Pars gas field.

Other plans were initiated in the 1990s to construct new pipelines
and engage in activities that also seem likely to violate the provisions of
ILSA and undermine U.S. policy toward Iran. For example, at a meeting
of regional states in May 1997, Kazakhstan, Turkmenistan, and Iran
signed a declaration calling for the construction of a 2,000-kilometer pipeline from Kazakhstan to the Persian Gulf via Iran. In December 1997, the

---

49. Proposal from Bijan Mossavar-Rahmani, President of Mondoil, as outlined in interview with the author on February 23, 1999.

three countries endorsed a feasibility study for the pipeline, estimated to cost between $2 and $2.5 billion. In 1998, France's Total completed a feasibility study on the possibility of such a pipeline with projected construction costs of between $3.2 and $4.5 billion, depending on the capacity of the pipeline.

In addition, in early 1999, the Iran Power Plant Management Company (MAPNA) announced the construction of a 392-kilometer oil pipeline, costing between $300 and $400 million from Iran's Caspian Sea port of Neka to Tehran, which would be capable of transporting 380,000 barrels per day of crude oil. This pipeline would permit Iran to engage in large volume oil swaps from the Caspian to its port on the Persian Gulf and strengthen its position as a major conduit for Caspian energy. U.S. oil companies Mobil (now ExxonMobil) and Conoco also pushed for restrictions under ILSA to be lifted by the U.S. government to allow oil swaps of Caspian Sea oil for Iranian crude to go forward. Mobil applied for a swap waiver in April 1998 and subsequently placed advertisements in U.S. newspapers asking for restrictions to be eased. Kazakhstan also explored the potential of oil swaps with Iran, where its oil would be shipped to refineries in northern Iran. In return, Iran would transfer an equivalent amount of its oil in the Gulf to Kazakhstan for shipment to world markets.[50] These Kazakh-Iranian swaps have not, however, been implemented because of differences in the quality of Kazakh and Iranian oil and insufficient refining capacity in northern Iran.

OBSTACLES POSED BY U.S. POLICY

This Iranian route and the prospect of increased oil swaps may pose a threat to Turkey in the future, on one level, but Turkey has also adopted a dual policy toward Iran which has run contrary to stated U.S. policy in the region. Turkey's increasing energy needs have become a major economic and political issue, and the search for new energy sources a particular challenge. Turkey has argued the need to diversify its sources of natural gas supplies and not rely almost exclusively on Russia. Iran with its giant South Pars gas fields and its border with Turkey is a viable alternative, as is Turkmenistan. U.S. policy against Iran has become a major obstacle to the realization of this diversification, in spite of the preferences on the part of the United States that Turkey should seek suppliers beyond Russia.

In 1996, Turkey concluded a $20 billion gas import agreement with Iran to ship gas from its fields to Turkey. This was scheduled to begin in 1999, with supplies increasing until 2005, and would require the con-

---

50. Oil swaps do not constitute a sanctionable investment under the terms of ILSA.

struction of three new gas pipelines from the Iranian border. Although this agreement was put on hold in October 1997, after protests from the United States, it was not shelved entirely.[51] In August 2000, Iran and Turkey signed a new protocol to finalize the operational terms of this agreement. Iranian gas deliveries to Turkey began in December 2001, but were suspended in September 2002, ostensibly because of quality issues. A major factor in the suspension was Turkey's economic crisis in 2001–02, which led to dramatic decreases in energy consumption, and thus in gas demand. In October 2002, Turkey initiated a round of negotiations with Iran to try to reduce Turkish import commitments and the contract price.[52]

In addition to the direct bilateral agreement with Iran, in 1996 and 1997, Turkey concluded agreements with Turkmenistan for gas exports that would include shipments through Iran, and under which Iran would receive transit fees. Again, the United States protested against these agreements. In response, in early 1999, when the Turkish government signed an additional 20-year contract with Turkmenistan, it undertook to receive this gas only through the Trans-Caspian gas pipeline.[53] But in the absence of the Trans-Caspian pipeline, deliveries through Iran remain the only option beyond Blue Stream for satisfying Turkey's gas demand— once its economy begins to grow again.

Turkey also expressed interest in the 1990s in increasing its natural gas imports from Iraq after the lifting of UN sanctions, concluding a preliminary deal with Iraq in May 1997 for the development of gas fields in northern Iraq and the construction of a pipeline to southeastern Turkey. Iraq has considerable gas reserves, and constructing a pipeline parallel to the existing oil line to Ceyhan would be a relatively low-cost and short-time option, especially given the high projected costs and long time-line of any Trans-Caspian pipeline construction. Again, this was a departure in policy from the United States, which opposed the lifting of UN sanctions and the redevelopment of Iraq's previously lucrative oil and gas industry. Although Turkey is central to U.S. Caspian policy, its energy needs, geographic position, and regional relations point to a different set of partners from U.S. preferences in future energy calculations.

51. Kelly Couturier, "Turkey Aims to Satisfy Its Fuel Needs: International Politics Rewrites Pipeline Deals," *Washington Post,* October 20, 1997, p. A17.

52. Hooman Peimani, "Turkey Squeezes Iran for Better Gas Deal," *Asia Times,* October 15, 2002. U.S. pressure on Turkey to forgo gas imports from Iran at this juncture, with the BTC pipeline project underway, was also seen as a factor in the suspension.

53. Leyla Boulton, "Turkey Acts to Encourage Foreign Energy Investors," *Financial Times,* February 16, 1999, p. 6.

COMPETITION WITH RUSSIA

The growing emphasis on oil, gas, communications routes, and commercial interests in the Caspian has also shaped Turkey's relations with Russia. Although Turkey's relations with the Russian Federation have been pragmatic and involve a great deal of bilateral trade, the incursion of Western oil companies into the region, the machinations about pipelines, Turkey's insistence that Caspian oil flows should be routed long-term through the proposed MEP from Baku to Ceyhan, and the thrust of U.S. policy have resulted in friction.

Since the collapse of the Soviet Union, Russia has seen Turkey as blocking all of its approaches from the Black Sea to the Mediterranean and the world's seaways and as harboring long-term ambitions for the political and economic penetration of Central Asia, the Caucasus, the Balkans, and the Middle East. Turkey has also been viewed by Russia as the proxy for the United States in this broader region. In the immediate post–Cold War era, Russia and Turkey fell into diametrically opposed camps on crucial issues such as Bosnia, Kosovo, and Chechnya, due to Turkey's close involvement with the Turkic Muslim peoples of the region and the presence of significant Balkan and Caucasian Muslim diasporas on Turkish territory. NATO expansion and Turkey's position in NATO further rankled Russia and set the scene for geopolitical competition between the two countries.

In spite of the difficulties in the bilateral relationship, however, Turkey has pursued an expedient and conciliatory policy toward Russia on commercial issues. Since the dissolution of the Soviet Union, Turkey has established itself as one of Russia's most important trading partners, concluding a ten-year agreement to promote ties in trade, industry, science, and technology. Turkish construction companies, such as Enka, have undertaken a total of $5 billion worth of contracts in Russia, including a number of high-profile projects in Moscow. Russian tourists have also made Turkey a leading vacation destination, with more than 800,000 visiting annually, dominating resorts such as Antalya on Turkey's Mediterranean coast.[54]

Energy trade, particularly gas, has been emphasized in these commercial relations. Turkey is a major market for Russia, where domestic demand is depressed because of persistent economic crisis, sluggish industrial development, and a glut of supply. Turkey has purchased more than 10 billion cubic meters of gas a year from Russia, and Gazprom has concluded deals to supply Turkey with natural gas that puts the Rus-

---

54. See the Embassy of Turkey in the United States information on economic relations with Russia at <www.turkey.org/governmentpolitics/regiosrussianfed.htm>.

sian-Turkish relationship on a solid business footing over the next several decades. In addition to the Blue Stream pipeline and gas export project, in spring 1997, Gazprom signed a $13.5 billion deal with Turkey to construct gas pipelines and carry out equipment upgrades—one of the largest single deals in foreign investment in Russia in the 1990s.[55] Russia and Turkey have also discussed future gas pipelines from Russia through Georgia and Armenia, and a possible extension under the Mediterranean to Haifa in Israel, which would capitalize on Turkey's strategic partnership with Israel in the Middle East, as well as an ambitious Middle East gas loop stretching to the Gulf of Oman.[56] In each of these cases, Turkey and Russia have a shared interest—Turkey in purchasing energy and levying transit fees, and Russia in exporting its gas and earning hard currency from the energy sales. Russia also has control over the supply and a direct stake in the transportation routes.

Developments in Pipeline Politics, and Prognoses

As stated earlier, the extent of Turkey's influence in the region will be determined by the ultimate fate of the BTC pipeline. While considerable progress has been made on BTC, serious obstacles remain and many factors will affect the outcome.

In early 1999, the governments of Azerbaijan, Georgia, and Turkey—with the support of the United States—moved ahead to conclude the framework agreements necessary for construction of the BTC. However, the oil companies held back. Given industry estimates that the route could cost at least $1 billion more than an expansion and refurbishment of the Baku-Novorossiisk or Baku-Supsa pipelines for "main oil" export, members of the AIOC opposed BTC on commercial grounds. The EU also promoted the development and construction of a range of alternative pipelines more economical than BTC. In February 1999, at a meeting in Brussels of Caspian and Black Sea regional states on energy supplies and the Caspian Sea, the EU discussed various options that would bring oil to Europe via existing and new pipeline routes through Romania, Bulgaria, and Ukraine, after shipment by tanker from Georgia.

---

55.   Cited in Sheila Heslin, "Caspian Energy Development: Strategies, Perspectives and Regional Context," paper presented to the Aspen Institute (May 1, 1997), p. 9; see also Sanobar Shermatova, "Gas Brings Turkey and Russia Closer," *Moscow News*, December 25, 1997, p. 6.

56.   U.S. Department of Energy, Energy Information Administration Country Report on Turkey, July 1998, at <www.eia.doe.gov/emeu/international/turkey/html>.

In an attempt to counter these proposals and to push the BTC project forward, in April 1999, in Istanbul, the U.S. government persuaded Turkey to offer a maximum cost or completion guarantee to the AIOC for the pipeline construction. The United States would also offer financing assistance for the pipeline through the TDA, OPIC, and Ex-Im.[57] In November 1999, after several months of negotiations—and against a backdrop of war in Chechnya and the rupture of the pipeline to Novorossiisk—a new framework agreement was signed during the OSCE summit in Istanbul between BP, on behalf of the AIOC, and the Turkish, Azeri, and Georgian presidents. In this agreement, the construction of the pipeline was set to begin in 2001 with a deadline of 2004 for bringing it into full operation.[58] BP/AIOC undertook to secure the financing for the construction of the pipeline, and the Turkish government agreed to pay for cost overruns in excess of $1.4 billion on its portion of the pipeline. The Azerbaijani and Georgian governments were much more reluctant to provide comparable guarantees for the portions of the Baku-Tbilisi-Ceyhan pipeline that traverse their territory.

Cost overruns on the Baku-Tbilisi-Ceyhan pipeline are likely. In the case of the much shorter line from Baku to Supsa for "early oil," unforeseen costs ran to at least an additional $275 million (a more than 72 percent cost overrun).[59] As the construction of the pipeline moves forward, the Turkish government will have to decide if there is a maximum ceiling up to which it is prepared to go, or if it is prepared to absorb the total cost of its portion, whatever the figure ultimately may be (bearing in mind the higher estimates by the AIOC of $3.8 billion for the construction of the line). In the event that cost overrun guarantees provided by the Azerbaijani and Georgian governments prove insufficient, Turkey could also find itself in a dispute over who is responsible for the remaining portion of the pipeline. With a high level of commitment already made, Turkey may find itself in the predicament of covering the cost overruns along the entire pipeline to ensure its completion.

The experience of Baku-Supsa, and the dispute that resulted then between the AIOC and the Azerbaijani government over which should pay the overage, does not augur well for Turkey. The ultimate costs could be a

57. Haitham Haddadin, "United States, Turkey Try to Speed Baku-Ceyhan Pipeline," *Journal of Commerce*, April 23, 1999, p. 8A.

58. The groundbreaking ceremony for BTC took place in September 2002, well behind schedule, with construction beginning in spring 2003.

59. See Carlotta Gall and Robert Corzine, "Pipeline Cost Dispute May Hit Azeri Oil Development," *Financial Times*, July 23, 1998, p. 5.

very high price to pay for securing Turkey's role as the MEP transit country—and may not be offset by the transit fees from the pipeline, especially as Turkey will also purchase much of the oil for the domestic market.

In addition, the AIOC, under the chairmanship of BP, set an initial deadline at the Istanbul OSCE summit of October 2000 for securing the private sector financing for the construction of the BTC pipeline. This timeline was then revised to 2001 while technical feasibility studies and cost estimates were carried out, and financing negotiations were still underway in early 2003. Financing has to be secured and guaranteed even though ultimate oil volumes in the Caspian are uncertain, oil prices are not guaranteed (in spite of the 2000 ten-year high), and regional conflicts persist. Low transit tariffs will also be key for oil companies in determining the commercial viability of the pipeline if oil prices fall for a prolonged period—not only those tariffs levied by Turkey, but also by Azerbaijan and Georgia. In February 1999, for example, Chevron halted shipments of Tengiz oil through Azerbaijan because of a dispute over tariffs. The Georgian government had agreed to reduce its fees, but Azerbaijan initially resisted Chevron's demands that its tariff be similarly reduced.

If sufficient financing for the pipeline is not secured, and BTC is perhaps deemed non-viable by the AIOC and other international players, then contingency plans—including the expansion of the existing Baku-Supsa line—may be implemented to prevent Caspian oil production from being stranded in Baku.[60] Turkey will then face some difficult choices.

It will have to decide whether or not to increase its level of financial commitment to the pipeline to cover the major costs of construction, not just the cost overruns. If it is not prepared to increase its financial commitment, it will have to lower its resistance to increased tanker traffic through the Bosphorus, and seek ways of improving navigation and marine safety in the strait. Turkey has no legal right to restrict shipping in the Bosphorus, which is controlled by the International Maritime Organization in London. If BTC is not completed on time, and Turkey continues its resistance, it runs the risk of encouraging the reorientation of oil flows toward pipelines through other Black Sea littoral states, and the increased pursuit of Iran as a transit route by international oil companies over the longer term.

---

60. Presentation by Wreford Digings, vice president Azerbaijan Export Development, BP, during panel on "Caspian Oil Strategy: Potential of Hydrocarbon Resources and their Transportation to World Markets," at the 4th Annual U.S.-Azerbaijan Chamber of Commerce conference, Washington, D.C., September 11, 2000.

In the final analysis, the consistency of U.S. policy toward Iran is also key. If there is a change in this policy—under pressure from U.S. oil companies operating in the Caspian and other regional lobbies, or through the dramatic evolution of domestic politics in both countries—then Turkey's role as the strategic transit country is diminished. To mitigate this, one potential strategy for Turkey might be to intensify and build upon the successful commercial partnerships it has already developed with Russia for gas exports, to engage it more actively in Caspian and other energy projects.

Turkey and Russia share a mutual interest in the transport of Caspian oil. If it is routed long-term through Iran to Persian Gulf ports, this will also threaten the viability of the Baku-Novorossiisk pipeline and Russia's Black Sea ports. An alliance with Turkey might draw Russia away from its partnership with Iran and actually facilitate the construction of BTC. It might also ultimately encourage Russia to view Turkey as a transit country for its own energy resources rather than simply as an export market.

In this case, however, Russia will have to be given some stake in both the supply of oil and the transportation routes and guaranteed a continued market for its gas supplies. The legacy of geopolitical competition with Russia in Central Asia, the Caucasus, the Balkans, and the Middle East will also be a formidable challenge for Turkey to overcome—even if the political will to pursue such a policy were to exist. Turkey and Russia are potential but, for the immediate future, uncertain partners in the developing pipeline and energy networks in the broader Caspian region.

*The Domestic Political Dimension of
Turkish Foreign Policy*

Chapter 12

Changes in Domestic Politics and the Foreign Policy Orientation of the AK Party

Sencer Ayata

Human rights issues, civil society, and democracy have recently become the core aspects of a new political discourse articulated by Turkey's moderate Islamic politicians, intellectuals, and writers. The discourse has had two major implications in terms of Turkey's foreign policy and foreign relations. First, the leaders of the Islamic parties, prominent Islamic writers, and Islamic intellectuals have started a new dialogue with political authorities, journalists, and academics in the Western world, mainly on the basis of themes of human rights, civil society, and democracy. Secondly, in the Western world, human rights issues centered on religious and ethnic demands and Turkey's way of dealing with them have received increased government attention and media coverage.[1] What is novel about this change of orientation is that until it was closed by a decision of the Constitutional Court on May 21, 1997, the Islamist Refah (Welfare Party, WP) had tended to differentiate itself sharply from the secular parties, in its ideology and program, often accusing them of being renegades, "imitators of the West," and puppets of Western imperialism. The party ideology and a vast body of Islamist literature proclaimed the corrupting effects of Western culture on the lives of devout Muslims and the devastating consequences of Western political and economic domination for Muslim societies. Among other things, democracy was seen as a com-

With the permission of the editors, an earlier version of this paper was read at the Campagna-Dervan lecture at Boston University on April 9, 2003.

1. Bergedorfer Gesprächkreis (109th: 1997, Istanbul, Turkey), *Im Kreuzungspunkt der Kräfte: die Türkei in einer veränderten politischen Umwelt* [Herausgeber, Körber-Stiftung], (Hamburg: Die Stiftung, 1997).

ponent of an infected Western system. By contrast, the new discourse as elaborated by the Islamic moderates involves a major stress on civil society and praise for Western democracy.[2] Furthermore, in foreign policy the tendency of moderate Islam has been toward the deepening of Turkey's relations with the Western world mainly through the promotion of Turkey's EU membership. Although it represented mainstream political Islam in Turkey, the WP was neither strongly radical nor militant. It nevertheless had a powerful zeal for Islamizing the society and the state and regulating both according to Islamic ideals and precepts. The changes that took place in the foreign policy outlook of the Islamist parties went parallel to significant changes taking place in the composition, structure, and ideology of the Islamist movement. This chapter examines the change of orientation in Islamist foreign policy in the context of changes taking place in domestic and international politics. The discussion also emphasizes the social and cultural inertia of Islamist conservatism and the persistence of anti-Western attitudes and sentiments among traditional and radical Islamist groups and constituencies.

The 28 February Process and the Rise of Moderate Islam

In order to understand the changes taking place in the profile and structure of the Islamist movement it would be useful to begin with the "28 February process" of 1997, identified by the Islamists, whether radical or moderate, as a form of indirect military rule in which power was usurped from democratically elected bodies, popular opposition was silenced, and the will of the nation forcefully undermined. As the largest party, with 22.5 percent of the votes in the December 1995 general elections, the WP managed six months later, in July 1996, to form a new government in which the WP leader, Necmettin Erbakan, became the prime minister. Although, in their first few months in government, the WP leaders tried to consolidate the image of a moderate Islamic party, they were unable to please either the secular opposition in the country or their own radical Islamist constituencies. The ensuing secular Islamist showdown eventually led to the resignation of Erbakan only one year after he came to power.[3]

---

2. The newspaper survey was done by the late Sevin Ünlü, who was a second year student in the Department of Sociology at the Middle East Technical University. I would like to express my gratitude to her and my deep sorrow at her tragic death.

3. Aryeh Shmuelevitz, *Turkey's Experiment in Islamist Government, 1996–1997* (Tel Aviv: Moshe Dayan Center for Middle Eastern and African Studies, 1999).

The campaign against Erbakan's party was a broad and intensive one, involving, above all, psychological combat against the Refah–Doğru Yol (True Path) Party coalition government. Secular women, for instance, promoted informal networks to defend the advancement of equality between the sexes, increased participation of women in public life, and individual liberties, against which Islamic fundamentalism, they thought, posed a major threat. The members of the Alevi sect,[4] who make up nearly 20 percent of Turkey's population, waged a major political struggle against Islamist encroachment on their communal existence and identity. An invigorated secular civil society composed of a host of associations, discussion groups, and philanthropic ventures began to protest the rise of political Islam. With the so-called "Civilian Initiative," the country's trade unions, small enterprise confederations, and business associations—other than the Islamic ones—established a platform to adopt a common strategy of opposition against the rising fundamentalist menace. The political parties also ardently defended secularism. The secularist movement received massive support from the urban middle classes and the leading mass media institutions. In a matter of a few months it became quite clear to many, including the Islamists themselves, that secularism was more than an obsessive concern of the military—though the role of the military was always pivotal—but also a major issue for wide sections of the population.

In order to confine what they saw as "the number one threat to the security of the country," the military leaders, rather than attempting to rule the country directly, enforced their policies through the National Security Council (NSC), a powerful organ of state composed of the president, the prime minister, the cabinet members responsible for security affairs, and the top military officers. The intervention of the military in politics reached a climax on February 28, 1997, with NSC recommendations that included a long list of measures targeting "reactionary Islam" (*irtica*). The strategy adopted by the military was one of total combat against this particular threat, aiming at both the Islamic political parties and the whole ensemble of Islamic educational, social, and economic in-

---

4. The Alevi have their origins among the Turcoman tribes that resisted the increasing centralization of the Ottoman state. Since the fifteenth century, they have emerged as a highly resistant subculture, based on religious heterodoxy developed under Iranian Shiite influences. Although the Alevi were seen as a subversive force in Ottoman society, threatening the Sunni Islam of the state, they nevertheless became insistent supporters of Atatürk's secularization reforms that aimed to separate state and religion and maintain equality between the two major religious sects.

stitutions.[5] These measures included increased financial scrutiny over the operations of Islamic firms; tightened control over the activities of religious associations, foundations, and communities; the closure of the WP Party and then its successor, Fazilet (Virtue Party, VP); court decisions that restricted political activity for a few members of parliaments and mayors of the WP, including both Erbakan himself and Recep Tayyip Erdoğan, then the mayor of Istanbul, and later the leader of the Adalet ve Kalkınma Partisi (Justice and Development Party, AKP). The NSC recommendations also included the extension of the period of compulsory elementary education to an uninterrupted eight years. This legislation foresaw the closure of the first stage of the religious schools, which, with enrollment reaching a record high level of 550,000 in 1997, constituted the basis on which the whole Islamist movement in Turkey rested. Many of the graduates of these schools continued on to higher education in order to give support to the Islamist cause as government officials, professionals, entrepreneurs, and, of course, as party activists and militants.

The 28 February NSC resolutions and their implementation were interpreted by the Islamist politicians and the Islamist press as a form of military coup and military rule.[6] They were seen above all as a legacy of the top-down Turkish modernization process and the undemocratic single party regime of the early republican period. In this view, the implementation of the 28 February resolutions involved unlawful measures that aimed to undermine the basic rights and freedoms of Muslim individuals and communities and of Muslim power in politics, society, and economy. The Islamist press continuously reported on Muslim entrepreneurs harassed and intimidated by government authorities and the grievances of victimized students in the religious schools, their parents, and public opinion sympathetic to their cause. The ban on the wearing of headscarves in schools and universities was characterized as a restriction of freedom of education. The Islamist press also reported on Muslims in the military and bureaucracy who were suspected, questioned, interrogated, and even dismissed by their superiors. Even more significant for the Islamist writers was the argument that the courts had ceased to be independent institutions as the whole judicial system was increasingly brought under the control of political authorities. The Islamic point of view essentially concentrated on the theme of the changing balance of power between the civilian authorities and the military, holding that the

5. Sencer Ayata and Ayşe Güneş-Ayata, "Religious Communities, Secularism, and Security in Turkey," in Lenore G. Martin, ed., *New Frontiers in Middle East Security* (New York: St. Martin's Press, 1999), pp. 107–126.

6. The Islamically inspired newspapers surveyed are *Yeni Şafak, Zaman,* and *Akit.*

latter tended to penetrate every aspect of social and political life. In addition to the military, the Islamists accused the Westernized elites, the leftist groups and parties, the Alevi conspiracy, the mass media institutions controlled by giant business corporations, and the privileged business stratum of lending support to the authoritarian regime. Islamist intellectuals and politicians argued that in Turkey, the state, which is in the hands of a small elite minority, is not at all subservient to the nation. Turkey was generally characterized as a Jacobin republic without a democracy, where people are denied their basic rights and liberties. Thus they proposed a drastic alteration to the existing constitution that would enable the extension of human rights, the maintenance of the rule of law, and the sustaining of the supremacy of civilian over military authority.

The 28 February process led to profound changes in the composition, ideology, and leadership of the Islamic movement. In the only general election in which it took part, in April 1999, the VP claimed only 16 percent of the votes, a significant decline from the previous WP vote. In the aftermath of the elections, the politically restricted Erbakan found it increasingly difficult to meet the challenge to the leadership of his caretaker, Recai Kutan, who came from the younger generation of politicians in the party. The VP thus began to suffer from growing internal strife and tension as the rift between the old guard and the so-called reformist moderates (yenilikçi) tended to widen. The moderates took the closing down of the party by the constitutional court in 2001 as an opportunity to establish a new party of their own. The Islamic movement was then divided into the two rival factions of Erbakan-controlled Saadet (Felicity Party, FP), and the AKP of the young Recep Tayyip Erdoğan and his friends. The AKP had a clear victory in the November 4, 2002, general elections with 34.4 percent of the votes and 363 of the 550 seats in parliament, enough to form a single party government and almost sufficient to change the constitution. Since the Turkish constitution stipulates that the prime minister must be an elected member of parliament, the president asked Abdullah Gül to form the first AKP government. Erdoğan replaced Gül three months later, in March 2003, when he was elected as member of parliament for the southeastern province of Siirt where the elections were renewed for procedural reasons.

The shift from a religious to a secular discourse was noticeable in both parties but it was mainly the AKP that gave the impression to the wider public of a major move toward to the center of the political spectrum. In the campaign before the November 2002 elections, the leaders of the AKP emphasized that they had thoroughly adopted liberal economic and political values. Nevertheless, the question of whether the AKP is genuinely committed to secularism and democracy, as well as to Turkey's

historical ambition of integrating with the Western world, draws the attention of a wide national and international public. This chapter argues
that the future domestic and foreign policies of the AKP will be shaped
and determined by the way its leaders cope with tensions within the
party, economic and social welfare problems, the challenge from secular
groups and forces, and the demands of international actors and global
players such as the European Union (EU), the United States and the International Monetary Fund. The related political, ideological, social and economic changes are discussed in the following sections.

Party, Parliament, and Politics

The ideological and organizational legacy of the Islamic movement, with
its mission of Islamizing the state and society, has not completely disappeared, even in the case of the AKP. An Islamic ethos is still powerful in
both the party and the wider Islamic movement; many of its proponents
emphasize the differences between the rightly guided and the misguided,
the believers and the non-believers. Islamic references continue to frame
the basic values and goals for political activity among many party activists, executives, and parliamentarians. Some members have joined the
party not as single individuals, but as part of the support that their communities lend to the party leaders. Their loyalty is primarily to their community rather than to the party.

It is also true that the Islamic political parties have changed and moderated as an outcome of various political factors and developments. Two
major political events had a profound impact on the political attitudes
and behavior of the AKP leaders. The secularist-Islamist conflict of the
1990s taught the Islamic politicians that secularism is a well-entrenched
force in Turkish society and politics. Hence, the AKP leaders tended to
moderate their views as they increasingly recognized the resilience and
strength of the secularist forces in Turkey. As part of the same experience
they became clearly aware that fomenting unnecessary political tension
was generally disapproved by the majority of the voters who prefer
peace, order, and stability in their everyday lives and in politics. Mainly
under the influence of television, which is present in almost every home,
voters developed a clear distaste for what is described as a "belligerent
outlook," closely identified with a thoroughly unproductive, rigidly doc-
trinaire, and highly conflict-oriented political style. Finally, despite their
overwhelming majority in the parliament, the leaders of the AKP see
themselves as encircled by a host of powerful domestic and international
actors and forces that can easily challenge their power.

A second lesson has to do with the extreme volatility that has characterized the Turkish electoral system since the 1990s. For instance, the support for the three coalition partners in the previous government was reduced from 54 percent to 15 percent in the course of only three years,
from 1999 to 2002. The voters swept aside the Ecevit government despite
the remarkable economic and political reforms it achieved. The AKP
leaders themselves frequently admit that they did not win all their votes
primarily for religious reasons. What many voters expect from them is
neither a major Islamist offense nor a decisive campaign against the military and the state. The frustration and anger of the majority that have
been the demise of many governments in the past can easily turn against
the AKP if it too fails to create more jobs and reduce poverty.

Although much has been said about the efficiency of the Islamic parties in mobilizing votes and attracting followers, an account of the impact
of electoral party politics on Islamic politicians has remained a widely neglected subject. In the three decades following the 1973 elections, when
the National Salvation Party entered the parliament for the first time, the
Islamic parties were represented in parliament for 21 years and shared
government power three times with other political parties. By and large
this is a unique experience in the Islamic world. Just as other parties, the
Islamic parties had to deal primarily with the practical problems of
everyday politics: securing power in the party; choosing between factions
that competed for positions and resources; finding party bosses to sponsor party activity; and cooperating with professional election agents to
organize party propaganda. As parliamentarians, the Islamic politicians
devoted most of their time and energy to approving or refusing legislation. Functioning in the parliamentary committees they learned the
mechanisms of government, ways of dealing with bureaucrats, and how
to build coalitions with other political parties. The parliamentary experience also involves taking divergent viewpoints into account. Meanwhile,
as mayors, deputies, and ministers, many developed external political experience in their encounters with Western politicians, experts, journalists,
NGOs, and other institutions. Thus the ideologically motivated Islamists
were transformed into professional party politicians who recognized the
need to secularize the content of everyday political activity. The experience of party, municipal, and parliamentary politics, both in opposition
and in power, fostered a pragmatic approach as some leaders became
more aware of the subtleties and complexities of the polity, economy, and
society. Thanks to Turkey's vast experience in electoral and representative party politics over nearly six decades, many Islamic politicians had
the opportunity to receive intensive political education.

Finally, the AKP is in some ways a new party that differs considerably from its predecessors. First, in addition to the traditional Islamist groups, its support comes from new constituencies, for example, the overwhelming conservative center-right and nationalist-right voters. In addition, the composition of the politicians has changed considerably: new recruits proliferated among frustrated grassroots politicians and activists in these constituencies. Finally, though ministers with a WP background hold the upper hand in the cabinet, and even more so in the parliamentary group, both contain deputies of diverse political origins. Thus, the AKP is not simply a survival of the past; it is a new mix of voters, cadres, and politicians who are led by a new Muslim elite.

The Elements of a New Political Discourse

As the WP and the VP became the major targets of military intervention, the party leaders began to recognize the significance of finding new partners and forging new tactical and strategic alliances. The cooperation of other groups and organizations was also essential for extending the AKP's constituency and enjoying wider legitimacy in public opinion. This required a change in political terminology and discourse, which fundamentally meant incorporating a body of liberal as well as conservative themes in party ideology to show that the new party had many aspects in common with other political parties and contemporary Turkish and Western politics. As a result the Islamic discourse is significantly abandoned at the public level; it survives however, in the small-scale, closed, and informal meetings that politicians hold with the more conservative and radical Islamic groups. In this context, the impact of three major political processes and discourses were crucial: nationalism, liberalism, and the center-right.

The political discourse of nationalism and moderate Islam in Turkey incorporates a peculiar blend of Ottomanism, Islam, nationalism, and modernism. The Milliyetçi Hareket Partisi (Nationalist Action Party, MHP) and the AKP, originally highly radical political movements, share the same voting basis in the central Anatolian provinces and stress a common set of values and viewpoints to appeal to the conservative Sunni-Turkish majority there, despite significant differences in their ideologies. The competition for votes between the Islamic and nationalist movements has intensified as both now claim to move to the center in order to fill the void created by the decline of the center-right parties. The volatility of votes is particularly high among the nationalist, religious, and center-right parties in the same constituencies in central Anatolia. The ideological overlap between Islam and nationalism should therefore be considered in the specific instance of appeal to the conservative Sunni-Turkish electorate.

For the MHP, founded in 1967, nationalism and militant anti-communism were the two major ideological and political objectives, very much counterpoised against the cosmopolitan values of the Westernized elites. Despite the early emphasis on secular-racist Turkism, Islam was later gradually incorporated into the party doctrine in order to appeal to the religious masses and to extend the popular base of the movement. The Turkish Islamic Synthesis (TIS) aimed to bring together two cultural/ideological poles of the right, nationalism and religion, in order to strengthen both the state and the right wing of the political spectrum against communism.[7] Against the Westernist elites' objective of wholesale adoption of Western culture and institutions, the TIS, following the views of early Ottoman reformists, argued that, while borrowing Western science and technology, a country should jealously safeguard its own tradition, that is, the national culture of the people. A core aspect of the indigenous, authentic, and national culture is Islam. The TIS sought a balance between the values of the modern nation-state and Islam, instead of polarizing the two, with the explicit purpose of reinforcing the state ideologically.

For the nationalists, Islam is indispensable for a number of reasons. First, religion is the major source of ethics, morality, spiritual life, and culture. Second, it is believed that strong religious faith and higher ethical values based on Islam will uphold traditional values, thus cementing the national community.[8] Religion also maintains and protects the core institutions of society, such as the family, against the ill effects of Western cultural imperialism. Thus, in the nationalist perspective, Islam is an essential component of national culture and identity and a more religious state and society is highly desirable. Taking the Turkish nation as their fundamental point of departure, the nationalists assume the existence of a perfect harmony between Islam and Turks; Islam in this view is the religion that fits best with the national character of Turks, who have throughout history been the vanguards of Islam, carrying its flag all over the world, and who have developed Islamic civilization and learning to its utmost extent. The Turkish interpretation of Islam is seen as flexible, and the Turkic states, such as the Seljuks and the Ottomans, are regarded as essentially secular, in that they separated religion from state. It is also argued that Sunni Islam reinforces political stability rather than unrest, and

---

7. Tanıl Bora and Kemal Can, *Devlet, Ocak, Dergâh* (Istanbul: İletişim, 1991).

8. Bozkurt Güvenç, et al., *Türk İslam Sentezi* (Istanbul: Sarmal Yayinevi, 1991).

effectively complements the state rather than opposing it.[9] Furthermore, since the most contemporary, urban, and civilized interpretations of Islam have been developed by Turks, Turkey's Muslims should not be looking for precedents and models developed in other Islamic countries.[10]

Moderate forms of Islam and nationalism have some characteristics in common. First, a search for a popular base in traditional values and hierarchical, patriarchal, and communitarian social relations is explicit in the plea of both political movements for the institutions of traditional civil society such as family and kinship, village and neighborhood communities, and the guild system. Similarly, for nationalism as well as Islam, religion constitutes the main fabric of the society and the source of social cohesion. The two viewpoints also insist on the necessity for increased state intervention in spiritual and moral life in order to prevent social atomization, anomie, and alienation. They share in common the glorification of the Ottoman past, placing an equal stress on cultural distinctiveness and the moral superiority of Turkey's traditional Muslim community. Finally, for both moderate Islamists and the nationalists the world is divided into nations and nation-states and they both express their ultimate goal in politics as one of elevating Turkey to the right place among the hierarchy of nations.[11] The increasingly national orientation of the Islamic movement in Turkey can be seen as a sign of its growing divergence from the more universalistic Islamist movements in the Middle East.

A group of liberal intellectuals who have recently introduced highly controversial ideas and views into political discussion emphasize in their writings the centralizing, authoritarian, and militarist nature of the state and the inward-looking and exclusive nature of political activity in Turkey.[12] Their arguments and insights have provided Islamic leaders and

---

9. Taha Akyol, *Osmanlı'da ve İran'da Mezhep ve Devlet* (Istanbul: Milliyet Yayınları, 1999).

10. Mümtaz'er Türköne, "İslamlaşma, Laiklik ve Demokrasi," *Türkiye Günlüğü*, Vol. 13 (Winter 1990), pp. 17–21.

11. Hugh Poulton, *Top Hat, Grey Wolf, and Crescent* (New York: New York University Press, 1997).

12. The ideas of liberal writers and intellectuals have influenced some prominent businessmen and politicians on the center-right and center-left, and very recently, a few among the state establishment. In the early 1990s, a group of liberals founded a political party to promote their ideas and objectives under the leadership of Cem Boyner, a leading businessmen and then president of Turkey's most prestigious businessmen's association, TÜSİAD. Despite considerable support from the media, in the first elections it entered the New Democracy Movement won less than 1 percent of the vote

writers with a contemporary critique of the role of the state in the economy and in society. One of the basic liberal contentions is that the state ideology in Turkey has an exclusive understanding of secularism and nationalism and is intolerant of religious belief and the ethnic identities of the people. In their conception, society is seen as an entity separate from the state, characterized by its highly pluralistic structure consisting of competing groups with divergent interests.[13] The liberals portray the state-society relationship in Turkey as dichotomous, polarized, and overtly hierarchical; specifically, this is not a relationship among equals since the state places itself above society, subordinating and controlling it to safeguard its own interests. The state pervades every realm of social and economic life, undermining the autonomy and diversity of its institutions. Individuals and groups that resist the homogenizing ideology of the state and its official citizenship identity are regarded as dissidents and deviants. Paradoxically, however, globalizing forces, social change, and economic development generate new patterns of social differentiation and introduce new groups that forge new identities and raise new demands that cannot be contained within the official framework.[14] The eventual outcome is described as an ever-deepening crisis of political legitimacy. The civil society discourse of the liberal intellectuals presents a fundamental questioning of the hegemony of the state ideology in Turkey.[15] In this context, the cases of two excluded groups are particularly highlighted: Kurds and Muslims. One of the major liberal contentions is that the republican modernity project has created a major conflict between the authoritarian secularism of the state and the religious culture and sensitivities of the people.

The new Islamist discourse tends to draw specifically on the following ideas of the liberals. First, the liberal insistence on a new democratic constitution for Turkey encourages the Islamist writers who are questioning the legitimacy of the regime in Turkey. Second, the liberal portrayal of the regime as a republic without a democratic substance is a view that is widely echoed by Islamist politicians and writers. Third, the two groups have in common their criticism of, and attacks on, "Kemalism," which

---

and soon disappeared from the political scene. The neoliberal trend survives in a diffuse form in Turkish politics, in the writings and speeches of a group of journalists, academicians, businessmen, and intellectuals.

13. Etyen Mahçupyan, *Radikal Yazilar* (Istanbul: Patika, 1998).

14. Ali Bayramoğlu, "Değişim ve Merkez Partiler," *Yeni Yüzyil,* February 1, 1999.

15. Metin Sever and Cem Dizdar, 2. *Cumhuriyet Tartışmaları* (Istanbul: Başak Yayinlari, 1993).

they identify both with the official ideology of the state and the devoted defenders of the secular regime. Fourth, and perhaps the most important, is the strong liberal challenge to the role of the military in Turkish politics, specifically the identification of the NSC as an organ of state that dominates the government, the parliament, and the people. At a time of increased tension in the relationship between the Islamic movement and the military, the liberal emphasis on the militaristic nature of the Turkish state is embraced as an argument that justifies the moderate Islamic case. Finally, crucial liberal support for the Islamic groups and parties came through their introduction to European and U.S. journalists, scholars, politicians, and institutions.

The VP and later the AKP leaders and the prominent Islamic writers increasingly tended to associate their political identity with a thoroughly indigenous political party and political movement, the Democrat Party (DP) of Adnan Menderes. The so-called "spirit of '46," epitomizing the foundation of the DP as a challenge to the single-party regime (1923–45), has since then become the major source of inspiration for all center-right parties in Turkey. Although the DP leaders, unlike those of the WP, had remained loyal to the secular principle of separation of state and religion, the Islamic politicians who now pay increased attention to the legacy of the "spirit of '46" argue that the political struggles of the WP and the VP as well as the AKP resemble the case of the DP in a number of ways. The political mission of the DP is conceived as one of upholding the national will, the establishment of the supremacy of civilian over military authority, and full-fledged democratization of the country. In their opposition to single-party rule, the Democrats advocated the extension of political freedoms, the relaxation of state control over religious activity, the reduction of bureaucratic regulation, and the democratization of the authoritarian and centralized state using bottom-up policies instigated through increased popular participation. The DP also attempted to redefine the role of religion in politics and society. In their propaganda, the leaders of the party emphasized that there was no imminent threat of religious reaction in the country and that Islam was not an impediment to economic development and modernization.[16]

The moderate Islamic AKP, along the same lines as the DP, is seen as introducing new political elites with popular backgrounds into the political scene to challenge the power of the established elites, and as having greater respect for traditional values. The DP and the WP/VP/AK have both claimed unique access to popular support and political legitimacy,

---

16. Feroz Ahmad, *The Making of Modern Turkey* (London: Routledge, 1993); Erik Jan Zürcher, *Turkey: A Modern History* (London: I.B. Tauris, 1993).

generally espousing a strongly majoritarian view of politics and power. The military coup of 1960 toppled the DP government, sent the majority of its members of parliament to prison, and executed its charismatic leader, Adnan Menderes, together with his two close companions. Thus, the FP and AK rhetoric in the Islamic press and media underlines the victimization of the DP as well as the WP and the VP by anti-democratic and unpopular forces and the political restrictions imposed on their leaders. In the last decade, there has been a major shift in Turkey of votes toward the ethnic, nationalist, and religious parties at the expense of the erosion of the parties on the center-right. For instance, in the November 2002 elections neither of the two major center-right parties was able to pass the 10 percent threshold necessary to enter parliament. The AKP tries to fill the vacuum in the political spectrum created by the absence of the center-right parties by identifying itself closely with the two charismatic leaders of the center-left: Adnan Menderes, the symbol of freedom and popular will, and Turgut Özal, who stands for liberalism and openness to the world.

The development of a new and comprehensive political ideology that synthesizes the competing and conflicting religious, nationalist, liberal, and conservative traditions in Turkish politics is an extremely ambitious project that cannot easily be undertaken by any of the existing political groups and parties on the right. Therefore the increasing similarities and convergences between the political discourse of moderate Islam and other political viewpoints should be interpreted as a search for wider legitimacy on part of the AKP leaders. But the main impact of such ideological influences, including some borrowing from the left of the vocabulary of social equality, has been the secularization of the political discourse of moderate Islam.

Islam, Civil Society, and Democracy

In the course of only a few decades the Islamic movement has created a vast social space that is identified as Islamic civil society by Islamic intellectuals and writers who argue that this particular formation has become the main foundation on which the nascent democracy in Turkey now tends to rest. This section examines the scope and nature of Islamic civil society and raises three major inter-related questions regarding its composition, constitution, and impact. First, what do Islamic activism, and the vast array of Islamic networks, groups, and communities that form the social basis of the Islamic movement, have in common with the ideal-typical Western notion of civil society? Second, do such groupings really accept and integrate the basic values and norms of democracy?

Third, what impact does Islamic civil society have on the political outlook of the Islamic parties?

The core idea and the constitutive unit of civil society is the rational individual, who can make free choices to pursue his or her individual ideas and interests. In this peculiarly Western discourse on civil society, the emphasis on individual liberties involves a negation of Puritan values that generate intense loyalties by binding the individual to the group and submerging his or her identity under a broader communal one. Hence, the emancipation of the individual from the pressure of the community is a constitutive principle of modern civil society.[17] But civil society also involves the association of free individuals on a voluntary basis so that they can promote peaceful and cooperative activities among themselves. Here the stress is on the self-mobilization and self-supporting capacities of such associations. Civil society is conceived as a self-regulating system that has autonomy vis-à-vis the political society and the state and as such its main function is to inform, monitor, check, and pressurize the state and not to win political power to rule. The autonomy of the civil society also derives from a legal and cultural framework that maintains a diversity and plurality in society.[18] The civil society is fundamentally embodied in institutions intermediate between the family and the state: trade unions, pressure groups, voluntary and professional associations, social movements, platforms, networks, and citizens' initiatives. Puritan-type exclusive and inward-looking group activity, and organizations controlled by or aiming to control the state, as well as patriarchal, hierarchical, and patronage-based networks that impose their power over individuals, are considered to be outside the concept of modern civil society.[19]

In the Islamic world, modernist and moderate Islamic intellectuals showed particular vigor in appropriating and developing a civil society discourse. According to this outlook, a perfect compatibility exists between Islam, identified as the basic constituent element of the community, and the notion of civil society. The Islamist opposition, embodying the civil society, is perceived as pushing for increased popular participation in politics, and thus challenging the legitimacy of the authoritarian

---

17. John Keane, "Despotism and Democracy," in John Keane, ed., *Civil Society and the State* (London: Verso, 1988), pp. 35–71.

18. Ergun Özbudun, "Civil Society and Democratic Consolidation in Turkey," in Elisabeth Özdalga and Sune Persson, eds., *Civil Society, Democracy and the Muslim World* (Istanbul: Swedish Research Institution in Istanbul, 1997), pp. 85–92.

19. Robert Nisbet, *The Quest for Community* (San Francisco: ICS Press, 1990); Amitai Etzioni, *The Spirit of Community* (New York: Touchstone, 1991).

and corrupt ruling groups and elites.[20] Intellectually too, attempts are made to emphasize the civilian nature of traditional institutions, such as the learned men of Islam, medieval guilds, Sufi orders, the mosque, and the neighborhood community.[21]

For moderate Islamic writers in Turkey, civil society as a concept has political, economic, and social dimensions. Politically, the Islamist movement, with a monopolistic claim for representing the authentic culture and interests of the people, tends to see itself on the side of civil society. Civil society is perceived as a major source of popular mobilization against the Westernist-secular state. The Islamist movement holds itself to be the only truly indigenous popular identity and the keeper of Islamic values and traditions. It believes that society should have primacy over the state, which at present is only a repressive, irresponsive, corrupt, and inefficient institution. Islam as a new political force has a powerful participatory dimension as it carries new social groups into the political arena. The Islamist movement, with a wide appeal and support from the underprivileged and the excluded, promotes the increased inclusion and participation of new groups and forces in politics and society. This particular outlook identifies the state/society divide as the main cleavage in Turkish politics; Islam, in this perspective, stands for civil society and the state for secularist authoritarianism. Clearly lacking a notion of complementary state-society relationships, Islamic groups and parties tend to conceive of civil society as any political force and ideology opposing the state.[22] Another specifically political aspect of the relationship between Islam and civil society is the recent emphasis on pluralism. As first the WP and the VP and then the AKP and the FP came to recognize the power and influence of the secular forces in Turkey, they tended to postpone or even abandon their claim for hegemony, to argue instead for a separate and autonomous Islamic field. Such autonomy in a pluralistic society is expected to guarantee for the Muslims the free practice of an "Islamic way of life," one, for instance, that would enable Islamist women to wear the headscarf in schools and in government offices. The demand for autonomy is also presented as a democratic step toward accepting the different other, which in this particular case would include the non-Muslims and non-believers.

---

20. Augustus Richard Norton, ed., *Civil Society in the Middle East*, Vol. 1 (Leiden: E.J. Brill, 1995).

21. Ahmad S. Mousalli, "Modern Islamic Fundamentalist Discourses on Civil Society, Pluralism and Democracy," in Norton, *Civil Society in the Middle East*, vol. 1, pp. 51–78.

22. Nur Vergin, *Türkiye'ye Tanık Olmak* (Istanbul: Sabah Yayınları, 1998).

The idea of civil society as an engine of social solidarity is most widely echoed in the vast array of Islamic associations, foundations, informal networks, and local organizations.[23] Islamic communities and networks have been well known for their self-mobilization capacity and high proclivity for spontaneous organization based on mutual trust. At its social base, Islam is most visible in the welfare-oriented activities of the Sufi orders and Islamic communities. These institutions help poor and deprived people to overcome their practical difficulties in everyday life. The best-known example is providing students, tens of thousands of them, with dormitories and other educational facilities. As Augustus Richard Norton describes them, the Islamists are "highly skilled populists."[24] They have also managed to establish organizations parallel to their secular counterparts in virtually every aspect of professional life: employers' associations, trade unions, and professional organizations. Such communal energy leads them to argue that the most dynamic aspect of civil society in Turkey is the religious one and that Islamically inspired civil society that comes from below is the main propellant of democratization in Turkey. More specifically, the moderate Islamic associations promote the strengthening of the civil society, the intermediate level that exists between the individual and the state. The dynamism of the Islamic movement has been most visible in the economic sphere with the emergence and expansion of a new class of Islamic entrepreneurs. This subject is addressed in the next section.

Despite its promotion of political participation, community development, social solidarity, and entrepreneurship, Islamic activism in some of its forms and manifestations deviates significantly from the Western model. The first divergence can be seen in the case of the Islamic conception of the relationship between religion and politics. The tendency among conservative Islamic communities is to insist on the view that the sacred texts of Islam should provide the primary reference for rules and laws that regulate society and politics. At the level of doctrine and ideology, if not always in the world of everyday politics, the traditional communities argue for the unity of religion and politics and of faith and power. In this perspective, religion is not solely a matter of individual be-

---

23. For a comprehensive discussion and ethnographic evidence on Islamic activism at the urban grass roots, see Jenny B. White, "Civic Culture and Islam in Urban Turkey," in Chris Hann and Elizabeth Dunn, eds., *Civil Society: Challenging Western Models* (London: Routledge, 1996), pp. 143–155; and Jenny B. White, *Islamist Mobilization in Turkey* (Seattle: University of Washington Press, 2002).

24. Norton, *Civil Society*, vol. 1.

lief and worship: as a much broader and integral system, Islamic "faith" embraces a code for the social, economic, and political conduct of the individual and the community. Hence, "religious freedom" and "faith" are highly nebulous concepts whose boundaries tend to extend indefinitely. In the Islamic framework the demand for religious freedom is not exclusively about religious belief and practices. Matters pertaining to belief, worship, and religious inquiry such as praying, fasting, pilgrimage, religious contemplation, scholarly study of divinity, and even performing ecstatic rituals are hardly restricted in Turkish society. Instead the assertion for religious freedom primarily involves an attempt to establish an autonomous Islamic community and an Islamic way of life, one that the Islamists are willing to disseminate among a wider Muslim population. Unlike the Muslim communities in Europe who demand minority rights for the Muslims, the Islamic communities in Turkey, sometimes even the moderate ones, divert their activities to strictly political ends such as making Islam reign supreme in the local neighborhood communities, educational system, and bureaucracy. Thus, as Bernard Lewis[25] argues, in the case of Islam what matters is not only the independence of civil society from the state but also the autonomy of the state in the face of religion itself since the general orientation of Islamic community activity is toward strengthening the ties between the state and religion. Again, however, the differences in approach between the conservatives and the moderates are significant. The former insist that religious commandments lay down a comprehensive and detailed legal code that pervades every aspect of social and political life while moderates believe that Islam should be adapted to a general moral and ethical framework for the society.

Islamic social activism has flourished mainly in the urban environment in order to address specifically urban problems. The Islamic networks and communities give their individual members the sense of belonging to a social group and these typically promote the interests and the mobility of their members. Those that have relatively affluent and educated members do uphold individualistic values,[26] but the majority tend to reinforce patriarchal, hierarchical, and authoritarian relations. As Tibi argues, these values and relations persist for the very reason that the social basis of political Islam in isolated villages and poor urban neighborhoods is one of educational backwardness, illiteracy, widespread poverty,

25. Bernard Lewis, *What Went Wrong?* (New York: Perennial, 2002).

26. Elisabeth Özdalga, "Civil Society and Its Enemies: Reflections on a Debate in the Light of Recent Developments within the Islamic Student Movement in Turkey," in Özdalga and Persson, *Civil Society*, pp. 73–84.

and blind submission to authority.[27] In these areas, especially in central and east Anatolia, individuals are forced by the conservative religious leaders to conform to the strongly binding demands and obligations of the community. Social ties in these communities are often rigid and methods of social control are traditional in nature, involving practices such as constant surveillance, strong moral punishment, and social ostracism. Even in the urban context and among students, girls who do not want to cover their heads are identified as having a weak character and since boys deliberately shun them, they may risk not finding good husbands in the community.[28] It is frequently reported that working class women "have to obtain permission from their husbands in order to leave their homes, adhere to strict sex segregation in many public and private settings and are often forbidden to work after marriage."[29]

Islamic groups and communities tend to lay great stress on the symbolic boundaries between themselves and other groups, emphasizing exclusivity and fostering voluntary segregation. Within the group there is a tendency to create a highly uniform lifestyle, which helps the members to distinguish themselves sharply from others. The emphasis on distinctiveness makes the group inward looking and it cultivates sentiments of hostility and intolerance toward others.[30] In the context of everyday life the Islamist groups and communities have little tolerance for plurality and diversity in society. For instance, among the Alevi sect, those who drink alcohol or even men who allow their women to work outside of the home can be dismissed as blasphemous unbelievers.

Islamic activism challenges the authoritarian tendencies in Turkish politics. The richness of associational life in the Islamic realm fosters an active civil society that strengthens the intermediate social level between the individual and the state. The Islamically inspired small group movement promotes the society's capabilities for self-organization and self-help. But Islamist associations have a major difficulty in combining individual freedom with social solidarity as they do not provide enough scope for individual autonomy, privacy, and liberty. At the grassroots level, the bulk of Islamist communities typically retain, reproduce, and

27. Bassam Tibi, "The Cultural Underpinning of Civil Society in Islamic Civilization: Islam and Democracy: Bridges between the Civilizations," in Özdalga and Persson, *Civil Society*, pp. 23–31.

28. Özdalga, "Civil Society."

29. Laura Secor, "What Went Right?" *Boston Sunday Globe*, February 9, 2003.

30. Ruşen Çakır, "Political Alevism Versus Political Sunnism: Convergences and Divergences," in Tord Olsson, Elisabeth Özdalga, and Catharina Raudvere, eds., *Alevi Identity* (Stockholm: Swedish Research Institute in Istanbul, 1998), pp. 63–64.

even reinforce the existing authoritarian and patriarchal relations exercised through traditional mechanisms of control. They also tend to isolate their members from the wider society and this leads to increased social segregation and cultural fragmentation. Finally, most Islamist associations are highly politicized.

Is Islam compatible with democracy? The following discussion focuses on only a few aspects of this extremely complex relationship. First it needs to be emphasized that Islam as a religious belief and political Islam are different things. Political Islam is a contemporary political project and a political discourse created mainly by contemporary forces.[31] Political Islam has rejected democracy, which is conceived as a political system imposed on the local people from outside, and as a system that is believed to be incompatible with Islamic belief, mainly on the grounds that it confers sovereignty on people instead of on God.[32] The Islamic movement in Turkey as well as the WP adopted a negative attitude toward democracy from the very beginning. For instance, even Recep Tayyip Erdoğan, when he was the WP mayor of Istanbul, stated that democracy has only instrumental value for Islam.[33]

The secular political parties and secularist writers often describe the Islamic democracy discourse as "*takiye.*" In its original usage the term refers to temporary avoidance of religious obligations out of necessity, threat of damage, or personal suffering; in more general terms it refers to any religious justification for hiding religious affiliation under such circumstances.[34] In the present context, it implies the instrumental use of democracy in order to win political power to establish an Islamic regime. For instance, very few, even among moderates such as Abdullah Gül, openly renounce the Islamic ideal of unity of state and religion; more prefer to remain obscure and ambiguous about the notion of separation of state and religion, raising instead an enigmatic polemic on the "irreligious Turkish version of secularism" in order to avoid extensive discussion of the subject. Furthermore, the Islamic insistence on presenting the Islamic movement as the only legitimate bearer of the popular will and on dismissing all others as alien is seen by the secular political parties as both incorrect and unfair. The Islamists assume that the Muslim popula-

---

31. Fred Halliday, *Islam and the West: The Myth of Confrontation* (London: I.B. Tauris, 1995).

32. Tibi, "Cultural Underpinning of Civil Society."

33. Pazar Sohbeti, interview with Recep Tayyip Erdoğan, "Demokrasi Bizim için Araştır," *Milliyet*, July 26, 1996.

34. Robert Strothman, "Takiye," *İslam Ansiklopedisi*, Vol. 2 (Istanbul: MEB, 1976).

tion of Turkey, which is almost everyone, naturally prefers an Islamic way of life, provided that they are given free choice. Had they to make a choice between Islamic belief and atheism, even the half-hearted Muslims would opt for Islam in order to avoid being labeled as apostates. Then the non-believers and the non-Muslims would remain as only negligible minorities while the Muslims would constitute the majority population. Hence, the implication is a plural system under the absolute supremacy and domination of Sunni Islam. The fundamental problem with this view is that Muslim believers are conceived as a single undifferentiated entity; thus, a separate space is recognized neither for the Alevi nor the so-called "laic Muslims," the majority Sunni population, who see themselves as Muslims, but who practice Islam in varying degrees.[35] The Islamist movement in Turkey still holds a missionary zeal for Islamizing society, with the understanding that misguided Muslims would eventually correct their behavior. Such intolerant elements are pervasive in the individual attitudes of the majority of Islamic politicians and grassroots activists.

In addition, the highly contested issues between Islam and secularism can have negative consequences for political stability and democracy. First, the use of excessive doses of Islamic symbols and ideology for maintaining party cohesion and increased Islamic political mobilization can create a major secularist backlash. Second, the AKP envisages Islam as an integral way of life that needs to be dominant and visible in most aspects and sections of society. The dissemination of the values and virtues of an Islamic way of life through education, now significantly under the control of the AKP government, can generate increased Islamic-secular tension in schools and in politics. In addition, the government is expected to address the highly disputed *türban* issue, which would polarize public opinion. The regulation of office hours in the work place and the calendar according to religious practices and events is another contested area. Furthermore, changing the status of the Directorate of Religious Affairs to make it more autonomous in passing judgment on moral and ethical issues has long been in the minds of some Islamic politicians and groups. The government is particularly keen in appointing its loyal followers to the bureaucracy in order to make this once bastion of secularism a stronghold of its own. In Islamized government offices the authorities tend to impose their own morality and standards on others by compelling them to join communal prayers, fast in Ramadan, and,

35. David Shankland, "Changing Gender Relations among Alevi and Sunni in Turkey," in Gabriele Rasuly-Palaczek, ed., *Turkish Families in Transition* (Frankfurt: Peter Lang, 1996), pp. 83–97.

specifically in the case of women, to adopt various dress codes. While the Islamists often complain about restrictions that come from the secular authorities when they are in opposition, when in power they too punish dissent using such measures as exclusion, intimidation, and forestalling promotions. Finally, perhaps most significantly, the existence of a government that appears relatively tolerant, if not necessarily approving, of patriarchal, hierarchical, and authoritarian values and relations that are still so powerful in Turkish society tends to unleash, encourage, and reinvigorate the sources of oppressive traditional authority. In Turkey the threat to individual liberty comes from tradition, community, and society as much as from the state. Women are the main losers.

By contrast, at the leadership level the AKP tends to accept fundamental liberal views and values to a greater extent than its predecessors. The attitudes of the moderates toward democracy have initially been "assimilationist" and "appropriationist," as Halliday uses the terms.[36] The first involves emphasizing the similarities between Islam and democracy, following the modernist tradition of explaining democratic notions and principles with an Islamic vocabulary. Democratic ideals such as rule of law, national will, and equality of citizens, freedom of expression and thought, and individual and minority rights are appropriated as originally and essentially Islamic. However, the AKP now goes beyond this to claim that it will bring Western democracy to Turkey. The moderates make it clear that they have no ambition to replace the existing constitution and the civil, penal, and commercial codes with a comprehensive Islamic one. Similarly, giving a constitutional status to Islam is not mentioned among the political objectives of the government. The AKP manifesto emphasizes that human rights and liberties should be implemented as universal standards in order to make Turkey part of the democratic world. These standards are defined according to international agreements such as the Helsinki Final Act, the Paris Charter, and the European Convention of Human Rights. The party's commitment to implement the Copenhagen political criteria of the EU is also noteworthy.

In the Turkish political context, the compatibility of Islam with democracy primarily requires the accommodation of the Islamic movement itself to democratic values and institutions. The citizens of Turkey, the vast majority of whom are Muslims, have adapted to the rules and principles of political democracy, and the country's two major secular traditions, the center-right and center-left, despite hurdles and obstacles in

36. Halliday, *Islam and the West*.

their way and their own shortcomings in meeting the new challenges for democratic reform, have struggled hard to expand the scope of democracy.[37] Moderate Islam has now joined this trend. Provided that the AKP can keep the repressive Islamizing tendencies under control, Turkish democracy can emerge as one that is by and large unique in the Muslim world.

Islamic Business

The relationship between entrepreneurship and Islamic politics, the economic dimension of Islamic civil society, gained a new momentum with the rise of the Islamic bourgeoisie. The Islamic parties have found in the Islamic bourgeoisie a partner, indeed a main pillar, whose economic muscle proved highly productive in sponsoring and financing Islamic religious, educational, political, and social welfare activism.[38] For instance, the Islamic Association of Independent Businessmen (MÜSIAD) has several thousand members spread all over the country. As Buğra indicates,[39] the association aims to develop cooperation, solidarity, and trust among its members through promoting reciprocal business ties and commercial links—subcontracting, outsourcing, information sharing, collaboration in marketing, and distributing representative agencies. However, Islamic capital constitutes only a part of the broader category of the Small and Medium Scale Enterprises (KOBİ) that have flourished in the new growth poles, towns and cities popularly known as the "Anatolian Tigers," as well as the leading metropolitan centers.

The Islamic businessmen and their associations such as the MÜSIAD have until recently remained committed to the principle of centrality of religious identity, arguing for the extension of religious freedoms. The business groups have also shared the anti-Western and anti-capitalist discourse of the Islamic movement. The MÜSIAD set its major organizational goal as one of promoting solidarity among Islamic countries. Its advocacy of the East Asian model of economic development as an alternative to the highly contested Western capitalist type is based on the role

37. Sabri Sayarı and Yılmaz Esmer, eds., *Politics, Parties, and Elections in Turkey* (Boulder, Colo.: Lynne Rienner, 2002).

38. Ayşe Buğra, "Class, Culture and State: An Analysis of Interest Representation by Two Turkish Business Associations," *International Journal of Middle East Studies,* Vol. 30, No. 4 (1998), pp. 521–539.

39. Ayşe Buğra, *Islam in Economic Organizations* (Istanbul: Friedrich Ebert Stiftung, 1999).

that the former attributes to traditional culture and the emphasis it lays on the need for providing a strong moral framework for economic action. The Asian model is also praised for the priority it gives to family and religion, communitarian and paternalistic values in industrial relations, and the significant role that social capital can play in business transactions.[40]

The evolution of Islamic capital has been mainly in the direction of greater integration with the market economy and a search for stability in domestic politics. The Islamic businessmen who suffered both politically and economically from the negative impact of the 28 February process now tend to favor peaceful and conciliatory approaches and policies. Thanks to the social mobility that they achieved, Muslim businessmen have become more content. They want to show that Islam does not necessarily entail poverty and that provided a Muslim man of substance is rightly guided, religious belief is perfectly compatible with prosperity and wealth. The Muslim business stratum enjoys the comforts, luxuries, and joys of middle-class life. Although the Islamic political discourse highlights their political and cultural exclusion, both socially and economically they are well integrated in urban middle-class society. Many of the leading AKP politicians are members of the Islamic bourgeoisie. In summary, the growth of a professional and entrepreneurial middle class constituency and the intensification of global connections among some sections of this particular class impose toleration, moderation, and liberal views on Islamic politicians and writers.

Although the WP government was short-lived, increased access to the municipalities under the control of the Islamic parties, including those in Ankara and Istanbul with their huge budgets, has strengthened Islamic capital and swelled the ranks of the Islamic bourgeoisie. Nevertheless, the Islamic entrepreneurs strongly resent the system of distribution of state resources that favors established business interests and their privileged position in society. In their economic discourse, the Islamic businessmen portray the Turkish economy as a domain of predatory and exploitative monopolies and cartels. The established large-scale corporations—generally characterized as "rentier"—are criticized for lending money to the government with exorbitant interest rates. The Islamic businessmen share with other industrialists the view that during the economic crash of 2001, the huge loans that Turkey received from the international banks were all used to save corrupt banks while the industrial sector and even more so the KOBİ were denied any access to credit.

---

40. Ibid.

In a context marked by the "extreme politicization of rent distribution,"[41] the Islamic bourgeoisie is anxious to increase its own share of the
cake. According to Buğra, the Islamic businessmen speak a double-edged
language of disadvantage. They resent the policies of previous governments, which tended to protect the interests of the politically favored
businessmen. The paradox, however, is that instead of challenging an unjust resource distribution system that favors special interests, Islamic capital now demands preferential treatment from the government for itself,
as a reward for its past loyalty. The AKP government, by contrast, wants
to consolidate its own economic power base by strengthening Islamic
capital. It would be difficult for the AKP to dismiss the demands of the Islamic business community, which is overwhelmingly represented in the
party and the parliament and which for a long time gave life and dynamism to the whole Islamic movement. Yet, adopting partisan policies in
resource distribution risks the danger of alienating those sections of the
KOBİ who in the last elections supported the AKP. Their opposition
could give a new vigor to the center-right parties whom they convention-
ally used to support. Furthermore, positive discrimination in favor of Islamic capital could also fuel opposition from the Istanbul-based big businesses that control the leading mass media companies and institutions.
But if Islamic capital is seriously neglected its support can easily shift to
the rival FP. Önis and Türem characterize the situation as a typical distributional conflict where groups and parties compete to provide more favorable access to state resources for their members.[42] In this kind of situation, the implementation of policies that satisfied all the parties involved
would best serve the interests of the government but this would require
sustained economic growth.

Prospects and Challenges

What then are the prospects for moderation, electoral success, and political stability for the AKP government? First, can the party successfully
combine its moderate Islamic orientation with the traditional values of its
conservative social base? The new leadership has strong support among
the Islamic urban middle class, which, however, is still relatively small

---

41. Ziya Öniş, "The Political Economy of Islamic Resurgence in Turkey: The Rise of the
Welfare Party in Perspective," *Third World Quarterly*, Vol. 18, No. 4 (1997), pp. 743–766.

42.   Ziya Öniş and Umut Türem, "Business Globalization and Democracy: A Comparative Analysis of Turkish Business Associations" *Turkish Studies*, Vol. 2, No. 2
(2001), pp. 94–120.

and weak and technically and professionally not as competent as its secular counterpart. Its hold on the traditional Islamist constituency is not very strong. The floating protest voters judge parties according to economic performance rather than ideology. The AKP is made up of different elements and suffers from lack of homogeneity, cohesiveness, and harmony; past and present, new and old, moderate and conservative, local and global are all in a state of flux and tension in the party. If the AKP were to move further to the center-right position in the political spectrum in order to accommodate democracy, the secular forces, and the Western world then it would risk alienating its Islamist voting base. For instance, a possible alliance with the United States in the war on Iraq seemed to pose such a threat; it aggravated internal strife and tension in the party between those of center-right origin and the Islamic moderates on the one hand and the hard-line Islamists on the other. Furthermore, if the party's foreign and economic policies do not prove successful, the rival SP may benefit by appealing to the conservative AKP members of parliament and voters. With regard to all these issues the danger for the AKP is that of factionalism and political disarray that could create major fractures and divisions in the future.

Second, can the AKP government prevent a major secular Islamic confrontation? There are many sources of anxiety and strain that threaten political stability: the continuing mutual mistrust between the secularists and the adherents of the Islamic movement; conflicts over the highly emotive politico-religious symbols such as wearing the *türban* in public places; the ongoing debate on revitalizing the religious school system; the Islamic infiltration of the bureaucracy and the army; attempts by the secular forces of the state to confine the activities of the AKP government; and the distributional conflict between secular and Islamic capital. Increased tension and conflict between the secular and Islamic blocs could reinforce and solidify Islamic support for the AKP government, strengthening it against the SP. Then, however, the party would risk losing moderate votes to the center-right parties. The government would then confront serious opposition not only from the secular parties and the military but also from the business community and the secular media.

Third, the majority of the voters tend to evaluate government performance on the basis of economic and social policy, most specifically the government's capacity to create jobs, increase living standards, and provide social security for more people. Equally significant for the voters is the government's determination to fight against corruption and bring more transparency and accountability to the system. For the vast majority of the voters increased prosperity and better justice are far more important objectives than ideology and cultural policy. In the area of governmental achievement, the AKP is vulnerable to criticism from all opposition whether right or left.

The Changing Foreign Policy Outlook

Political Islam in Turkey has opposed Western political, economic, and cultural domination, introducing Islam as an alternative system to resist, challenge, and replace the Western system. The West is conceived as a system contrary to Islam, a rival religion and culture, a source of external domination, an unjust economic system, and a sick society on the verge of ethical collapse. The West, it is argued, has lost the original message of Christ and ended up with secularism, an ideology that is marked by the neglect of religion and that has bred a society solely guided by material interests and the pursuit of power for its own sake. Western domination in the form of colonialism and imperialism has involved the violent repression, economic exploitation, and cultural exclusion of non-Western peoples. Capitalism, the economic system of the West, has brought exploitation, extreme disparities of income, misery, and poverty. From this perspective, the consumerist culture of the West is believed to lie at the basis of the moral breakdown in modern society and its social ills, such as rising crime rates, collapse of family life, illicit sexual relations, and alcohol and drug abuse. Finally, the West is specifically blamed for its racism, intolerance of other cultures, and violence against excluded outsiders.[43]

In foreign policy, Islamist writers and politicians before the 28 February process took a clearly anti-Western stance. The United States, for instance, was generally characterized as a superpower that acts according to double standards, that is always involved in vicious plotting to destabilize individual nation states, specifically those that are Islamic. Europe used to be seen as colonial, racist, ethnocentric, and exclusive. Turkey's integration with the EU was again rejected by the Islamists on grounds of fundamental civilization differences based on religion and the dangers of possible limitations on national sovereignty. By contrast, an alternative Islamic international system to provide a base for political action, security, and economic cooperation for all Muslims was advocated. Anti-Westernism used to lie at the core of Islamist identity and the political discourse of the WP. Islamist ideology was also based on a critique of Turkey's modernization process and Turkey's close relations with the

---

43. Sencer Ayata, "Perceptions of Foreign Policy and International Relations in the Islamic Press," workshop paper, Washington Institute of Near Eastern Studies, July 25–27, 1997.

Western world.[44] The WP introduced itself as the antithesis of the West, calling the Muslim world to wage a major combat against Western imperialism. The Islamists tended to see Turkey historically, geographically, and culturally as part of the Islamic world and its identity as totally indigenous, based on its traditional Muslim culture. The WP envisaged foreign policy as highly instrumental in achieving its domestic political project: total national independence and rapid economic development to counter Western power and hegemony. Turkey was assigned the role of the leading Islamic country to initiate an alternative block.

However, in the course of only five years, from 1997 to 2002, the foreign policy orientation of the Islamic parties changed so radically that at least in the case of the AKP the previous anti-Westernism was replaced by Euro-enthusiasm. Moderate Islam in Turkey has no major objections to Turkey's role in NATO and no longer argues for an alternative Islamic defense organization. Similarly, it has abandoned its project of an Islamic commonwealth to challenge Western economic cooperation organizations. Furthermore, at least at the leadership level, though not necessarily at its social base, there is a great willingness to see Turkey in the EU. The AKP manifesto, for instance, stresses mutual national interests as the guiding principle in foreign policy without making any reference to the role of religion and Islam in international relations.[45] The significance of Turkey's relations with the European countries is underlined and the party is committed to fulfill the EU membership requirements. On security issues the manifesto emphasizes Turkey's commitment to NATO, also asserting, however, that Turkey deserves increased participation in the new European security system. It also proposes that relations with the United States be broadened by stimulating U.S. direct investments in Turkey and increased cooperation in the fields of science and technology to transcend the existing hard security–centered relationship. Deepening Turkey's relations with the Turkic states in the Caucasus and Central Asia and specifically the Islamic world is advocated as a means of diversifying foreign relations.

When the AKP came to power, the government launched a campaign in the EU countries to promote Turkey's membership. Its then politically restricted leader, Erdoğan, visited almost every European capital negotiating with leading statesmen to set a date for starting accession negotiations between Turkey and the EU. It was ironic that at a time of crucial decision-making about Turkey's membership, the secular Turkish Repub-

---

44. İhsan Dağı, *Kimlik Söylem ve Siyaset* (Ankara: İmge Kitabevi, 1998).

45. "Adelet ve kalkinma partisi Programi 2001" at <www.akparti.org.tr>.

lic was represented at the EU Copenhagen summit of 2001 by a party with Islamist roots that had long seen Europe as a major source of evil and conspiracy against Islam and Turkey.

Two questions are crucial in relation to the changing foreign policy orientation of moderate Islam: what accounts for this abrupt change of attitude and how stable is it? The major impetus behind this change was the gradual moderation of the Islamic movement analyzed in this chapter. Nevertheless, additional factors can be taken into consideration. To begin with, significant changes have been taking place in the economic sphere. Islamic business associations such as the MUSIAD began to argue for Turkey's accession to the EU in search of a democratic anchor to guarantee freedom for political activity. Muslim businessmen acknowledge that they function in an economy that is increasingly geared to external markets and specifically to Europe. For instance, Turkey has been trying to overcome economic stagnation through boosting its export of manufactured goods, the demand for which comes mainly from the EU countries. Companies, whether Islamic or secular, especially as they grow bigger in size and use more sophisticated technologies, tend to join this trend as intermediaries, subcontractors, and direct exporters. They become ever more dependent on the Western economies for markets, technology, advertising, consulting, and production services. Islamic entrepreneurs also recognize that EU membership could stimulate foreign investments and thereby increase the overall level of economic prosperity in the country. Thus, despite their strong religious and cultural bent toward intensifying business ties with Muslim, Eastern, and Asian countries, many Islamic companies tend to join the increasingly Western and European oriented orbit of the Turkish economy.

Islamic businessmen have developed a new kind of relationship with the European countries; they collect the savings of tens of thousands of Turkish immigrants in Europe and invest these in joint ventures in Turkey that function on the principle of sharing of capital gains and losses. This venture or participation capital involves the mobilization of Islamic networks and communities for raising funds to promote the establishment of new enterprises. This system has created a new bridge between the Islamic movement in Turkey and Europe as the Islamic businessmen visit European countries frequently, have first-hand experience of them and develop a permanent interest in the state of business of the immigrant communities and their host societies.

Another significant aspect of the EU relationship is that three and a half million Turkish immigrants in Europe constitute a culturally heterogeneous, politically divided, and socially stratified community having a diversity of political and religious orientations and viewpoints. Among them are secularists, the Alevi, Islamic moderates, and radical Islamists. A growing number of immigrant individuals have in the past one or two decades integrated further into the adopted society, becoming established workers, retired pensioners, and small-scale entrepreneurs. Meanwhile the second and even third generation migrants have also expanded in numbers. The Islamically inspired immigrants still have many complaints about European society: the mutual mistrust between Muslims and non-Muslims, high unemployment among the immigrants, problems that their youth experience in schools and in urban life, exclusion from various political and social institutions, and threats to Islamic family values and relations that come from a sexually more permissive and more individualistic society. It is also true that people in the immigrant community naturalize and take part in various ethnically- and religiously-based networks and voluntary activities—generally the males of course. What makes them content about their life in Europe is that while they maintain their customs and cultural practices and preserve their Islamic identity they can improve their living standards and benefit from comprehensive governmental social security services. Although they strongly reject cultural integration and have only minimal encounters with the non-Muslim host population they no longer see their new environment as a realm of war for the Muslims, as do many among the radicals.[46] They have most of their encounters in the world of work and in the segregated neighborhood communities where they live. As such they develop an awareness of urban society and the plurality of the host country with its diversity of groups, cultures, and lifestyles. They observe that modern citizenship in a multicultural society allows socioeconomic integration while retaining cultural distinctiveness. Muslims in Turkey learned of this cultural autonomy from their counterparts in Europe at a time when their freedoms and sometimes businesses were under threat in the aftermath of the 28 February process. This new positive image of the West, fundamentally a pluralist society granting freedom and autonomy to Muslims, had a strong appeal to those Islamic politicians in Turkey who had close encounters with Muslims in Europe.

At a different level, direct encounters of Islamic politicians, intellectuals, and writers with Europe and the Western world have intensified. The proliferation of conferences, round-table discussions, and dialogue platforms organized by Western NGOs and institutions has offered represen-

46. For very recent data and discussion on the subject of Muslim identity in Europe, see "A Survey of France," *Economist*, November 16, 2002; "A Survey of Germany," *Economist*, November 23, 2002; and "Special Report on Islam in Europe," *Time*, December 16, 2002.

tatives from Islamic parties and associations the chance to present their views in organized debates and discussions. Islamically-inspired intellectuals, scientists, students, and writers who live abroad have formed a globally well-connected intelligentsia that has appropriated the basic values of democracy. This new generation of "Young Muslims" have both influenced the AKP leaders with their ideas and also acted as political intermediaries between them and the representatives of various European and U.S. institutions.

The change in foreign policy orientation is also the outcome of a set of political factors. The WP approach came up against a major dilemma when it became apparent to the leaders that the party's foreign policy objectives, including creating an alternative Islamic bloc, had virtually no chance of realization. After WP's closure the new leadership of the VP abandoned the claim for a distinctive Islamic foreign policy. In the late 1990s and early 2000s the leading Islamist movements and regimes were all losing power and prestige and Islamic sources of support and inspiration in the Middle East were notably absent. The political moderation of the Islamic movement and its diminishing emphasis of a distinctive Islamic foreign policy were in tandem; it was as though once the dream of creating an alternative Islamic world order was gone the domestic political project had also collapsed. The party presented its defense against the 28 February measures as one of fighting for democratic rights and freedoms: it appealed to Western governments, institutions, and public opinion in order to strengthen itself vis-à-vis the secular forces in Turkey. For the moderates, this involved a major reconsideration and reinterpretation of Islamist identity and politics, which they increasingly found incompatible with Western values and democracy.[47]

The primary interest of the AKP was to win the election, come to power, and consolidate its hold on the government. The leaders of the party know that their rule is always subject to constraints imposed by a vigilant secularist elite, the mass media, and institutions of the state such as the military. The two most powerful actors in domestic politics—the big business community that controls the media, and the military—had strained relations with the Islamist parties in the past and are still highly suspicious of the activities of the AKP. In its efforts to prevent military encroachment, the AKP considers the EU, which as part of the accession criteria insists on the civilian control over the military, as a major ally. Hence, deepening integration with the EU is a top policy priority of the

---

47. İhsan Dağı, *Ortadoğu'da Islam ve Siyaset* (Istanbul: Boyut Kitaplari, 1998).

AKP government to win the support of the Euro-enthusiast business community and to widen its scope of action in domestic politics.

As inexperienced zealots, the AKP leaders took power at a time of great ordeal. Turkey had to make ultimate and binding decisions with regard to cooperation with the United States in the war on Iraq. The future of Cyprus and EU membership were also among the monumental issues in foreign policy. In their first months in power the party leaders found themselves in the midst of extremely intensive diplomatic relations that brought them into contact with many leaders of the Western world. Having been restricted in Turkish politics only a few months earlier, the leaders of the AKP dined with and talked to the most eminent statesmen and politicians in the Western world. Force of circumstances placed them at the center of developments and events requiring cooperation with almost all their previous opponents and rivals, including Turkey's military leaders, the Europeans, and the Americans. A few months of experience in the affairs of the Western world and heightened sense of involvement in extraordinary diplomatic events also helped to change the views and attitudes of the AKP leaders toward the Western world, which became increasingly familiar to them.

The AKP leaders acknowledge that they live in a world where the leading Western powers—despite significant competition and conflicts among them—have established global economic, political, and military supremacy and are keen to impose their liberal democratic norms and values on other societies. The dominant groups in Turkey respond positively to this challenge: the big business community is seeking to intensify and reinforce its global economic links, while the military is determined to remain within the framework of Western security systems. Due to the country's enormous foreign debt, any Turkish government has to come to terms with the demands of international economic organizations that are controlled by the leading Western governments. Beginning in the 1970s, Islamic politicians emphasized the close relationship between economic development, political influence, and military power. The AKP is sensitive about economic considerations for other reasons too; first, only a buoyant economy will maintain the government's popular support and second, in the party itself the single most powerful group is the Islamic bourgeoisie, which is enthusiastic about developing economic relations with the Western world. Finally, the AKP needs political support from outside, primarily the EU and the United States, in order to strengthen its position in domestic politics against the secular parties and the military.

Countervailing tendencies and forces are also powerful. The AKP has the highest proportion of Euro-skeptic voters and the multitude of groups and associations constituting the organizational infrastructure of the Islamic movement still holds strong anti-Western attitudes. Islamic politicians also insist on discrediting the views, values, and symbols of the secular professional, bureaucratic, and entrepreneurial middle classes whom they deeply mistrust. The secular middle class is, however, the main repository of political experience, professional competence, and intellectual vision; its exclusion would deprive Turkey of one of its most valuable assets in its economic and diplomatic encounters with the Western world. Also, though moderate Islamic politicians have accepted the basic values of civil society, democracy, and pluralism, the strength of their commitment to these values has not yet been seriously tested by time and conditions. Yet the Islamic politicians carry a whole stock of ideas and sensitivities, indeed an ethos or world-view that they received from their Islamist past. What influence will this have on their political behavior when they find themselves at a crossroads facing crucial moral or ideological dilemmas in decision-making? For such questions there are no simple answers. Lastly, for many countries in the world, specifically for those in the Middle East, the international and regional context of foreign policy has become more uncertain, unstable, and risky after the U.S. intervention in Iraq. Thus, the divergent trends in the new international environment coupled with the internal contradictions and conflicts of the Islamic movement could make Turkey's foreign policy more inconsistent, ambivalent, and volatile during the AKP rule.

Conclusion

An important segment of the Islamic movement in Turkey has recently made a major Western turn in its foreign policy. The main thrust of Turkey's foreign policy is unlikely to change and the AKP government will remain loyal—despite some new nuances and sensitivities—to modern Turkey's historical commitment to fuller integration with Europe and the Western world.

But it is also possible that Islamic anti-Westernism is likely to persist as a powerful trend in two major areas. First, Muslims—as well as some other political groups in Turkey and the Middle East—are extremely suspicious of the West and specifically the United States as an intrusive and corruptive power. The mainstay of Islamic anti-Westernism, however, is based in the realm of culture: this involves an emphasis on the role of religion in the defense of society against Westernizing influences. The Western way of life is perceived as a major threat to the traditional gender role definitions, communal solidarity, and the religious devotion of the people. Modernist Islam in Turkey has stressed that Islamic countries can and should adopt Western science and technology—and to these objectives moderate Islam now adds the incorporation of Western political institutions of civil society and democracy. The immediate implication for the AKP's foreign policy orientation is that in the near future, the moderate Islamic strategies emphasizing dialogue and enhanced cooperation with the Western world in the economic and political spheres will go in tandem with a cultural protectionism against the encroachment of Western values and lifestyles.

Chapter 13

The Kurdish Question and Turkish Foreign Policy

Kemal Kirişci

The end of the Cold War and the collapse of the Soviet Union and former Yugoslavia brought to light the challenge of multi-ethnic and multicultural demands facing nation-states. The violence that surrounded Iraq's repression of the Kurdish rebellion at the end of the Gulf War in 1991 and the many ethnic conflicts in the Balkans and the Caucasus have been the more brutal manifestations of the difficulties associated with the failure of governments to adjust to what political scientist Crawford Young called "the rising tide of cultural pluralism" and "the disuniting of the nation."[1] During the 1990s, Turkey also faced an ever intensifying questioning of its national identity and unity, particularly from its Kurdish population. The failure to accommodate Kurdish ethnicity and culture has been an important factor that has led to the deaths of thousands of civilians and the displacement of masses of people, as well as severe human rights violations.[2] This failure has also caused many governments and international political actors to be drawn into the conflict between Turkey and the Kurds. As a result, the Kurdish question became interna-

---

1. Crawford Young, "The Dialectics of Cultural Pluralism: Concept and Reality," in Crawford Young, ed., *The Rising Tide of Cultural Pluralism: The Nation-State at Bay?* (Madison: University of Wisconsin Press, 1993).

2. There is a very large body of literature examining the Kurdish problem in Turkey. Among these publications are Robert W. Olson, ed., *The Kurdish Nationalist Movement in the 1990s: Its Impact on Turkey and the Middle East* (Lexington: University Press of Kentucky, 1996); Michael M. Gunter, *The Kurds and the Future of Turkey* (New York: St. Martin's Press, 1997); Kemal Kirişci and Gareth M. Winrow, *The Kurdish Question and Turkey* (London: Frank Cass, 1997); Henri J. Barkey and Graham E. Fuller, *Turkey's Kurdish Question* (Lanham, Md.: Rowman and Littlefield Publishers, 1998).

tionalized and came to dominate a significant proportion of Turkey's foreign policy. Issues ranging from Turkey's membership of the European Union (EU) to getting the international community to choose to transport Caspian and Central Asian oil through Turkey became linked to this question.

The extent to which the Kurdish problem came to dominate Turkish foreign policy was probably best exemplified by the saga concerning the capture of the leader of the Kurdistan Workers' Party (PKK), Abdullah Öcalan, by Turkish authorities in Kenya in February 1999.[3] The saga started in October 1998, the very month that the seventy-fifth anniversary of the foundation of the Turkish Republic was being celebrated. Syria expelled Öcalan, subsequent to a Turkish threat of military intervention. In November, matters reached a climax when Öcalan was arrested in Italy on his way from Russia, where his initial demand for asylum had not been granted. A legal and diplomatic battle occurred between Turkey and Italy over the extradition of Öcalan to face trial in Turkey. A wide assortment of political actors participated in this battle. They ranged from those calling for the extradition of Öcalan to Turkey, such as the U.S. government, to former Italian communist parties seeking to grant him asylum. There were also many non-governmental organizations (NGOs) involved in this battle, for example, the Helsinki Watch, a prominent U.S.-based human rights organization, which called for Öcalan's trial for crimes against humanity in an international tribunal. Eventually, Öcalan was forced to slip out of Italy (in January 1999) and for days flew the skies of Europe in an unsuccessful attempt to find refuge until he was captured in Kenya.

Öcalan was tried and sentenced to death in June 1999. However, during and after his trial, he substantially moderated his views. He advocated greater democratization and pluralism in Turkey as a solution to the Kurdish problem, rather than secessionism or a federal solution.[4] In August, he even called for an end to the use of violence by the PKK and urged his militants to turn themselves in to the Turkish authorities as a gesture of good will. This was followed by general moderation on the part of Kurds in Turkey. Relations with the West took an unprecedented turn for the better, resulting in a major improvement in Turkey's relations with the EU and the United States. This new trend culminated in the visit

---

3. For a chronology of the saga, see CNN and *Milliyet* (<www.milyet.com.tr/>), February 16, 1999.

4. For the full text of Öcalan's defense statement, see Oktay Pirim and Süha Örtülü, *Ömerli Köyünden İmralı'ya PKK'nın 20 Yıllık Öyküsü* (Istanbul: Boyut Kitaplari, 1999), pp. 293–361.

of President Clinton to Turkey in November and the EU's decision in December to accept Turkey as a candidate for membership. Subsequently, the EU required Turkey to meet a minimum set of democratic criteria for accession negotiations to start. These developments were accompanied by a growing commitment on the part of the Turkish government and political leaders to support greater democratization and reforms in Turkey. In October 2001 the Turkish parliament adopted a series of critical amendments to the Turkish constitution and in August 2002 and June 2003 was able to adopt the necessary legislation to give effect to these amendments, as a result of which broadcasting and education in Kurdish became legal for the first time in the history of the Turkish Republic. This was accompanied by a decision abolishing capital punishment, enabling Öcalan's death sentence to be commuted to life imprisonment in October 2002. These reforms have been recognized as a sign of the Turkish government's commitment to join the EU as well as a manifestation of the EU's ability to instigate political transformation in a candidate country.

The Kurdish question in Turkey had been a function of the state's failure to reconsider the definition of its national identity in a manner that would allow Kurds to express and live their ethnic and cultural identity in public. The problem was also aggravated by the PKK's armed struggle to set up a separate Kurdish state. Turkish security forces fought to prevent the PKK from achieving its goal. Traditionally, there were two approaches to the Kurdish question in Turkey.[5] The dominant and hard-line approach had seen the problem as externally driven and has pursued what is basically a military way of dealing with it. The more moderate and liberal approach has seen the problem mostly as a denial of Kurdish cultural and ethnic identity, and has advocated political reforms in support of greater democracy and pluralism in Turkey, and economic reforms aimed at achieving greater development in the east and southeast of Turkey, where traditionally most Kurds have lived. The hard-line approach long dominated governmental decision-making in Turkey, regarding both domestic and foreign policymaking. However, after the capture of Öcalan, the gap between moderates and hard-liners diminished. A number of factors have played a role in this development, most importantly the improvement of relations with the West. The prospects of EU membership strengthened the commitment to introduce political reforms. At the same time, many Kurdish politicians and leaders expressed a desire to work within the political system to find a solution to the

---

5. Şahin Alpay, "Kürt Kapanı," *Milliyet* (Turkish daily), October 3, 1998.

Kurdish problem. This clearly made it much easier to raise and debate reforms in respect to the Kurdish problem, without risking the wrath of hard-liners.

The focus of this chapter is Turkey's relations with its neighbors, as well as with Europe and the United States. The manner in which Turkish foreign policy and Turkey's relations with the external world have been affected by the Kurdish problem is also analyzed. The chapter argues that the conspicuous improvement in Turkey's relations with the West, and especially the EU's decision to open the way to Turkish membership, has created an environment conducive to solving the Kurdish problem. Those who have long argued that the West, and particularly the EU, could play a critical role in helping to improve and consolidate democratic pluralism in Turkey may actually be proved right. It is also in such a climate that the liberal and hard-line views on the Kurdish problem may stand the best chance of being reconciled. This reconciliation is much more likely to occur and to be consolidated if the EU remains engaged in efforts to bring about Turkey's membership. A concrete manifestation of this would be the offer by the EU of a date for starting accession negotiations.

Turkey and the Kurdish Problem

The founders of the Turkish Republic led by Atatürk aimed to transform the decrepit Ottoman Empire into a modern and secular republic. In this respect emphasis was given to developing a sense of nationhood based on the Turkish language. In the context of the 1920s, this was an important step in transforming a traditional society where identities were local and often religiously defined. In the Ottoman Empire, particularly, ethnic identities among the Muslim population did not carry much significance beyond the cultural and the linguistic. The common bond was Islam. This emphasis remained an important driving force behind the national resistance and liberation struggle from 1919 to 1922. Kurdish tribal leaders held important positions in this struggle, as well as in the first national assembly formed in April 1920. Interestingly, during this period, of the 23 rebellions that occurred, only three were Kurdish. The most important of the three was the Alevi Koçgiri rebellion in 1921, to which Sunni Kurdish tribes refused to lend support.[6]

However, with the declaration of the Republic in 1923 and the abolition of the caliphate in 1924, accompanied by a series of social and political reforms, the newly born state took an increasingly modernist and sec-

---

6. For rebellions during this period, see *Türk İstiklal Tarihi*, Vol. 6: *İstiklal Harbinde Ayaklanmalar (1919–1921)* (Ankara: Gnkur Basimevi, 1974).

ularist character. This process included a redefinition of the national identity, with an emphasis on territoriality rather than religion. For the founders of the Turkish Republic, the European, and in particular, the French, experience of the past century was central to their project.[7] The 1924 constitution defined a "Turk" as anyone living within the boundaries of Turkey and attached to Turkey by bonds of citizenship. Legally, the state would be indifferent to a citizen's religious or ethnic identity. Yet, right from the very start it was clear that, in practice, matters would evolve differently. The indication of this divergence came during the assembly debate on citizenship, when a member of the assembly, with striking frankness, remarked that the legal definition was fine, but that the "real" citizens of Turkey were Hanafi Muslims who spoke Turkish.[8] Such an approach risked leaving not only Kurds, who mostly did not speak Turkish and belonged to the Shafi branch of Sunni Islam, outside the definition of "real" citizenship in the new Turkish Republic, but also Arabs and Alevis.

Building a modern, secular, and national state was not an easy task. Considerable resistance was encountered from many quarters, but the most persistent was that which came from Kurdish-populated areas of the country. Of the 18 rebellions that broke out against the government between 1924 and 1938, 17 were in eastern Anatolia, and 16 of them involved Kurds.[9] Interestingly, none of these rebellions included Kurdish Alevi tribes. Clearly, a secular state, in which the bias against the Alevis had not yet made itself evident, seemed preferable to the Ottoman state that had traditionally discriminated against them. The Alevi Koçgiri tribe, which had rebelled earlier, refused to join the infamous Shaykh Said rebellion of 1925 led by Sunni Kurds.[10] The Kurdish rebellions were fueled partly by a local elite, who resented the centralized power of the modernist state, and partly by a sense of Kurdish political consciousness.

---

7. There is an impressive body of literature that examines the origins and evolution of Turkish nationalism and the formation of the Turkish Republic. A study covering these topics and offering a critical analysis of the formation of the Turkish national identity is Hugh Poulton, *Top Hat, Grey Wolf, and Crescent: Turkish Nationalism and the Turkish Republic* (London: Hurst, 1997).

8. Şeref Gözübüyük and Zekai Zengin, *1924 Anayasası Metinleri Hakkındaki Meclis Görüşmeleri* (Ankara: Balkanoğlu Matbaacılık, 1957), pp. 439–440.

9. For a detailed coverage of each rebellion, see *Türkiye Cumhuriyeti'nde Ayaklanmalar (1924–1938)* (Ankara: Gnkur Basimevi, 1972).

10. For a detailed study of the Shaykh Said rebellion see Robert W. Olson, *The Emergence of Kurdish Nationalism and the Sheikh Said Rebellion, 1880–1925* (Austin, Tex.: University of Texas Press, 1991).

By 1939, all such insurrections had been suppressed, and the authority of the central state stood unchallenged.

In the first decades of the republican era, policies aiming to mold a diverse mosaic of ethnic and cultural identities into a Turkish national identity were also undertaken. Emphasis was put on the Turkish language, as well as Turkish culture and history, as interpreted by the Turkish Language and History Societies.[11] The efforts of these two societies were focused on developing and disseminating arguments to mobilize the public behind a homogenous identity characterized by the Turkish language and the idea that all persons living in Turkey were Turks who were descendants of a people who migrated out of Central Asia, as bearers of civilization. The government also introduced immigration and resettlement policies to assimilate diverse ethnic and cultural identities into a Turkish identity. A conscious effort was made to settle Turkish-speaking immigrants from the Balkans among the Kurds, while resettling some of the more rebellious tribes in western parts of Turkey.[12]

The mid-1930s coincided with government efforts to deny the very existence of a separate ethnic Kurdish identity and instead advocate the notion that Kurds were "mountain Turks." By the 1950s, it seemed that this approach had achieved reasonable success, as many Kurds and other ethnic groups in Turkey melted into a Turkish national identity. But by the late 1960s, a number of leftist groups began to raise the Kurdish question as an issue. The government met the challenge by adopting policies ranging from co-option to repression and continued to deny the existence of a separate Kurdish identity. The Kurdish problem became aggravated in the mid-1980s, as the PKK emerged as an organization seeking secession and began to attack civilian as well as military targets. This violence and the human rights violations resulting from the operations of the security forces against the PKK, together with the activities of Kurdish organizations, helped to raise consciousness among Turkish citizens of Kurdish origin.[13]

This growing sense of ethnic and cultural consciousness among many Kurds engendered two main and competing approaches toward the problem on the part of policymakers. Each approach defines the prob-

---

11. For the details of the formation of these societies and their politics, see Poulton, *Top Hat, Grey Wolf, and Crescent;* and Büşra Ersanli-Behar, *İktidar ve Tarih: Türkiye'de "Resmi Tarih" Tezinin Olusumu (1929–1937)* (Istanbul: AFA Yayınları, 1992).

12. For a detailed analysis of these policies and their implication for the Turkish national identity, see Kemal Kirişci, "Disaggregating Turkish Citizenship and Immigration Practices," *Middle Eastern Studies,* Vol. 36, No. 3 (July 2000), pp. 14–17.

13. See especially chapters 2 and 3 in Barkey and Fuller, *Turkey's Kurdish Question.*

lem differently, and the policies it propounds reflect its particular bias in analysis.

The hard-line approach, very briefly, is the one that argues that there is no Kurdish problem, but a problem of terror, aggravated by the economic and social problems of southeastern Turkey and the support given to the PKK by the international community. This way of thinking was for a long time supported by the military as well as the government. This approach had the upper hand beginning in 1993, when Tansu Çiller formed the government, following the death of President Turgut Özal and the ascent of former Prime Minister Süleyman Demirel to the presidency. One reason why the strictly military response prevailed was the fact that in 1993, the PKK seemed to be on the verge of leading a popular uprising. At that time, the PKK could almost run "liberated zones" and impose its own law and order (extorting taxes, preventing political parties from operating, banning the Turkish media, and punishing "collaborators" from these areas). Once the policy was adopted, the PKK was substantially weakened by a long series of security operations in southeastern and eastern Turkey and in northern Iraq.[14]

The advocates of this hard-line approach have argued that once terrorism is eradicated, then economic and social programs associated with the Southeastern Anatolia Project (GAP) would resolve the problems of the region.[15] Immediately after Öcalan's capture, this position was reinforced. Süleyman Demirel, in an interview with the Turkish daily *Milliyet*, dismissed the possibility of any language reforms for Kurds, arguing that Turkey had one official language. He went on to say that in Turkey there were many ethnic groups with their own languages, and that the only way to protect the unity of the country was with one language; he added that he was against broadcasting in Kurdish.[16] His remarks were accompanied by Prime Minister Bülent Ecevit's announcement in March 1999 of a special financial package to boost the economy of the Kurdish-populated provinces of southeastern Turkey. There was also a promise of

---

14. According to a report by the General Staff of the Turkish military summarized in *Milliyet*, September 29, 1999, the number of PKK acts of violence (*eylem*) fell steadily from 3,328 in 1994, to 1,500 in 1996, and to 589 in 1998. Similarly, the number of PKK militants dropped from approximately 10,000 (both inside and outside Turkey) in 1994 to 4,000 in 1999, and the PKK was able to keep only 25 percent of them within the country, compared to 65 percent in 1994.

15. Ali Çarkoğlu and Mine Eder, "Domestic Concerns and the Water Conflict over the Euphrates-Tigris Basin," *Middle Eastern Studies*, Vol. 37, No. 1 (January 2001), pp. 41–71.

16. *Milliyet*, February 19, 1999.

a repentance law for PKK members who turned themselves in. Ecevit's package did not make any reference to a Kurdish problem, even when he went to the most Kurdish of cities in Turkey, Diyarbakır, to launch it.[17] In the national elections of April 1999, this hard-line approach appeared to receive public endorsement. Ecevit's Demokratik Sol Partisi (Democratic Left Party, DSP) received the highest percentage of the votes, followed by the right-wing Milliyetçi Hareket Partisi (Nationalist Action Party, MHP)—long a supporter of the hard-line approach.

However, soon after the formation of a coalition government led by Ecevit's DSP and including the MHP and the Anavatan Partisi (Motherland Party, ANAP), this hard-line approach began to erode. One important factor was the discourse that Öcalan adopted during his trial throughout May and June. In his defense statements, he repented the death and destruction caused by the PKK and promised that he would be willing to serve Turkey, if his life were spared. His advocacy of greater democracy and pluralism coincided with the new government's aim of a more liberal democracy and an improvement in Turkey's human rights record. Ecevit played a critical role in this respect, and in a personal letter to the newly elected social democrat chancellor of Germany, Gerard Schröder, just before the EU's June summit in Cologne, he expressed his government's determination to meet the Copenhagen criteria of the EU.[18] According to these criteria, prospects of membership require that a candidate country achieve stability of institutions guaranteeing democracy, the rule of law, human rights, and respect for and protection of minorities. This was the turning point at which the political process was set in motion that led to the EU's formal acceptance of Turkey's candidacy. In June, the government also succeeded in pushing through parliament a constitutional amendment removing the military judge who was to hear Öcalan's case from the state security courts. This reform had been demanded earlier by a decision of the European Court of Human Rights and was considered in Europe to be an important step toward ensuring a fair trial for Öcalan.

During the course of 1999, a series of unprecedented developments occurred. After the August 1999 earthquake disaster in Turkey, the government took a relatively constructive attitude in the face of a massive amount of public criticism. This was manifested in a willingness to work with the international community in disaster relief but, more importantly,

17. *Milliyet,* March 8, 1999.

18. The letter was originally sent secretly on May 26. However, it was subsequently leaked and published in *Hürriyet* (Turkish daily), June 5, 1999, together with Chancellor Schröder's answer.

also demonstrated a new readiness to work with Turkish civilian groups. In October 1999, the minister responsible for human rights in Turkey, Mehmet Ali Irtemçelik, held a conference with human rights organizations and other NGOs and expressed a willingness to work more closely with them.[19] Just before the Organization for Security and Cooperation in Europe (OSCE) summit held in Istanbul, the government allowed the pre-summit gathering of NGOs to take place without any interference, thus reflecting a major change in attitude compared to the treatment that many NGOs had received during the UN Habitat II summit held in Istanbul in June 1996. During this summit some events organized by NGOs were interrupted by the police or prevented from taking place. Furthermore, during the OSCE summit, government officials, including the president, made statements about the need to improve Turkey's democracy and human rights. Most striking was, of course, the occasion when President Demirel, during his meeting with President Clinton, publicly acknowledged that Turkey had a problem concerning the use of torture and that the government was determined to address it.[20]

Another critical development weakening the hard-line position on the Kurdish problem was the shift in position of the PKK and the increase in the number of moderate Kurdish views. Kurdish opinion throughout the 1990s was largely dominated by the PKK. Few Kurdish public figures dared to deviate from this position, and those who did, did not find a very receptive environment for their views, so far as the Turkish government was concerned. Many remained silent, and some simply advocated the government line. The PKK's decision to drop its armed struggle and its secessionist agenda in support of democratization and pluralism helped to generate a lively debate in Kurdish circles. A number of political movements supportive of a moderate Kurdish agenda emerged. This was very much reflected in an interview given by the mayor of Diyarbakır, Ferridun Çelik, a member of the pro-Kurdish Halkın Demokrasi Partisi (People's Democracy Party, HADEP). He argued that the violence and separatist agenda of the Kurdish movement had not helped solve the Kurdish problem in Turkey and maintained that his party was committed to seeking a solution to the problem through democratization and pluralism in Turkey.[21] This approach probably explains why, compared to previous years, the relationship between

---

19. The proceedings of this meeting were published in *Hukukun Üstünlüğü Demokrasi İnsan Haklari: Sivil Toplum Örgütleriyle Düzenlenen Çalışma Toplantısı—Ankara Palas,* 14 Ekim 1999 (Ankara: Başbakanlik Basimevi, 1999).

20. *Radikal* (Turkish daily), *November 15, 1999.*

21. *Radikal,* January 17, 2000.

HADEP and the Turkish state was much more positive, or at least much less confrontational. Earlier in 1999, attempts by state prosecutors to have the party closed down on the grounds of its advocacy of separatism were overruled by the constitutional court. HADEP participated in the elections of April 1999. Although it was unable to win seats at the parliament during the national elections, it won mayoral positions in 37 districts, mostly in Kurdish-populated parts of the country. The central government appears to have learned to live with HADEP-led local governments.

Lastly, the decision to dissolve the "Kurdish parliament in exile," mostly dominated by the PKK, at its session in Brussels in September 1999, also helped to improve the political climate.[22] This parliament had long been a source of serious tension between Turkey and the many European countries where it held its sessions.

The effects of moderation became visible among the military too. Early in September 1999, the chief of general staff pointed out that there was in Turkey *de facto* broadcasting in Kurdish. In December he also declared that the military did not want to become involved in the decision as to whether or not the execution of Öcalan should be carried out. That decision, he argued, lay with the government.[23] At its end-of-year meeting, the National Security Council (NSC) discussed the possibility of lifting the emergency rule, which severely restricted civil rights and gave the authorities overarching security powers over a number of Kurdish-populated areas.[24] This rule had been in place since 1987 and was frequently blamed as the cause of human rights violations. Its termination has long been called for by moderates, and all political parties represented in the parliament gave their support to this change.[25] In parallel with efforts to adopt EU-related reforms, the number of Kurdish provinces under emergency rule was progressively reduced and the rule in the last two remaining provinces of Diyarbakır and Sırnak was extended for the final time in June 2002.

In spite of these developments, it should be noted that the hard-liners in Turkey argue that reforms granting cultural rights to Kurds constitute

---

22.   In their analysis of this parliament, Barkey and Fuller note the close relationship between the membership of the parliament-in-exile and the PKK. Barkey and Fuller, *Turkey's Kurdish Question*, p. 34.

23.   *Radikal*, December 17, 1999.

24.   *Radikal*, December 30, 1999.

25.   *Radikal*, December 28, 1999.

a threat to the unity and territorial integrity of Turkey. Members of the parliament belonging to MHP voted against these reforms as well as the lifting of the capital punishment. They accused other members of the parliament of wanting to save the life of Öcalan for the sake of pleasing the EU rather than giving priority to Turkey's national interest.[26] But the MHP was decisively defeated in the November 2002 elections and left with no seats in the parliament. This has weakened the ability of the hard-liners to obstruct the adoption and implementation of political reforms directly addressing the Kurdish problem.

The second, more liberal, approach starts with the premise that in essence, the Kurdish problem is a product of increasing demands by Kurds to express their cultural and ethnic identity and the inability of Turkey to adjust to these demands. After a decades-old policy of denial, this new approach first officially surfaced in the late 1980s under Turgut Özal's presidency. He made it known that he was partly of Kurdish descent and initiated contacts with the Kurdish leadership in northern Iraq, just before the refugee crisis of April 1991. He also played a critical role in seeing through the adoption of legislation that rescinded the law that had banned the public use of the Kurdish language. Following the 1991 national elections, Süleyman Demirel, the new prime minister and leader of the Doğru Yol Partisi (True Path Party, DYP), in the company of his coalition partner, Erdal İnönü, made what at the time was considered to be a historic speech. He argued that Turkey had to recognize the Kurdish reality and could not continue to pretend that Kurds were Turks who had originally come from Central Asia.[27] The speech and the program of the newly formed coalition seemed to be offering the possibility of introducing measures that would eventually enable the Kurds in Turkey to maintain their Kurdish ethnic and cultural identity as Turkish citizens.

This was a period when society debated the Kurdish problem at length, but it was also a period marred by violence, coinciding as it did with the saga of Halkin Emek Partisi (People's Labor Party, HEP) and its successor, Demokrasi Partisi (Democracy Party, DEP). The radical nationalist rhetoric adopted by the leaderships of these two Kurdish nationalist parties provoked the hard-liners in the parliament into action. Both parties were shut down, and this action was followed by the sentencing of DEP members of parliament to varying lengths of prison terms for advocating separatism and supporting the PKK. This development signaled

26. *Radikal,* August 5, 2002.

27. *Milliyet* and *Hürriyet,* December 9, 1991.

the fall of the more liberal approach from favor.[28] Subsequently, many intellectuals (members of the civil society), as well as some politicians and members of government, continued to express support for this approach, but rather meekly and intermittently. To all intents and purposes, the liberal approach remained very much in the background until recently.

This situation began to change significantly by the summer of 1999. The expression of liberal views and opinions concerning the Kurdish problem became much more common, even popular, both within and outside government circles. One of the first striking expressions of such views came from Sükrü Elekdağ, a former influential ambassador previously associated with hard-line views on the Kurdish problem.[29] In a set of articles, Elekdağ argued that Turkey did not need to fear anything in allowing broadcasting in Kurdish and added that, in effect, this was already taking place. He also supported the idea that there should be some possibility of education in Kurdish.[30] Similar ideas had for a long time been put forward by many columnists, especially in liberal newspapers, but that a former high level bureaucrat should become their proponent showed the shift in opinion regarding the Kurdish problem. The liberal approach received a significant boost when the chief judge of the High Court of Appeals (Yargıtay), Sami Selçuk, made a historic speech in which he stated that the current constitution had lost its legitimacy. He advocated a constitution and legal system that would open the way to a truly democratic and pluralist society with complete freedom of expression. Although he did not refer to the Kurdish problem directly, he did not leave any room for doubt as to where he thought the ideal solution lay when he maintained that individuals should be able to express their cultural identity freely.[31]

---

28. For the closure of these political parties and the ascendancy of hard-liners, see Philip Robins, "The Overlord State: Turkish Policy and the Kurdish Issue," *International Affairs*, Vol. 69, No. 4 (October 1993), pp. 657–676; and Henri J. Barkey and Graham E. Fuller, "Turkey's Kurdish Question: Critical Turning Points and Missed Opportunities," *Middle East Journal*, Vol. 51, No. 1 (Winter 1997), pp. 59–79.

29. Elekdağ had advocated the view that Turkey's Kurdish problem was mostly foreign-instigated, emphasizing the role of Greece and Syria in particular, and arguing that Turkey should be prepared to fight two and a half wars simultaneously, with these two countries and internally with the PKK. Şükrü Elekdağ, "2½ War Strategy," *Perceptions: Journal of International Affairs* (Ankara) Vol. 1, No. 1 (March–May 1996) <www.mfa.gov.tr/grupa/percept/i1/per1–3.htm>.

30. *Milliyet*, June 21, June 28, and September 10, 1999.

31. Excerpts from the speech can be found in *Milliyet* and *Radikal*, September 7, 1999. The full speech can be found at <yargitay.gov.tr/bilgi/adli/99–20.html#d126>. See especially the section on "Cultural Identity" (Kültürel Kimlik).

The chief judge's speech marks the beginning of a period during which an increasing number of politicians and members of the government energetically called for political reforms in support of greater democracy. However, until after the adoption of the constitutional amendments of October 2001 few politicians expressed support for reforms regarding the Kurdish populated provinces. The exceptions in government were Deputy Prime Minister Mesut Yılmaz, the leader of ANAP, and Foreign Minister İsmail Cem. Yılmaz had, on a number of occasions, supported the idea of political reforms to allow for broadcasting and education in Kurdish. In December 1999, he paid a visit to Diyarbakır, the largest Kurdish-populated city in Turkey and a city whose population has been most directly affected by the violence and repression resulting from the confrontation between the PKK and security forces. There, he implied that Turkey's membership in the EU was linked to an improvement in the political and economic lot of the Kurds. Cem, by the same token, suggested during an interview that it might be possible to allow education in Kurdish.[32] Both Yılmaz and Cem met considerable criticism from hard-liners. Yılmaz was bitterly criticized by members of the MHP, including Deputy Prime Minister Devlet Bahçeli. An MHP member of the cabinet even went as far as accusing Yılmaz of "speaking like the PKK," adding that Turkey was a unitary state with one flag and one language.[33] In the case of Cem, there were calls that he should actually be prosecuted and tried for expressing such divisive views.[34]

The constitutional reforms of October 2001 ushered in a new era in Turkish politics. In particular an amendment to Article 26 of the constitution opened the way to the possibility of the public use of languages other than Turkish.[35] Subsequently, a massive debate on broadcasting and education in Kurdish started that at times became very acrimonious. Ultimately, the moderate approach prevailed and the parliament adopted a series of specific reforms in August to meet the requirements to respect

---

32. *Radikal,* December 14, 1999.

33. Speech by Abdullah Çay, *Radikal,* January 5, 2000.

34. These calls were turned down by the prosecutor, who argued that there were no grounds for prosecution, and that people were free to express their views; *Radikal,* January 5, 2000.

35. For an analysis of the meaning and consequences of this amendment see Kemal Kirişci, "Evaluating the Question of Minorities in Turkey in the Light of Turkish-EU Relations," in Bertil Duner, ed., *Turkey: The Road Ahead?* (Stockholm: Swedish Institute of International Affairs, 2002); for a detailed analysis of the package of amendments, see Bertil Emrah Oder, "Enhancing the Human Face of Reality in Turkey Through Accession Partnership with the EU," in ibid.

cultural rights of minorities in an attempt to meet the Copenhagen criteria of the EU. The parliament was also able to rise above the populist calls of the MHP to prevent the lifting of the death penalty. Undoubtedly, Turkey's aspirations to become a member of the EU and the pressing need to start negotiations for accession played a critical role in the political transformation of the Kurdish problem in Turkey that helped the moderate approach to prevail over the hard-line one. Nevertheless, the U.S. intervention against Saddam Hussein in March 2003 and the ensuing instability in Iraq have revived hard-liners' fears that a Kurdish state in northern Iraq could emerge and threaten Turkey's national unity and territorial integrity.

Turkish Foreign Policy and the Kurdish Question

In the late 1990s, Turkish foreign policy had been characterized by a conspicuous assertiveness. This can to a large extent be seen as an outcome of the hard-line policy adopted toward the PKK and the Kurdish problem during the 1990s. By 1995, the military was already confident that it had seriously weakened the PKK's presence in Turkey. In a series of military operations in the mountainous areas of southeastern Turkey, the PKK was driven mostly into northern Iraq.[36] As a part of Turkey's denial of the existence of a Kurdish problem, the PKK had always been portrayed as an externally-supported organization whose aim was to weaken and divide Turkey. Such a portrayal is very much part of what in Turkey is commonly referred to as the "Sèvres syndrome," a concept popular among nationalist, as well as bureaucratic and military circles. It is based on the belief in a conspiracy and embodies the fear that the Treaty of Sèvres will be revived. (This was the treaty drawn up by the victorious powers at the end of the First World War that carved up the remaining Anatolian regions of the Ottoman Empire into small states and occupation zones.) Turkey is seen as surrounded by enemies who are efficient and can act in unison. The PKK is depicted as a tool of such a conspiracy. The conspirators are most of Turkey's neighbors and the West, including the United States.[37]

---

36. For reporting by prominent journalists on an improved security situation in the southeast as early as 1994, see *Sabah* (Turkish daily), May 13, 1994. The *Turkish Daily News* (TDN), January 8, 1996, reported a significant drop in 1995 in PKK-led terrorist incidents. The *Economist*, December 17, 1995, also noted that the military had won the upper hand, but at the cost of alienating ordinary Kurds.

37. For a brief analysis of the "Sèvres syndrome" and its impact on foreign policy, see Kemal Kirişci, "Turkey: Foreign Policy Making and the Mediterranean," in Theodore

The immediate focus of attention became northern Iraq, where the PKK had succeeded in establishing a series of military bases from where they were able to mount attacks on Turkey. The infighting between the two opposing Kurdish groups in northern Iraq, the Kurdistan Democratic Party (KDP) and the Patriotic Union of Kurdistan (PUK), had created an environment conducive for the PKK to consolidate itself there.[38] In March 1995, Turkey mounted a massive military operation involving 35,000 troops and lasting six weeks.[39] This was an operation very different from the frequent previous incursions mounted in pursuit of the PKK. It signaled the beginning of a new strategy that aimed to deny northern Iraq to the PKK.

Turkey had played a leading role in the adoption of Security Council Resolution 688, and then the establishment of a safe haven north of the 36th parallel, in an effort to ensure the repatriation of almost half a million mostly Kurdish refugees who had fled from the Iraqi military.[40] The task of managing the return of these refugees and then ensuring their safety fell to Operation Provide Comfort (OPC), composed of mostly U.S. and British military personnel. Once the repatriation was completed, the military wing was withdrawn to a NATO base in southern Turkey, from where they have continued to operate on six-month mandates granted by the Turkish parliament. From its earliest days, OPC was highly controversial in Turkey, and many suspected that it was helping the PKK as well as assisting the establishment of a Kurdish state in northern Iraq.[41]

A. Couloumbis, et al., eds., *The Foreign Policies of the European Union's Mediterranean States and Applicant Countries in the 1990s: A Comparative Analysis* (London: Macmillan, 1999), pp. 25–60.

38. On the conflict between the two Kurdish groups in northern Iraq and the PKK, see Michael Gunter, "Kurdish Infighting: The PKK-KDP Conflict," in Olson, *The Kurdish Nationalist Movement*, pp. 50–64.

39. For details of this operation and its background, see Kemal Kirişci, "Turkey and the Kurdish Safe-Haven in Northern Iraq," *Journal of South Asian and Middle Eastern Studies*, Vol. 19, No. 3 (1996), pp. 21–39.

40. For the text of the resolution, see UN Security Council Document S/RES/688 (1991), April 5, 1991. The resolution called on Iraq to cease its military operations against Kurds that had precipitated the flight of more than a million refugees towards Iran and Turkey, and called on the government to cooperate with the international community in resolving the refugee crisis. For an analysis of the adoption of the resolution and its importance from Turkey's point of view, see Kemal Kirişci, "'Provide Comfort' and Turkey: Decision Making for Refugee Assistance," *Low Intensity Conflict and Law Enforcement*, Vol. 2, No. 2 (Autumn 1993), pp. 227–253.

41. Baskın Oran, *"Kalkik Horoz": Çekiç Güç ve Kürt Devleti* (Ankara: Bilgi Yayınevı, 1996); Ümit Özdağ, "Kuzey Irak ve PKK," *Avrasya Dosyası*, Vol. 3, No. 1 (Spring 1996); and Ümit Özdağ, *Türkiye-PKK ve Kuzey Irak* (Ankara: Avrasya Dosyası Yayınları, 1999).

The presence of a large number of NGOs, together with a forward military office of OPC in Zakho, known as the Military Coordination Command (MCC), remained a continuous source of friction between Turkey and the United States. The problem was also aggravated by U.S. policies aimed at organizing Iraqi opposition to the regime of Saddam Hussein, using as cover the NGOs operating in the area.

In the fall of 1994, in an attempt to address the problem, Foreign Minister Mümtaz Soysal introduced new, more stringent rules to regulate the entry of NGOs into northern Iraq from Turkey.[42] However, the security problem in northern Iraq from Turkey's perspective was not resolved until 1996. First, in May 1996, yet another massive Turkish military operation into northern Iraq took place after the PKK forced out villagers from KDP-controlled areas near the border.[43] The operation uprooted the PKK from the area, with the cooperation of the KDP, and then left behind significant units to support the KDP in patrolling the area. Second, in August 1996, the KDP mounted an attack on PUK-held territory, with the support of the Iraqi military. This led to panic among NGO workers and the locally hired personnel, culminating in a U.S. decision to evacuate. The closure of the MCC office and the departure of Americans significantly strengthened the hand of Turkey and that of its local ally, the KDP, in continuing to confront the PKK. Last, in November of the same year, the KDP and the PUK signed a cease-fire. From the Turkish military's point of view, this was a significant development that increased the possibility that the KDP would confront the PKK. A diplomatic effort that became known as the "Ankara process" was launched, with the aim of consolidating both the cease-fire and Turkey's influence in northern Iraq. Both parties were reminded of their economic and security dependence on Turkey. Turkey was northern Iraq's only major access to the external world and was also the host of OPC, policing the safety zone against the Iraqi military. By 1997, there had already been a significant fall in the PKK's ability to operate in northern Iraq and attack Turkey from there. In 1998, another major blow was inflicted on the PKK, when one of its leading commanders, Semdin Sakık, after having broken ranks with the PKK leadership, was apprehended and brought for trial to Turkey.[44] Since Öcalan's call for an end to the armed struggle, most PKK militants have

42. Oran, "Kalkık Horoz," pp. 128–130.

43. On PKK attacks, see TDN, March 14, 1996. On PKK-PUK conflicts, see Gunter, "Kurdish Infighting," pp. 51, 56.

44. TDN, April 14, 1998.

left Turkey and retreated into northern Iraq. At its Seventh Congress meeting in January 2000 in northern Iraq, the PKK leadership endorsed Öcalan as their leader and approved his decision to end the armed struggle. The congress also decided to reorganize various branches of the PKK to wage a political rather than an armed struggle.[45] Furthermore, Turkey has continued to maintain a small but effective military presence in northern Iraq as well as considerable influence over KDP and PUK leadership to preempt remaining PKK militants from contemplating any attacks on Turkey. The September 11, 2001, attacks on the twin towers in New York and the Pentagon and the subsequent war on terrorism also facilitated Turkey's efforts to keep the PKK subdued. Nevertheless, Turkey continues to be concerned about the prospects of a "Kurdish state" emerging in northern Iraq, particularly in the aftermath of the U.S. military intervention against Saddam Hussein's regime.[46] This concern was expressed in a very forceful manner immediately after the reconvening of the Kurdish parliament in Erbil in October 2002.

A greater assertiveness in foreign policy was also reflected in Turkey's relations with Iran and Syria. After the revolution in Iran, relations between it and Turkey have frequently suffered a downturn. Turkey often accused Iran of supporting Islamic fundamentalist groups operating in Turkey. Yet, in spite of these crises, the two countries by and large managed to maintain a working relationship. However, as the military operations against the PKK in Turkey and in northern Iraq intensified, Turkey increasingly accused Iran of harboring the PKK and providing it with logistical support. Iran has always rejected these accusations, but continued PKK attacks in areas adjacent to the Iranian border increased the tension between the two countries.[47] It has even been rumored that a frustrated

---

45. For a detailed reporting on the congress, see *Özgür Politika* (biweekly bulletin published by the Kurdistan Information Centre London), February 10, 2000. For a general evaluation of the PKK since Öcalan's capture see Michael Radu, "The Rise and Fall of the PKK," *Orbis*, Vol. 45, No. 1 (Winter 2001), pp. 47–63.

46. For an evaluation of Turkish concerns about northern Iraq after Öcalan's capture, see Nihat Ali Özcan, "Türkiye'nin Kronikleşen Baş Ağrısı: Kuzey Irak," *Stratejik Analiz*, Vol. 1, No. 12 (April 2001); and Armağan Kuloğlu, "11 Eylül Sonrası Değişen Dengeler Çerçevesinde Türkiye'nin Irak Politikası," *Stratejik Analiz*, Vol. 2, No. 23 (March 2002).

47. For a detailed analysis of Iran's relationship with the PKK, see Nihat Ali Özcan, "Iran'in Türkiye Politikasinda Ucuz ama Etkili Manivela: PKK," *Avrasya Dosyası*, Vol. 5, No. 3 (Fall 1999). For a briefer coverage of the issue in English, see Alan Makovsky, "Turkish-Iranian Tension: A New Regional Flashpoint?" *Policy Watch* (Washington Institute for Near East Policy), No. 404 (August 9, 1999) <www.

Turkish government considered a military attack on PKK bases in Iran in May 1995.[48] In April 1996, a major crisis occurred when the two countries exchanged accusations of espionage and support for terrorism. Yet another crisis erupted in July 1996, when the PKK mounted an attack on a Turkish military post on the Iranian border. The president visited the border and criticized Iran bitterly.[49]

During his premiership from July 1996 to June 1997, Necmettin Erbakan, the leader of the Islamist Refah (Welfare Party, WP) made visible efforts and expressed great enthusiasm to improve relations with Iran, but soon encountered bureaucratic and public objections. In August 1996, he was loudly censured for visiting a country considered to be supporting anti-Turkish terrorism. Similarly, in December 1996, during the visit by Iranian President Akbar Hashemi Rafsanjani, Erbakan's desire to reach a defense cooperation agreement with Iran was vetoed by General Staff and Defense Minister Turhan Tayan of the DYP. The following month, the Turkish foreign ministry accused Iran of supplying the PKK with heavy weapons, including Katyusha rockets. Relations with Iran deteriorated further when the Iranian ambassador in Ankara became embroiled in an Islamic fundamentalist gathering in a suburb of Ankara in February 1997, which eventually, under heavy military pressure, triggered the dissolution of the WP-led coalition government.[50] This led to a recall of ambassadors, and in December 1997, President Demirel found himself leaving the Islamic Conference Organization's summit in Tehran early, when his Iranian hosts tried to censure Turkey for its relations with Israel. Subsequent relations with Iran appear to have improved somewhat, partly through the launching by Foreign Minister Cem, in February 1998, of the "Neighborhood Forum," which aimed to improve relations with neighboring Middle Eastern countries. The improvement of relations has become relatively easier since the PKK stopped mounting armed operations out of Iran. During the visit of Iranian Foreign Minister Kamal Harrazi, his Turkish counterpart insisted that a difference in style of regimes should not constitute an obstacle to friendly and cooperative

---

washingtoninstitute.org/watch/Policywatch/policywatch1999/404.htm>; and Kemal Kirişci, "Turkey and the Muslim Middle East," in Sabri Sayarı and Alan Makovsky, eds., *Turkey's New World: Changing Dynamics in Turkish Foreign Policy* (Washington D.C.: Washington Institute for Near East Policy, 2000), pp. 51–52.

48. *Tempo* (Turkish magazine), No. 18, May 1, 1996.

49. TDN, July 18, 1996.

50. For a thorough and detailed analysis of the Erbakan government's foreign policy, see Gencer Özcan, ed., *Onbir Aylık Saltanat: Siyaset, Ekonomi ve Dış Politikada Refahyol Dönemi* (Istanbul: Boyut Kitapları, 1998), pp. 179–242.

relations. Harrazi in his turn announced that his government was opposed to the PKK and did not support its activities.[51] But Prime Minister Bülent Ecevit had argued, only a month earlier, that the new sponsor of the PKK was Iran.[52] Against the pragmatism of the foreign ministry, the Turkish military also continued to believe that Iran supports terrorism in Turkey. This belief was reinforced and led to bitter accusations against Iran when, in February 2000, a series of gruesome graves of victims of Turkish Hezbollah violence were unearthed and the culprits apprehended by the police. With Iran's national elections during the Spring of 2000 producing a parliament dominated by reformists and Iran's conscious efforts to distance itself from terrorism since the September 11, 2001, attacks there has also been a marked improvement in Iranian-Turkish relations. The improvement was marked by the Turkish president's visit to Iran in June 2002. The visit itself and the support for Turkey's membership of the EU expressed by his counterpart Mohammed Khatami, as well as the latter's recognition of Turkey's Western and indirectly secular vocation, were regarded as an important signs of reconciliation.[53] These may be indications that the bitterness resulting from Turkish accusations of Iranian support for the PKK may have been left in the past.

Turkey had long maintained that Syria was harboring Öcalan in Damascus, but this was denied by Syria on every occasion. Erbakan had argued, in a major break from well-established practice, just before forming his coalition government, and in an effort to improve relations with Syria, that Syria was not supporting the PKK.[54] In late 1997 and early 1998, a number of meetings took place between Syrian and Turkish foreign ministry officials. However, before these meetings could produce any positive results, relations soured when, during a radio program, the Syrian ambassador to the United States raised the sensitive issue of the province of Hatay.[55] Turkish authorities protested at what they considered to be an irredentist claim from Syria directed at Turkey's territorial integrity. The situation worsened in September 1998. Chief of General Staff Hüseyin Kıvrıkoğlu argued that, because of Syrian support for the PKK, there actually was an undeclared war going on between Turkey and Syria. The Turkish government called on Syria to stop its support for Öcalan, while the Turkish military began to mass on the border. Prime Minister Mesut

51. *Radikal,* January 19 and 20, 2000.

52. *Radikal,* December 15, 1999.

53. *Radikal,* June 19, 2002.

54. *Yeni Yüzyıl* (Turkish daily), May 7, 1996.

55. Reported by *Milliyet,* May 7, 1998.

Yılmaz argued that Turkey was determined to end Syrian support for
Öcalan. Since the PKK had been defeated, Syria had to stop supporting
Öcalan in order to end the threat posed by the PKK.[56] The crisis was resolved without violence when the Egyptian president's mediation paid
off, and Syria eventually expelled Öcalan. The hard-liners had clearly
achieved a major victory. The PKK had been weakened substantially, first
within Turkey, then in northern Iraq, and now the actual leader of the
PKK had been forced out of Syria. Since then, bilateral relations have
started to improve. A symbolic expression of this occurred during the
Muslim holidays in January 2000 at the end of Ramadan, when the two
governments allowed local people living in the region of the border town
of Ceylanpınar to visit their friends and families.[57] For decades the border
had been closed for such visits. Societal interactions as well as trade between the two countries have significantly increased.

The elite of Turkey, loyal to the concept of a modern and secular Turkey, always considered membership in the EU and integration with Europe to be their ultimate goal. As Süleyman Demirel put it, "one of the
main thrusts of Turkish foreign policy is to realize Turkey's perennial
drive to integrate fully with Europe."[58] The long relationship that had begun in the early 1960s was always expected to evolve naturally into membership in the EU.[59] In 1989, when the European Commission finally
turned down a Turkish application for membership, many in Turkey considered it a temporary setback. The general belief was that further democratization and the consolidation of the liberalization of the Turkish
economy would eventually create the circumstances for membership.[60]
But relations between Turkey and the EU began to deteriorate in 1993, as
the Kurdish problem in Turkey became aggravated and the PKK in Europe became increasingly successful in mobilizing the Kurdish diaspora
and leading campaigns against Turkey. This was reflected in a growing

56. *Radikal,* October 12, 1998.

57. For a very positive reporting of this decision in the media, see *Radikal,* January 10
and 11, 1999.

58. Süleyman Demirel, "Commentary," *Middle East Journal,* Vol. 51, No. 1 (Winter
1997).

59. Meltem Müftüler-Bac, "The Never-Ending Story: Turkey and the European
Union," *Middle Eastern Studies,* Vol. 34, No. 4 (October 1998), p. 243; Ziya Öniş, "Tur-
key, Europe and Paradoxes of Identity: Perspectives on the International Context of
Democratization," *Mediterranean Quarterly,* Vol. 10, No. 3 (August 1999), p. 107.

60. See, for example, remarks by Hikmet Çetin, a former foreign minister and
speaker of the Turkish parliament, after the EU's ruling, in *Milliyet,* December 10, 1989.

barrage of criticisms directed against Turkey for violating the human rights of Kurds. As a result of such public censure, some governments imposed arms embargoes on Turkey, and the European Parliament (EP) suspended financial assistance to Turkey.

One important factor that has influenced Western European attitudes toward Turkey is the presence of an active Kurdish community. There are no reliable statistics on the number of Kurds living in Europe. The director of the Kurdish Institute in Paris, Kendal Nazan, puts their number at 850,000 and estimates 10 percent to be supporters of the PKK.[61] The majority reside in Germany, and most of them arrived as part of a massive labor migration from Turkey to Germany during the 1960s and, to a lesser extent, in the 1970s. In the 1980s, after the military coup in Turkey, a growing number of Kurds, often supporters or activists of the PKK, sought asylum in Germany and some of the other European countries.[62] Many of the asylum seekers came to constitute the cadre of PKK front organizations in Europe. These organizations are involved in numerous activities, ranging from running nationalist publications to raising, often through extortion and drug trafficking, large sums of money for the PKK. The PKK also runs MED-TV, a television station broadcasting across Europe. It founded the Kurdish parliament-in-exile in April 1995. Because of PKK dominance in this parliament, a number of Kurdish organizations, for example, the Kurdish Socialist Party, led by the veteran and moderate Kemal Burkay, as well as the KDP and PUK, declined to join it.[63] Before its dissolution in September 1999, the parliament met in a number of capitals around Europe and developed extensive contacts with representatives from various European political parties. This enabled the PKK to mobilize considerable support among politicians and public figures in Europe. The activities of the PKK across Europe and among the Kurdish diaspora played a central and critical role in raising awareness of Kurdish national identity.[64] The success of the PKK was very much reflected by the large number of Kurds it mobilized across Europe to protest the capture of Öcalan. At the same time, however, the PKK to a great extent also

---

61. Quoted in the *New York Times*, February 19, 1999.

62. Anita Bocker, "Refugee and Asylum Seeking Migration from Turkey to Western Europe," *Boğaziçi Journal*, Vol. 10, Nos. 1–2 (1996), pp. 55–57, 61.

63. Barkey and Fuller, *Turkey's Kurdish Question*, pp. 37–38.

64. For a detailed analysis, see A.J. Lyon and E.M. Uçarer, "The Transnational Mobilization of Ethnic Conflict: Kurdish Separatism in Germany," paper prepared for the International Studies Association annual meeting, Minneapolis, March 1998.

stifled alternative voices among the Kurds in Europe. One important consequence of this was that many among the European public and politicians came to consider the PKK as representing the Kurds in Turkey.[65]

This situation is possibly best demonstrated in a resolution adopted by the EP in December 1998, following the crisis between Turkey and Italy over the extradition of Öcalan to Turkey. The resolution bitterly criticized Turkey and called for an international conference to find a political solution to the Kurdish problem in Turkey. What was particularly striking was that the resolution referred to "terrorist activities of certain Kurdish organizations" but did not mention the PKK by name. This vividly demonstrates the legitimization that the PKK appears to have received in the EP. In 1992, for example, Jas Gawronski had resisted efforts by some left-wing members of the parliament to introduce amendments to his EP report recognizing the "Kurdish people's right to self-determination including independence." Instead the report had called the PKK a terrorist organization and had acknowledged Turkey's right to defend itself against terrorism.[66] However, the fact that the Kurds were referred to as a minority[67] was enough for the Turkish government to distance itself from the report and the EP. Nevertheless, this report was clearly much more balanced and less partisan than the December 1998 resolution of the EP. A retired ambassador, Gündüz Aktan, in a general study of EP resolutions on Turkey, considers the December 1998 resolution a violation of Turkey's sovereignty.[68]

The difference between the 1992 report and the December 1998 resolution is indicative of the extent to which relations between Turkey and the EP deteriorated, as a result of the Kurdish question. The shutdown of the DEP, a Kurdish nationalist party, and the removal of its members' immunity in the Turkish parliament in March 1994, followed by their being sentenced to prison in December, provoked adverse reactions from the EP. As a result, the EU found itself having to postpone the signing of the Customs Union (CU) treaty with Turkey until March 1995. The EP held

---

65. V. Eccarius-Kelly, "Inter-Community Ethnic Conflict in Post-Unification Germany: The Kurdish Conundrum," paper prepared for the International Studies Association annual meeting, Minneapolis, March 1998.

66. Kirişci and Winrow, *The Kurdish Question*, p. 171.

67. Turkey does not recognize any ethnic or religious minorities in the legal sense of the word, other than the ones recognized in the Treaty of Lausanne of 1923. For a discussion of this issue as it relates to Kurds, see ibid., pp. 44–49.

68. Gündüz Aktan, "The European Parliament and Turkey," *Perceptions: Journal of International Affairs*, Vol. 3, No. 4 (December 1998–February 1999), p. 84, <www.mfa. gov.tr/grupa/percept/iii-4/default.htm>.

up the ratification of the treaty until after Turkey amended the constitution and other laws to introduce greater freedom of expression and association.[69]

The ratification was also the product of considerable lobbying and
pressuring emanating from the larger members of the EU and the European Commission. An important argument used was that closer economic relations with Turkey would give the EU considerable leverage on
human rights issues and greater democratization.[70] The EP did eventually yield to this pressure, but soon after ratifying the treaty it flexed its
muscles against Turkey. During the budget discussions in October 1996,
the EP decided to suspend some of the financial aid package agreed upon
in the context of the CU, on the grounds of continuing violations of human rights in Turkey.[71] The resignation of Erbakan's coalition government in June 1997, under pressure from the military, and the subsequent
closure of the Islamic WP worsened relations between Turkey and the EP
and provoked strong criticisms of Turkish democracy and the military.
The wave of Kurdish asylum seekers that arrived on the shores of Italy in
November 1997 became another source of conflict between Turkey and
the EP. During this period, Turkey refused to maintain any relations or dialogue with the EP. This was part of the government decision to suspend
political relations with the EU in protest at the decision taken at the EU
Luxembourg Summit not to include Turkey among the next group of
countries eligible for accession to the EU. This, in many ways, neutralized
any leverage that the EP could have enjoyed over Turkey. One concrete
manifestation of this was the refusal by the Turkish government to allow
a group of members of the EP to visit Öcalan in prison.[72]

The negative impact of the Kurdish question on Turkey's relations
with the European Commission and the major members of the EU has
been more limited.[73] Turkey is a major trading partner of the EU, and
leading EU countries such as Germany, France, and Italy have large investments in Turkey. These interests, together with a preference for a policy of engagement, rather than the confrontation adopted by the EP, have
led the EU to follow a more finely tuned policy toward Turkey. However,

---

69. S. Klaus, "The European Parliament in the EU External Relations: The Customs
Union with Turkey," *European Foreign Affairs Review*, Vol. 5, No. 2 (June 2000).

70. Philip Robins, "More Apparent Than Real? The Impact of the Kurdish Issue on
Euro-Turkish Relations," in Olson, *The Kurdish Nationalist Movement*, p. 128.

71. TDN, October 25, 1996.

72. TDN, March 6, 1999.

73. Robins, "More Apparent Than Real?"

this does not mean that relations between the EU and Turkey have always been smooth. Germany, for example, imposed arms embargoes on Turkey, albeit temporarily. Leading members of the EU have on a number of occasions found themselves being critical of the military approach adopted by Turkey and suggested the need to seek a political solution to the Kurdish problem in Turkey. Calls for a political solution for the Kurdish problem coming from Europe were often evaluated through the perspective of the "Sèvres syndrome" and engendered strong reactions in Turkey. For example, in 1995, Süleyman Demirel reacted in an unusually forceful way when he interpreted remarks made by French Minister of Foreign Affairs Alain Juppé that Turkey should find a political solution to the Kurdish problem. Demirel argued that Juppé's statement was unequivocal evidence of Western intentions to create a Kurdish state in Turkey.[74]

A similar reaction was evoked by the report on Turkey that was prepared by the European Commission in November 1998. The report aimed to assess Turkey's progress toward accession to the EU on the basis of the political criteria adopted at the Copenhagen Summit in June 1993. The report found Turkey wanting in all of these criteria. Regarding the Kurdish problem, the report noted that "Turkey will have to find a political and non-military solution to the problem."[75] The references to minority rights and the need for a political solution provoked criticisms and even led to accusations of European aspiration to undermine Turkey's territorial integrity.[76] During an interview, President Demirel also expressed his discomfort over the need to meet the Copenhagen criteria on minority rights because of Turkey's genuine fear of separatism. He argued that such criteria imposed on Turkey could complicate its prospects of membership of the EU.[77]

Clearly, the Kurdish question is among one of the most important obstacles in the way of Turkey's membership in the EU. However, the stance that the EU took toward Turkey's membership also aggravated the prospects of Turkish democratization and liberalization, and in turn com-

---

74.   TDN, May 10, 1995.

75.   European Commission, *Regular Report from the Commission on Progress towards Accession: Turkey* (Brussels: European Commission, November 1998).

76.   See, for example, the commentary by Mehmet Ali Kislali, "Sèvres Korkusu," *Radikal,* December 12, 1998. For a general review of reactions to the report and a more moderate approach, see the commentary by a retired ambassador and former minister of foreign affairs, Ilter Türkmen, "AB Raporuna Tepki," *Radikal,* November 13, 1998.

77.   *Radikal,* February 4, 1999.

plicated the possibility of resolving the Kurdish conflict peacefully. This became very apparent in the light of significant political changes that occurred in Turkey after the EU opened the way to possible eventual Turkish membership, which had been preceded by the failure of the EU meeting in Vienna in December 1998 to endorse the European Commission's November 1998 report. The Turkish ambassador to the EU, Nihat Akyol, criticized the meeting for failing to respond positively to the new approach adopted by the European Commission and considered the meeting to have been a missed opportunity to improve relations between Turkey and the EU.[78]

Europe's earlier exclusion of Turkey caused the EU to lose its leverage over Turkey in terms of encouraging greater democratization and moderation on the Kurdish question. "The mixed messages coming from the EU unfortunately undermine its legitimacy, thereby decreasing Turkish trust and weakening the pro-European and pro-democratic arguments of the modernizing, Western oriented forces in Turkey."[79] This in turn played into the hands of hard-liners. As a journalist noted, as a result of the snub "most Turks no longer care what the EP has to say and the Turkish military feels less compunction about intervening assertively in political matters."[80] This was illustrated by the policies adopted toward the Kurdish question during the course of 1998. Once hard-liners felt Turkey did not have anything to lose, the way was open to carry the hard-line approach to the Kurdish problem to the external world and take greater risks in order to defeat the PKK outside the country. Turkey not only remained deaf to European criticism of Turkey's threat to use force against Syria, but around the same time rigorously confronted Italy for allowing the Kurdish parliament-in-exile to hold a session at the Italian parliament. The Kurdish parliament-in-exile had met previously in a number of European cities and attracted protests from Turkey, but none had been this intense. This turned out to be relatively mild compared to what was to come when Öcalan was found to be in Rome. Turkey entered into a bitter diplomatic and legal confrontation of a kind that had never been seen between Turkey and a Western European country, let alone a member of the NATO alliance. The Turkish public boycotted Italian products, and many big businesses canceled their contracts with Italian com-

78. *Radikal,* December 25, 1998.

79. Müftüler-Bac, "Never-Ending Story," p. 257.

80. R. Dale, "EU Needs to Make Up With Turkey," *International Herald Tribune,* May 5, 1998.

panies. This pressure has been cited as one of the important reasons why the Italian government forced Öcalan to leave the country, even before his asylum request had actually been decided upon.

The role of political and economic pressure in the Italian decision to expel Öcalan and the consequent reluctance of any European government to accept him on their territory did not go unnoticed by the hard-liners. This must have emboldened the Turkish authorities to contemplate apprehending Öcalan and then to actually succeed in doing it. One other important development that strengthened the determination of the hard-liners to push their pursuit of Öcalan to its limit was the German decision not to seek the extradition of Öcalan to Germany to face trial for crimes committed there by the PKK under his instructions. Originally, Öcalan had been arrested under a German warrant. Germany had put political considerations ahead of legal ones when the newly formed coalition government led by Gerhard Schröder feared that putting Öcalan on trial could lead to unrest among the large Kurdish and Turkish communities in Germany. From the hard-line point of view, trying Öcalan in Turkey seemed to entail the least risk. It meant that they could be in control of the process and domestically enjoy the political capital that would come with the trial of the person whom the majority of the Turkish population considered to be guilty of more than a decade's violence, sacrifice, and suffering.

At least domestically, this strategy paid off. Two political parties, the DSP and the MHP, most closely associated with hard-line policies toward the EU and the Kurdish question emerged triumphant from the national election in April 1999. In 1995, the MHP had failed to win votes above the 10 percent national threshold required to enter parliament. Commentators attributed the performance of the MHP partly to the general public's frustration with the treatment of Turkey by the EU and partly to its uncompromising stance against the PKK and moderate approaches to addressing the Kurdish question in Turkey.[81] The leaders of both parties were known for their reluctance toward fostering better relations with the EU. Bülent Ecevit, the leader of the DSP, had long been an advocate of the notion of developing much closer ties with countries from surrounding regions, in place of aggressively pursuing membership in the EU.[82] The MHP, on the other hand, traditionally has been apprehensive of member-

---

81. For these explanations, see remarks by the former president of Turkey and leader of the military coup in 1980, Kenan Evren, in *Milliyet,* April 23, 1999, and the analysis by two academics, Sencer Ayata and Ümit Özdağ, in *Milliyet,* April 22 and 23, 1999.

82. For Bülent Ecevit's views on foreign policy, see B. Ecevit, "Bölge-Merkezli Dış Politika," *Yeni Türkiye Dergisi,* March/April 1995, pp. 64–70.

ship in the EU on grounds of devolution of Turkish sovereignty, and instead favored much more intimate relations with Turkic states, as well as some of the states of the region, such as Israel, Jordan, Egypt, Georgia, and others.[83]

Nevertheless, relations between Turkey and the EU improved steadily after the formation of the new coalition government in June 1999 by Bülent Ecevit. The new climate even led Prime Minister Ecevit to change his previous views about the EU and become a vocal advocate of joining the EU and making the necessary reforms. His commitment to political reforms in support of greater democracy in Turkey, and the EU's positive response, brought the two sides much closer to each other, especially after the EU's decision to accept Turkey's candidacy for membership in December 1999. The pressures for political reforms in Turkey increased following the presentation to Turkey of the Accession Partnership document by the EU in November 2000. The document laid down a long list of economic, legal, and political reforms Turkey needed to introduce to be able to meet the Copenhagen criteria for starting accession negotiations. These included the adoption of cultural rights for minorities in Turkey. However, in a marked departure from the past and the progress report of 1998 mentioned above, the document shied from using the term "minority," the use of which on many occasions had marred EU-Turkish relations. Instead, the EU, in this document and the new discourse it adopted, chose to use a much more subtle, inoffensive, and nuanced language. It called for lifting of restrictions that deny Turkish citizens the possibility of broadcasting in their mother tongues as well as the need to assist cultural diversity and secure the cultural rights, including education in the mother tongue, of all Turkish citizens irrespective of their origin. The wording chosen not only manifested a conscious effort to avoid the use of "minority" but also emphasized cultural rather than minority rights. This situation gave the moderates in Turkey the opportunity to disarm the arguments of hard-liners in Turkey. The absence of references to minority rights and political solutions specially referring to Kurds meant that hard-liners could not argue their classic case centered on the notion of the Sèvres syndrome. Furthermore, it also became much more difficult to accuse moderates of being traitors. Undoubtedly, these developments were very significant in opening the way to the adoption of critical reforms in October 2001 and August 2002 that have helped to defuse the Kurdish problem to an important extent in Turkey. However, this should not mean that the problem has completely been resolved. In its

83. Sami Kohen, "MHP Dış Politikası," *Milliyet*, April 22, 1999.

most recent report in October 2002 the European Commission welcomed the reforms but pointed out that their implementation remained problematic. As a result, to the dismay of the Turkish government and public, the report failed to recommend the beginning of negotiations for membership.[84]

Then in a historic parliamentary election in November 2002 the Turkish electorate swept out of power the political parties that had made up the coalition that had governed since 1999. A critical member of this coalition, the right-wing nationalist MHP that had long been associated with hard-line views on the Kurdish question, was decisively defeated. Instead the Adalet ve Kalkınma Partisi (Justice and Development Party, AKP) won an absolute majority of the seats enabling it to form a government on its own. The Cumhuriyet Halk Partisi (Peoples' Republican Party, CHP) became the only opposition party in parliament. The AKP leadership and the government came out in a forceful and unequivocal manner in support of Turkey's membership of the EU as well as of a program of political reforms to meet the Copenhagen criteria. In an effort to mobilize support for setting a date for the beginning of accession negotiations with the EU, the government embarked on an intense campaign to lobby EU member governments during the run-up to the European Council Summit in Copenhagen of December 12–13, 2002. However, the government failed to obtain a clear date for the start of negotiations. Instead, Turkey was given December 2004 as a deadline for reviewing its progress in meeting the criteria for membership; depending on the progress achieved, an actual date for negotiations to start could be given for 2005. Many factors played a role in this decision. One of them clearly concerned the EU's desire to see whether the new government would actually see through the implementation of political reforms adopted in August 2002 that promised education and broadcasting in Kurdish. On numerous subsequent occasions the government has expressed its commitment to implementing reforms. However, at the same time the government continues to meet resistance from various quarters within the Turkish state apparatus with regard to the implementation of these reforms. Paradoxically, many in Turkey have also argued that the EU indecisiveness in offering a date for Turkey has complicated the hand of the government against the hard-liners.

Compared to Europe, U.S. relations with Turkey on the Kurdish question were more ambiguous. The United States made an unequivocal distinction between the PKK and the Kurdish question. On the one hand,

---

84. European Commission, *Regular Report from the Commission on Progress towards Accession: Turkey* (Brussels: European Commission, October 2002).

it did not hesitate to criticize Turkey bitterly on its human rights violations, and on the other, was unambiguously critical of the PKK and supported Turkey's struggle against the PKK. The United States for a long
time listed the PKK among the terrorist groups monitored and covered
by the *Global Terrorism Report*. For Turkish hard-liners, the U.S. position
on the PKK was always in stark contrast to the ambiguous position toward the PKK taken in Europe. When Turkey's confrontation with Syria
occurred, it was generally recognized that the United States brought pressure on Syria in favor of Öcalan's expulsion. Similarly, Öcalan's inability
to stay on in Russia for very long before traveling to Italy was also attributed to U.S. influence behind the scenes. During the crisis between Italy
and Turkey, the United States called for Öcalan's extradition to Turkey
and took a stand against his being granted asylum, engendering considerable resentment from Italian Prime Minister Massimo D'Alema, who
was known for his sympathetic feeling toward Kurds.[85] Lastly, the U.S.
extended critical assistance to Turkey to enable Öcalan's capture in
Kenya.[86] Hence, it was not surprising that Prime Minister Ecevit, soon after the capture of Öcalan, praised U.S. understanding and support for
Turkey against the PKK.[87]

Yet, at the same time, the U.S. government, particularly the Congress,
was deeply critical of human rights violations in Turkey. Turkey was regularly condemned in reports issued by the State Department. In 1995, one
such report, prepared under instructions from the Congress, suggested
that Turkey was using U.S. weapons against Kurdish civilians.[88] This led
to reluctance on the part of the State Department to issue export licenses
for a Turkish order of Super Cobra helicopters. These helicopters were
particularly valued by the Turkish military because they were effective
against the PKK in rugged and inaccessible mountainous terrain.[89] The
importance attached to them prompted President Demirel, during his
March 1996 visit to the United States, to bring up the issue personally

85. Reported by Alessandra Stanley, *New York Times*, March 4, 1999.

86. According to a prominent Turkish journalist, it was actually the CIA that proposed assistance to the MIT, the Turkish intelligence service, in capturing Öcalan, in
return for a commitment to put him through a fair trial. See Tuncay Özkan, *Operasyon*
(Istanbul: Dogan Kitapçılık, 2000).

87. *Milliyet*, February 20, 1999.

88. See *Report on Allegations of Human Rights Abuses by the Turkish Military and on the
Situation in Cyprus* (U.S. State Department Report, June 1, 1995).

89. Öcalan himself revealed the important role that helicopters played in weakening
his organization during an interview he gave while in Rome to *Jane's Intelligence Review* (February 19, 1999), reported in *Milliyet*, February 24, 1999.

with President Clinton. This had little effect, and the Turkish general staff, receiving a letter from President Clinton critical of Turkey's human rights record, decided to cancel the order.[90]

A speech by U.S. Deputy Secretary of State Strobe Talbott in October 1998, in memory of the late Turgut Özal, provides another example of how the Kurdish question could sour relations between the two allies. Talbott noted that, as much as the importance of the strategic location of Turkey, what provided the driving force behind the friendship between the two countries was values central to the United States. In this regard, he was censorious of Turkey's human rights record and its failure to protect freedom of expression. While asserting that the United States was firmly behind Turkey's right to fight terrorism and defend its territorial integrity, he also noted that there could not be a solely military solution to the problems plaguing the southeast.[91] The speech was not particularly well received by hard-liners. A journalist who was present and known for holding views close to those of the government called the speech an "unexpected attack" and a "betrayal." He accused the United States of holding Turkey to double standards.[92]

Nevertheless, such criticisms and setbacks did not significantly undermine relations between Turkey and the United States. One important reason was the interdependence between the two countries on a number of strategically important issues. The United States was concerned about maintaining Turkey's Western orientation and energetically supported Turkey's membership in the EU. It attached great importance to Turkey's close cooperation with Israel and saw Turkey as a key player in its dual-containment policy toward Iran and Iraq. Also significant was Turkey's role in the Caucasus and Central Asia. In turn, Turkish decision-makers recognized the advantages of maintaining good relations with the United States—the last superpower. They also greatly valued U.S. support for Turkish membership in the EU, as well as for the construction of a pipeline from Baku to Ceyhan to carry oil from the Caspian region to the Mediterranean Sea. Turkish decision-makers were very aware, too, of U.S. policy analysts' assessment of Turkey's role in world politics as a pivotal state.[93] Finally, as a U.S. expert on relations with Turkey noted:

90. *Yeni Yüzyıl,* November 19 and 21, 1996.

91. Strobe Talbott, "U.S.-Turkish Relations in an Age of Interdependence," Washington Institute for Near East Policy, October 14, 1998, <www.washingtoninstitute.org>.

92. Commentary by Sedat Sertoğlu, *Sabah,* October 16, 1998.

93. A number of prominent U.S. analysts have underlined the significance of Turkey to U.S. policies in Eurasia: Zbigniew Brzezinski, *The Grand Chessboard: American Pri-*

"United States policy toward Turkey attempts to balance support for Turkey as a strategic ally facing terrorism with advocacy of improvements in human rights. Most of the time the former appears to get greater emphasis from policy makers."[94]

The balance in favor of strategic considerations benefited the hard-liners in Turkey and created a climate conducive to pragmatic cooperation between the decision-makers of both countries. This pragmatism was best captured with regard to northern Iraq. The United States was keen to see the two Kurdish groups in northern Iraq cooperate and effectively administer the Kurdish-controlled enclave in northern Iraq. But Turkish policy on Iraq is significantly different from that of the United States. Turkey is extremely sensitive to Iraq's territorial integrity and fears the development of a Kurdish state in northern Iraq. Thus, relations between the United States and Turkey do occasionally reach a crisis point over U.S. involvement in Kurdish affairs in northern Iraq.

Turkish authorities became particularly upset when, in September 1998, the United States succeeded in bringing the representatives of two Kurdish groups to Washington, D.C., to sign an agreement.[95] The agreement aimed to revive the Kurdish parliament and administration that had originally been set up in 1992, but had quickly lost effectiveness when the two Kurdish groups fell into a violent conflict. The agreement was a critical step in the implementation of the new U.S. policy of actively organizing and supporting opposition forces against Saddam Hussein. Turkish decision-makers immediately objected to certain aspects of this agreement. In November, they very assertively brought the leaders of the two groups to Ankara to refine the agreement in a way that addressed Turkish interests.[96] Most important was the need to ensure that Turkey could continue to operate in northern Iraq militarily to prevent the PKK from using the area. Turkey also needed to receive assurances that references to the term "federation" in the Washington agree-

---

macy and Its Geostrategic Imperatives (New York: Basic Books, 1997); Robert Chase, Emily Hill, and Paul Kennedy, "Pivotal States and United States Strategy," *Foreign Affairs* (January–February 1996), pp. 37, 46–48; Stephen J. Blank, et al., *Turkey's Strategic Position at the Crossroads of World Affairs* (Carlisle Barracks, Pa.: Strategic Studies Institute, U.S. Army War College, 1993).

94.   E-mail correspondence with Carol Migdalovitz, March 8, 1999.

95.   Details of the agreement reached at this meeting were reported in *Milliyet*, October 2, 1998. For evaluations of this agreement from the perspective of Turkish national interests, see Sami Kohen's commentary in the same issue; and Ümit Özdağ, "Türk-Amerikan politikaları cakışıyor," *Milliyet*, October 6, 1998.

96.   For the coverage of the meeting, see *Yeni Yüzyıl*, November 9, 1998.

ment would not undermine Iraqi territorial and political integrity. The United States did not seem to object to these revisions. The whole episode is very telling in terms of the differing interests of the United States and Turkey in northern Iraq, accompanied by a Turkish governmental desire to assert itself.[97]

Turkish concerns about developments in northern Iraq and the prospects of the establishment of a Kurdish state became a contentious issue between the United States and Turkey in the context of the war against terrorism launched by the Bush administration after the September 11, 2001, attacks. Turkey has cooperated extensively with the United States against the Taliban and al Qaeda in Afghanistan. Turkey contributed to the International Stability Force in Afghanistan and also took over its command for six months in June 2002. However, Turkey has expressed major differences in respect to U.S. policy towards Saddam Hussein and Iraq. In this respect Turkey's major concern has been that a U.S. military intervention could precipitate the disintegration of Iraq and the emergence of an independent Kurdish state in the north. The visit of the deputy secretary of defense Paul Wolfowitz in July 2002 and his reassurances that the United States was against such a state and recognized that such an eventuality would be a source of instability for the region did not allay Turkish public and official concerns. Instead, U.S. efforts to reconcile warring Kurdish factions and support given to the reopening of the Kurdish parliament in October 2002 refueled Turkish fears that there is a fundamental conflict between the two countries over northern Iraq. In the meantime, during the run-up to the U.S. intervention in Iraq, Turkish officials repeatedly stated that they would intervene militarily if a Kurdish state were to emerge. If it does and Turkey does intervene militarily in northern Iraq this could clearly set back many of the gains achieved through the recent political reforms and reignite the Kurdish problem in Turkey.

In contrast, after the trial of Öcalan was completed and the new government expressed a conspicuous commitment to introduce political reforms and improve Turkey's human rights record, there was a marked warming in U.S.-Turkish relations. This was reflected in President Clinton's close interest in Turkey's relations with the EU and Turkey's acceptance as a candidate. More importantly, the U.S. administration played a vital part in ensuring the holding of the OSCE summit in Istanbul. In the Congress, the Commission on Security and Cooperation in Eu-

---

97. Malik Mufti, "Daring and Caution in Turkish Foreign Policy," *Middle East Journal*, Vol. 52, No. 1 (Winter 1998), p. 48, quotes Turkish officials who assert their right to have policies on Iraq that differ from those of the United States.

rope (CSCE) had long been objecting to this summit on the grounds that Turkey did not deserve such prestige, given its negative human rights record. The CSCE had also demanded that the U.S. administration do its best to have the venue of the summit changed. However, the administration argued in support of a policy of engagement, putting forward the view that such a summit would benefit democracy and civil society in Turkey.[98] The administration succeeded in getting the congressional opposition withdrawn and President Clinton actually led the U.S. delegation to the summit, the first visit of its kind since President George Bush's visit in 1991. The president addressed the Turkish parliament and argued that Turkey had a very important role to play in ensuring security and stability in the region, but also urged Turkey to introduce political reforms. He received a standing ovation from the members of parliament and much praise in the Turkish media.[99] After this visit, and especially with the arrival of the Bush administration, the Kurdish problem was minimized in U.S.-Turkish relations. The attacks of September 11, 2001, reinforced Turkey's strategic importance to the United States due to the war on terrorism. U.S. officials frequently referred to Turkey as a model to the Muslim world.

The new government that came to power during January and February 2003 experienced intense pressure from the United States to support a military intervention against Saddam Hussein by allowing U.S. troops to travel through Kurdish-populated southeastern Turkey to enter Iraq and open up a northern front. Long and tedious negotiations between U.S. and Turkish officials failed to secure an agreement and the parliament, somewhat to the surprise of the AKP leadership, on March 1, 2003, refused to support the decision to allow U.S. troops through Turkey. Relations between the United States and Turkey became strained. The deal that the government had reached would have provided Turkey with a generous financial compensation package and would also have placated Turkish fears about the emergence of a Kurdish state in northern Iraq by allowing a Turkish military presence there. Massive public opposition

98. For details of the relevant debate at the CSCE, see "The Road to the Istanbul Summit and Human Rights in the Republic of Turkey," Hearing before the Commission on Security and Cooperation in Europe, 106th Cong., First Sess. (Washington, D.C.: U.S. Government Printing Office, March 18, 1999). For an analysis of U.S.-Turkish relations in general, and in respect of the Kurdish problem, see Kemal Kirişci, "U.S.-Turkish Relations: New Uncertainties in a Renewed Partnership," in Kemal Kirişci and Barry Rubin, eds., *Turkey and Its World: Emergence of a Multi-Regional Power* (Boulder, Colo.: Lynne Rienner, 2001).

99. For coverage of Clinton's speech and responses, see *Radikal, Milliyet, Sabah,* and other Turkish dailies, November 16, 1999.

against the war in Turkey and also the reluctance of many Kurdish members of parliament from the AKP to support the government resolution left the government defeated.

Once the U.S. military intervention started without Turkey, the fear especially among hard-liners that the U.S. would now help to support the establishment of a Kurdish state in northern Iraq became aggravated. There was considerable agitation in Turkey in support of a Turkish military intervention in northern Iraq. However, intense negotiations with the Kurdish leadership in northern Iraq, accompanied by U.S. and EU pressure not to intervene, led the Turkish chief of general staff to shelve the plans of intervention in early April, leaving Turkey in a precarious position. Will the United States be able to bring stability to Iraq and keep Iraq from disintegrating? Will the United States be able to convince the Kurds in northern Iraq to be sensitive to Turkey's interests? Will they be able to prevent the PKK, now KADEK, from becoming active again? The answers to these questions will invariably have important implications in terms of what happens to U.S. and Turkish relations as well as what happens to the implementation of the political reforms concerning Kurds in Turkey.

Curiously, there is one area where Turkish foreign policy appears to have been much more subdued than might be expected, if it were not for the Kurdish problem's tying the hands of decision-makers. One important consequence of the eruption of ethnic conflicts in the Balkans and the Caucasus after the end of the Cold War was that Turkey became much more sensitive toward the well-being of Muslim ethnic groups. These groups range from Albanians, Bosnians, and Turks in the Balkans, to Abkhazians, Azeris, Chechens, and a multitude of other ethnic groups in the northern Caucasus. Turkey adopted a very active foreign policy during the conflict in the former Yugoslavia and pressed for military intervention against the Serbs to protect the Bosnians.[100] In the case of the conflict in Chechnya, by contrast, despite loud public support for Chechens, the government followed a policy that shied away from alienating Russia. Clearly, there was a fear that Russia could use the "Kurdish

---

100. For detailed analysis of this assertiveness in Turkish foreign policy in the Balkans, see Şule Kut, "Turkish Diplomatic Initiatives for Bosnia-Herzegovina," in Günay Göksu Özdoğan and Kemâli Saybaşılı, eds., *Balkans: A Mirror of the New International Order* (Istanbul: Eren, 1995), pp. 295–315; Şule Kut, "Yugoslavya Bunalımı ve Türkiye'nin Bosna-Hersek ve Makendonya Politikası: 1990–1993," in Faruk Sönmezoğlu, ed., *Türk Dış Politikasının Analizi* (Istanbul: Der Yayınları, 1994); İlhan Üzgel, "Doksanlarda Türkiye İçin Bir İşbirliği ve Rekabet Alanı Olarak Balkanlar," in Gencer Özcan and Şule Kut, eds., *En Uzun Onyıl: Türkiye'nin Ulusal Güvenlik ve Dış Politika Gündeminde Doksanlı Yıllar* (Istanbul: Boyut Kitapları, 1998).

card" against Turkey if Turkey were to follow an assertive policy in support of the Chechens.[101] Recognizing the parallels to the Kurdish question in Turkey, Turkish decision-makers considered the Chechen problem an internal one to Russia.[102] This was stated in a most conspicuous manner when, just before an official visit to Moscow in November 1999, the Turkish prime minister referred to Chechnya as a problem internal to Russia. In many ways this was an acknowledgement of the Russian government's decision not to grant political asylum to Öcalan after the latter fled to Russia from Syria in 1998. The Russian parliament had actually called on the government to grant him refugee status. Since then Russia and Turkey appear to have avoided each other's ethnic problems, and relations, especially in the area of trade and economics, have grown extensively.

Similarly, after the violence in Kosovo erupted early in 1998, Turkey was much less active and assertive than it had been in the case of Bosnia. Both Prime Minister Yılmaz and Foreign Minister Cem conferred with Slobodan Milosevic personally and assured him that they supported a solution to the Kosovo problem that respected Serbian territorial integrity.[103] The uncomfortable similarity between the problems of the Kosovo region of Serbia and the Kurdish-populated southeastern region of Turkey is an important factor.[104] Italian Prime Minister Massimo D'Alema made a point, during his visit to the United States in March 1999, of drawing this parallel. He said, "If we defend the rights of the Albanians in Kosovo, and rightly so, then I think we have to also defend the rights of the Kurdish minority."[105] However, after the massive refugee exodus and NATO operations against Serbia started in March 1999, the Turkish government became supportive of a more interventionist policy. Subsequently, Turkey lent active support to NATO's operation and sent a Turkish military unit to assist in humanitarian work and peacekeeping. Nevertheless, the alarming parallels go a long way in explaining why, in the case of Kosovo and Chechnya, Turkish decision-makers tended to argue

101. For a detailed analysis of how the Kurdish problem has constrained Turkey's policy on the Chechen conflict, see Robert W. Olson, "Turkish and Russian Foreign Policies, 1991–1997: The Kurdish and Chechnya Questions," *Journal of Muslim Minority Affairs* (Abingdon, U.K.), Vol. 18, No. 2 (October 1998), pp. 209–228.

102. T. Yıldırım, "Cecenistan Sorunu ve Türkiye," in Faruk Sönmezoğlu, ed., *Değişen Dünya ve Türkiye* (Istanbul: Bağlam, 1996), pp. 214–215.

103. TDN, March 8 and 9, 1998.

104. Üzgel, "Doksanlarda Türkiye," p. 423, also points at this parallel.

105. *New York Times*, March 4, 1999, p. A12.

that these were internal problems needing to be resolved in a manner that paid heed to the territorial integrity of Russia and Serbia.

Conclusion

Since the capture of Öcalan in February 1999 and his decision to repent and order the PKK to end armed struggle, Turkey has entered a new era. His capture can be seen as the outcome of a process that started in 1993. This was when the hard-liners' argument that Turkey was facing a grave threat from terrorism to its security and territorial integrity prevailed, and the military approach to the Kurdish problem was adopted. Öcalan's capture was received with great jubilation by the overwhelming majority of the population, and President Demirel identified it as the most important event in the history of the Turkish Republic.[106] This success has been attributed to the resolution and determination of the policies advocated by the hard-liners. Ironically, this new era has eroded the influence of hard-liners on policymaking while the liberal approach gained the upper hand in addressing the Kurdish problem. This is likely to be a long process, but one that would have been unthinkable at the time of Öcalan's capture.

In February 1999, Turkey was at odds with the external world, especially several of its neighbors and the EU. The Kurdish problem was central to this state of affairs. Turkey had almost gone to war with Syria in October 1998 in an effort to stop Syrian support for the PKK. Its relations with members of the EU were at a low ebb, especially after the Luxembourg Summit in December 1997, when Turkey was excluded from a new list of candidates. Criticism of Turkish treatment of Kurds and Turkish unwillingness to introduce political reforms played an important role in this decision. Relations with the United States, although not as bad, were also going through ups and downs. But with the capture of Öcalan, relations began to improve. A new government in Turkey that was determined to improve democracy, accompanied by the changing attitude in Europe, marked the beginnings of the new phase. Undoubtedly, the EU decision to engage Turkey positively and open the way to eventual membership was a critical factor that reinforced the emergence of a will to introduce political reform toward greater democracy and liberalism. Whether or not the political reforms adopted during the course of 2001 and 2002 actually gain root and Turkey emerges as a liberal and pluralist democracy with room for cultural rights for minorities will depend very

---

106. *Milliyet*, March 19, 1999.

much on how Turkey's relations with the EU evolve. Positive relations, especially with the EU, whereby Turkey slowly but surely becomes integrated with the EU, will not only strengthen the hand of liberals, but also allay the concerns and fears of hard-liners for Turkey's stability and territorial integrity. This would be the most promising outcome in terms of the resolution of the Kurdish problem.

Since the capture of Öcalan, Turkey's relations with Iran and Syria have steadily improved. Turkey still has major conflicts with Syria, especially over the waters of the Euphrates, and with Iran because of deep mutual distrust. However, with Öcalan and the PKK removed from the equation, it might be possible to make progress on the other outstanding issues between Turkey and its Middle Eastern neighbors. Clearly, such progress would go a long way in alleviating the concerns of hard-liners about threats to Turkey's security originating from these countries. It is ironic that if these regimes were to become more democratic, open, and liberal, hard-liners in Turkey might feel more at ease. However, in the meantime, the aftermath of the U.S. intervention in Iraq has fueled concerns particularly of hard-liners in Turkey. They fear and suspect that the current unstable situation in Iraq could lead to the emergence of an independent Kurdish state and to the re-emergence of a threat to Turkish national security. Furthermore, the U.S. intervention in Iraq has left U.S.-Turkish relations soured. This comes after a decades-old strategic relationship that had been further strengthened by Turkey's close cooperation with the United States in its war against terrorism since the September 11, 2001, attacks. Turkey had also cooperated very closely with the United States in efforts to bring security and stability to the Balkans. The U.S. commitment to Turkey's membership to the EU and the U.S. assistance to Turkey in capturing the leader of the PKK had contributed to facilitate democratization in Turkey. Over the last few years, violation of human rights of Kurds in Turkey had not been on the agenda of U.S.-Turkish relations. Yet, ironically, there is also a concern that the U.S. intervention against Saddam Hussein could still create a situation that could reverse the positive developments in Turkey with regard to the Kurdish problem.

Ultimately, of course, what happens regarding the Kurdish problem will depend on developments within Turkey. Much rests on how the present government fares in introducing and pushing through their package of political reforms. In turn, these developments will also very much depend on what Öcalan, the PKK, and leading Kurdish politicians in Turkey choose to do. Since the beginning of this new era, many Kurds once associated with radical and nationalist views have significantly moderated their opinions. There are no more calls for secession, federalism, or even autonomy. Instead, the emphasis is on playing the game of democracy and pluralism and emphasizing the rights of Kurds as individual Turkish citizens, rather than group or minority rights. Furthermore, the change in the PKK's position has also enabled moderate Kurds who feared the wrath of the PKK and nationalists to come forward. These developments will definitely strengthen the force of the liberal approach and, more importantly, relieve the concerns of hard-liners about Turkish unity. Nevertheless, the process of addressing the Kurdish problem in this new era will be very long and difficult. Keeping hard-liners on both sides from making a common cause to bring the new era to an end will be a challenge in itself.

Much rests on how successful the new AK Party is in implementing political reforms already adopted and pushing forward with new reforms. This will likely deepen EU-Turkish relations. A clear prospect of EU membership would inject a major boost to both the Turkish economy and politics. In return this would clearly benefit the consolidation of the cultural rights of Kurds. If the AK Party is not successful and EU-Turkish relations are weakened, and if the situation in Iraq following the U.S. intervention does not stabilize, Turkey's democratization might be put at risk, especially if this leads to the return of hard-liners on the Turkish side and of Kurdish nationalists with a secessionist agenda. Such an outcome would not bode well for Turkey, for the region, the EU, or the United States.

Chapter 14

The Impact of Foreign Relations on Human Rights in Turkey

Elizabeth Andersen

This chapter highlights the major obstacles to influencing human rights practices in Turkey in the context of its foreign relations. A country's foreign relations are typically a critical context for the promotion of human rights. Aid, trade, and political relationships with other countries and intergovernmental bodies, conditional on human rights progress, are among the most important tools of the human rights activist's trade. Turkey presents the human rights community with a particular challenge, however, since so often these traditional techniques of human rights promotion seem to backfire. Frequently, the inconsistent promotion of human rights in Turkey by key foreign interlocutors—especially the United States and the European Union (EU)—has undermined the cause. The result has been stutter-step progress on human rights in Turkey, driven substantially by internal dynamics rather than external pressure imposed on Turkey.

Any discussion of this topic should acknowledge at the outset that Turkey is not alone in facing serious human rights–related problems. Indeed, one important difficulty that human rights advocates face in promoting greater respect for human rights in Turkey is that the countries that might otherwise effectively encourage human rights improvements in Turkey have compromised their credibility in doing so, because they have failed to put their own houses in order. Thus, for example, the United States has been hard-pressed to advocate abolition of the death penalty or measures to ameliorate isolation conditions in Turkey's high-

The views expressed in this chapter are the author's and do not necessarily reflect the views of Human Rights Watch or the American Bar Association.

security prisons, and when it comes to pressing for an end to incommunicado detention in Turkey, a number of EU member states do not have a leg to stand on.

This cannot, however, excuse Turkey's human rights record, which, notwithstanding significant recent progress, remains seriously substandard. Human Rights Watch's *World Report 2003*, an annual survey of human rights conditions throughout the world, describes continued serious violations of human rights in Turkey, including widespread torture in detention, with substantial impunity for its perpetrators; arbitrary and abusive restrictions on freedom of expression; repression of human rights advocates; continued failure of the government to facilitate the return home of hundreds of thousands of Kurds displaced by conflict in the southeast; and in general, a role for the military in political affairs that is inconsistent with standard democratic principles.

After years of limited progress on human rights, 2002 saw several significant steps forward, including abolition of the death penalty, an end to restrictions on the use of minority languages, including Kurdish, and progress toward the elimination of incommunicado detention. Certainly Turkey's foreign relations, especially the prospect of setting a date to start negotiating Turkey's entry into the EU, were an important catalyst of this reform. Nonetheless, the continuation of reform efforts, even after the December 2002 EU decision to refuse Turkey a negotiation date, suggests that other, internal factors have been at least as influential in stimulating human rights progress.

The failure of Turkey's foreign relations to consistently yield substantial human rights progress is as much a function of the inconsistent approach to human rights taken by Turkey's foreign interlocutors as it is attributable to Turkey's resistance to reform. Too often, human rights concerns in Turkey are subverted to its allies' competing economic, political, and security agendas. This has been the case, for example, when notwithstanding their expressed concern over Turkey's handling of the conflict in the southeast, Western governments have rubber-stamped transfers of the very arms used by Turkish security forces to commit violations of international humanitarian law against the civilian population. The U.S. record on arms transfers to Turkey is mixed. It barred the transfer of cluster bombs in 1995 and raised sufficient obstacles to the sale of attack helicopters in 1996 that Turkey withdrew its offer to buy the equipment. In September 1998, the U.S. government determined that human rights concerns would prevent it from financing a sale of armored personnel carriers to Turkey's abusive anti-terror police.[1] At the same time,

---

1. Amnesty International, Press Release, "Amnesty International USA Urges U.S.

U.S. law prohibiting arms sales to countries that perpetrate gross violations of human rights is, with respect to Turkey (as with all other abusive but strategically important states), more honored in the breach. Throughout the late 1990s, U.S. manufacturer Bell Helicopter Textron received U.S. support for its efforts to win a lucrative $4 billion contract for 145 attack helicopters for Turkey, although there had at that time been only limited progress toward meeting the human rights commitments made by then Prime Minister Mesut Yılmaz in December 1997 in exchange for the marketing license for the helicopters.

In the case of the EU, the ironies were compounded. Italian and Franco-German arms manufacturers bid for the helicopter contract, apparently unhindered by the EU's concerns about Turkey's methods in the southeast, not to mention the resultant influxes into Europe of Kurdish refugees and migrants.

The EU's approach to the Kurdish influx itself provides a good illustration of the inconsistency of EU human rights policy toward Turkey. EU member states have been aggressively and appropriately critical of Turkey's treatment of its Kurdish minority and its failure to protect refugees. But these concerns flew out the window in early 1998, when a few thousand Kurds arrived on the Italian coastline. Eurocrats panicked at the prospect of increases in their substantial Turkish and Kurdish immigrant populations and quickly adopted an "Action Plan" to deal with the influx, primarily by tightening border controls and pressing Turkey to stem the flow of migrants. The plan gave little consideration to the potentially legitimate causes for the Kurds' flight or Turkey's capacity or willingness to absorb them and treat them humanely.[2] This dissonance in EU policy toward human rights in Turkey was evidenced again in late 2002. Even as EU member states expressed concern about the humanitarian implications of war in Iraq and Turkey's potential involvement, they voted to give the European Commission negotiating authority to conclude a readmission agreement with Turkey, requiring Turkey to accept the return of migrants and asylum seekers who had traveled from or through Turkey.[3] Such an agreement could be applied to those fleeing the war in Iraq via

State Department to Block Sale of Police Equipment to Turkey," September 4, 1998; Jennifer Washburn, "Isn't It Time for the U.S. to Stop Aiding Turkish Repression?" *Washington Times*, September 14, 1998.

2. Council of the European Union, "Influx of Migrants for Iraq and the Neighboring Region: E.U. Action Plan," adopted January 26, 1998.

3. Council of the European Union, Press Release, "Conclusions of the 2469th Council Meeting—Justice and Home Affairs," November 28–29, 2002, Document 14872/02, p. 8.

Turkey, without specifying safeguards to ensure appropriate treatment of those returned to Turkey.

The greatest irony is, of course, that in adopting such policies, the Europeans have not only ignored human rights concerns in Turkey, but have done so, at least in part, because of domestic political pressure that stems from their failure to deal with their own human rights problem at home—the acceptance and integration of significant immigrant communities.

From the Turkish perspective, the international critique of its human rights practices might begin to seem not very serious at best and two-faced at worst. The problem is not solely, however, that the international community maintains a fair-weather human rights policy toward Turkey, ignoring human rights concerns when they clash with competing interests. In the case of the EU, there has been a secondary problem of creating an appearance of co-opting and misusing the human rights agenda as an excuse for slowing Turkey's progress toward EU accession. The December 1997 decision to refuse Turkey the status of a candidate for EU accession, though substantially couched in human rights terms, seemed to be actually driven, at least in part, by political and economic considerations—some of them inconsistent with human rights principles of non-discrimination.[4] Comments that a Muslim state might have no place in Europe, such as that notably made in 1997 by then Dutch Foreign Minister and President of the EU Council of Ministers Hans Van Mierlo,[5] substantially undermined the credibility of the legitimate human rights–related reasons that the EU might advance for a cautious approach to Turkey's accession. In short, this kind of human rights dialogue gave human rights a bad name in Turkey.

Once Turkey cleared the political hurdle of obtaining EU candidate status in 1999, one might have hoped for a new era of principled, consistent, and productive human rights dialogue between the EU and Turkey. Unfortunately, the first two years of Turkey's candidacy yielded little reform. One important factor during this period was the EU's failure to dispel suspicions of its human rights agenda with transparent, specific demands for reform to be achieved prior to formal negotiations on accession. The European Commission's Accession Partnership for Turkey, adopted in November 2000, highlighted areas of reform needed in the

---

4. See, generally, Özdem Sanberk (Turkish ambassador to the United Kingdom), "The Outlook for Relations between Turkey and the European Union after the Cardiff Summit," Washington Institute for Near East Policy, July 20, 1998.

5. Human Rights Watch, *Human Rights Watch World Report 1998* (New York: Human Rights Watch, 1997), p. 288.

context of EU membership. At the same time, the lack of unambiguous specificity—particularly on key subjects such as safeguards against torture and protection of freedom of expression—left the EU's accession plan open to political manipulation by both sides.[6]

Why would Turkey undertake reform in response to vague EU requests, for example, "that it strengthen legal and constitutional guarantees of the right to freedom of expression,"[7] only to learn subsequently that the EU had shifted the goal and that the enacted reform is inadequate? Not surprisingly, Turkey's response to the EU Accession Partnership document—its March 2001 National Program for the EU Accession Partnership Agreement—was an even less ambitious and less specific plan for reform.[8] Only in October 2001, two years into Turkey's EU candidacy, did the EU take advantage of its Regular Report on accession countries to provide a detailed critique of Turkey's human rights record and identify with greater specificity the steps required for Turkey to advance toward membership.[9]

The following year saw Turkey get serious about ticking off those demands, but the reform came too late to demonstrate a satisfactory level of implementation before the December 2002 Copenhagen Summit. The EU could justifiably cite human rights grounds to postpone negotiations on Turkey's entry for another two years. Unfortunately, once again, the human rights concerns that informed the EU decision were largely discredited in light of xenophobic statements that a Muslim country does not belong in Europe, made by a prominent European figure (this time President of the Convention on the Future of Europe, Valéry Giscard d'Estaing). A principled EU assessment of Turkey's on-going human rights challenges might have encouraged Turkey to take the remaining steps required to commence accession negotiations; but against the backdrop of Giscard d'Estaing's comments, the EU has little legitimacy in using its Copenhagen summit decision to promote further reform in Turkey.

---

6. See Human Rights Watch, *Turkey: Human Rights and the European Union Accession Partnership* (September 2000).

7. Council of the European Union, "Council Decision of 8 March 2001 on the principles, priorities, and immediate objectives and conditions contained in the Accession Partnership with the Republic of Turkey" (2001/235/EC), *Official Journal of the European Communities,* March 24, 2001, para. 4.1, p. L 85/13.

8. See Human Rights Watch, Press Backgrounder, "Comments on Turkey's National Program for the E.U. Accession Partnership Agreement," April 2001, available at <www.hrw.org/press/2001/06/turkey-plan.htm>.

9. See Human Rights Watch, Press Backgrounder, "Analysis of the 2001 Regular Report on Turkey," December 2001, available at </hrw.org/backgrounder/eca/ turkey-analysis.htm>.

It is interesting therefore that in the aftermath of the December 2002 Copenhagen Summit, the Turkish government has vowed nonetheless to follow through with reform, and indeed has done so. Immediately after being rebuffed by the EU, Turkey adopted a number of reform measures, including a law aimed at giving all detainees access to counsel. Even more remarkable, in early February 2003, Turkey adopted legislation paving the way for a new trial for its longest serving political prisoners—four Kurdish former parliamentarians, imprisoned in 1994 following a trial the European Court for Human Rights concluded was unfair. The EU has long sought resolution of their case, and yet this was achieved only after the EU refused an early date for membership negotiations. That Turkey seems to be making human rights progress in spite of the EU's actions, rather than in response to them, strongly suggests there are other powerful forces behind this progress.

Indeed, hope for human rights improvements in Turkey today generally comes not from the international context in which it is situated, but primarily from within, from the growth in Turkey of a vibrant civil society with a significant stake in reform. The media, though subject to ongoing arbitrary restrictions on the coverage of certain controversial topics, is substantially unrestricted and lively.[10] Recent years have also seen the emergence of a vocal and effective civil society supportive of human rights and populated not only by human rights organizations, but also by business and professional organizations—those who are increasingly frustrated by the political and economic instability and uncertainty that too often accompany repression. The Islamic movement in Turkey has also begun to articulate its demands in human rights terms. If they are successful in achieving their goals using those tools, then they too will in the process become important stakeholders in a progressive development toward greater respect for fundamental human rights.

In conclusion, until Turkey addresses its remaining human rights problems, human rights issues will remain a persistent feature of its international relations. At the same time, because the human rights agenda is, vis-à-vis Turkey, too often compromised or co-opted by the United States and the EU, Turkey's foreign relations with them can be expected to yield only limited human rights progress. Fortunately, notwithstanding the mixed signals from abroad, that progress, though halting and flawed, would appear to be an increasingly inevitable outgrowth of Turkey's dynamic civil society.

10. See, generally, Human Rights Watch, *Free Expression in Turkey* (February 1999).

Chapter 15

Foreign Strategies and Domestic Choices: Balancing between Power Politics and Interdependence

Dimitris Keridis

In 2002, Turkey experienced a major political realignment as the political elites that had governed the country for decades were thrown out of office and a new Islamic and democratic leadership was elected to power. In addition, the demise of Saddam Hussein's regime and the occupation of Iraq by U.S. and U.K. forces, coupled with the eastward enlargement of the European Union (EU) (including Cyprus) have created a radically different geostrategic environment within which Turkey needs to operate. Dramatic change at home and abroad has made Turkish foreign policy-making volatile and often unpredictable and confusing. Change has faced Turkey's new leaders with serious policy dilemmas, the like of which they have no previous experience of dealing with, and has accentuated a certain crisis of identity.

The election of the Justice and Development (AK) Party to power with a strong parliamentary majority was greeted by many of Turkey's friends abroad as a boost for Turkish democracy and a fresh start away from the corrupt and ineffective squabblings of the fragmented coalition governments of the past. Many non-Islamist reformers at home were happy to see the Kemalist establishment being punished and discredited. Indeed, the new government signaled its willingness to take a new look at Turkey's foreign policy by pushing ahead with Turkey's bid for EU membership while supporting the plan of Kofi Annan, the UN secretary-general, for the reunification of Cyprus. However, the initial momentum was quickly squandered as the government lost its nerve and found itself under fire from the Kemalist-nationalist establishment led by the opposition, from the military, and from Turkish-Cypriot leader Rauf

Denktas.[1] It also failed to reconcile Turkish public opinion with the demands of the transatlantic superpower regarding Iraq and to balance national sentiment with national interest. As a result, Turkey disappointed its European friends and was viciously criticized by some of its strongest supporters in the U.S. policy establishment for withholding its support for the U.S. military effort in Iraq.[2]

In the first half of 2003, Turkey appeared disloyal and irrelevant in the eyes of many U.S. and Western strategists. By not allowing for the opening of a northern front in Iraq, Turkey—for years the beneficiary of military, economic, and political aid—did not deliver. However, even without Turkey's help, the U.S. military campaign went ahead successfully. If Iraq is turned into a U.S. protectorate, Turkey's Middle Eastern role would appear much reduced and complicated by the emergence of an autonomous Kurdistan.

The Iraqi crisis has rekindled Turkey's identity crisis. How much eastward and how much westward should Turkey orient itself? What should be the role of Kurdish and Islamic identities in Turkish society, now that Iraqi Kurds and Muslims (Shiite and Sunni, liberated from three decades of Ba'athist nationalist secularism) are allowed to co-determine Iraq's future? After the recent disappointment, what should be the future relationship with the United States, which for 50 years was the most important anchor of Turkish foreign policy? Finally, what is Turkey's position in a united Europe?

Of course, Turkey remains a large country of vital strategic significance for regional stability and Western interests. But it is time for the country's policymakers and public opinion alike to realize that in the era of globalization, accelerating European integration and major regional realignments, size is not everything. Turkey will join the EU sooner than many Europeans wish but later than Turks hope, and take its rightful place in the European family of nations—mostly on Europe's, not Turkey's, terms. Turkey has a large military but remains dependent on Western capital and technology. Europe and the United States need a friendly, stable and prosperous Turkey but Turkey needs Europe and the United States even more.

---

1. International Institute for Strategic Studies (IISS), *Strategic Survey 2002/03* (Oxford, U.K.: IISS, 2003), pp. 134–135.

2. William Safire, writing in the *New York Times:* "New Take on Turkey," May 29, 2003, p. 25; "Jubilant V-I Day," April 10, 2003, p. 27; "On Rewarding Friends," April 3, 2003, p. 21; "Snap Judgments," March 31, 2003, p. 13; "Turkey's Wrong Turn," March 24, 2003, p. 15; "Getting On With It," March 17, 2003, p. 23.

Turkish foreign policymakers are confronted with challenges of great variety and complexity, ranging from conventional bilateral disputes, such as that between Turkey and Greece in the Aegean, to less conventional threats, such as ethnic separatism, terrorism, religious extremism, environmental deprivation, and securing water and energy supplies. For Turkish foreign policymakers, these are demanding times, which require new thinking and creative and resourceful strategies.

In the aftermath of the Cold War, Turkey emerged from the periphery to the very center of Eurasian security. This is attributable to Turkey's geography and demography. With a land mass and a population larger than France's, Turkey is an important Eurasian power. Stretching from Thrace and the Aegean in the west and the Caucasus in the east, Turkey controls the land route between Europe and the Middle East and the sea lanes between the Black Sea and the Mediterranean.[3]

But more than its geostrategic endowments, Turkey's contemporary rise is a result of the success of economic reforms initiated in January 1980 and the significant, if erratic and unequal, economic expansion that followed. In a region of chronic economic mismanagement and slow development, Turkey stands out as a powerhouse, even after the severe 2001–02 recession. With a GDP of $250 billion, the Turkish economy is three times the size of Egypt's and as large as the economies of all the Balkan countries combined. Turkey's recent medium-term performance becomes more startling when contrasted to that of all of its neighbors, barring Greece. Since 1980, the regional balance of power vis-à-vis countries such as Iran, Iraq, Syria, Bulgaria, the former Soviet Union, and even Greece has undoubtedly turned in Turkey's favor.[4]

This combination of natural and human resources has put Turkey in a unique position. No longer concerned with its own survival, as was the case in much of the Ottoman and early republican era, for the first time in its modern history Turkey is able to project its influence beyond its borders and transform itself into a regional leader. The collapse of the Soviet Union offers great economic and political opportunities for Turkey. From the Adriatic to China and from the Black Sea to the Persian Gulf, a vast region exists in which Turkey can exercise its authority.

---

3. Turkey's land area is 779,452 square kilometers and its population in 2000 stood at 63.5 million, according to the State Planning Organization, as reported in Economist Intelligence Unit, *Country Profile: Turkey 2002* (London: Economist Intelligence Unit), p. 3.

4. According to the World Bank and other international organizations, Turkey's aver-

In this process, Turkey is supported and impeded by past legacies and present realities. Since 1989, Turks have rediscovered their ethnic kinsmen in the Balkans, the Caucasus, and Central Asia, as well as the legacy of the Ottoman Empire. Whereas ethnic and cultural affinity have been helpful in promoting relations, old historical antagonisms, such as those with Armenians and Greeks, have impeded them.

These antagonisms are made worse by the fact that Turkey lives in a difficult and unstable neighborhood of weak states prone to ethnic and religious conflicts. Since 1989, the Turkish foreign policy agenda has expanded dramatically. Turkey has interests in the Balkans, the Caucasus, the Middle East, and the Mediterranean. Turkey itself has often contributed to regional instability by refusing to deal politically with the Kurdish insurgency, by its willingness to use force, its unwillingness to submit disputes with foreign nations to international arbitration, and by its activism abroad, such as in the Caucasus.

Most troubling is a certain imperialist, hegemonic, neo-Ottoman discourse that, however useful it might be for domestic political consumption, can lead to serious policy blunders. Since 1989, the Turkish public has been fed—to the horror of many of its neighbors—a constant diet of multi-billion dollar infrastructural projects of great geostrategic significance, from highways to oil and water pipes, that has amounted to very little so far. Turkey confidently engaged the Balkans in 1991, only to withdraw with the exception of Bosnia in 1995, as Albania drew closer to Greece; Bulgaria and Romania focused on their accession to NATO and the EU, and Yugoslavia fell apart. Turkey's greatest disappointment by far has been its engagement in the Caucasus and Central Asia. Heralded as Turkey's backyard or "Near Abroad," it soon became apparent that Turkey did not have the resources to play the leadership role it had envisioned. More recently, this initial enthusiasm gave way to a more sober and realistic approach, thus relegating Turkey to an important, but more supportive, role in the region.

The vast majority of Turks take great pride in the legacy of the founder of the modern Turkish Republic, Kemal Atatürk. In the past, however, they abandoned his cherished foreign policy principles, which sanctioned neutrality and non-intervention abroad, in at least two important respects. First, after the Second World War, Turkey moved away from its interwar neutrality and special understanding with the Soviet Union in order to be actively linked to the West. It became a member of NATO, and it leased military bases to the United States. Second, after

age annual GDP growth after 1980 has been a healthy 4 percent; see <www.world bank.org/Turkey>.

1989, Turkey abandoned Kemalist inwardness to take an active interest in the well-being of Turkic and Muslim populations in its Near Abroad. This is a process that had started with its entanglement in Cyprus in the 1950s but intensified with the end of the Cold War.

These developments cannot be understood without an appreciation of the dramatic internal changes that Turkey has experienced over the last 50 years. What used to be a conservative, religious, patriarchal, peasant, immobile, and illiterate society has been transformed into an urban, industrialized, highly mobile, and reasonably educated nation that is increasingly open and cosmopolitan. For Turkey, modernization meant a certain Westernization that was interlinked with its Western foreign policy orientation. In parallel, populist and nationalist concerns, following the opening of the political system to mass participation after the first competitive elections in 1950, have made it difficult, if not impossible, to ignore the fate and welfare of fellow Turks abroad.

The arrival of "modernity" was bound to create tensions and cause enormous dislocations. As a result, the democratic political process was "rebalanced" by the intervention of the army—three, if not four, times. Contrary to what obtained in the past, today's foreign policymakers operate within the context of an aspiring civil society, vibrant media, and powerful private economic interests that to a great extent impede the army's rebalancing acts and facilitate the domestication of Turkish foreign policy.

As Turkey moves closer to Europe and aspires to obtain EU membership, it is not surprising that its domestic politics are coming under increased international scrutiny. The stability and quality of Turkish democracy, the state of human and minority rights, the level of economic development and income, and regional inequalities have become, especially after 1989, issues of European concern.

Since the end of the Motherland Party's (ANAP) hegemony in Turkish politics in the early 1990s, Turkey and the Kemalist establishment have been challenged by two groups: the Islamists and the Kurdish nationalists. Both challenges and the policy responses they generate have serious implications for the image and position of contemporary Turkey in the world. Both have their roots in Kemalism's exclusionary vision and intolerance towards religion and ethnic diversity. As an elite-driven, top-down, authoritarian movement, Kemalism allowed little room for social pluralism and strove to build a modern, homogeneous, and secular society.

The present incarnations of the Islamic and Kurdish challenges are the result of both the successes and the limitations of Kemalist modernization. Success can be measured in the social pluralization of Turkey and the emergence of a vibrant, diversified, complicated, and sophisticated civil society outside the reach of the official state. The exclusionary nature of the Kemalist program has impeded the expression of popular ethnic and religious identities and has polarized Turkish politics around contrasting heroic grand narratives that are ill-suited to today's consensual politics in the era of globalization. The fact that political Islam and Kurdish nationalism have found fertile ground at the intersection of modernity and tradition, that is, among recent peasant immigrants in the urban peripheries and in the southeast, demonstrates the failure of Kemalist modernization to achieve completion. The Islamists have captured the protest vote of the populous lower social strata that feel inadequately represented by the official Kemalist political establishment, due, in part, to the collapse of the Turkish left. Taking advantage of the opening of the Turkish economy, the Islamists have established an extensive network of business, informational, and educational activities to finance and spread, implicitly or explicitly, their Islamic message, often to the frustration of liberal reformers.

The military took action after the 1980 coup in order, as they viewed it, to restore social order and balance to Turkish politics. Many of Turkey's Islamic and Kurdish problems have their roots in these policies. First, in their effort to weaken the left's influence and Kurdish assertiveness, the generals, and later Turgut Özal, supported "law-abiding, conservative Islam," and even tolerated Hezbollah as a counterweight to the Kurdistan Workers' Party (PKK), thereby allowing the opening and consolidation of thousands of religious schools that in the 1990s the military tried to close down. Second, by imprisoning many moderate Kurdish nationalists, the military provided fertile ground for the rise of the most maverick, ruthless, and uncompromising of all challenges, the PKK, whose leadership had already escaped safely to Syria on the eve of the coup.

Besides being Kemalism's staunch opponents, Islam and Kurdish nationalism are also connected in other ways. First, and possibly most importantly, Islam and the Kurds figure prominently in the Euro-Turkish agenda and have negatively affected Turkey's image abroad. Europe criticizes Turkey for human rights violations, disrespect for minorities, and the military's "guardianship" of the democratic process. In December 1997, the EU refused to recognize Turkey as a candidate for accession because it failed the political preconditions for membership. Given the priority Turkey attaches to its relationship with Europe, this was a serious foreign policy blow and caused an anti-European popular uproar and Ankara's harsh official response. Second, much of the parliamentary support for Refah (Welfare Party, WP) in 1995 came from southeast Turkey.

Kurds voted directly for the WP, due to its more relaxed attitude toward co-religionist Sunni Kurds, and WP deputies were elected in wholly Kurdish constituencies because the People's Democratic Party (HADEP) and other Kurdish candidates failed to secure the necessary 10 percent of the national vote.[5]

Euro-Turkish relations carry their own heavy historical baggage. At the height of Ottoman power in the sixteenth century, Turkey was an important European power and participant in maintaining the balance of power of the time by allying itself to France against the Habsburgs. Europe-inspired reforms did not start with Atatürk, but were more than a century old by the time he came to power. A reformist discourse is discernible from the Ottoman Tulip Era in the first half of the eighteenth century onwards. After the Second World War, Turkey oriented itself fully toward the West, abandoned its immediate neighborhood in the troubled Middle East, and strove to integrate politically into the Euro-Atlantic alliance. It entered NATO in 1952 and signed an association treaty with the European Communities in 1963. As European integration accelerated in the 1980s, Turkey aspired to a full membership in the EU. However, the end of the Cold War and the emergence of Central Europe suddenly put Turkey further behind in the line for accession, while renewed interest in the strict observance of democratic preconditions for membership further complicated Turkey's efforts.

Turks object to Europe's allegations on two grounds: they suspect Brussels of a "Christian Club" bias at best or neocolonialism and racism at worst. Modern Turkey cannot but carry the traumas of the Ottoman Empire and the memories of the repeated, quasi-colonial interventions of Europe's great powers in its internal affairs, culminating in the nightmare of the Treaty of Sèvres of 1920 and the dismemberment of not just the empire, but the Turks' very homeland in Anatolia. Thus, most Turks, particularly of the most nationalist vocation, are especially sensitive when dictated to by foreigners and tend to share a strict and traditional understanding of state sovereignty. But the very nature of EU membership in-

---

5. For an excellent overview of Turkey's recent electoral trends see Ali Çarkoglu, "Turkey's November 2002 Elections: A New Beginning," *Middle East Review of International Affairs*, Vol. 6, No. 4 (December 2002), <meria.idc.ac.il/journal/2002/issue4/jv6n4a4.html>. According to Çarkoglu, "since HADEP and [its ethnic Kurdish successor] DEHAP's regionally concentrated electoral support is unrepresented in parliament this fact favors the parties that capture the second largest vote shares in those provinces. In 1995 and 1999 the pro-Islamist RP and FP benefited from HADEP being left out of the parliament. In 2002, it was the AK party, which on average gained less than half of the electoral support that DEHAP obtained in the East and Southeastern provinces, that benefited from this representational threshold." Ibid., p. 34.

volves the voluntary surrendering of parts of state sovereignty to a supranational organization. The EU cannot and does not draw a line at "internal affairs." European unification can only work if German concerns are also those of Italy, Greece, France, and the rest. This must also be true for Turkey: the privilege of participating in the club of the most advanced democracies in the world carries some costs.

Most Turks believe that whatever Turkey does, Europe will still consider it an Islamic, non-European outsider. Occasional statements by Christian Democrats and far-rightists regarding Turkey's non-European racial and Oriental cultural character only reinforce Turkish suspicions. There is no doubt that many Europeans share such beliefs. However, Europe has not officially endorsed them and contrary to its treatment of other applications for membership (such as that of Tunisia), the EU has carefully considered Turkey's case and has established a well-structured process, the Euro-Turkish dialogue, which should culminate one day in membership. After all, no matter what European public opinion believes about Turkey's membership, the project of European unification has always been more elite-driven than popularly supported. Europe itself is changing, as is evident in the new German citizenship law after the center-left's victory in the last two elections. Racism is present in Europe, but it would be a mistake to think of it as rampant. There are many Europeans, including Greeks, who genuinely believe in Turkish membership. European leaders endorsed, in principle, Turkey's membership in the European Summits of Helsinki in 1999 and Copenhagen in 2002 and have declared that in December 2004 a decision on accession negotiations will be made provided that certain criteria are met. Turkey's celebrated "otherness" could enrich the European project and serve important European strategic interests.

Traditional left-right political distinctions in the conventional European sense carry little meaning in Turkey. The Kemalist body politic (some three-fifths of the total, if the Islamists, Kurdish nationalists, and radical left and right-wing groups are excluded) is roughly divided along two main poles: Jacobins and reformers. The former adhere to a strict interpretation of Kemalism and reject any deviation from secularism and uni-culturalism. They are to be found mostly in the center-left, the military, and the top bureaucracy. For this group, secularism does not mean simply the separation of church and state, but the suppression of religion from the public sphere and its privatization. In the event that this is not possible, then secularism is taken to mean religion's complete submission to the state. Using similar logic, minority rights are suspect tools of foreign agents who want to belittle modern Turkey in the same way nineteenth-century European concern for Ottoman Christians led to the dismemberment of the empire and the Treaty of Sèvres. Being all too ready to exaggerate risks abroad into foreign threats, they appear as hard-line nationalists, defining Turkey's national interest in narrow security terms and feeling uncomfortable with the rapid economic liberalization of the last two decades.

On the contrary, present-day reformers, the progeny of the late president Özal, understand the limits of Kemalism and the need for reaching a new post-Kemalist consensus, and are better suited to a society that has developed dramatically and pluralized radically during the last half century. Kemalism served its modernizing purpose well, but in this new phase, it is a straitjacket ill-suited to Turkish society, as it inhibits the full consolidation of an open, liberal, and democratic polity. Reformers, most numerous in the center-right, the left, and the cosmopolitan business elites of Istanbul, would like to see recent economic openness translated to further political openness. Normalization of Turkish politics must include constitutional reform involving the permanent retreat of the army to the barracks; the consolidation of the party system around two or three poles and its modernization away from today's personality-based, patriarchical, and clientelist formations toward mechanisms for effective and consensual governance; and the guarantee of the rights, including cultural, of all citizens in an often intrusive, secretive, and authoritarian state. The reformers recognize Turkey's multicultural and multi-ethnic background but, taking pride in Turkey's recent successes, remain confident that Turkey has nothing to fear and much to gain from a more open, relaxed, and cooperative policy abroad. For them, national interest is not just military strength and security. They want Turkey to be rich in not only "hard," "pushing" power but in "soft," "pulling" power as well.

Turkish reality has often been conceptualized in terms of dualities and antitheses: for example, between developed Western and backward Eastern Turkey or between modernizing Kemalist and traditionalist Islamist Turkey. But the conference upon which this study rests made clear that there exists another antithesis, that between Ankara and Istanbul. This antithesis should not escape foreigners who are all too ready to talk of one static, monolithic Turkey, and who tend to ignore the plurality and internal fragmentation among competing interests with different policy preferences of contemporary Turkey. Reflecting official Turkey, Ankara representatives at this conference, which took place at Harvard University in October 1998, gave a conservative, nationalist, often defensive, reading of Turkish foreign policy. Istanbul representatives, however, startled the audience by the vision and assertiveness of a new Turkey that wants to be fully integrated into Europe, build economic, cultural, and political bridges with all its neighbors, and project its influence across its region from the Middle East to Central Asia and the Balkans.[6]

For this to be possible, Istanbul representatives need to successfully resolve the dilemma all reformers are confronted with: how to manage change safely. In other words, how to make sure that political openness will not bring a fundamentalist regime to power, and how to ensure that the recognition of Kurdish rights will not lead to secession. In broader terms, the question is how to build up the efficiency and the policy-making capacity of a democratically accountable political leadership. A helpful framework within which Turkey could navigate through change is Europe. The success of the structural transformation of southern Europe in the 1970s and central Europe in the 1990s shows that Europe can provide a safe anchor. With European guidance and resources, most Turks could claim a stake in an open, pluralist system against a closed, monolithic one.

The economic crisis that hit Turkey hard in 2001 made clear the limits of muddling through and lent special urgency to the reformist agenda. Uncompetitive sectors such as agriculture and state enterprises proved too much of a drain on the public treasury; dubious private business interests appeared too close to the state; rampant corruption diverted resources and fundamentally distorted the economic environment; and party fragmentation made policymaking a frustrating and often vain balancing act. Despite the success of Kemal Dervis in macroeconomic stabilization and in avoiding an Argentina-type implosion, the Ecevit-Bahcheli-Yılmaz tri-party government fell apart and was swept from power in November 2002, paying a heavy price for the wrath of the middle and lower classes. The Turks' appetite for change was effectively exploited by the reformed Islamists led by the charismatic Tayyip Erdogan and helped by the fragmentation of the Kemalist camp.

The election of Erdogan as prime minister marks a momentous new beginning. Despite the inexperience, inertia, and frequent incompetence of the new government, its election has already served Turkish democracy well. Political reforms proceed apace even if economic ones are stalled by special interests. Aware of the limits of his power, Erdogan has, to a great extent, depolarized Turkish politics by refusing to press for an "Islamic" agenda, focusing instead on expanding the liberal space for self-expression. He has temporarily and conditionally secured the help of

---

6. According to Çarkoglu, Turkish politics is polarized between the conservative Anatolian plain provinces around Ankara and the Western-oriented coastal provinces around Istanbul; ibid., p. 33.

many Kemalist reformers while hardliners are licking the wounds of their recent defeat at the polls.

It seems that in Europe today there exist two types of politics: traditional power politics that emphasize security, military might, and state sovereignty, and the postmodern politics of political and economic integration that downplay the need for a powerful military and do not recognize "internal matters." The former is best understood through a realist reading of international relations as a zero-sum game. The latter tends to seek liberal positive-sum cooperative situations, where all parties involved have something to gain. The politics of interdependence acknowledge the supremacy of the state in international affairs, but recognize that in an era of rapid globalization, identities, loyalties, and sovereignties are increasingly overlapping and shared. From nationalist Britain to federalist Germany, European politics are dominated by this dichotomy. Turkey's U.S.-supported alliance with Israel points toward traditional realism and the politics of balance of power. Acceptance of EU candidate status and its conditions points to a liberal direction.

In 2003, Turkish foreign policy seems to stand at a crossroads. The decision of the European Council in Helsinki on December 10, 1999, to grant Turkey the candidate status it sought, signifies a great historical opportunity. Turkey is at last recognized as a European nation. However, the road to membership passes through the full adherence to the liberal European norms and values, the so-called *acquis communautaire*. This involves, at a minimum, the peaceful resolution of bilateral disputes and respect for human rights. For Turkey, concrete steps would be to acknowledge the general jurisdiction of the International Court of Justice, comply with the European Convention on Human Rights, and resolve the Cyprus problem.

In fact, Cyprus provides a first rate battleground between European and nationalist forces. The Annan Plan and the prospect of EU membership exposed severe divisions inside the Turkish-Cypriot community that could lead to the isolation and departure of Denktas in the near future. After 40 years of division, Denktas's politics of ethnic separatism appear bankrupt. But it remains to be seen if Ankara, which ultimately calls the shots in Northern Cyprus, makes the great leap forward to pressing for a reunification that secures a prosperous, European future for the Turkish Cypriots and paves the way for its own EU accession.

For a country with Turkey's democratic deficit and socioeconomic problems, the accession road to Europe will be long and taxing. But for the time being, liberal reformers have every right to hail the EU's decision as a great victory. Many Islamists and Kurds feel equally happy looking to Europe as a guarantor of their right to free expression. It should not go unnoticed that nationalists, including Turkish Cypriot leader Rauf Denktas, reacted negatively to the Helsinki decision. A repetition of Luxembourg would have increased their popularity and strengthened their agenda.

As Turkey tries to adapt and take full advantage of globalization and build a society well integrated into the world, Europe will increasingly dominate Turkey's foreign and domestic policy, even if EU membership remains a goal rather than a reality. Having proved its reformist zeal and economic dynamism, "Europeanization," that is, the structural transformation toward a stable and prosperous democracy, is Turkey's greatest challenge.

Conclusions

Chapter 16

Conclusions

Lenore G. Martin and Dimitris Keridis

Each of the contributors to this book has given the reader a rich and nuanced understanding of the critical issues facing Turkish foreign policymakers in the turbulent times of the early twenty-first century. For every issue, however, there seems to be a complex set of choices and a competing set of philosophies advocating opposite resolutions. The very complexity of these foreign policy challenges and apparent irreconcilability of the competing philosophies jeopardizes Turkey's chances of realizing its future potential.

The challenges to the future of Turkish foreign policy arise from the fact that its foreign policymaking is a three-dimensional exercise. One dimension in this matrix consists of the philosophical foundations for foreign policymaking. In this we observe a spectrum of world-views, typified at one end by proponents of the conservative interpretation of the Kemalist tradition and at the other by proponents of change. We see some of this in the lively debate between Mümtaz Soysal who endorses a very conservative approach and Cengiz Çandar who urges reform. Echoes of the debate are also heard in other chapters, such as Kemal Kirişci's counterposing of the conservative and liberal views on the Kurdish question; they are also audible in the proposals for, and resistance to, human rights reforms described by Elizabeth Andersen.

These opposing philosophies, however, do not fit neatly within boundaries demarcating Turkey's political actors or elites. Opposite views may develop under the same political label and within the same political institution. As we learned from Sencer Ayata, the ruling AK Party had its roots in the conservative Islamist tradition represented by its predecessor, the Welfare Party, which was suspicious of Westernization and opposed European integration. Yet the moderate AK leadership strongly endorses Turkey's European integration. The process of accession to the European Union (EU) promotes the lessening of the involvement of the military in Turkish politics as well as human rights reforms that will safeguard the exercise of Islamic rights. Moreover, as Cengiz Çandar observed, the Turkish military itself, which ordinarily serves as a standard bearer for Kemalism and its Western orientation, has been split on European integration. One faction within the military power structure has opposed European integration and advocated the pursuit of Turkish alignments in Asia.

The second dimension consists of the pursuit of Turkey's geostrategic interests. Here we observe a plethora of foreign policy issues facing Turkey from all the principal points of the strategic compass. Looking west, we see that in order to promote its national interests Turkey must carefully balance good relations with Europe and the United States. In the future, however, the balance may not be so easy. Divining this future means anticipating whether Turkey will still be able to maintain its close strategic relationship with the United States if the Republic is truly integrated into the EU. What if Europe pulls away from the United States, or a European defense force loosens the bonds of NATO? On the other hand, to gain accession to the EU, Turkey needs to be able to resolve its trenchant territorial disputes with Greece over the Aegean and accommodate the reduction of Turkey's military presence and political role in Northern Cyprus and allow for the reunification of the island. Will the cooperative efforts of the reformers to mend relations between Turkey and Greece succeed, or will the unbending conservatism within the establishments of Ankara and Athens prevail to the detriment of any settlement?

Looking north and to the east we observe Turkey engaged in a similar balancing act, seeking simultaneously to compete with Russia for influence in the Caucasus and Central Asia and to cooperate with its former adversary for mutual economic advantage. The balance is precarious and may tip if there is a recrudescence of ethnic strife in the Caucasus that aligns Turkey and Russia with opposite factions. It would certainly tip toward greater competition if there were a resurgence of Russian imperialism. Would it tip toward greater cooperation with Russia if Europe barred Turkey's accession?

Looking to the south and east, we see Turkish foreign policymakers seeking to improve diplomatic and economic relations with Iran and Syria while at the same time remaining concerned over Iranian and Syrian support for Kurds and Islamists who challenge the Turkish regime. Turkey is also concerned about the strategic threats from Syria and Iran posed by their interest in developing weapons of mass destruction. Turkey's military cooperation with Israel enhances Ankara's ability to deter these threats. But Turkey's relationship with Israel raises domestic concerns among Turks as long as the Palestinian-Israeli conflict rages. Will the future portend peaceful relations between Israel and a Palestinian state, the final destination on the international road map for peace? Or will a failure to achieve peace turn the Israeli alignment into a greater problem for Turkey, because of domestic popular sympathy for the Palestinians and the continuing antipathy to Israel of Turkey's Middle Eastern neighbors?

Equally complex are Turkey's future policies concerning Iraq after the overthrow of Saddam Hussein and U.S. occupation of Iraq. Turkey's policymakers are clearly concerned about the development of autonomous Kurdish rule in northern Iraq. In this they share a common cause with Syria and Iran, both of whom have the potential for intervention into the affairs of Iraq. But it is also true that Iran, Syria, and Turkey could find themselves supporting opposing factions in Iraq in order to maintain their own base of power in the state. The destiny of Iraq's Kurds appears to be in the hands of the United States who will not take kindly to any intervention by Iraq's neighbors. Thus, in order to gain a greater say in the shaping of northern Iraq, Ankara will need to strengthen its rapport with the Iraqi Kurdish factions and repair its relations with Washington after its refusal of military support for the U.S. invasion. Will a realignment of Turkey's interests with U.S. plans for Iraq lead to a deterioration of the Republic's relations with Iran and Syria and possibly revive their interests in supporting opposition groups not only in Turkey but in Iraq as well?

One of the ways in which Turkey has in the past tried to build stronger relations with the Arab Middle East has been to offer to provide water from rivers running into the Mediterranean. Such offers were rejected at a time when Arab states supported Syrian (and Iraqi) grievances against Turkey for not sharing sufficient water from the Euphrates and Tigris. After Syria's renunciation of support for the PKK and the general improvement of relations with Turkey, there are indications that Turkey may be able to resolve its water issues with Syria. Is then a final settlement of their water issues possible? If so, could the ability of Syria and Turkey to overcome deep mutual suspicions carry over generally into the Arab world and enable Arabs and Turks to overcome the mutual suspicions they developed from the legacy of Ottoman imperialism?

Turkey's geostrategic location has created opportunities for it to become a valuable bridge for oil and gas destined for Europe from the Caucasus and Central Asia. Transiting Caucasian oil to the terminus at Ceyhan is also an economic stimulus to this key Turkish port. Alternatively, Turkey's rivals could design transit routes to bypass Turkey. Could Russia persuade Europe to invest in pipelines through more politically stable routes across the Black Sea into Bulgaria and Romania? Or could political reform in Iran persuade the United States to renounce its opposition to more economical pipeline routes through Iran to the Gulf? Any of these events would have a major impact on the furtherance of Turkey's geopolitical importance as well as on its ability to obtain critical oil supplies and transit fees.

The third dimension to Turkish foreign policymaking results from domestic policies that affect the Republic's foreign relations. Thus we have seen that domestic political opposition to the conservative Kemalist tradition—from Islamists who challenge its principle of secularism and from Kurds who challenge its principle of national homogeneity—garners foreign political support. Europeans who control Turkey's accession to the EU support reforms for Turkey's Kurdish community, and Middle Eastern states whose political legitimacy stands upon Islamist principles support rights for Islamists and feel challenged by Turkey's democratic, secular regime. By contrast, will the more moderate Islamists in the AK Party, if they gain more popularity and institute more Islamic practices in the future, unnerve the EU and lead to rejection of Turkey's accession? If so, will the Islamists reverse their pro-European integration approach in favor of stronger relations with Turkey's Middle East neighbors, as did the Islamists under Necmettin Erbekan? The promotion of Kurdish identity and cultural rights, as favored by foreign policy reformers, enhances Turkey's chances for accession to the EU. Yet the foreign policy conservatives fear that acknowledging a separate Kurdish identity and allowing free expression of Kurdish culture will only encourage demands for more Kurdish autonomy in Southeast Anatolia and create additional opportunities for pressure points from Turkey's neighbors. Whichever of the philosophical traditions most strongly influences the direction of Turkey's domestic politics, there will be repercussions for Turkey's geopolitical position.

Although the multidimensionality of Turkish foreign policy raises critical issues that have at times stymied the Republic, Turkey clearly has the potential for growth in its economy, domestic political stability, national security, and civil society. The Republic can apply its prodigious energy to realizing its potential as a Westernized democracy that is actively involved in the geopolitics of its surrounding communities—Europe, the Balkans, the Caucasus, Central Asia, and the Middle East. With the cooperation of others in the international community it can resolve the fundamental issues that restrain its foreign policy: integration of the Turkish community in Cyprus, demarcation of boundaries and rights in the Aegean, reaching agreements on allocating the waters of the Euphrates and Tigris with Syria and Iraq, reconciliation of secular politics and Islamic society, implementing the laws that allow the open recognition of Kurdish cultural identity, and conformity to the norms of international human rights. The resolution of these issues will enable the Republic to expedite its accession to the EU, revive its flagging strategic partnership with the United States, increase its cooperative relations with Russia, expand its trade and pipeline network with the Caucasus and Central Asia, and increase its security vis-à-vis the Middle East, thereby allowing it to successfully pursue its national interests in the future.

Contributors

Feroz Ahmad is Professor of History Emeritus, University of Massachusetts, Boston.

Elizabeth Andersen, formerly Executive Director of the Europe and Central Asia Division, Human Rights Watch, is now Executive Director of the American Bar Association Central European and Eurasian Law Initiative (ABA/CEELI), Washington, D.C.

Sencer Ayata is Professor and Chair of the Department of Sociology, Middle East Technical University, Ankara.

Cengiz Çandar is a journalist in Istanbul, and was special advisor to President Turgut Özal of Turkey (1991–93).

Thanos P. Dokos is Director of Studies, Hellenic Foundation for European Foreign Policy (ELIAMEP), Athens.

Atila Eralp is Jean Monnet Professor of European Political Integration, Chair of the Department of International Relations, and Director of the Centre For European Studies, Middle East Technical University, Ankara.

Fiona Hill is a Senior Fellow in the Foreign Policy Studies Program at The Brookings Institution, Washington, D.C.

Dimitris Keridis is Assistant Professor of International Politics, University of Macedonia, Thessaloniki, and Director of The Kokkalis Foundation, Athens.

Kemal Kirişci is Jean Monnet Professor of European Political Integration at the Department of Political Science, and Director of the Centre for European Studies, Boğaziçi University, Istanbul.

Ian O. Lesser is Vice President and Director of Studies at the Pacific Council on International Policy, and a former member of the Policy Planning Staff, U.S. State Department.

Lenore G. Martin is Professor and Chair of the Department of Political Science, Emmanuel College, and Associate at the Weatherhead Center for International Affairs and Co-Chair of the Study Group on Modern Turkey at the Center for Middle Eastern Studies, Harvard University, Cambridge.

Mümtaz Soysal is former Minister of Foreign Affairs of the Republic of Turkey, and Professor of Constitutional Law and Comparative Government, Ankara University, Ankara.

Oktay F. Tanrısever is Assistant Professor in the Department of International Relations, Middle East Technical University, Ankara.

Panayotis J. Tsakonas is Assistant Professor, Department of Mediterranean Studies, University of the Aegean, and Senior Advisor, Ministry of Foreign Affairs, Athens.

İlter Turan is Professor of Political Science, Department of International Relations, Istanbul Bilgi University, Istanbul.

Index

BCSIA Studies in International Security

Published by The MIT Press

Sean M. Lynn-Jones and Steven E. Miller, series editors
Karen Motley, executive editor
Belfer Center for Science and International Affairs (BCSIA)
John F. Kennedy School of Government, Harvard University

Allison, Graham T., Owen R. Coté, Jr., Richard A. Falkenrath, and Steven E. Miller, *Avoiding Nuclear Anarchy: Containing the Threat of Loose Russian Nuclear Weapons and Fissile Material* (1996)

Allison, Graham T., and Kalypso Nicolaïdis, eds., *The Greek Paradox: Promise vs. Performance* (1996)

Arbatov, Alexei, Abram Chayes, Antonia Handler Chayes, and Lara Olson, eds., *Managing Conflict in the Former Soviet Union: Russian and American Perspectives* (1997)

Bennett, Andrew, *Condemned to Repetition? The Rise, Fall, and Reprise of Soviet-Russian Military Interventionism, 1973–1996* (1999)

Blackwill, Robert D., and Michael Stürmer, eds., *Allies Divided: Transatlantic Policies for the Greater Middle East* (1997)

Blackwill, Robert D., and Paul Dibb, eds., *America's Asian Alliances* (2000)

Brom, Shlomo, and Yiftah Shapir, eds., *The Middle East Military Balance 1999–2000* (1999)

Brom, Shlomo, and Yiftah Shapir, eds., *The Middle East Military Balance 2001–2002* (2002)

Brown, Michael E., ed., *The International Dimensions of Internal Conflict* (1996)

Brown, Michael E., and Šumit Ganguly, eds., *Fighting Words: Language Policy and Ethnic Relations in Asia* (2003)

Brown, Michael E., and Šumit Ganguly, eds., *Government Policies and Ethnic Relations in Asia and the Pacific* (1997)

Carter, Ashton B., and John P. White, eds., *Keeping the Edge: Managing Defense for the Future* (2001)

de Nevers, Renée, *Comrades No More: The Seeds of Political Change in Eastern Europe* (2003)

Elman, Colin, and Miriam Fendius Elman, eds., *Progress in International Relations Theory: Appraising the Field* (2003)

Elman, Colin, and Miriam Fendius Elman, eds., *Bridges and Boundaries: Historians, Political Scientists, and the Study of International Relations* (2001)

Elman, Miriam Fendius, ed., *Paths to Peace: Is Democracy the Answer?* (1997)

Falkenrath, Richard A., *Shaping Europe's Military Order: The Origins and Consequences of the CFE Treaty* (1994)

Falkenrath, Richard A., Robert D. Newman, and Bradley A. Thayer, *America's Achilles' Heel: Nuclear, Biological, and Chemical Terrorism and Covert Attack* (1998)

Feaver, Peter D., and Richard H. Kohn, eds., *Soldiers and Civilians: The Civil-Military Gap and American National Security* (2001)

Feldman, Shai, *Nuclear Weapons and Arms Control in the Middle East* (1996)

Feldman, Shai, and Yiftah Shapir, eds., *The Middle East Military Balance 2000–2001* (2001)

Forsberg, Randall, ed., *The Arms Production Dilemma: Contraction and Restraint in the World Combat Aircraft Industry* (1994)

Hagerty, Devin T., *The Consequences of Nuclear Proliferation: Lessons from South Asia* (1998)

Heymann, Philip B., *Terrorism and America: A Commonsense Strategy for a Democratic Society* (1998)

Heymann, Philip B., *Terrorism, Freedom, and Security Winning without War* (2003)

Howitt, Arnold M., and Robyn L. Pangi, eds., *Countering Terrorism: Dimensions of Preparedness* (2003)

Kayyem, Juliette N., and Robyn L. Pangi, eds., *First to Arrive: State and Local Responses to Terrorism* (2003)

Kokoshin, Andrei A., *Soviet Strategic Thought, 1917–91* (1998)

Lederberg, Joshua, ed., *Biological Weapons: Limiting the Threat* (1999)

Shaffer, Brenda, *Borders and Brethren: Iran and the Challenge of Azerbaijani Identity* (2002)

Shields, John M., and William C. Potter, eds., *Dismantling the Cold War: U.S. and NIS Perspectives on the Nunn-Lugar Cooperative Threat Reduction Program* (1997)

Tucker, Jonathan B., ed., *Toxic Terror: Assessing Terrorist Use of Chemical and Biological Weapons* (2000)

Utgoff, Victor A., ed., *The Coming Crisis: Nuclear Proliferation, U.S. Interests, and World Order* (2000)

Williams, Cindy, ed., *Holding the Line: U.S. Defense Alternatives for the Early 21st Century* (2001)

The Robert and Renée Belfer Center for Science and International Affairs

Graham T. Allison, Director
John F. Kennedy School of Government
Harvard University
79 JFK Street, Cambridge, MA 02138
(617) 495-1400
http://www.ksg.harvard.edu/bcsia   bcsia_ksg@harvard.edu

The Belfer Center for Science and International Affairs (BCSIA) is the hub of research, teaching and training in international security affairs, environmental and resource issues, science and technology policy, human rights and conflict studies at Harvard's John F. Kennedy School of Government. The Center's mission is to provide leadership in advancing policy-relevant knowledge about the most important challenges of international security and other critical issues where science, technology, and international affairs intersect.

BCSIA's leadership begins with the recognition of science and technology as driving forces transforming international affairs. The Center integrates insights of social scientists, natural scientists, technologists, and practitioners with experience in government, diplomacy, the military, and business to address these challenges. The Center pursues its mission in four complementary research programs:

- The **International Security Program** (ISP) addresses the most pressing threats to U.S. national interests and international security.

- The **Environment and Natural Resources Program** (ENRP) is the locus of Harvard's interdisciplinary research on resource and environmental problems and policy responses.

- The **Science, Technology and Public Policy** (STPP) program analyzes ways in which science and technology policy influence international security, resources, environment, and development, and such cross-cutting issues as technological innovation and information infrastructure.

- The **WPF Program on Intrastate Conflict, Conflict Prevention and Conflict Resolution** analyzes the causes of ethnic, religious, and other conflicts, and seeks to identify practical ways to prevent and limit such conflicts.

The heart of the Center is its resident research community of more than 140 scholars: Harvard faculty, analysts, practitioners, and each year a new, interdisciplinary group of research fellows. BCSIA sponsors frequent seminars, workshops and conferences, maintains a substantial specialized library, and publishes books, monographs, and discussion papers.

The Center's International Security Program, directed by Steven E. Miller, publishes the BCSIA Studies in International Security, and sponsors and edits the quarterly journal *International Security*.

The Center is supported by an endowment established with funds from Robert and Renée Belfer, the Ford Foundation and Harvard University, by foundation grants, by individual gifts, and by occasional government contracts.